Pemberville Public Library
RALE3

**THE NIXON
NOBODY KNOWS**

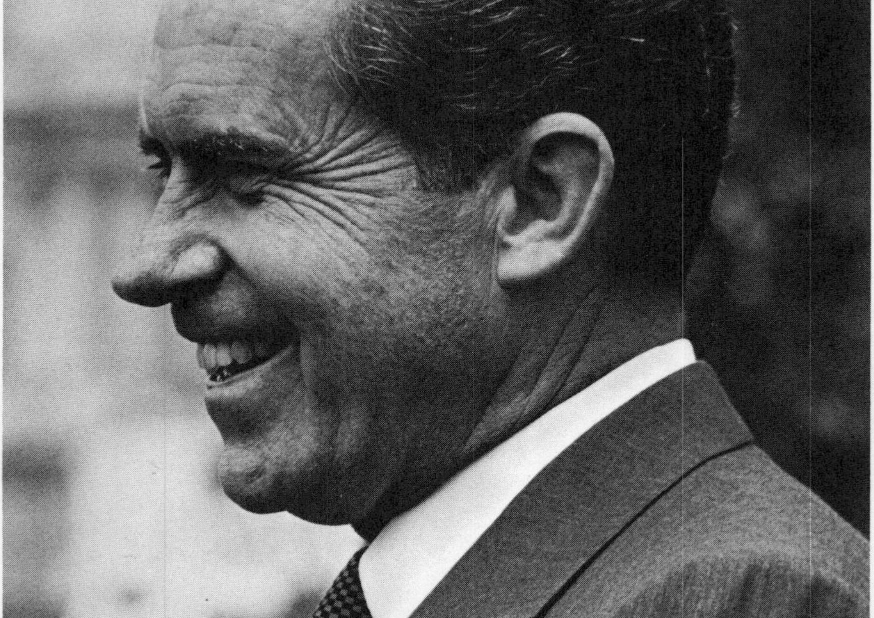

the Nixon nobody knows

by HENRY D. SPALDING

PEMBERVILLE
PUBLIC
LIBRARY

jD | JONATHAN DAVID PUBLISHERS
MIDDLE VILLAGE, N.Y. 11379

THE NIXON NOBODY KNOWS

Copyright © 1972

by

Henry D. Spalding

No part of this book may be reproduced in any manner without written permission from the publishers.

Address all inquiries to:

JONATHAN DAVID PUBLISHERS

Middle Village, New York 11379

Library of Congress Catalogue Card No. 70-188240

ISBN 0-8246-0139-4

Printed in the United States of America

TO MY YOUNG FRIEND
JONATHAN KOLATCH
WHO SUGGESTED THAT
I WRITE THIS BOOK.

TABLE OF CONTENTS

1. The Nixon-Milhous Saga 1
2. Years of Struggle—Years of Toil 27
3. A Fledgling Spreads His Wings 111
4. The Political Arena 145
5. Nixon in Congress 176
6. The Hiss Case 200
7. The Nixon-Douglas "Debate" 261
8. Senator Nixon Behind the Scenes 281
9. The Fund 304
10. Vice-President Richard M. Nixon 369
11. 1960: The Nixon-Kennedy Campaign 397
12. The Waiting Years 418
13. Fulfillment 441
    Index 453

1
The Nixon-Milhous Saga

RICHARD NIXON, by virtue of his mighty office, is the most influential man in the United States of America—and one of the most controversial. Not since the days of Martin Van Buren, who once presided over the Senate with cocked pistols in each hand, has a President or Vice President been disliked with such intensity. Nor has any President, with the possible exception of Franklin Delano Roosevelt, been supported with such profound fervor. Somewhere between these two extremes of unbridled hatred and blind approval—extremes that shroud the man in fold upon fold of myth and legend—stands Nixon himself, a figure of mystery despite the millions of words that have been written about him in newspapers, magazines and books.

Who is this man who, in spectacular Horatio Alger style, has managed to become a living example of the American success story. How did this grocer's son manage to become President of a nation infinitely more powerful than ancient

Rome at its zenith? What mysterious inner forces propelled, shaped and guided his destiny? Certainly, Richard Nixon, the President, did not spring from the head of Dick Nixon, the boy, like Athena from the brow of Zeus. Nor were there any Olympian flashes that illuminated his long and zig-zagged career leading to the White House. No prodigy, he was a hard-working, bright and rather lonely boy who advanced in life through his own determined efforts, with little assistance or succor from Lady Luck. Milton wrote: "The childhood shows the man, as morning shows the day," but nowhere in Nixon's youth was there the slightest hint of his ultimate achievement. How, then, was it accomplished?

An obviously over-simple answer was given by the President's wife, Pat: "We come from typical, everyday American families who have had to work for what they got out of life, but always knew that unlimited opportunity was possible. . . ."

The *Washington Post,* vehemently anti-Nixon, was not so laudatory. Referring to the difference in campaign styles between Harry Truman and Richard Nixon, the *Post* commented: ". . . [their techniques] are the difference between a warmhearted fellow who plows into a fist-fight for the sheer joy of it; and the grim-minded man who charges in with a pipe wrench."

In their own particular ways, the statements made by Mrs. Nixon and the *Post* are both significant. Richard Nixon is, indeed, a product of his environment and probably of heredity as well. But he is also a man obsessed by an overwhelming *need* for triumph. For him, life is a battleground in a war in which there are no successes or failures. There is only complete victory or complete defeat. And Nixon has taught himself to pursue victory with single-minded purpose. Indeed, without that compulsive drive he could never have reached the White House.

Richard Nixon's career—and his accomplishments as President—has also been enhanced by an intuitive ability to recognize sudden and unexpected opportunity, to grasp it with an iron hand, and to wring from it whatever advantage it might yield. This trait—this opportunistic sense—is characteristic of most candidates for high office. The bare-bones truth is that no leader can ever expect to survive in the jungle we call politics without a strong sense of opportunism.

The paradox, however, is that despite his manipulative ability, in situations where the twists and turns of fortune are prone to play havoc, Nixon usually remains the calm, cautious political scientist in the finest pragmatic sense of the word. He is a President who dissects, analyzes, weighs and measures a problem in the laboratory of his mind before announcing a decision.

But this is not a manifestation of the "new" Nixon. "Dick always planned things out; he didn't do things accidentally," said his younger brother Don. "He would never explode, but saved his thoughts until he needed them. He wouldn't argue much with me, but once, when we were boys, I did something that finally made him angry. He didn't just criticize me for that one incident; he went back a whole *year,* listing everything I had done wrong. He kept at it for half an hour and didn't leave out a thing. It really made me think, believe me! I've had a great deal of respect for that memory of his ever since."

To carry the paradox still further: He is a remarkably compassionate man, a quality imbued in him by his mother, and one which is often concealed behind the taciturn facade he acquired from his father.

The President himself affirmed the comparison. "I have never known anyone as patient or completely dedicated to the needs of others as was my mother, but I must say that my father was impatient and—well—rather grouchy with most people."

Rather grouchy! Frank Nixon could, and did, breathe fire and brimstone. Yet, he too was a complex personality and, like his famous son, would sometimes surprise everyone with a sudden display of genuine warmth.

Richard Nixon's Antecedents

In a real sense, the career of Richard Nixon was influenced by his very earliest antecedents in the New World. From the day of their arrival, the Nixon*-Milhous families epitomized the traditional American values represented by those who tilled the soil; worked with their hands as artisans or laborers; became storekeepers, teachers and ministers of the gospel; served in the military establishment; and helped broaden our frontiers. They were the plain people, always close to the good earth. Had he not decided on a career in law, it is not too difficult to imagine Nixon as a farmer, rancher, teacher or, yes, as a minister.

Of Scot-Irish extraction, the paternal side of the family traces its ancestry in America to James Nixon who arrived in colonial America from Ireland in 1753, and settled in New Castle County, Brandywine Hundred, Delaware, some five miles north of Wilmington. James died in 1775 and was survived by two sons: John, and an older brother, George. Both fought in the Revolutionary War, John as a colonel in the Continental Army, and George as an ensign, later promoted to the rank of lieutenant.

Both brothers distinguished themselves. George crossed the Delaware with Washington in the crucial months of the War and also participated in the Battle of Trenton. He recounted his experiences in a letter of application for a pension, in 1833:

> . . . together with my Company, we joined the Army of General George Washington, crossed the Delaware with him, and were stationed with him at Trenton on

---

*The family name, a derivation of the Gaelic words, "he faileth not," has been variously spelled Nicholl, Nichols, Nicholls, Nicholson, McNichols, MacNichols, Nicholas, Nickson and, of course, Nixon.

the memorable second of January, 1777, when the British marched to attack the Americans.

The American troops were marched towards Princeton. . . . They met the rear of the British troops where a battle was fought, and the latter defeated, in which this deponent bore his share to the best of his skill and understanding as Ensign in said Company, and has now in his possession the very sword and spontoon* by him carried on that occasion.

The younger brother, John, also established his niche in history when, as Sheriff of Philadelphia, it devolved upon him to offer the first public reading of the newly-proclaimed Declaration of Independence.

Upon his death, the senior Nixon, James, bequeathed to his wife, Mary, $300 in cash and ". . . a third of the place where I now live, and the bed and bedding and furniture for one room." His three married daughters each received $225. James' last will and testament further stipulated: "To my son George, I leave the plantation whereon I now live consisting of one hundred acres. To my loving son, John, I leave the two Negro slaves, Ned, the male, and Nance, the female." The sons received, additionally, $250 each and some cattle.**

On August 17, 1775, in Wilmington, Delaware, George married Sarah Seeds in Holy Trinity Church. After the Revolutionary War, fired by romantic tales of frontier life, he and his wife joined the westward trek. They settled first near Washington, Pennsylvania, and finally in Clinton County, Ohio, where he died seven years later at the age of ninety. His son George II, born in 1784, was twenty-two when he married

---

*The spontoon is also known as a half-pike, a pointed weapon with a blade at the head of the shaft and a cross-bar at the base. It was used by infantry officers in the 17th and 18th centuries.

**The bequests, stated in dollars, were originally written as English pounds. The figures used here approximate the exchange rate of five dollars to the pound, current for that time.

sixteen-year-old Hannah Wilson, daughter of a blacksmith. Although her mother was a Quaker, Hannah and George were Methodists as, indeed, were all the Nixons for four generations. Their son, George III, was born in 1821 in a log cabin in Washington, Pennsylvania. He, in turn, married seventeen-year-old Margaret Ann Trimmer, a girl of Dutch ancestry, bringing the only non-Scot-Irish blood into the Nixon line.

George III and Margaret Ann moved to Elk Township, Ohio, in 1853, where he became a farmer. A hero of the Civil War, he enlisted in Company B, 73rd Ohio Voluntary Infantry Regiment, and was killed in action on July 3, 1863, one of the last to die in the sanguinary struggle that marked the Battle of Gettysburg. He was buried there, not far from the late President Eisenhower's farm. He was only forty-two when he lost his life, but the tragedy was compounded when his wife died less than two years later, leaving eight children. Of these, the couple's second son, Samuel Brady Nixon, born October 9, 1847, was Richard Nixon's grandfather. Only eighteen at the time of his mother's death, he helped manage the farm, taught school and carried the mail part time. On April 10, 1873, he married Sarah Ann Wadsworth, twenty-one year old daughter of a storekeeper.* The mother of five children (three sons and two daughters), she died of tuberculosis, as did two of her grandsons, Harold and Arthur. At the time of her death, her son Francis Anthony, born December 3, 1878, was seven years old. He was to become Richard Nixon's father.

---

*Genealogists trace Sarah Ann Wadsworth, Richard Nixon's paternal grandmother, to General "Mad Anthony" Wayne (1745-1796), an outstanding general of the Revolutionary War and later a distinguished statesman in the new Republic. Wayne earned his "Mad Anthony" sobriquet because of his impetuous, hot-headed nature. He quarreled with everyone, including his fellow officers, a characteristic that was to manifest itself in the President's father, Francis Anthony (Frank) Nixon. Some members of the Wayne family, staunch Democrats, heatedly deny any kinship with the Nixons.

Richard Nixon's paternal grandfather, Samuel Brady Nixon.

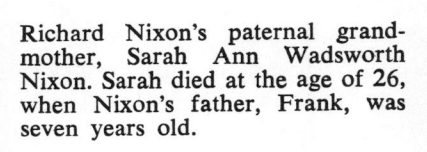

Richard Nixon's paternal grandmother, Sarah Ann Wadsworth Nixon. Sarah died at the age of 26, when Nixon's father, Frank, was seven years old.

Early Milhouses

On the President's maternal side, the first to reach the New World was the Quaker family of Thomas and Sarah Milhous, and their three children. Born in County Kildare, Ireland, they fled the waves of religious persecutions that were widespread in the early eighteenth century, and settled in Chester, Pennsylvania in 1729. Originally, the family name was Melhausen. Migrating from Germany to England in 1688 with the entourage of William, Prince of Orange, and his consort, Mary, they anglicized their name to Milhous, and were soon converted to the teachings of George Fox, founder of the Society of Friends (Quakers). A number of the Friends, including the Milhous family, soon moved to Ireland where they remained for about thirty-five years before emigrating to colonial America.

Clearly, neither the Nixons nor the Milhouses were part of the so-called "landed gentry" or aristocracy of the burgeoning New World. They were the toilers, the builders, the venturesome souls who brought civilization of sorts to the wilderness, and who, because of their abiding faith and resourcefulness, were able to make a better life for themselves and their children.

Despite the similarities, however, the two families were very different, and it is surprising that they were finally united at all. Whereas the Nixons personified the rash-and-brash Irish American pioneer who built our railroads and helped the nation expand, the Milhouses were quiet, gentle people; albeit possessed of their own brand of iron-willed toughness. The Nixons were fundamentalist Bible-thumping Methodists. The Milhouses were peaceful, devout Quakers. The Nixons pushed ever westward, while the descendants of Thomas and Sarah Milhous gradually migrated to the south. There, however, in the tense years that preceded the Civil War, many members of the Society of Friends found themselves in alien territory. Their Quaker teachings, which rejected the entire concept of bondage, forced them to reverse their southward movement and to head north again.*

Among these abolitionists were Franklin Milhous, a fruit-grower, and his wife Almira,** who settled in the vicinity of Butlerville, a small village in southeast Indiana. Here, amid their orchards, in a sturdy farmhouse as foursquare as its occupants, Hannah Milhous, destined to be the President's mother, was born.

For some time, Franklin and Almira had been hearing glowing reports of the new Quaker town of Whittier in far-off California. They learned of the agreeable climate, the orange groves, the lovely hills made lush by winter's greening rains, the fellowship shared by Friends living in their own community, and the opportunity afforded Quaker children to attend meeting houses and schools of their own faith. The lure of the west proved overpowering, and in 1897 Franklin loaded his furniture, tools, lumber and even some nursery stock aboard a freight car and, together with his wife, their nine children (two boys and seven girls), and Franklin's mother, Elizabeth, they journeyed to Southern California. Settling in Whittier only ten years after its founding as a community of the Society of Friends, Franklin built their home—the house in which Hannah grew up. It was here where she was to meet Frank Nixon, her future husband.

---

*Another Milhous, John William, operated an Underground Railroad station on the north bank of the Ohio River, where he aided fugitive slaves in their perilous escape to freedom in the northern states and in Canada. It is said that Columbus, Indiana, and its environs, still number many descendants of the slaves rescued by Milhous and his fellow abolitionists.

**Almira Burdg was Franklin's second wife. His first, Sarah Emily Armstrong, died in 1877, five years after their marriage. Their son, Griffith, Hannah's half-brother, was a skilled musician and became Richard Nixon's first music teacher. Franklin and Almira were married in 1879, two years after Sarah's death.

Nixon's maternal grandfather (Hannah's father), Franklin Milhous.

Dick Nixon's grandmother (Hannah's mother), Almira Burdg Milhous.

The Milhous home, in Butlerville, Indiana, where Franklin and Almira lived with their nine children and Franklin's mother, Elizabeth. Birthplace of Hannah Nixon.

Almira and Franklin Milhous (center row, right) with their children. Eight-year-old Hannah, top row, left.

Hannah, at eleven, was a quiet, studious girl already steeped in the Quaker faith.

For the remainder of her life, Grandmother Almira Milhous, who lived to age ninety-six, exerted a strong influence on the town of Whittier, as she did upon her grandson, Richard Nixon. The President recalled her vividly. "Grandmother admired Lincoln tremendously," he reminisced. "She worshipped him. I remember, on my thirteenth birthday, she made me a present of his picture, and underneath she wrote the ending of Longfellows' *Psalm of Life*."* The President paused and smiled. "She also sent me a very welcome five-dollar bill."

Nixon also recalled his grandmother's home, his voice nostalgic as he reminisced: "It was a large house on Whittier Boulevard. Each year, at Christmas, and usually once during the summer, we would have a family reunion. She kept the family together through the years. She was a prolific letter writer, and on birthdays she composed rhymes and couplets and sent them to us.

"My grandmother set the standards for the whole family," the President continued. "Honesty, hard work, do your best at all times—humanitarian ideals. She was always taking care of every tramp that came along the road, just as my own mother did. She had strong feelings about pacifism and very strong feelings on civil liberties. She probably affected me in that respect. At her house no servant ever ate at a separate table. They always ate with the family. There were Negroes, Indians, and people from Mexico—she was always taking somebody in."

The esteem in which Nixon held his grandmother is graphically illustrated in this letter which he sent to her in 1936, when he was twenty-three, and a senior at Duke University Law School:

---

*Nixon kept the picture on the wall above his bed throughout his high school and college years.

Dear Grandmother,

At this Christmas Season, I should like to be sending you a gift which would really express my love for you, but it will probably be several years before I reach such a high financial level—if ever.

So instead of sending you a card which would not express the feeling I wish to convey, I'm writing you this little Christmas note.

You will never know how much I've appreciated your remembrances, at Christmas, at Easter, on my birthdays—and on days which have no special significance at all. More than them, however, I believe that I appreciate the fact that I have been a member of a family with such an illustrious person at its head. Sometimes—in our spare moments, some of us indulge in reminiscing sessions here at school—and the boys are amazed at the remarkable person I describe as my Quaker grandmother. I myself share this respect.

So here is wishing for you a merry Christmas—and many more happy new Years.

Your loving Grandson
Richard Milhous Nixon

Richard Nixon is a composite of the virtues and shortcomings of his antecedents; the intellectualism of his grandparents, the stubborn instincts of his father, the gentle reasonableness of his mother. Whether these qualities, which he possesses in varying degrees, are due primarily to heredity or environment, remains a matter of lively controversy among psychologists, sociologists and anthropologists. But, whatever the source, he is unquestionably as individualistic as he is a new breed of president. Born of stalwart Quaker stock, he is, nevertheless, a son of the atomic age. The influence of his

Richard Nixon's Christmas letter to grandmother Almira Nixon, written in 1936.

mother, father and maternal grandmother cannot be discounted in any evaluation of his personal feelings, reactions and motivations.

The President's Parents: Frank and Hannah Nixon

Following the death of his mother, when he was seven, young Frank Nixon experienced the first stirrings of that rootlessness which was to propel him until his marriage. After quitting grade school, he went to work on his uncle Lyle's farm and on other farms in the area of Elk Township, Ohio. Here Frank Nixon, the President's father, was born.

Those were not easy times. "Fifty cents a day, sometimes seventy-five, was just about tops in wages for a farmhand," Frank recalled.

Always a loner, the wanderlust that gnawed at his nomadic spirit drove him from one place to another—city to city, state to state—forever seeking the one big break. He worked as a Pullman car painter, as a sheep rancher in Colorado, a carpenter, a telephone linesman, an oilfield roustabout, and a farmer. He had no formal education, but his wanderings helped him become a well educated man, taught through the practical experiences of life itself. Though his education lacked a formal structure, it was rich and creative, yielding the kind of knowledge that a man of independent spirit needed in order to cope with the realities of life.

Frank's brother, Dr. Ernest Leland Nixon, was Professor of Horticulture at State College, Pennsylvania. He once described his brother's mental abilities with this observation: "Frank had a grasp of the principles involving social, political and economic problems that was far beyond the level one would expect of a man with his limited schooling. He was not a formally educated man, but he was a discerning and perceptive one."

Frank Nixon's political direction was launched by two ob-

Richard Nixon's father, Francis Anthony Nixon, a few years after the turn of the century.

scure experiences. The first stamped him as a lifelong Republican; the other gave him his first taste of labor activism.

"Back in Ohio, the Nixons had always been Democrats," explained the President's younger brother, Don. "My father, who was about thirteen at the time, was a hired hand on a farm just outside of McArthur, and had a filly he was mighty proud of. William McKinley came to town during his presidential campaign tour and noticed the horse my father was riding in the parade. He left the bandstand, came over and patted and praised the horse. Then he asked my father if he would always vote Republican. The answer was, of course, 'Yes.' And to our knowledge, Father never broke faith with McKinley, although my mother suspected that he left the political fold in 1932 to vote for Franklin D. Roosevelt—but this was a suspicion he would never confirm or deny."*

A pair of frozen feet, like a ruse of destiny, accounted for Frank's brief experience as a labor agitator and for his moving to California, a move which was eventually to influence the course of history.

Having decided to give up farming for more lucrative work in the city, he found employment as a street-car motorman in Columbus, Ohio, where he was required to stand in the open vestibule of the vehicle—often in snow and ice. One particularly harsh winter, his feet were frostbitten—literally, frozen. Appeals to the management to enclose the vestibules were fruitless, so, with characteristic aggressiveness, he organized the trolley employees into a group to press for the passage of a law to improve their working conditions. His lobbying activities before the Ohio State Legislature were successful, and a law was passed requiring the transit company to enclose the vestibules.

---

*Richard Nixon states that his father may also have broken with the Republican Party in 1924 to vote for Farmer-Labor candidate Robert LaFollette in opposition to Calvin Coolidge, in the Presidential election of that year.

But the damage to his feet could not be undone. Even when healed, the pain would return during cold weather, and Frank finally realized that he would have to seek a warmer climate. He chose Southern California.

Whittier—The New Homestead

Whittier, at the turn of the century, was a peaceful little town of orange, lemon and avocado groves, and small farms. Nearly all of its inhabitants were Quakers who lived in simple homes and avoided the frills and fancies of Los Angeles, fifteen miles away—a distance to be reckoned with in those days of narrow roads built to accommodate only the horse and wagon. Founded in 1887 by the Society of Friends, it was named after the abolitionist Quaker poet, John Greenleaf Whittier.

It is no longer the tranquil community it once was. The town's population has grown from a few score hardy souls to about 35,000. Groves have largely been replaced by oil rigs, new housing and a spider-web of interlacing freeways. Where once the soil yielded its fruit, vegetables, grain and dairy products in abundance, it now lies dormant underneath huge factories that produce tools and parts for airplanes and missiles.

The city's main street runs north toward the slopes of the Puente Hills in whose shade rests Whittier College. On one side of the street, just before one reaches the college as he leaves the freeway from Los Angeles, stands the First Friends Church; on the other side is the William Penn Hotel. Today, Nixon's relatives attend the downtown First Friends Church, but the President, as a boy, was a member of the East Whittier Friends Church, on Whittier Boulevard, opposite the site of the old Nixon store.*

---

*The present East Whittier Friends Church is the replacement for the original structure which was moved across the street to the Nixon property. "Nixon's Market" is gone; a filling station now occupies the grounds.

Yet, despite all the overhead powerlines, the roar and fumes of passing trucks, the endless ribbons of auto traffic, the blatant neon signs that illumine the approaches of the city, Whittier still retains much of its natural beauty and early charm. It is not too difficult to visualize the pastoral setting nor the industrious Friends among whom Frank and Hannah came to live and to rear their family. The poet, Whittier may have had just such people in mind when he wrote:

> *We cross the prairies as of old*
> *The pilgrims crossed the sea,*
> *To make the West, as they the East,*
> *The homestead of the free.*

Frank Nixon arrived in Whittier in 1907, carrying with him a letter of recommendation from his old employer—the Columbus Street Car Company. He soon found a job as motorman on the now defunct Red Trolley System that served as the link between Los Angeles and Whittier. The climate suited him, the work was pleasant, and the pain in his feet almost gone. It was good to be alive here in this peaceful community.

Frank and Hannah Meet

On the evening of February 15, 1908—a date he remembered with affection for as long as he lived—Frank met Hannah Milhous at a party sponsored by the Friends Church in East Whittier. They were attracted to each other from the start. Frank walked her home that night, and four months later they were married, despite obviously pronounced differences in personality and background.

Frank Nixon was a stormy, argumentative man; Hannah was a soft-spoken woman. Frank's formal education was limited to the sixth grade grammar school; Hannah was a college graduate (Whittier, 1906). Frank was forever the disrupter;

Frank Nixon in 1907, at the age of 29 when he arrived in Whittier, California, from Columbus, Ohio.

Hannah, shortly before her marriage to Frank, in 1908.

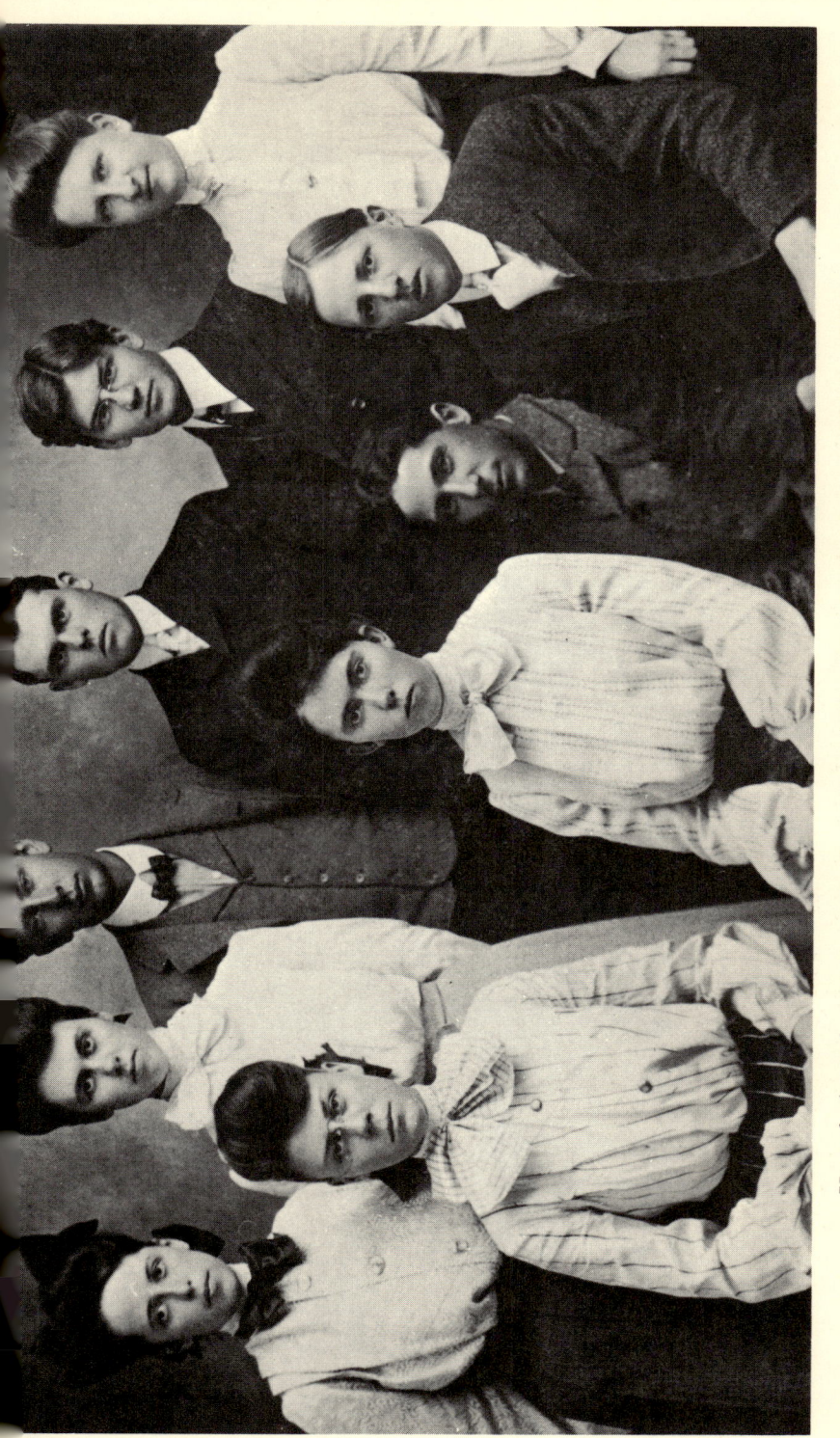

Hannah (seated, center), a pensive senior of 20, with her classmates at Whittier College.

Hannah, the eternal peacemaker. Yet, there was a bond between this high-strung, moody man, and this calm, forbearing woman—a silken cord whose threads were spun on the bobbin of mutual respect.

In the first years after their marriage Frank and Hannah lived in the Milhous home; and Frank became a Quaker. The early years were times of struggle, sorrows and deprivation, but they had pleasant experiences too; they had the security and contentment that characterized so many of the well-knit, small-town families of a past generation.

The first of their five sons, Harold, was born in 1909, while Frank and Hannah still lived with her parents. In February of 1911 Frank, Hannah and their two-year-old son Harold moved to nearby Yorba Linda, a recently settled rural community where Frank hoped his skill as a carpenter would be employed in the building of the new homes that were springing up in that desert town. He also planned to start a lemon grove, at that time the mainstay of the local economy.

They could not know, of course, that the next occupant of their Yorba Linda home would someday occupy the White House. But two years later, in 1913, Richard Nixon, the future President of the United States was born in this modest, simple setting.*

---

*Richard Nixon's brother, Donald, was born in 1914, and brother, Arthur, in 1918—both in Yorba Linda. Edward was born in Whittier in 1930 when Hannah was 45 years old.

2
Years of Struggle— Years of Toil

SOME THIRTY MILES southeast of Los Angeles, the tiny farming village of Yorba Linda had suffered through the furnace-heat of a mid-winter day, typical in that desert area. Now, with the setting of the sun, the night had turned quite cold, a not uncommon occurrence. The villagers, mostly farmers, accustomed to arising at dawn to begin their daily chores, had retired early, allowing the logs in the fireplace to smoulder in their own embers for whatever warmth they might produce. One by one, lamps were extinguished and the inhabitants made ready for bed. But one home was ablaze with light, the soft hum of voices somewhat restrained, yet vibrant with scarcely concealed excitement.

High atop a knoll, at its very summit, a solid, two-story white clapboard house attested to the skills of Frank Nixon who had built the family home with his own hands.* At the

---
*The house in which Richard Nixon was born, at 1806 Yorba Linda Boulevard, is still in perfect condition. It is now the property of the

base of the hill was the deep, swift-running Anaheim Irrigation Ditch. Overlooking the Ditch, on the parched and crumbly slope of the knoll, where nothing but weeds and desert plants had ever grown before, was Frank's lemon grove.

As a rule, the wintry nights were so cold that the Nixon family would dress in the kitchen near the warmth of the cooking stove. On this special night, however, Frank brought two wood stoves into the living room and placed them at either side of the fireplace. The entire house was now snug and warm. In the bedroom, just off the living room, Hannah Nixon was being attended by Mrs. Henrietta Shockney, a practical nurse who had been retained to assist with the delivery. Four-year-old Harold, apparently sensing the tension, and unable to sleep, had been taken in tow by his grandmother, Mrs. Almira Milhous, who kept him quiet and out of everyone's way.

At 9:30, on Thursday night, January 9, 1913, Richard Milhous Nixon was born—an eleven pound baby with a mass of dark brown hair, brown eyes and a howling screech that could be heard throughout the house.* Grandma Milhous turned to her son-in-law. "With a voice like that," she said, smiling, "he'll be either a lawyer or a preacher."

Years later, at the Eastern Star Masonic Home for Women, in Beverly Hills, nurse Shockney, then in her eighties, recalled that momentous evening. "I was recommended by the Nixons' family physician, Dr. H. P. Wilson, who practised in Whittier," she said. "I was paid $25.00 for the week, but I would have worked for Mrs. Nixon at less pay because everyone in the community seemed to love and respect her.

Yorba Linda Elementary School District. The house was dedicated as a historic site by the townspeople and the school board, January 9, 1959, on the occasion of Nixon's forty-sixth birthday.

*Richard Nixon was the first child to be born in the newly-founded town of Yorba Linda.

They had every reason to feel that way. She was a gracious, understanding and very kind lady, and I considered myself lucky to help with Richard's birth."

> Richard Milhous Nixon
> Thursday Nine Thirtyfive P.M.
> January Ninth
> Ninteen-hundred-thirteen
>
> Eleven Pounds

Nurse Henrietta Shockney used green ink to record the vital facts regarding the birth of Richard Milhous Nixon.

Richard Nixon has often been described as a serious and introspective boy by members of his family and by others who knew him as a youngster. And he was. His formative years left little time for frivolity, and undoubtedly his demeanor was a reflection of the strict Quaker standards and work ethic demanded by his loving but no-nonsense parents. "Richard was always mature—far beyond his age," recalled his mother. "Even as a small child he was thoughtful and serious."

Alan Gaines, an elementary school classmate, remembered him because of his sober personality. "I don't recall ever hearing him really laugh," he said. "Dick was friendly enough, and he had a nice sort of smile, but he always seemed like he was carrying the weight of the world on his shoulders."

During the years in which the Nixons lived in Yorba Linda, father Frank worked at whatever job he could find. His skill as a carpenter was soon recognized and he helped build many of the houses which are still standing and occupied in the

The Yorba Linda house in which Richard Nixon was born in 1913.

Main Street, in the newly-founded settlement of Yorba Linda at the time of Nixon's birth in 1913.

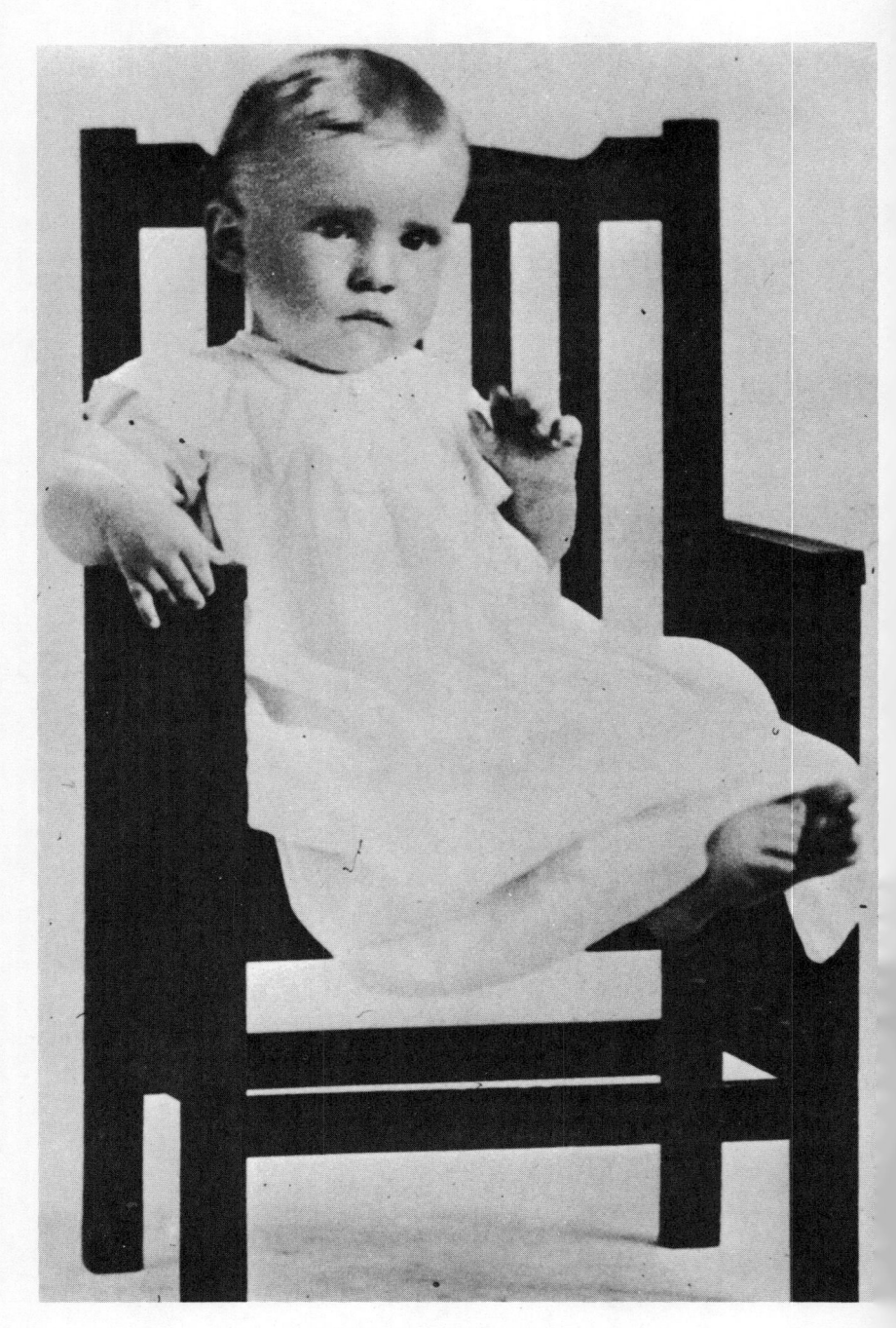

Richard, age nine months.

Twenty-two-month-old Richard, surrounded by Thanksgiving and Christmas pumpkins. Brother Harold (left) shades his eyes.

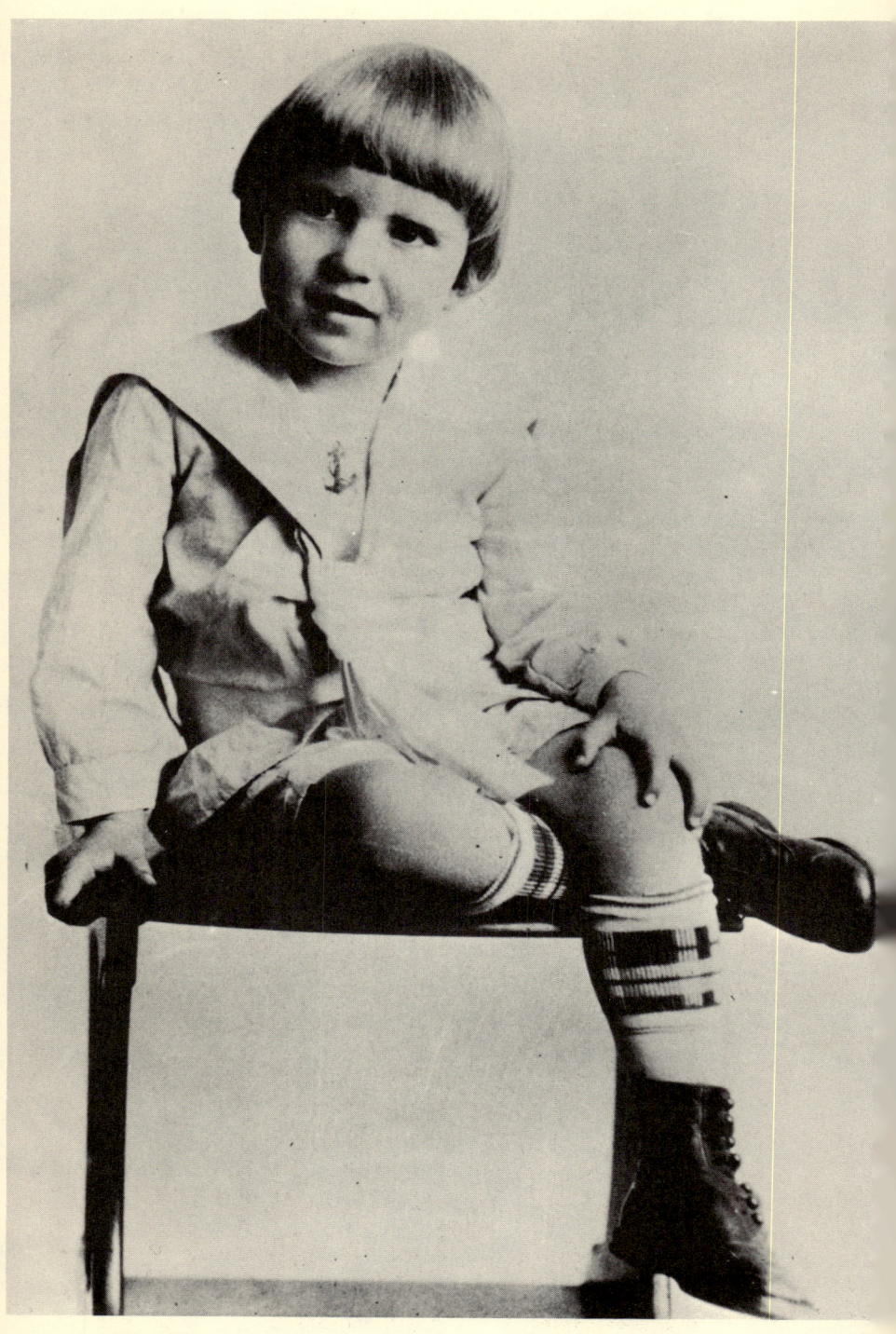

Richard Nixon, age four, had just recovered from a near-fatal horse-and-buggy accident.

Frank and Hannah Nixon with (left to right) Harold 8, Donald 5, and Richard 4.

town. Employment was far from steady, however, and he was hard put to support his family. "Those were not easy times," said Donald Nixon, in modest understatement. He was no doubt recalling some of his father's unsuccessful business ventures.*

But, whatever their financial circumstances, the children never went hungry; nor did they lack clothes or any of the other essentials—a tribute to their father who never allowed his dignity to interfere with honest toil. This was an impressive and unforgettable example that he set for his sons. The boys received no "allowance" or spending money. When they needed something important, it was provided. But, normally, the boys worked in order to earn the wherewithal to meet their other needs.

Reared to observe the strict requirements of their faith, Richard accompanied Frank, Hannah and his brothers to church every Wednesday evening and three times on Sunday. As he grew older, Richard taught Sunday School, as did his father, and played the organ at services.

The Nixons lived frugally, of course, but nevertheless managed to accumulate some savings, all of which were wiped out in 1916 when a horse-and-buggy accident almost killed three-year-old Richard. It happened as Hannah was driving a two-horse buggy, returning from the railroad station in neighboring Placentia where she had picked up her visiting aunt.

---

*Characteristic of Frank Nixon's bad luck, he lost his chance of attaining wealth when he sold the "worthless" property on which his lemon grove was planted. The new owners struck oil on the land. The senior Nixon's unlucky streak continued when he moved to Whittier. He was given his choice of two locations for a gas station—one in East Whittier, the other in nearby Santa Fe Springs. After much deep thought and a personal inspection of both sites, he decided on the East Whittier property. History repeated itself: within a year oil was discovered on the rejected Santa Fe Springs site which he could have purchased for the tiniest fraction of its true value. The Santa Fe's very first well burst forth with a gusher yielding 25 barrels a day. Once again, the hard-pressed Nixons had narrowly missed becoming oilionaires.

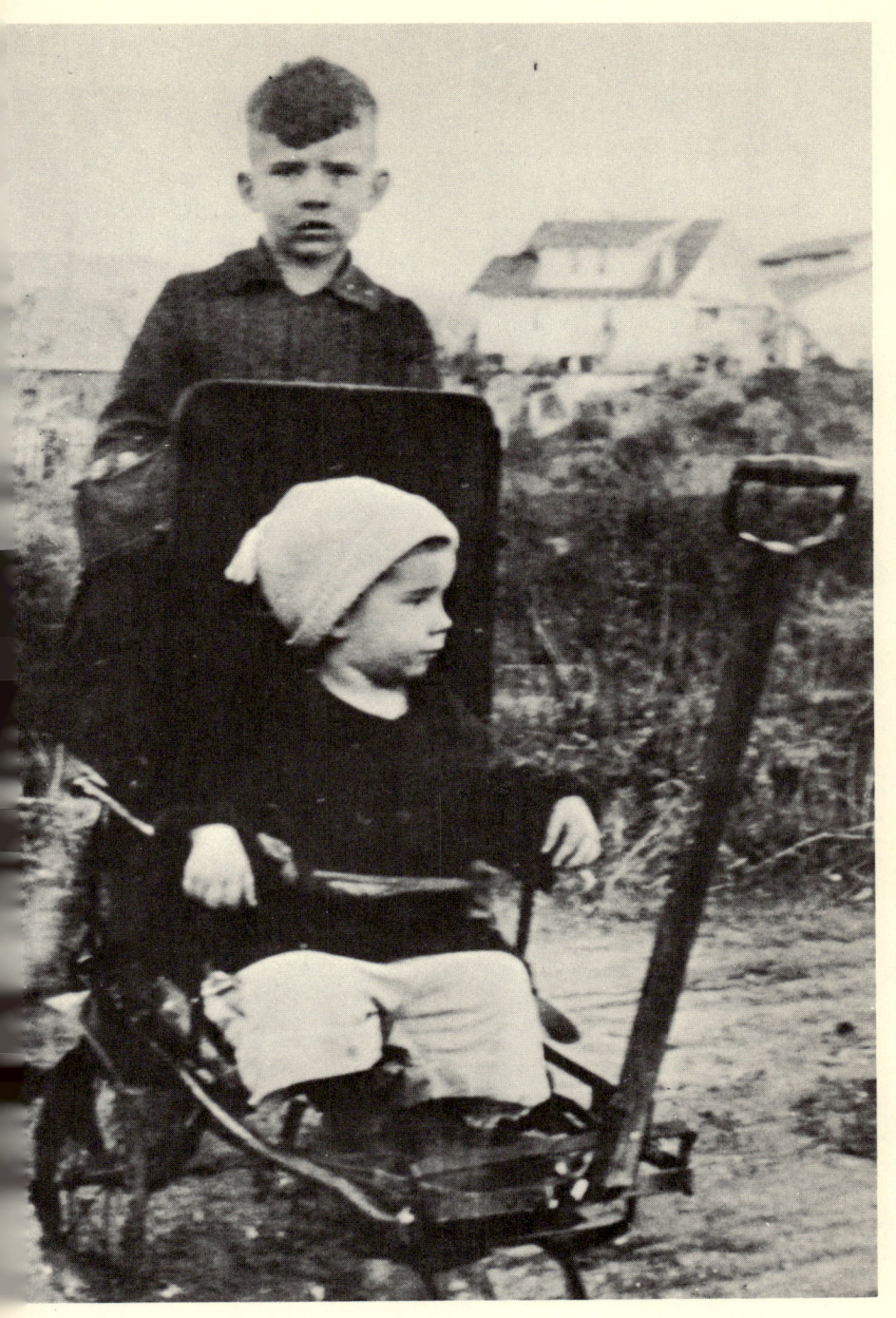

Richard, age eight, helping his brother Arthur, age two, through a mud puddle.

In their Sunday-go-to-meetin' clothes (left to right): Harold, Richard, Arthur and Donald.

"I was holding Donald, the baby, in my lap while driving the buggy," explained Mrs. Nixon. "Richard was being held by a little neighbor girl because I had all I could do to manage the horses and the baby without trying to watch my three-year-old boy too. As we were rounding the curve at the Anaheim Irrigation Ditch, something startled the horses and they bolted. The buggy swayed wildly from side to side and the little girl lost her hold on Richard. He fell out onto the road and a wheel cut into the side of his head. His scalp was badly lacerated, and blood spurted from a long, jagged gash that separated his scalp from the bone."

Fortunately, the Quigleys, neighbors of the Nixons and owners of the only car in Yorba Linda, were able to drive young Richard to the hospital, some 25 miles distant. "Had he reached the hospital emergency room just a few minutes later," observed Dr. A. L. Roberts, "Richard would have been dead on arrival."

The ugly scar, beginning just above the forehead and extending down to the neck, is now hidden by judicious use of a comb—which explains why the President always parts his hair on the right side.

A year after the buggy accident, the life of little Richard was again in jeopardy—this time from pneumonia.

And thirteen years later, during his final year at Whittier High School, he once again almost lost his life after contracting undulant fever. The crisis lasted a full week, with his temperature rising to 104° every day.

"But my prayers were answered," said his mother fervently. "It was a miracle."

Richard's recovery was slow. He was unable to attend classes in that final year, but he pursued his studies at home —often while bedridden—and graduated with honors. He even managed to maintain his four-year "A" average in Latin.

One of the honors that he received in his early years was the Harvard Club of California Prize, awarded to the school's foremost all-around scholar. But the prizes he cherished most were those connected with victory in the debates he had entered before the onslaught of his illness. Indeed, his skill as a debater had long since become a topic of conversation in every school in the area.

The picture that emerges is that of a boy dedicated to work and study, without a single hobby to afford him pleasant hours of relaxation; a boy leading a life that was austere even when compared with other Quaker youths in his neighborhood. Nowhere in the several biographies about Richard Nixon is there any mention of a carefree youngster, a fun-loving boy enjoying boyish pranks and escapades; nor has Nixon himself ever alluded to such activity.

Novelist Jessamyn West* reports young Richard's sole act of misconduct; a bit of coltish exuberance that is so innocuous it would scarcely merit reporting were it not for the fact that it represents the one and only incident wherein he disobeyed his parents.

It seems that Richard and his older brother, Harold, would occasionally swim in the fast-running current of the Anaheim Ditch despite their mother's stern warnings and the *No Swimming Allowed* signs posted on the banks. This transgression resulted in one of the very few spankings he ever received, the punishment administered by his mother. Mrs. Nixon proudly claimed that this was his only lapse from good behavior.

"Most boys go through an age of revolt and mischief," Mrs. Nixon declared. "When they reach their teens they think they know all the answers and they tend to get a little difficult around the house. But except for that one swimming incident, Richard [she never called him Dick] was never like that. Even when he was six or seven he was interested in things you would expect of a much older boy."

---

*Jessamyn West, cousin of the Nixons, is the author of *The Friendly Persuasion*, a novel revolving around Richard Nixon's great-grandfather, Joshua Milhous, a red-headed Irish Quaker who stunned the Friends' community by purchasing an organ for his home. Gary Cooper starred in the Motion picture version.

The Nixon boys around 1923. Inside the tire is Don. Standing (left to right) are Richard, Harold and little Arthur who had already begun to badger his mother for a "real boy's haircut."

Hannah Nixon's estimate of her son cannot be brushed aside as the exaggeration of a doting mother; there is ample evidence that he was indeed precocious. While the other boys in the neighborhood were absorbed by children's picture books, young Richard was avidly reading newspapers and constantly asking the meaning of words he did not understand.

"Dick was the studious one in the family," said Donald. "He was always reading and studying while the rest of us were out having fun." Proof of his serious nature, his initiative and industry came early in life. At age 11, Richard wrote his first formal letter of application for a job. It was to the Los Angeles Times in answer to an ad:

                                        Whittier, Calif.
                                        Jan. 24, 1924

Times Office,
K, Box 240

Dear Sir:—

    Please consider me for the position of office boy mentioned in the Times paper. I am eleven years of age and I am in the Sixth grade of the East Whittier Grammar School.

    I am very willing to work and would like the money for a vacation trip. I am willing to come to your office at any time and I will accept any pay offered. My address is Whittier boulevard and Leffingwell road. The phone number is 5274. For reference you can see Miss Flowers, princaple of the East Whittier School.

    Hoping that you will accept me for your service, I am, Yours truly

                                          Richard M. Nixon

> Whittier, Calif.
> Jan. 24, 1924.
>
> Times Office,
> X. Box 240
> Dear Sir:—
>
> Please consider me for the position of office boy mentioned in the Times paper. I am eleven years of age and I am in the sixth grade of the East Whittier Grammar School.
>
> I am very willing to work and would like the money for a vacation trip. I am willing to come to your office at any time and I will accept any pay offered. My address is Whittier Boulavard and Leffingwell road. The phone number is 5274. For Reference you can see Miss Flowers, principle of the East Whittier School.
>
> Hoping that you will accept me for your service, I am, Yours truly,
>
> Richard M. Nixon

Sixth-grader Richard Nixon applies for the job of office boy to earn his vacation money.

In their spare time, Richard and Donald worked as farm laborers, picking fruit for citrus growers in the area, and string beans and peas in the neighborhood's truck gardens.

"It taught us the value of a dollar," commented the President. "We would work twelve long hard hours to earn that one dollar." He grinned and added, "I still hate the sight of string beans."

There were a number of reasons why the Nixons finally decided to move from Yorba Linda. For Hannah, the deep and dangerous Irrigation Ditch that skirted their property aroused her concern for the safety of the children. Further, she longed to be nearer the Quaker meeting house that meant so much to her spiritual life. As for Frank, it was a matter of earning a better living.

Thus, in 1922, ten years after their arrival, they left the penury of Yorba Linda and relocated in the town of Whittier.

Here, in their new home, Father Frank's wanderings finally came to an end. And here, Richard Nixon grew to manhood.

The Making of a Man

When Frank purchased the land on which his filling station was to be located—a desolate corner on East Whittier Boulevard, at that time about three miles from town—it represented what was probably the only successful business venture he had ever entered into. "At least I can walk to work," laughed Frank, pointing to their home on Santa Gertrudes, which was immediately to the rear of the gas pumps.

"The house was a simple one," Richard Nixon recalled during his terms as Vice President, "but in the living room was a mahogany upright piano that Mother insisted on having, although I was the only one in the family who played it. Next door was the garage with connecting stairs that led to three bedrooms and a bath above the garage. The downstairs bedroom, off the living room, was where two of my brothers died."

Nixon, in recalling the old-fashioned piano, noted that it was the only activity in his early boyhood that was not directly associated with school or his daily chores.

He made his first "public appearance" as an entertainer at a recital when he was in the eighth grade of grammar school, playing *Rustle of Spring*.

"Richard played it very well—I was proud of him," said his mother. Obviously she cannot be termed an objective, disinterested critic, but she was, nevertheless, a good judge of music. Like all small boys, he invented all sorts of stratagems to avoid practice (he hated the monotony of doing the scales), but under his mother's watchful eye he practiced until he became quite proficient. At the age of twelve, he could play Brahms and Bach with fair skill for a youngster, and with evident enjoyment.*

In the early 1920's the automobile had not yet come into its own, and consequently few of the roads were paved. However, there were already enough cars on the dirt roads to support a strategically located station. This one was well situated indeed. "We had the only one between Whittier and La Habra," said Donald. "We often had the customers lined up waiting for gas."

Industrious Frank, at Hannah's suggestion, built an addition to the station, installed a refrigerator, and began selling milk, eggs and bread. Across the street, congregants of the East Whittier Friends Church decided to build a new and larger building, so Frank bought the old meeting house and

---

*Nixon's skill as a pianist approaches professional standards, and had he not chosen the law as a career he might have done well as a musician. Today, the President's range of musical preference is wide and varied; he likes country folk music, the better pop tunes and the classics. In the past three years, he and Mrs. Nixon have attended the opera, and both have been quite knowledgeable about the performers as well as the performances. In 1971, Nixon played the piano at the White House celebration of Mamie Eisenhower's 75th birthday, prompting a television commentator to quip: "He played for all three networks, and they didn't even offer to pay him a dime."

moved it onto his site. This became "Nixon's Market."

The bell tower served as the store's office, and it was there that Richard would often study at night. The tower held a certain nostalgia for him. "That's where he had gone to Bible class, taught by our Uncle West," explained Donald.

The filling station and the market began to prosper, with Frank at first dispensing gasoline while Hannah tended the store. It was bone-wearying labor, especially for Hannah. Her day would begin at dawn and, until the boys were old enough to help, continue for eighteen straight hours until nearly midnight, when she would sink into bed for a few blessed hours of sleep. Her final task, before retiring, was to cull the small or bruised fruit and berries, then sort and wash them for filling the pies which she baked at night and sold in the store the next morning. Most popular, according to the family, was her cherry pie.

Yet, no matter how busy her day, she always prepared breakfast for her husband and sons, and ate with them. "It was the ritual that started our day, with prayers and recitatations of Bible verses," said Hannah Nixon. "We all participated—it helped to remind us that we were a family unit."

Father Frank also worked hard and long in the store. His assistance was so badly needed that there were times when the gentle, long-suffering Hannah wished he were more the grocer and less the orator, for Nixon's Market had become—in true cracker-barrel, country style—a favorite gathering place. Here Frank expounded his liberal political philosophy, vehemently debating whatever issues were the topic of the day. The arguments often grew heated, and Hannah would step in to cool tempers, mollify Frank's cronies, placate customers, and generally play the peacemaker. His outbursts may well have cost them many customers.

"People not only avoided him at the store, but even when they just phoned in their orders they would ask to talk to Hannah, not Frank," recalled Evelyn Dorn, Richard Nixon's secretary during the period he practiced law in California.

By Hannah Nixon

Cherry Pie –

Crust: 1½ cups flour
½ cup shortening
½ tsp salt
3 or 4 tbsp ice water

Cut shortening into salted flour and lightly mix in ice water

Filling: 1 number 2 can sour pitted cherries
1 cup sugar
2 tbsp cornstarch mixed into a thin paste with water –

Bring cherries and sugar to a boil. Stir in thickening, let cool. Put in unbaked pie shell, dot with butter. Thoroughly moisten edge with water before firmly pressing down top crust. After crimping edge – circle the pie 8 times with wet fingers. Slightly moisten top crust with pastry brush dipped in milk. Bake in moderate oven 35 min or until done.

Hannah Nixon's secret recipe for cherry pie, a favorite with her family and a best-seller at "Nixon's Market." Years later she added her name to the top of the page saying, laughingly, "Don't forget to give me author's credit."

To this, brother Donald added, "Father would rather argue, than do anything else—and he'd take any side of an issue."

A compromise of sorts was finally reached: Frank was to confine himself to cutting meat, driving to Los Angeles to do the buying, and performing whatever heavy work was necessary. The happy result was a tribute to Hannah's diplomacy in the handling of her obstreperous husband. Nevertheless, it was Frank's diligence that brought a modest degree of prosperity to his family.

"My father was fairly successful," Richard Nixon agreed, as he recalled that it had been his father's idea to buy the old Quaker meeting house which had helped their store and filling station to prosper.

There was never the slightest evidence of rancor in Richard Nixon's recollections of his father. On the contrary, he admired and respected him, knowing that his towering rages would eventually reduce themselves to moody reflection. There was also the further consideration that his excess of energy boiled and bubbled within him as in a pressure-cooker; his penchant for debate the only way he could let off steam. And, of course, an additional reason for his irritability was the pain from his arthritis, his partial deafness and his ulcers.

"The main reason for Frank's attitude, I think, was that he had led a very active life," said Mrs. Dorn. "When he could no longer do the many things he did in the past he became frustrated."

People in Whittier, especially those who had felt the sting of his tongue, are unanimous in recalling that Frank was a liberal thinker whose impassioned expositions deeply impressed his young son. If that assessment is correct, then the President's political antecedents have long been obscured by his self-evaluation as a conservative. Indeed, he was an activist and "liberal" in college, and was hailed in the campus newspaper as a "liberal and outspoken president of the student body," after winning the election to that post in his senior year at Whittier College.

The Nixon Nobody Knows 49

Perhaps it was after Richard Nixon became the chief executive of the nation that his father's liberal influence really came to the fore. It was then that he surprised his opponents, and antagonized his conservative supporters, by listening attentively to the shrill demands of the "liberals," turning down the decibels to a realistic volume and revealing the "real Nixon"—in stereo—with the treble notes pitched for the maximum comfort of those on the left of the political spectrum, and the bass tones designed to soften the moans of the ultra-rightists. The so-called "Nixon method," of course, was a carefully-constructed device to appropriate the best of diverse opinions and approaches, and mold them into a workable program.*

There is little question that Richard Nixon's basic philosophy of government, and his style were influenced, in some measure, by the bombast and forthrightness that he saw in his father—that fighting Irishman whose declamations may be likened to those of a Bible Belt evangelist denouncing the Imps of Satan.

How might Frank Nixon have fared in the political arena? Richard Nixon himself speculated on the possibility. "Dad loved the excitement and the battles of political life," he wrote in *Six Crises*.** "During the two years he was bedridden, before his death [which came just at the start of the 1956 campaign], his one request of me was that I send him the *Congressional Record*. He used to read it daily, cover-to-

---

*This "method" or "game plan" is what Washington correspondents—the White House watchers—like to call "style." It is evident in his ambitious legislation in the field of domestic policy, and in his handling of the nation's foreign affairs—a style and performance that cannot be construed, in the political sense, as either liberal or conservative. Nixon, as President, shed the customary labels and emerged as a contemporary Progressive Republican, attuned to the needs of the "now" generation, but steadfast in his belief that two centuries of constitutional government have demonstrated the merit of the American political system.

**This book by the President will be discussed later on.

cover, something I never had the patience to do. I have often thought that with his fierce competitive drive and his intense interest in political issues, he might have been more successful than I in political life had he had the opportunity to continue his education."

Tendencies of the past are to be discerned, not only in the President's political approach to many matters, but also in his association with people. Mrs. Rose Olive Marshburn, Hannah's youngest sister, affectionately called "Aunt Ollie" by her nephews, recalled that Richard, after a long day at the store, enjoyed lying on the grass and losing himself in daydreams. "He always seemed to have something else on his mind," she said. "Sometimes he would walk past people he knew well, and he would look right through them. They thought he was stuck up, but he was so immersed in his own deep thoughts, he just didn't see them."

This habit of a half-century ago is still one that the President falls victim to as he lapses into sporadic periods of silent contemplation, as his best friend, Charles Gregory (Bebe) Rebozo, has attested. (These are periods during which Rebozo never intrudes.) But whether these are moments of reflection associated with affairs of State, or simply wool-gathering, no one knows, but the President himself.

"I have never seen a man with such highly developed powers of concentration," said Mrs. Dorn, recalling him as a young lawyer. "There were times when I would be working at my desk for fifteen minutes or more before he realized I was there. He would then look up from his desk and greet me with, 'Oh, good morning, Evelyn.'"

Did his boyhood dreams contribute towards his later ambitions? Did he bow to family suggestions? "The last thing my mother, a devout Quaker, wanted me to do was go into the warfare of politics," said Nixon. "I recall she once expressed the hope that I might become a missionary to our Quaker mission fields in Central America. But true to her Quaker tradition, she never tried to force me in the direction she herself might have preferred." Clearly then, his earliest childhood ambitions were not inspired through "friendly persuasion," but through the fantasies that took root and blossomed in the fertile recesses of his mind.

As a small boy, before the family moved to Whittier, Richard was fascinated by the Santa Fe spurline that ran close to the Nixon home, crossing the Irrigation Ditch and the dirt road that led to town. This preoccupation was heightened by the vivid anecdotes told by a railroad man who would occasionally stop by for a chat.

"He was a good friend of the family whom we had known back in Indiana, before we moved west," explained Aunt Ollie Marshburn. "He was a Santa Fe engineer who lived in Needles, here in California. Whenever he visited Frank he would tell the boys about his work and travels. Richard would listen, spellbound."

The Santa Fe filled his impressionable young mind. From his bedroom window he watched the freight trains chug past and thrilled to their rumblings as they vibrated the timbers of the house. The long box cars, linked in a seemingly endless chain, carried oranges and lemons—California's golden flow of citrus wealth—to the heartland of America.

Night after night he listened to the eerie hoot of the steam whistle of the giant train plunging into the darkness. The Iron Horse of western lore raced down the twin tracks of adventure, going nowhere, going everywhere, its yellow-bronze canteloupe lights shining palely into the night until they were indistinguishable from the glimmering stars on the horizon.

Richard was no more than seven or eight years old when he became enthralled with the vision of a Casey Jones in his own likeness, his hand on the throttle of a speeding, roaring, fire-spitting locomotive.

"Yes, my first ambition as a child was to become a railroad engineer," affirmed the President; "not because of any interest in engines—I have no mechanical aptitude whatever—

but because I wanted to travel and see the United States and the world."

It was not until he was twelve that he abandoned the Casey Jones dreams which had captivated him. It was then that he decided to become a lawyer.

What propelled him in the direction of law were the fascinating Senate disclosures of the corruption attending the Teapot Dome transactions involving government-owned oil reserves in Wyoming and California.* The scandals reached into President Harding's cabinet itself, and implicated many well-known politicians, businessmen and lawyers who had hitherto enjoyed impeccable reputations. One attorney even committed suicide.

As the dramatic sequence of revelations made the headlines daily, Frank Nixon, who could not forget that he himself had missed out on great oil wealth by only the breadth of an eyelash, launched into a frenzy of vituperation that reverberated from the walls of his store and his home. The recriminations, which lasted for weeks, made a deep impression on his son—the scholarly, grave youngster who preferred reading newspapers to the usual children's literary fare.

"Shortly before her death on October 1, 1967, his mother reached back into her memory to recall the incident. "Richard could not help but hear and, to some extent, share his father's indignation about the Teapot Dome scandals.

"One evening Richard was lying on the floor, the news-

---

*Teapot Dome refers to the area near Casper, Wyoming, established in 1915 by President Woodrow Wilson as an oil reserve for the United States Navy. Without explanation, and by executive decree, President Warren G. Harding, in 1921, transferred control from the Navy to the Department of Interior. A year later, ignoring the requirement for competitive bidding, Secretary of the Interior Albert F. Fall leased the Teapot Dome fields to Harry F. Sinclair and leased another government-owned oil field at Elk Hills, California to Edward L. Doheny. In 1923 these secret activities resulted in a Senate investigation, conducted by Senator J. Walsh. Fall resigned his cabinet post amid great notoriety and a number of prominent persons were subjected to criminal prosecution. In 1929, ex-Secretary Fall was convicted for accepting bribes and was sentenced to a year in prison and

paper spread out around him, reading an account of the corrupt officials and attorneys who had been on the front pages for many days. Suddenly, he looked up and solemnly announced, 'Mother, I just made up my mind: I'm going to be a lawyer—a lawyer who can't be bought by crooks.' "*

Frank Nixon's influence carried over into his son's scholastic life as well. Aside from the youth's natural penchant for learning, two factors were instrumental in his competitive drive to achieve distinction in school. "One was economic, the other personal," the President explained. "From an economic standpoint, I knew that I could not go on to college and to law school unless I was able to earn scholarships. It was as simple as that. The personal factor was contributed by my father. . . . Never a day went by when he did not tell me and my four brothers how fortunate we were to be able to go to school. I was determined not to let him down. My biggest thrill in those years was to see the light in his eyes when I brought home a good report card."

Young Nixon pursued his education with the same kind of determination with which he was later to conduct his political campaigns, eschewing all that might conceivably interfere with his plans. Not for him were the camaraderie or the laughter shared with other boys at the end of a high school day; or even the pleasantries of casual flirtations and dates. The tales of sex and romance that his schoolmates told (with the usual exaggerations and naivete expected of school boys— at least in those days) were of little interest to Nixon.

Certainly he was no Lochinvar, this strait-laced youth who did not learn to dance until he was a sophomore at Whittier College—and even then, very poorly. Yet, one anonymous

---

fined $100,000. Sinclair and Doheny were acquitted, though Sinclair was subsequently sentenced to prison for contempt of Congress and for hiring private detectives to shadow members of the jury in the case. In 1927, the Supreme Court restored the Teapot Dome oil fields to the government.

* President Eisenhower once said of Richard Nixon: "He's as clean as a hound's tooth."

student with a sense of humor wrote in Whittier's Yearbook: "Richard left a trail blazed with fluttering feminine hearts." Nixon, who had never sown his Quaker oats, was highly embarrassed by the quip.

A casual girlfriend and fellow student at Whittier recalled, "He was a nice-looking boy and I liked him, as did the other girls, but he was too preoccupied with his studies, too aloof to be much fun."

For a while he dated the daughter of the Whittier Chief of Police, a relationship that ended when he left to attend law school at Duke University. But even there, one could never accuse him of being a ladies' man. "It wasn't that Dick disliked girls," commented Lyman Brownfield, Nixon's roommate and fellow law student at Duke. "He enjoyed their company, as did the rest of us. But we just couldn't afford the good times the other fellows used to have; consequently we dated very infrequently."

If these comments about Nixon's youthful appeal to the fair sex seem sparse, consider the blank verse recently expressed by Mrs. Marjorie Hildreth Knighton, his date for the Whittier College senior prom of 1934:

"I knew Richard Nixon very well at college: I was in his class, and I was his date for the prom; but I'm sorry, I just can't remember any anecdotes I could tell you about him."

As President, 34 years later, Nixon laughed aloud when he heard the statement. "And to think! all this time I was under the impression I'd made a big hit with her."

After Richard transferred to the elementary school in Whittier, he continued attaining the high grades which he had earned in the Yorba Linda grammar school. There, in the seventh grade, he encountered and passed the first milestone in the career that he was to follow when he made his debut as a debater, taking the affirmative side of the proposition, "Resolved, That Insects Are More Beneficial Than Harmful." Opposing him and another boy was a girls' team—

Richard (top row, second from right) with his seventh grade class at East Whittier Grammar School. His burning ambition, at the time, was to be a railroad engineer.

a confrontation he did not particularly relish. His team won handily, but not before he had searched the library for several days and, with his usual thoroughness, had consulted every book on the subject. He then discussed the question with his uncle, Dr. Philip H. Timberlake, Professor of Entomology (retired) at the University of California, Riverside. That initial venture into the field of disciplined argument taught him the value of systematic, controlled presentation of ideas and the need for advance preparation—doing his homework and marshalling his facts in a methodical manner. It was at this point that the so-called "Nixon method" was born—a method he has further refined and polished and honed as the years progressed.

But let us not get ahead of our story.

After being graduated from grammar school, Richard entered Fullerton High School, a short distance from Whittier. To enable him to earn the necessary money for school expenses and personal needs, his parents placed him in complete charge of the vegetable department at Nixon's Market. This responsibility required that he arise before dawn each day and drive the family truck to Los Angeles to do the buying at the wholesale markets, bargain with the produce growers, load the truck and drive back to Whittier. Back at the store, he washed and sorted his vegetables, then displayed them for sale. When all this was done, he went to school.

In the afternoon, he returned to the store and waited on customers until closing time. Often, he studied until two in the morning, sitting in the kitchen beside the gas oven where his mother cooked their meals and baked her famous pies. Incredibly enough, he not only wedged in the time to continue his piano lessons, but also took up the violin. It was a hard life, but the profit derived from the sale of the vegetables at the store was all his.

Richard's determination to become a lawyer now started to take on the flesh and bone of reality, for during his first

Richard Nixon, 1926, while in his first year at Fullerton High School found time to add violin lessons to his daily piano practice.

year as a high school student he was able to start a college fund at the local bank.

As a sophomore at Fullerton High, he took an extraordinary interest in the Constitution of the United States. The early stages of a philosophy that was to permeate his lifelong beliefs was born; and undoubtedly had a bearing on decisions made fifty years later when he was called upon, in his first three years as President to select four new Supreme Court justices. Throughout the two years he attended Fullerton, his debating skills continued to grow. He represented the school in the National Oratorical Contest and won the Constitutional Oratorical Contest—a pair of accomplishments he was to duplicate at Whittier High, where he transferred for his junior and senior years because it was much closer to his home.

The speech that he wrote and delivered in his junior year at Whittier has been preserved in the pages of *Cardinal and White*, the school's yearbook. Here is Richard Nixon, age 16, speaking on "Our Privileges Under the Constitution:"

> During the struggle for freedom, our forefathers were in constant danger of punishment for exercising the rights of freedom of speech and freedom of the press. Again the cause of their danger was the intolerance of men in power toward others with different views. The framers of the Constitution provided that we, their descendants, need not fear to express our sentiments as they did.
>
> Yet the question arises: How much ground do these privileges cover? There are some who use them as a cloak for covering libelous, indecent, and injurious statements against their fellow men. Should the morals of this nation be offended and polluted in the name of freedom of speech or freedom of the press?
>
> In the words of Lincoln, the individual can have no

rights against the best interests of society. Furthermore, there are those who, under the pretense of freedom of speech and freedom of the press, have incited riots, assailed our patriotism, and denounced the Constitution itself. They have used Constitutional privileges to protect the very act by which they wished to destroy the Constitution. Consequently laws have justly been provided for punishing those who abuse their Constitutional privileges—laws which do not limit these privileges, but which provide that they may not be instrumental in destroying the Constitution which insures them. We must obey these laws, for they have been passed for our own welfare. . . .

. . . In times past, the right to hold office was given only to those of the nobility. We, however, have our Lincolns and our Jacksons—men who needed only a chance to prove their worth, that they might rise to the highest office in the land.

Truly it is a great privilege to hold office, but it is also a great responsibility. The officeholder is elected by his fellow men, who expect him to represent them wisely and justly. It is his duty to give his services willingly, no matter how insignificant the position; to perform his work to the best of his ability; and to defend, maintain and uphold the Constitution.

In his senior year, Nixon again won the Oratorical Contest with his speech: "America's Progress—Its Dependence Upon the Constitution." One paragraph from the 1930 edition of *Cardinal and White* is especially significant, because it illustrates that Dick Nixon the student and Richard Nixon the President hold the same "constructionist" interpretation of the Constitution. The connection becomes clear as one examines the new philosophy of the Burger court, appointed by President Nixon, and the philosophy of its predecessor, the Warren court.

This is what Richard Nixon of Whittier High School said in 1930:

> Fellow citizens: We have seen that without question the Constitution has been the underlying force in America's progress. We know that our forefathers have championed this document to the extent of giving their lives—that we might enjoy its benefits. Yet, in view of these facts, at the present time, a great wave of indifference to the Constitution's authority, disrespect of its law, and opposition to its basic principles threatens its very foundations. Shall we of the present generation allow this instrument to be cast in disrepute? Shall we be responsible for its downfall?
>
> If this nation wishes its progress to continue, this wave of indifference to the laws of the Constitution must cease. For as long as the Constitution is respected, its laws obeyed and its principles enforced, America will continue to progress, but if the time should ever come when America will consider this document too obsolete to cope with changed ideals of government, then the time will have arrived when the American people as an individual nation must come back to normal and change their ideals to conform with those mighty principles set forth in our incomparable Constitution.

For all the earnest rhetoric one might expect of a schoolboy (even a gifted one, as he unquestionably was), those early speeches clearly reflect his fundamental beliefs today, and lend added credence to the observation that the only difference between the oft-mentioned "old" and "new" Nixon is that he has grown wiser as a result of experience and maturity, and has succeeded in coming to grips with a modern, changing society without forsaking his basic convictions.

In his last year at Whittier High School, Richard acquired a girl friend, Ola Florence Welch, whom he dated more or less steadily for five years. He had already exhibited a keen interest in the theatre and considerable talent as an actor—surprising in view of his reticent nature. When his Latin class decided to present a drama, he was chosen to play the lead. Appearing opposite him in the romantic lead was Ola Florence.

Ola Florence Welch

"The play was based on Virgil's *Aenid*," Ola reminisced recently. "Aeneas is a nomad who reaches Carthage where he falls in love with Queen Dido. At the end of the play she throws herself on a bier. We all wore white gowns. It was so romantic. It must have been contagious, because after that Dick and I started going together.

"Dick was a kind and considerate boy, but deep down a little unsure of himself," Ola recalled. "Sometimes, like other couples, we would argue. When we did, his face would cloud and he'd make a conscious effort to restrain himself. He was always a gentleman—then as now. But when the argument grew heated Dick could get quite harsh. He'd make me cry.

But then we'd make up and he would be sweet and gentle again."

What did they argue about? Politics, for one thing. "I was a Democrat, and still am," she explained. He was very conservative, young as he was. And, as you can see, for all our arguing, neither of us changed the other's political opinion."

Not all of their friends shared Ola Florence's evaluation of young Nixon. "I don't know what she saw in him," said a classmate who had dated him a few times. "He was good-looking enough, but he wasn't a mixer. He was kind of stuffy."

Another girl remembered him as a fellow who was something less than personable. "He just didn't know how to be sexy with girls," she complained. "Who wants a date with a boy whose main topic of conversation is football or books? Sometimes, when he'd be off on Cloud 9 about some philosophical subject, I'd want to blurt out, 'Oh, for heaven's sake, we're supposed to be having fun!'"

But Ola Florence did have fun with Dick. They enjoyed going to the movies—when he had the price of two tickets. Sundays, always after church services, they went to the beach. He was well aware of her fondness for dancing and it annoyed him when she would date someone else because, as she would explain, "I love floating to dreamy music." Without letting her know about it, he took dancing lessons and managed to learn the simple waltz, and, when in high spirits, a slow fox trot: no Fred Astaire, he.

The Richard Nixon of Whittier High was a thoughtful, amiable lad of high intelligence (in an intelligence test where the norm was 35, he scored 59); not quite the loner he had been heretofore, but still far from gregarious. The incipient political talents that were to come to the fore during his college years were already in evidence. He was never lionized as are football heroes (although he did play soccer), but he did win the respect of his fellow students—a remarkable tribute when one considers that he exerted only the quiet force of

When he was not studying, debating, or working in the family store, Richard Nixon, somehow, found time to play on the soccer team at Whittier High School.

his personality, and his articulate speech, to achieve school-wide recognition. "I think of Dick as a 'fighting Quaker'," said O. C. Albertson, his principal at Whittier High. "He was a leader in scholastic and student activities, but he was never so far in advance of his supporters that they lost sight of him —and this, I believe is the mark of true leadership. He was quite popular."

The years of drudgery and sacrifice that had been devoted to the expansion of the Nixon filling station and store finally began to pay a modest dividend. The Nixons were able to meet their immediate modest needs. "If it hadn't been for the expense of my brothers' sicknesses we would not have had any problems at all," observed Richard Nixon in the late 1950's.

But the river of life runs deep, with many eddies and undercurrents. The family was caught up in the swirl of its dark waters; first with the death of Richard's younger brother, Arthur, and then the passing of his oldest brother, Harold. The financial security that was intended to help the young Nixon through his college years had become dissipated.

Small wonder that those who knew him as a youth invariably described him as "serious."

Threnody for Two Brothers

Prayer is the burden of a sigh,
The falling of a tear;
The upward glancing of an eye,
When none but God is near.
                             James Montgomery

Appeals to the Almighty are non-denominational; they are also highly personal. We express our private griefs, our approach to the divine, in whatever manner fulfills the needs of our most heartfelt longings.

Schoolboy Richard offered his silent prayers that his brothers be spared, and if a furtive tear coursed down his cheek, he turned his face. Thus, early in life he learned to conceal his inner torment instead of wearing sorrow on his coatsleeve as a public proclamation.

This discipline of restraint has caused many Americans, including some of his ardent supporters, to regard him as a stereo-typical cold fish, devoid of warmth and sensitivity. Categorized in this way, when he reveals his congenial self, expresses sadness because of someone's misfortune, or even offers a friendly smile, he is often accused of "grandstanding." This evaluation, widespread though it may be, is simply incorrect.

"One cannot know President Nixon for even a short time without realizing that he is a very warm human being, said evangelist Billy Graham. "I have known him for many years and I assure you he is a warm-hearted, compassionate gentleman."

The key word in Dr. Graham's assessment is *gentleman*. Nixon's innate dignity accounts for much of the reserve which is so easily misconstrued as a kind of aloof arrogance. But from his earliest years, his family, friends, schoolmates and later, his political associates, all have agreed that he was, and still is, a warm-hearted and compassionate human being. His profound grief over the loss of his brothers illustrates his depth of feeling.

Of the five Nixon boys, Edward, the youngest, never knew his oldest brother, Arthur, who died in 1925 at the age of seven—five years before Edward was born. Harold was sixteen at the time; Richard was twelve and Donald eleven.

Arthur's death came as a stunning blow to the Nixons, as it would to any family, but the loss was made even more tragic by its unexpectedness. No one suspected, even remotely, that Arthur was dying, when he complained one morning of a stomach-ache. Mild cases of upset stomach are no novelty for small boys, and his mother treated him with the usual home remedies. Within a week, he developed a fever, grew listless, and found it difficult to remain awake. Hannah, now thoroughly alarmed at the possibility that he might have fallen victim to sleeping sickness, called a doctor who diagnosed the illness as tubercular encephalitis. Other medical men were also consulted, but in an incredibly short time the virus overwhelmed his vital organs and he lapsed into a deep sleep. Two days later he died.

Tucked away among the family's treasured mementos is a eulogy to Arthur, written by Richard Nixon when he was a junior at Whittier High School. The depth of his emotions, his sensitivity, his spiritual convictions present a picture of the real Nixon, with which his immediate family and intimate friends are acquainted, but which the outsider could not possibly know.

Here is seventeen-year-old Richard's composition, written five years after his brother's death, but with the memory still engraved in his heart and etched in his mind.

MY BROTHER, ARTHUR R. NIXON

We have a picture in our home that money could not buy. It is not a picture for which great art collectors would offer thousands of dollars. There is nothing outstanding about its frame or coloring. It is only about five inches tall and two inches wide. It is probably unnoticed by most of those who come to visit us, for they all have seen pictures of small boys and probably could not be interested in this one.

However, let us examine the picture closely. The first thing we notice, perhaps, is that this particular boy has unusually beautiful black eyes which seem to sparkle with hidden fire and to beckon us to come on some secret journey which will carry us to the land of make-believe. Then we would probably admire his neat appearance; his well-pressed, little dark-blue sailor's suit; his shoe strings, tied in bows which match each other exactly. Even his hands are crossed in front of him to complete a perfectly balanced picture. We find that only his hair is unlike what we would expect in a portrait of a boy. For instead of neatly combed locks, we see a mass of brown curls which seem never to have known the touch of a comb. This, in brief, is our picture. There are some who might not even notice these small features which I have been mentioning, but nevertheless, I still say that money could not buy that picture, for it was the last one ever taken of my brother Arthur.

But I am starting at the wrong end of my story. Let me tell you, in a few words, something of my brother as I remember him.

One day in May, 1918, when I had reached the age of five years, my father came home from work a little later than usual. After talking with my grandmother, who was taking care of my two brothers and me while mother was away on a visit, he came over to where we boys were quarreling over some toys and told us that there was a little doll over at the hospital for us; a real live doll! Naturally we then began to quarrel over whose doll it would be, although each of us wished to have it merely to keep one of the others from getting it. My father, however, assured us that our rights would be equal, and then he asked us what name we should give our doll. After learning that it was not a "girl doll," we finally decided that its name should be Arthur.

Several days later, grandmother scrubbed us all up, especially gouging into the depths of our ears, and helped us to dress, for we were going to see "our doll," which we had learned by this time was a baby. At least, that was what brother Harold, who had reached the all-knowing age of nine, had said it was. He had told us secretly that it wasn't a doll but a baby. He warned us, though, not to let on he'd told us so.

Anyway, doll or baby, we were greatly excited over the prospective visit and could hardly control ourselves until the family Ford finally got us to the hospital. All I remember about the visit was the fact that I was rather disappointed in the baby, because, after all, a tiny baby is not as pretty as a doll, at least in outward appearances.

The first two or three years of my baby brother's life are rather indistinct in my memory for I was so engrossed in the first years of my grammar school education. However, there were certain things that concerned my little brother's early development which did impress me. For example, I remember how his eyes changed from their original baby-blue to an almost black shade; how his hair, blond at first, became dark brown; how his mouth, toothless for five months, was filled with tiny, white teeth which, by the way, were exceedingly sharp when applied on soft fingers or toes which happened to get within their reach; how those little, incoherent sounds of his finally developed into words and then into sentences; and how he learned to roll over, then to crawl and finally to walk.

Although I do not remember many incidents connected with my brother's early childhood, there were some which made a clear imprint on my mind. There was one time when he was asked to be a ring bearer at a wedding. I remember how my mother had to work with him for hours to get him to do it, because he disliked walking with the little flower girl. Another time, when he was about five years old, he showed the world that he was a man by getting some cigarettes out of our store and secretly smoking them in back of the house. Unfortunately for him, one of our gossipy neighbors happened to see him, and she promptly informed my mother. I have disliked that neighbor from that time on. Then I remember the grief he experienced over his hair. My parents wanted him to be a girl in the first place; consequently they attempted to make him one as much as possible. Each day he begged my mother for a boy's haircut, and when he finally did get it, there was not a happier boy in the state. Again, I shall never forget how he disliked wearing "sticky" wool suits. As soon as he was able to read, he used to search the mail order catalogues for suits that weren't "sticky."

To continue our story, let us come to the year 1925. My aunt had convinced my mother that I should go to her home, several hundred miles away, to continue my study of music. My young brother was then entering his first year of school, and I learned from letters sent from home that he was doing exceptionally well in all things except drawing. He absolutely would not take an interest in anything he thought common to girls. The school year ended finally, and my parents came to get me. Arthur was unchanged except for the fact that several teeth were lacking in the front of his mouth, which my father had told him was the result of too much candy. As soon as he saw me alone, he solemnly kissed me on the cheek. I learned later that he had dutifully asked my mother if it would be proper for him to kiss me, since I had been away for such a long time.

After my return home, nothing eventful happened until mid-summer. Arthur then became slightly ill; just a case of indigestion, we thought. But a week went by and his condition became worse instead of better. He began to become sleepy; he did not want to eat; he wanted to rest and sleep. Several doctors came to see him but none could see what his trouble was. Finally, my father sent me with my younger brother to the home of an aunt who lived nearby, fearing that we too would become ill. One night my aunt awakened us and told us to get dressed. Arthur was a little worse, she had said. We were bundled into the car, it happened to be a Ford again, and were carried home. My father met us with tears in his eyes. He did not need to tell us what we knew had happened.

I might leave the story here and let you decide why that picture means so much to me, but I shall atttempt to tell you in my own words. There is a growing tendency among college students to let their childhood beliefs be forgotten. Especially we find this true when we speak of the Divine Creator and His plans for us. I thought that I would also become that way, but I find that it is almost impossible for me to do so. Two days before my brother's death, he called my mother into the room. He put his arms around her and said that he wanted to pray before he went to sleep. Then, with eyes closed, he repeated that age-old child's prayer which ends with those simple yet beautiful words:

> If I should die before I awake,
> I pray Thee, Lord,
> My soul to take.

There is a grave now, out in the hills, but like the picture, it contains only the bodily image of my brother.

And so, when I am tired and worried, and am almost ready to quit trying to live as I should, I look up and see the picture of a little boy with sparkling eyes, and curly hair; I remember the child-like prayer; I pray that it may prove true for me as it did for my brother Arthur.

Woman of Valor

Memories of Arthur were still poignant when it was discovered that Harold had contracted tuberculosis—memories that were made more acute, now that a variant of the same malady had struck again. Father Frank, heretofore the bellicose, challenging, "fighting Irishman," attended to his duties in tight-lipped silence—a painful sight to those who understood his innate need to assert himself. Richard, like his father, worked harder than ever to supplement the family income in an effort to help reduce the drain of the medical bills which, to them, were monumental.

Mother Hannah Nixon, always the activist, took eighteen-year-old Harold to a sanitorium, high in the California mountains within a hundred miles of Whittier—but to no avail. The doctors suggested a drier climate, and Hannah, hopeful that his lungs might respond, left her family to take Harold to Prescott, Arizona.

The cost was staggering, and before long their modest resources were depleted. "My Dad sold half of the acre on which our house and store were located in order to pay our medical bills," recalled the President.

But the money from the half-acre was soon exhausted, and they could no longer afford the sanitorium. Hannah, driven by a desperation that only a frightened mother can know, worked as she had never worked before. Determined to remain in Prescott, she rented an old house and converted it into a nursing home so that she could look after her son as well as other tubercular children sent to her as paying patients.

Unable to pay for help, she cared for her little charges around the clock. She got up during the night to tend the youngsters whenever they needed her, and arose at dawn every morning whether or not she had slept well. She shovelled coal into the furnace to keep the children comfortable; she cooked, cleaned, changed linens, fed and bathed the young patients who were too ill to care for themselves—all this so that her first-born might have the proper care and climate.

The sighs that escaped her when she could lie down for a few moments of rest cannot be recorded; the tears she must have shed in the privacy of her spartan, upstairs bedroom will never be known. To the world—indeed, to her own loved ones—she always presented a spiritually courageous face, a face on which a scarcely discernible pained smile played at the corners of her mouth—the only indication of the inner anguish that wracked her soul. As a queen among mothers, as a lady in the fullest meaning of the word, sweet and brave Hannah Nixon had few peers.

The words of the Book of Proverbs were intended for her:

>A woman of valor who can find,
>She is more precious than rubies.

The Prescott Years—
Years of Privation

The two years that Mrs. Nixon remained in Prescott were frightfully difficult for the rest of the family back in Whittier. Frank and his sons redoubled their efforts to maintain themselves and their home, and to keep the store and filling station operating. Their savings long since depleted, Frank would go to the local post office each Friday and mail every penny he could spare to Hannah.

Meals in the Nixon home usually consisted of canned beans and soups; hamburgers and fried eggs. Preparing the meals became part of Richard's duties now that Mother was in Arizona. But despite the turmoil and added burden thrust upon him, he maintained his straight A's at school, attended Quaker services regularly, worked in the store and, after the store was closed, studied long into the night.

Sometimes he stared at his father whose face was drawn, and who no longer argued with his customers. How he longed for one of his healthy, hearty explosions! But Frank, lonely, weary and yearning for his wife, was too deeply disturbed to be his usually rambunctious self, and he remained silent for the most part.

Richard saw what was happening to his father and, somehow, in spite of his youth, understood the meaning and depth of his father's unexpressed sorrow. And he decided to do something to help the family.

During his last summer at Whittier High, and before entering college, Richard joined his mother and ailing brother in Prescott in order to help ease their financial burden. He soon found work as a field laborer on one of the many farms that dotted the outskirts of Prescott at that time. The pay was twenty-five cents an hour, standard for what was called "stoop labor." Afterwards, when the harvest season was over, he found a job as janitor of a swimming pool which included mopping and scrubbing the locker rooms.

Luck was with him, and soon he landed a "position" in which his debating experience could be utilized. He was now employed as a barker or "pitchman." He worked for Frontier Days, a concession featuring a "wheel of fortune" which offered prizes of hams, preserves and other foodstuffs to winning customers—a strange occupation for a Quaker lad with an almost puritanical moral code; a boy who had avoided such "frivolities" as dancing and gambling. As a spieler, Richard earned about fifty cents an hour, a munificent sum in those days, and all of his earnings were turned over to his mother.

It was a strange and mystical game they played, Hannah and her son. She must have known how Richard was earning his wages, but she said nothing. When he brought her his pay, she lovingly patted his cheek—and they both thought of Harold who was visibly sinking. There are times when the tongue and heart are poorly connected, and this was such a time. But they both knew.

Perhaps Harold experienced a premonition, for he implored his mother to take him home. There was little question that his stay in Arizona had not helped to arrest the disease that was consuming his lungs. So they returned to La Habra, a town close to Whittier, where the family had recently moved. Harold was now a ghost of the once robust young fellow he had been.

Some three weeks later, Harold asked Richard to drive him to Los Angeles—he wanted to buy an electric mixer to give to their mother for her birthday. He was in high spirits; the idea of surprising Mother with a new labor-saving device—an electric mixer which had only recently been introduced on the market—was exhilarating. Harold had taken on a verve and energy he had not known for many months. It was still early morning, and having purchased the gift, Harold and Richard joked and chatted as they drove back to La Habra.

"I feel tired, Dick," Harold said after they returned home. "I think I'll lie down for awhile before I tell Mom about her present." Richard smiled, exchanged a few pleasant words with his brother and hurried off to school.

Fifteen minutes later, as he entered the classroom, Richard's teacher handed him a message: "Come home. Your brother has died."

Whittier College

At the age of 17, Richard Nixon graduated from Whittier High School, with the California Interscholastic Federation Gold Seal Award for scholarship affixed to his diploma. He was also awarded the coveted Harvard Award for being the "best all-around student." Here was his great opportunity to get a scholarship from Harvard University! His daydream, however, ended at this point. The cold reality was that he simply could not afford the cost of supporting himself at an eastern Ivy League institution even if his tuition was paid for.

Instead, he enrolled at Whittier College, the local Quaker school whose academic standards were (and still are) among the highest in the nation. Here, from 1930 to 1934, he majored in history, achieved statewide renown as a debater, became active as a campus leader, and graduated second in his class—all the while continuing to work after school, paying his own way by running the fruit and vegetable section of the family market where he was now keeping the store's accounts as well. Whatever spare time he had, and the hours were few, he devoted to studying, and to some extracurricular activities such as campus politics and football. But he was no longer the loner he had once been. Whatever recollections his fellow students now have, revolve around his abilities as a student leader.

Whittier College is symbolic of the town's Quaker history, with its Greenleaf and Friends Avenues and its bustling Quaker Maid Dairy. As one enters Mendenhall, on the mantlepiece near the office of the president of Whittier College, there is an inscription borrowed from the college's namesake:*

> Early hath life's mighty question
> Thrilled within the heart of youth,
> With a deep and strong beseeching,
> What and where is Truth?

The school can no longer be regarded as the cloistered haven of Quakerism intended by its founding fathers, and it

---

*John Greenleaf Whittier (1807-1892) has been called "the gentle poet" for so long that many have forgotten that he was a fiery abolitionist, a thundering spokesman and one of the founders of the Republican Party. He was an elector in the Electoral College that chose Lincoln. The hoary-headed Quaker, who began writing verse at the age of 14, was an outspoken and often unpopular writer-editor and legislator (Massachusetts House of Representatives), who not only demanded freedom for the slaves, but one who energetically fought for peace, temperance and woman's suffrage. Despite these views, however, he was extremely conservative in his political, moral and economic outlook. In his time, he was considered the best poet America had produced, with the possible exception of Longfellow. His first poems were published in 1826, in the Newburyport (Massachusetts) *Free Press* edited by William Lloyd Garrison, the abolitionist who became his lifelong friend. See biographies by Whitman Bennett (1941) and J. B. Pickard (1961).

now has its share of student dissidents and radicals. Yet, it has somehow managed to retain an atmosphere of dignity, not terribly affected by current behavior and attitudes. It was here that the President's mother performed in college plays, and from where she was graduated in 1906—forerunner of her famous son who, on the very same campus scored so many forensic victories and scholastic achievements.

There is no question about Nixon's academic excellence during his four years at Whittier College; the records are clear. Although many of his after-school hours were confined to the store and devoted to study, he was nevertheless popular with his fellow students. That he excelled as a scholar, might have been expected; but, that he managed so quickly to play a dominant role in campus affairs seems anomalous—store clerks and bookworms are seldom made of the same stuff as leaders. Yet, that is precisely what happened.

Exploiting the Issues

Within thirty frenetic days, the raw freshman began his college political career as a co-founder of a school-wide club, the Orthagonian Society, in opposition to a hitherto entrenched group known as the Franklins, composed mainly of students from wealthy families. There were neither fraternities nor sororities represented at the small, restrictive, Quaker College, but members of the Franklins had long considered themselves as the literati, with superior social status and intellectual attainment. Needless to say, they exerted inordinate power over Whittier's student body. One can almost hear Father Frank's liberalism declaiming itself through his outraged son as young Nixon spearheaded a campaign to break the monopoly of the Franklins.

Every fraternity has its own symbol, and the Orthagonians, whose Greek derivative means "square-shooter," naturally enough chose the square—its four corners signifying: "Beans, Brawn, Brains and Bowels." Nixon, his few weeks at Whittier

Richard Nixon as a freshman at Whittier College. Already noticeable is his famous "ski" nose which was to delight the caricaturists of a later day.

notwithstanding, shrewdly gauged the sentiments of a majority of the other students, and launched a populist attack. The Orthagonians, he declared, would break from the Franklins' tradition of formal wear for school functions and photographs, by dressing in sweaters and tieless, open-collared shirts. This was not so much an act of defiance for its own sake, as a canny political evaluation. He knew full well that most of them could not afford formal clothes. Further, he promised that the new Society would welcome those engaged in school

Richard and Harold in their last snapshot together. Harold showed no outward effects of his illness until the last few months before his death in 1933.

athletics, a group not especially favored by the Franklins. It was a bold move for those days, considering the value that Whittier attached to scholastic achievement. But reformer Nixon had evolved a winning platform. Almost immediately, his name became among the best-known on campus.

Perhaps Nixon might have enjoyed a career in show business had he not chosen the law. He composed the club's theme song, a spirited tune called, "Ecrassons l'Infame," and played the male lead in the Orthagonians' first stage play, a melodrama called *The Trysting Place,* which he also co-wrote and directed. Soon, his new Society rivaled the Franklins in numbers and activities, with Nixon leading his cabal in an all-out membership drive. In this task, he was aided by "Chief" Wallace Newman, the full-blooded American Indian who was football coach of the Whittier Poets.

Competing against sophomores, juniors and seniors, newcomer Richard Nixon was unanimously elected as the Orthagonian's first president. He was also elected president of the freshman class, winning more than ninety per cent of the votes. And he was also elected to a seat on the college's Joint Council of Control. All these achievements in his first month as a Whittier student!

Throughout his four years at Whittier College he displayed a surprising gift for finding and successfully exploiting issues. That talent was later recalled by Nixon's classmate, Talbert Moorehead.

"I was running for the office of class president and I was expected to make a speech," Moorehead said. "I certainly had deep misgivings about my ability to deliver a creditable address, but I never mentioned that feeling of inadequacy to a soul. Nevertheless, Dick sensed that uneasiness and waited until we were alone. I can still see him, pacing up and down, jabbing his finger at me and firing instructions on how to deliver an effective speech: 'You have to find an issue and concentrate on *it*—forget yourself completely—think only of that issue!' "

As Nixon progressed through Whittier College, his debating skills were enhanced with the years, and he developed a talent for ferreting out issues that would evoke a popular response. In his senior year, for example, he won his race for president of the student body on a campaign pledge to change the school's policy of prohibiting dances on college grounds—a position that shocked the governing Quaker officials who had always frowned on such "self-indulgence." But Nixon won his point (and kept his platform promise) by convincing the board of trustees that it would be wiser to permit school dances where the college elders could keep an eye on the students rather than have them "carousing in the dens of iniquity" in Los Angeles. He also busied himself with a much more important campaign: To institute a program that would help prepare first and second year classmen to assume positions of student leadership. This platform pledge he was also able to honor after he won the election.

This unusual combination of issues—permission to hold school dances (for which he personally cared little), and training freshmen and sophomores for future leadership, were concerns calculated to appeal to the broadest spectrum of students, and no one knew this better than young Nixon whose left eye was on the sparrow while his right eye was on the hawk. Despite this pragmatism, however, he never assumed a moral or political stance that was offensive or that was calculated merely to win popular approval.

Despite his intellectual prowess and his debating ability, one cannot assert that student Nixon was brilliant while at Whittier (although there is no denying that he had already shown much promise, and possessed latent skills that were to develop as he matured). His triumphs on the rostrum, even during his freshman days, were the result, not of brilliance, but of a perceptive and pragmatic evaluation of his audiences; that is, a recognition that most people are seldom moved except when struck with the thunderbolt of an exclamation point. Nixon understood this, and utilized it, but he out-pointed his opponents by augmenting his purple prose with hard-nosed facts that no specious oppositional rhetoric could negate.

Facts, however, seldom spring to mind full grown. Dates, names, places and incidents do not appear out of thin air. They are the end product of labor—of concentrated, sometimes long and painstaking effort. It was this faculty for unearthing the core of a problem and fortifying it with supportive evidence that led some biographers to refer to his college oratory as that of a "genius." Nixon himself denies that he was a brilliant student. "I won my share of scholarships, and of speaking and debating prizes in school," Nixon explained, "not because I was smarter, but because I worked longer and harder than some of my more gifted colleagues."

Despite his protestations, Richard Nixon was clearly smarter and intellectually more alert than most of his fellow students, always ranking near or at the top of his class. The French Revolution held a particular fascination for him. He read Voltaire, Rousseau and other classical writers on the subject—mostly in the original French. His interest in sociopolitical philosophy was so intense that he read the entire works of Tolstoi, not as required reading, but for his own edification. How he found the time for such prodigious, extracurricular reading remains a mystery, because he still arose at 4:00 A.M. each day and drove the family truck to the wholesale markets in Los Angeles. Then he would return in time for an early class, without any record of his ever having been tardy.

Early Influences

During his formative years, Nixon had been influenced by his father and his political theories, who in turn had been influenced by Theodore Roosevelt, Robert LaFollette and, later, by Franklin D. Roosevelt. His mother's support of Woodrow Wilson and her Quaker philosophy of "Christian

Democracy" also influenced him as did Almira Milhous, his maternal grandmother and former teacher, who transferred to him her esteem for Lincoln.

Now, as a college student, there entered into his life a renowned and dedicated educator, Dr. Paul S. Smith, a professor of history and politics, who was to stimulate great interest in these subjects.

Dr. Smith, who was head of Whittier's History Department during Nixon's years there, was subsequently selected to be president of the college in 1956. An Indiana Quaker, as were the Nixon forebears, he had graduated from a Quaker university, and taught history at the University of Wisconsin before accepting a teaching post at Whittier. He was recognized by his colleagues as an outstanding authority and scholar in the area of American history and political science.

"A few students always stand out in a teacher's memory because of their diligence and their ability to learn and absorb," said Dr. Smith in an interview. "Dick Nixon was one of those students. I remember him well. In fact, I have no hesitation in saying that his confident approach to difficult assignments, his serious interest in his school work, and his intellectual capacity for assimilating knowledge made him one of the best students I ever taught."

Citing an example, Whittier President Smith described Nixon's test papers as models of brevity: "As a rule, Dick would complete on a half page an answer for which the average "A" student would require two pages. On a number of occasions I re-read his examination papers to determine whether he had omitted anything of significance, but my conclusions were always the same: He had gone to the very heart of the assignment and expressed himself in a simple, direct manner."

Dr. Smith paused, leaned back in his chair, and reflected on Nixon's high marks: "Dick was about eighteen during the academic year of 1930-1931. In that time he took three of my courses: The American Constitution, International Rela-

Dick Nixon (center) with some of his Whittier College classmates.

tions and Law, and History of the American People and British People. I gave him straight A's."

It was only natural that a student of Richard's aptitude and willingness would attract the attention of a dedicated teacher. "Obviously, Dick's ability—that fine mind of his—intrigued me," mused Dr. Smith. "During my years as a teacher I would select the top history-major students and assign them to cover the most authoritative, and often the most extensive, works in American history, to enhance what I felt was their already-demonstrated interest. On one occasion I decided on an analytical study of a ten volume history of America. This was a tough assignment that I gave only to "A" majors, and in this instance there were only two students who were advanced enough to qualify—Dick Nixon and Leonidas Dodson.* Both passed the examination with percentages to spare, but I cannot forget the enthusiasm with which Dick attacked the ten volumes. It was as though he had been waiting for just such an opportunity."

Richard Nixon believes that history is created by the style, the charisma, and the character of a nation's leaders to a greater extent than it is by the problems that may beset them. That "great man" concept, Dr. Smith is convinced, was established in Nixon's mind when he took the course about representative Americans.

"Dick could not help being influenced by Lincoln, Madison and other of our statesmen who contributed so effectively to America's progress and development," Dr. Smith reasoned. "In all candor, however, I thought he would some day become an outstanding teacher or an eminent attorney; it never occurred to me that he would attain such heights in the field of politics."

Whittier College did not offer a course in political science

---

*Leonidas Dodson went on to become a professor of history and archivist at the University of Pennsylvania. Dr. Smith also recalled novelist Jessamyn West, Nixon's cousin, as another of his outstanding students who achieved national eminence.

at the time Nixon was a student there, but he insists, understandably enough, that the omission proved no hindrance to his career. Looking back, he believes the limited number of courses offered was offset by the high quality of the teachers under whom he studied.

"History, literature, philosophy and the classics—taught by inspirational men—is the best foundation for a career in politics," Nixon maintains. "There will be plenty of time later to learn first hand the intricacies of political strategy and tactics by working in the precincts. There will be too little time later for gaining indispensable knowledge, in depth, about the nature of man and the institutions he has created—an understanding which, from my experience, can better be acquired from the classics than from the more 'practical' courses in politics."

The President hastened to add: "This is not a case against courses in political science. After all, had I been exposed to one, I might have won the last election [against John F. Kennedy] rather than losing it! I only express my opinion that if a choice has to be made, the college years—when the mind is quicker, more receptive, and more retentive than it will ever be again—can best be used to develop the whole man rather than the specialist. I would say that this is important whatever the field an individual may plan to enter. In the field of politics, it is an absolute must. It is not that people do not 'grow' after they finish their formal education and enter public life. But the capacity to grow will be determined by the breadth and depth of the intellectual base which is acquired during the college years. If a man comes out of college with only the narrow and thin background of the highly trained political specialist, he may win elections, but he will serve neither his country nor himself as well as he should. He will be a sitting duck for every half-baked idea or timeworn cliché that comes along."

The Purloined Privy

One amusing Nixon college incident bears repeating, for if ever a young fellow burst through his somber cocoon, Nixon did in his junior year at Whittier. As in many other universities, in those less-cynical days before World War II, it was traditional for the undergraduates to hold an annual bonfire celebration. Students would scour the countryside for days collecting logs, scrap lumber, broken furniture, fence posts, wood boxes—anything that would burn. The debris would be dragged to Fire Hill, where the bonfire was permitted by school officials. It was piled into a huge pyramid. As custom demanded, the chairman of the bonfire was expected to crown the mountain of wood with the *pièce de résistance*, an old-fashioned country privy. Ordinarily, the chairman would produce a one-holer, sometimes a two-holer, and legend has it that an enterprising chairman whose name has been lost to posterity once "borrowed" a three-holer from some unfortunate farmer. But in 1933, Richard Nixon scored his most popular student triumph with a record that still stands in glorious isolation—he showed up at the last minute with a *four*-holer. Somewhere in Whittier or its environs, the President of the United States still owes a farmer or his descendants the price of a purloined outhouse with four-on-the-floor.

Football Years

I Wanna Be a Football Hero, sang a nation of young people in the early 1930's. Nixon, too, was singing the popular song, but not with much hope. In all his four years at college, he tried doggedly to make the starring football team, but with the exception of a few instances in his freshman year, he warmed the bench.

As a high school student his weight of 138 pounds precluded anything other than a spectator role, although he did try out for the football team. His early failure to make the team was not attributed so much to his light weight, as to a lack of muscular coordination. In college, the problems were reversed; he barely attained the weight, but his coordination was excellent—despite the assertion by one teammate that "Dick had two left feet."

Nixon shrugged off the statement with a grin: "At least I always got a seat on the fifty yard line."

Occasionally, a humorous quip results in a connotation not intended by the jokester. One player made a tongue-in-cheek comment: "Dick didn't play very often, but once, when he was called to play in the last few minutes of a game, I said, 'Let's get out the five-yard penalty marker.' What I meant was that Dick was so eager to win he'd be offside about every play. That comment, which I only meant as a joke, was used many times against Dick in politics, though I sure never intended anything of the sort."

William Brock, a former Whittier football star who is now an electrical engineer in Pasadena, remembered his teammate with warmth and admiration. "Dick was a lot better football player than he's been given credit for," said Brock. "He was little, but he had more spunk than the big men."

A lifelong Democrat who has always voted for his party's choice, except when Nixon was a candidate, Brock is impatient with those who associate the President with racial prejudice. Brock is black. "I really get mad when I hear Democrats or anybody else accuse him of bigotry," he said. "That sort of thing is fantastic. Dick was my buddy in college many years before he or anybody else figured him to become a politician. He was one of the fellows who got me into the Orthagonians."

Nixon's temperament was hardly geared to the exigencies of football. Before each game, nervous tension built up in him to such a degree that he could neither eat nor sleep. Since this tendency was common knowledge among his teammates, they often helped themselves to his portion of steak and dessert which were served prior to each game.

Years later, when fighting for his political life against the charge that he had a secret, illegal fund, the same kind of nervousness gripped him. "In such periods of intense preparation for battle," he wrote, "most individuals experience all the physical symptoms of tension—they become edgy and short-tempered, some can't eat, others can't sleep. I had experienced all those symptoms in the days since our train left Pomona. I had a similar experience during the Hiss case. . . . But what I had learned was that feeling this way before a battle was not something to worry about. On the contrary, failing to feel this way would mean I was not adequately keyed up, mentally and emotionally, for the conflict ahead."

"Chief" Wallace Newman, the school's football coach, in his suburban Whittier home on what was once Murphy's orange grove, reminisced about Nixon shortly after his former protégé became Vice President: "I don't know how much sleep he lost before a game, but it's true that he was unable to eat. Dick was very serious about football. I never knew anyone so determined. There was a bulldog tenacity about him. When he got hold of something, he never let go. He was so light, he'd take an awful beating in scrimmage. But what an inspiration he was to the team! Weeks would go by and he wouldn't even play a minute, but he almost never missed a practice, and he worked hard.

"He was really wonderful for morale. Here was this second-string kid on the bench encouraging the other guys and telling them how well they'd played. I guess he saw it as his duty. It isn't easy to sit it out for four years, especially in the case of Dick who excelled in everything else at school. The way I see it, kids like that have more guts than the first-string heroes."

What Made Richard Run

One can only speculate upon his reasons for enduring the years of effort which, for him must have been emotionally

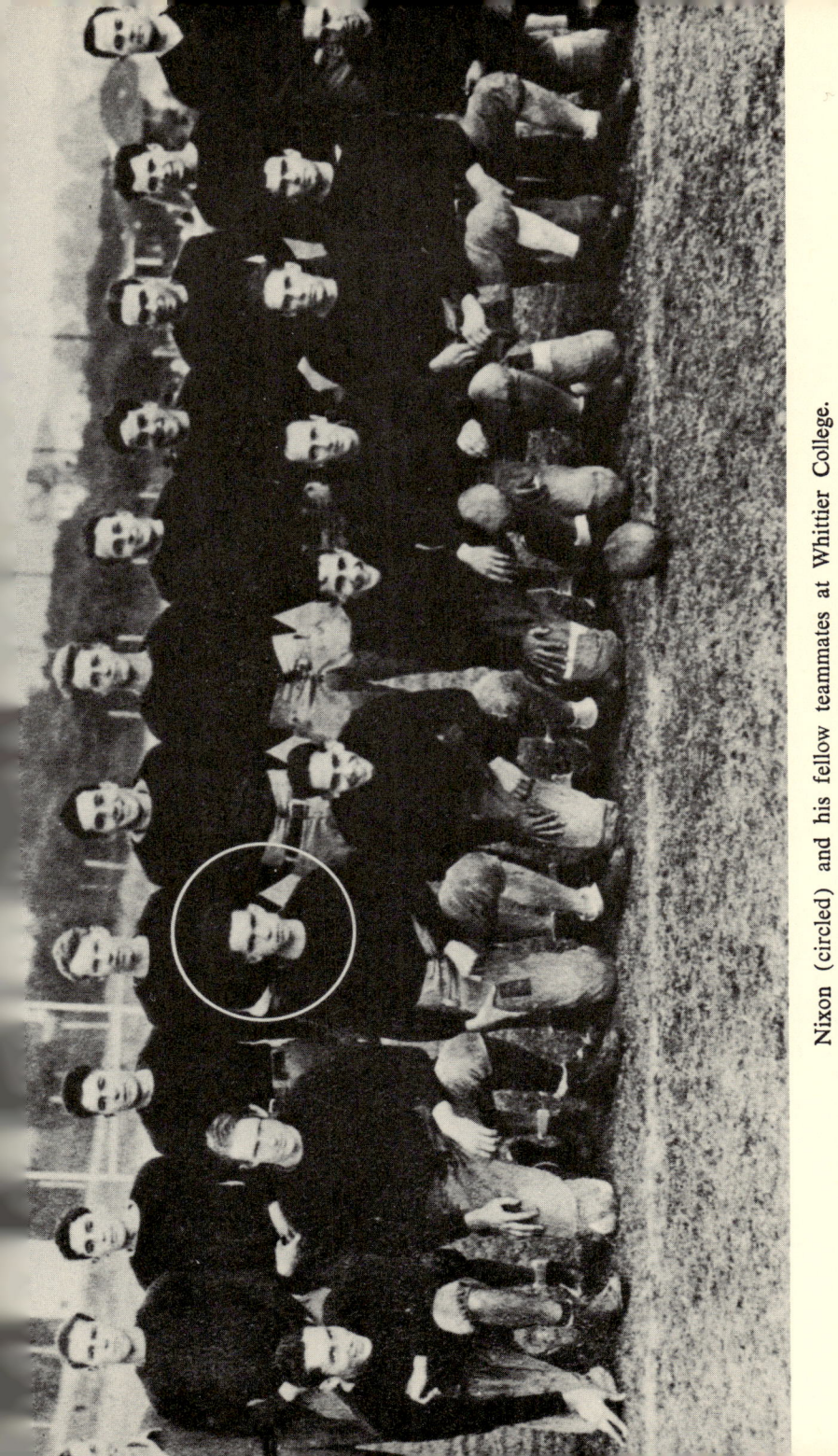

Nixon (circled) and his fellow teammates at Whittier College.

painful and thankless. Coach Newman ascribes it to his sense of duty. There is a measure of validity in this assumption, but Richard Nixon then, as now, was also a striver, an energetic doer who attacked his assignments vigorously and aggressively, often driving himself to gray-faced exhaustion. But, again, *why?* What made Richard run?

From his Quaker heritage he learned the importance of "doing the unpleasant, but necessary, without complaint." He was reared by the tenet that "the burdens of life sometimes outweigh the pleasures." He hinted at these subconscious beliefs, which at times emerge as a "sense of duty," in the introduction to his *Six Crises.* He wrote there: ". . . surely there is more to life than the search for enjoyment in the popular sense."

Yet, he did experience satisfaction and pleasure in being a member of the football team, even if—as was pointed out—his only contribution was to inspire his teammates with his morale-building comments and by his own example of determination.

It has been said that he basked in the reflected glory of the school's grid stars. But these armchair analysts forget the dominant trait in Nixon's character: Richard Nixon is psychically unable to derive pleasure by being in *anyone* else's shadow; he experiences no vicarious delight in the accomplishments of those outside his own immediate family. He is pleased with the successes of other people; he admires excellence in whatever form it takes, but never at his own expense. In one way or another, he is driven by a need to stand in his own light. Whether it be termed a defect or a virtue, it is a mark of leadership that has been observed in the character of every American President, with the possible exceptions of Taft and Harding.

An imaginative young fellow, his inner thoughts might well have been occupied with the comforting knowledge that the gridiron heroes, for all the adulation they received from their fellow students and the public, looked to *him* for inspiration:

'Here I am, Dick Nixon, the second-string guard, but still as well-known as anyone on the first team.' If such feelings did surface to conscious thought, they are entirely understandable. He did, after all, "excell in everything else" and, as his coach put it, it was only natural that he would use whatever resources he could muster to avoid the embarrassment of anonymity—or worse yet—mediocrity.

Should that be too harsh an assessment, there is another explanation for his grim pursuit of an athletic career—a pursuit that would have discouraged most other team hopefuls. Nixon was the product of a unique spiritual and moral environment that relished struggle for its own sake. The goal was always sublimated to the "honest toil and sweat" that led to whatever final success might be achieved. Nixon had heard these Quakerisms articulated in the town of Whittier for as long as he could remember, and had witnessed them in stark reality, as his parents pursued their arduous labors. Indeed, his personal life was evidence enough that the verities instilled in him as a child were sound: "The race is in the running. . . . The estimate of a man's worth is in the succeeding, not the success. . . . Pluck is its own reward." It is not too difficult to imagine that the lines written by Grantland Rice were composed especially for Dick Nixon:

> When the One Great Scorer comes to
>   write against your name—
> He marks—not that you won or lost—
>   but how you played the game.

So it was that this turn-of-the-century Victorian philosophy kept his spirits high during his four long years on the bench, yet ever shouting bravura cheers to his teammates. 'The game is in the playing,' he might have thought in self-consolation, but for him, football was more than a game: It was as grim a challenge as any of those he was to face in the rigors of his future political life.

Never Made The First Team

"I never did make the first team," Nixon recalled ruefully. "I was not heavy enough to play the line, not fast enough to play halfback, and not smart enough to be a quarterback." That statement notwithstanding, and in all fairness to him and the entire second team, the years 1930-1934 encompassed a period when an unusually large number of first-rate players, many of whom had distinguished themselves in high school football, went out for the team. He may have been too light, and perhaps not fast enough, as he stated, but no one has ever agreed with his self-evaluation that he wasn't "smart enough." Richard Nixon does not enter a game unless he is thoroughly familiar with its ground rules and knows how to react to them, whether in sports or in the business of government.

Drawing an analogy between football and politics, George Allen, head coach of the Washington Redskins, attributed Nixon's dedication to his competitive instincts. "The President looks at football as a way of life," he theorized. "He is a competitor! One of the things I admire about him is not that he came back and won, but that he came back after being beaten twice. The determination to come back shows that he is a competitor and that is why he likes football. He is a very dedicated man, and that's really what I look for most in my football players. We have players with less ability, but more dedication, and the dedication often makes the difference. President Nixon had that when he played football at Whittier, just as he has it now."

Young Richard was not popular in the classic sense; he was never acclaimed as were some of his teammates. He made no close friendships as did the other students. Nevertheless, he was well liked and respected. Classmates have little to say about his athletic prowess, but they still recall Nixon as a "progressive," able president of the student body, the most persuasive contemporary orator in California's college system, and an "intellect," if not an intellectual.

Planning A Career

In 1934, as Nixon was planning his future career, the nation was still in the throes of the Great Depression. And although Franklin D. Roosevelt's New Deal was making some inroads against a shattered economy, and had given a sorely needed lift to the country's morale, soup kitchens, "Hooverville" shantytowns, and other outer-signs of desperate poverty were quite visibly in evidence. Had Nixon sought a job after graduating from Whittier College, he might well have joined the millions of others who were among the unemployed—many of whom also held college diplomas.

Fortunately, the town of Whittier was beginning to expand. The Nixon market and the filling station began to enjoy a modest increase in business. Frank and Hannah were anything but prosperous, but they were determined that Richard's ambition to become a lawyer would be fulfilled.

"I could still see my little boy, lying on the floor with the newspapers spread around him like a fan, reading about the Teapot Dome scandals, and telling me he would someday be a lawyer who can't be bought," said his mother, a catch in her throat. Her husband nodded: "I wasn't about to let him down—not as long as I had the strength to keep working," he added. His voice was quiet, but brimming with tenderness. It was difficult to believe that this was the same old Frank Nixon whose tongue could clip a hedge. "I knew we'd have to sharpen our pencil if we were going to help make our son's dream come true," he continued proudly.

At twenty-one, Richard was a lean-jawed, slender young man, serious as ever, somewhat uncertain about his ability to carve out a future in law despite his demonstrated scholastic merit, yet determined to make an all-out attempt.

Duke University

A concomitance of sheer luck—the first "big break" of his life—put Nixon on the road towards his goal. On the other side of the continent, Duke University, formerly a small Methodist college, had been named as one of the beneficiaries of a $40,000,000. endowment fund (now grown to over $400,000,000.), by tobacco industrialist and philanthropist James Buchanan Duke. Formerly known as Trinity College, it adopted the name of its benefactor, and utilizing its new largesse, the faculty decided to establish a school of law. Soon, it began to seek extra-bright scholarship candidates in order to establish high academic standards from the outset.

Nineteen scholarships were being offered for Duke University's first class of thirty-eight students, Nixon discovered. The tuition grant required that the student maintain at least a B average, with the added proviso that the number of scholarships available would be reduced as the students advanced to their second and third years. The purpose of this condition was to develop strong competition and also to assure a continuing high standard for the university. Nixon applied for, and was awarded, one of the nineteen grants.

His application to Duke's law school was given more weight by two warm and somewhat prophetic letters of recommendation to Dean H. Claude Horack: "I believe Richard Nixon will become one of America's important, if not great leaders," wrote Dr. Walter F. Dexter, president of Whittier College. Nixon's faculty advisor addressed Dean Horack with this note: "At Whittier, Richard Nixon displayed a rich sense of humor, human understanding, personal eloquence, and a marked ability to lead. He is intellectually honest, modest, and youthfully enthusiastic. If he has any handicap, it is his lack of sophistication."

The eagerly awaited reply, dated May 19, 1934, informed Nixon that he had been awarded a full tuition scholarship for the academic year, 1934-1935. Written by Justin Miller,

Dean of Duke University's School of Law, the letter stated, in part: "... The value of this scholarship, as you have already been informed, is two hundred and fifty dollars, sufficient to cover the cost of tuition and matriculation fees for the year. ... It will be possible for you to receive a re-award of this scholarship for each of the two following years of your law course, provided that you are able to maintain a superior average of scholarship while you are in law school."

"We had often talked of the time he would be going to law school," Ola Welch remembered. "But the night he came to my house to tell me he had won that scholarship—oh, we had such a good time! He wasn't just fun, he was absolutely joyous, abandoned—the only time I can recall seeing him like that. He had bought an old 1930 Ford and we rode around in the car and just celebrated."

The Ola romance cooled before he left for Duke University. They had planned to go to a dance one evening when they had an argument. ("It was my fault," said Nixon gallantly.) Ola Florence went with another suitor, Gail Jobe, instead. Nevertheless, he would occasionally write to her. "He wasn't happy at law school in the beginning," she said. "A few times he sounded like he was on the verge of quitting and coming home." Two years later Nixon received a "Dear John" letter from Ola Florence: she had married Gail Jobe.

The struggle against adversity and the long hours of study he had experienced at Whittier College were to be repeated at Duke. His parents, true to their word, provided him with an income of thirty-five dollars a month—a stipend, small though it was, which taxed their meager resources to the limit. Without the money, Nixon could not have attended law school since he needed every cent of it to cover his expenses: food, clothing, books, rent and personal effects. To supplement his finances, he found a job in the university's law library, doing research for Dr. Horack at the rate of thirty-five cents an hour,

Duke University
DURHAM
NORTH CAROLINA

School of Law
Justin Miller, Dean

19 May 1934

Dear Mr. Nixon:

It is a great pleasure to be able to inform you that you have been awarded a scholarship in Duke University School of Law for the academic year 1934-1935. The value of this scholarship, as you have already been informed, is two hundred and fifty dollars, sufficient to cover the cost of tuition and matriculation fees for the year.

It will be possible for you to receive a reaward of this scholarship for each of the two following years of your law school course, provided that you are able to maintain a superior average of scholarship while you are in the law school. We are interpreting this to mean maintaining at least a B average. Please advise us at your earliest opportunity of your acceptance of the award.

I shall look forward to seeing you here in the fall. If there are any further questions which you would like to have answered, please do not hesitate to call upon me.

With best wishes and kindest regards to you, I am,

Very sincerely yours,

Justin Miller

Mr. Richard Milhous Nixon,
Whittier College,
Whittier, California.

JM:p

Justin Miller, Dean of the School of Law, notifies Richard Nixon that he has been awarded a full tuition scholarship.

the wages made possible by a grant from the New Deal's National Youth Administration.

Few families could afford the cost of tuition, to say nothing of the comparative luxury of a dormitory room, inexpensive though it was during those bleak years of the Depression. For Nixon, the problem was compounded. His requirements for a place to live were determined by his limited funds and the need for a quiet environment. Never for a moment could he allow himself to forget that his tuition depended on his maintaining a B average. The necessity for study in relative privacy was paramount.

Whippoorwill Manor

"The cost of a dormitory was far beyond my means," Nixon reminisced. "At first I stayed at a boardinghouse but I had to move because of the noise. I found myself living with fourteen divinity students whose elocution practice created so much bedlam it was impossible to think, let alone study."

The problem of suitable quarters was finally solved when Nixon and three other law students—William R. Perdue, Fred S. Albrink and Lyman Brownfield—pooled their resources and rented a back room in a ramshackle farmhouse located in Duke Forest, about one and one-half miles from the campus. Mrs. Rose Henderson, a widow who lived with her small son in the front part of the house, provided the quartet of aspiring attorneys with two brass beds. Nixon and Perdue shared one of the double beds, Brownfield and Albrink the other. There were no other furnishings in the big room, nor were there any lights or plumbing; but there was a pot-bellied stove that provided some heat. Water was drawn from a well, and a rickety outhouse stood sentinel in the back yard. The foursome promptly dubbed their new dwelling "Whippoorwill Manor."

Whippoorwill Manor had none of the coziness Nixon had known in the Whittier home where he had lived since childhood. The four students soon developed a ritual to fend off the cold that made their room as chilly as an open-door barn. In the evening they stuffed the sheet-iron stove with crumpled newspapers, and then took advantage of the few minutes of quick heat that the blazing fire provided, to undress. In the morning they reversed the procedure. And, in the best democratic tradition, the roommates evolved a system of rotation so that each, in turn, jumped out of bed, refueled the stove with paper, and started the fire. The others then threw off their blankets and dressed hurriedly before the room temperature dropped again.

In theory, the system worked fine. However, Nixon's after-school job in the law library left him with little time for study, and he found that the only hours available for study were the early morning hours before class began. Since he was the first to awaken—at 4:30 A.M.—it became his chore to light the early morning fire. Then he hurried off to the university gym where he showered and shaved, had a quick breakfast, and raced to the law library to study until classes started.

"There were times when the fire would go out before he left for school," recalled Brownfield years later, "but not once during those cold winter mornings did Dick ever leave without re-loading the stove with paper for the rest of us."

Fred Albrink was equally impressed. "We understood why he had to arise so early in the morning, long before the sun came out. But I can't forget the picture of that solitary figure, his teeth chattering in the cold semi-darkness, dressing and preparing the stove as quietly as possible to avoid disturbing the rest of us. I have never known a more determined, hard-working fellow than Dick."

One of the attractions of the austere accommodations was the nominal rent: $50 per month—$12.50 each. But more important was the congeniality of the occupants. They were not only good friends who respected one another; they were also intellectual equals. But even more, their financial circumstances were very much alike.

On those occasions when they could afford something more than candy bars and peanut butter sandwiches, they had their suppers at a boardinghouse where the proprietress, a Mrs. Pierce, prided herself on her "home cooking." It was a warm, convivial environment, made more pleasant by the knowledge that the cost of the meal was only twenty-five cents, and that one did not have to mind his table etiquette. The well known "boardinghouse reach" was the order of the day.

The Nixon Nickname

Like young folks everywhere, the boys delighted in their invention of breezy nicknames for one another. Albrink was known as "On-the-Brink Fred" or just "Freddie." Brownfield, as might be expected, became "Brownie." Perdue's inelegant moniker was "Boop-Boop-Perdue," and the soubriquet attached to Nixon was "Gloomy Gus."

Gloomy Gus was not really an accurate characterization of Richard Nixon, the student. "Concerned" or "anxious" might have been more appropriate.

An illuminating and popular story, one which the President himself enjoys repeating, reveals the depth of his concern during his early years at Duke. Late one evening, studying as usual in the library, homesick and weary, he closed the book he was reading and rested his eyes, thinking of the problems that confronted him. His face mirrored his anxiety.

"I was concerned about my ability to keep my scholarship in competition with the members of a class that numbered over twenty Phi Beta Kappas out of a total enrollment of fifty," said Nixon. "I had expressed this concern to Bill Adelson, a third-year man who ranked near the top of his class. Adelson, who had noted the long hours I spent studying in the law library, reassured me: 'You don't have to worry. You know what it takes to learn the law? An iron butt.' "

Despite his anxieties, life for Richard Nixon began to assume a cheerier outlook. His worries about attaining high averages proved to be groundless—before the end of his first year he was among the top scholars of his class. Even Whippoorwill Manor had its good points. He enjoyed the pastoral setting during warm weather, the long walks along the dusty footpath that led to the university, the wildflowers and songbirds that added charm to the rustic surroundings. It was all conducive to peace and relaxation. One was free to explore his own thoughts without disturbance.

Occasionally Nixon would take time off from his studies to listen to the campus bands. Among his favorites were the orchestras led by Johnny Long and Les Brown, two Duke undergraduates who eventually made the big time. "Dick enjoyed hearing their music," said Albrink, "but he never stayed longer than ten or fifteen minutes before he'd be back at his books."

Nixon's drive for academic success forestalled his interest in social life. For him there was the occasional handball or football game to keep himself physically fit. Once in a rare while, a date. His tight financial straits were a factor here. "There were a few girls I liked and would have enjoyed dating, but I didn't have the money," said Nixon briefly.

The soubriquet, Gloomy Gus, that had been attached to Nixon by his friends was unwarranted, although it had some degree of validity. "How will I ever learn all this law? There's so much of it," he would often sigh as his head bent over his books. But in the end, he always emerged with honor grades.

In his second year at Duke, he achieved a rare honor that falls only to the most distinguished students: He became a staff member of the *Law Review*, and contributed a number of scholarly papers to it. One was entitled "The Law and Contemporary Problems," and another, "Changing Rules of Liability in Automobile Accident Litigation." Only Nixon and one other student, from the entire Law School student body (including those holding Phi Beta Kappa keys), were invited to write articles during that year: 1936. He also contributed legal essays to the *Duke Bar Association Journal*.

In his third year Nixon was elected to the Order of the Coif, an exclusive honorary society whose membership is restricted to the law students whose grades are in the top 10 per cent of all those in the nation.

The local chapter of the national legal fraternity, Phi Delta Phi, eagerly sought his membership, but Nixon, instead, joined the Iredell Law Club, a fraternity whose emphasis was on study and "other free entertainments and pursuits."

In his senior year at Duke, Nixon decided to grant himself the luxury of getting involved in campus politics. He believed in starting at the top. He ran for the presidency of the Duke Bar Association—the most prestigious office of all student organizations—and won. According to some of his classmates it was more than sheer prestige that motivated Nixon's campaign for this high student office. For the past three years, he had been forced to keep his clothes in a trunk. Austere Whippoorwill Manor provided him with no closet-space; nor was there a bathroom there where he could keep his shaving materials. Now, as president of the Duke Bar Association, he finally had his own office where he could keep his clothes hanging neatly on hangers, and store his toilet articles within easy reach, without having to rummage for them, as he had on those dreary, cold North Carolina mornings.

Finding A Job

Nixon utilized his last Christmas holiday at Duke Law School by looking towards New York where he hoped to establish himself with an important law firm. Accompanied by two friends, roommate William Perdue, and classmate Harlan Leathers, the three job-seekers sought employment with the largest and most influential law firms in the country. But December, 1936 was not an auspicious time to launch a career, particularly in metropolitan New York where competition for the few available jobs was acute. Nevertheless, Perdue was accepted by the legal department of the Ethyl

The Iredell Law Club of Duke University. The residents of Whippoorwill Manor are fully represented: Richard Nixon is number 25, Fred Albrink 2, William Perdue 7, and Lyman Brownfield 22.

Corporation. Leathers found a position with the prominent firm of Millbank, Tweed, Hope and Well, specialists in tax and corporate law. But Nixon received only vague, inconclusive responses from the several firms to which he had applied. His greatest disappointment was his failure to interest the one firm in which he placed his highest hopes: Sullivan and Cromwell. The late John Foster Dulles was the senior partner of this distinguished firm.

"As I look back," said Nixon in 1958, "I think I was impressed more by the thick, luxuriant carpets and fine oak paneling of Sullivan and Cromwell's reception room, than by the possibility of being a minor associate of Dulles." Nixon paused, smiled and concluded: "I'm sure I would have been there today if they had given me the job; a corporation lawyer instead of Vice-President."

After assuming the Presidency, Richard Nixon, looking back at some of those early years of law school and trying to establish himself in the legal profession, offered this evaluation of the profession and its practitioners:

"To the extent that the study of law disciplines the mind, it can be most helpful in politics as well as in other fields," he said. "But as a lawyer I should add a *caveat* at this point: Lawyers tend to be nit-pickers. Too often, when confronted with a problem, they approach it from the standpoint of 'how not to do it' rather than 'how to do it.' Lawyers in politics need non-lawyers around them to keep them from being too legalistic, too unimaginative.

"Looking back on my own years in law school," Nixon continued, "the most valuable course I had from the standpoint of preparing for political life was one in jurisprudence, the philosophy of law. . . . It was not a required course for the degree, but it would be, in my opinion, an essential course for any law student who is planning to enter public life, because the public man must not only know what the law is—he must know how and why it got that way. And again, the time to acquire this background is during the college and university years when a man has the time to indulge in the luxury of reading and thinking. Later on, he may well find himself too busy acting and speaking; and if he does not acquire this perspective and background in his college years, he may never acquire it."

None of his contemporaries envisioned Nixon as a politician, and certainly not as the occupant of the White House. Albrink, Brownfield and Perdue, his closest friends at Duke, were unanimous in their opinion that he would become a prominent attorney in a distinguished firm specializing in taxation and corporate law. "It just never entered our minds that he would make a career of politics," said Albrink.

There were two men, however, who did not share this belief: Dean Claude Horack and Richard Nixon himself. They had formed a close and enduring friendship in the three years they had known each other, and during Nixon's hours of employment as the dean's research assistant, they had often discussed the possibility of a future in politics.

"Dick, if you ever decide to enter politics, my advice is that you return to Whittier where you will find it easier to establish a political base," counseled Horack. "Join a local law firm and get involved in community activities. Make your start in your own home town."

But Nixon, then as now, was a complete realist. He knew that at age 24 he was hardly likely to create even a ripple in the mainstream of American politics. There was even some question as to whether he would register as a Democrat or Republican. He leaned toward the philosophies expounded by Justices Brandeis, Cardozo and Hughes, who, at that time were the liberal minority of the Supreme Court. In nearly all of his pronouncements as a campus leader at Whittier College and Duke University, he stamped himself as a moderate liberal, and a fighter for liberal causes.

Yet, always present in the recesses of his mind was his Quaker belief in the essential nobility of man. Man is an individual, not a faceless cipher. He is not merely a member of the masses or the classes. It was the same attitude that inspired his forebears to take a stand in favor of the Abolitionists whether they found themselves in the south or in the north. They conducted integrated schools and mixed religious services when prevailing racial mores went the other way. For many, it cost them their lives as well as their livelihood.

As a result of this background, Nixon perceived the individual as something more than a voter, a producer or a consumer. He saw the American citizen as a sentient human being whose greatest strengths and aspirations could be best realized through an orthodox approach to the Constitution and its attendant Bill of Rights.

Harboring such "conservative" thoughts in an era when the New Deal's populist appeal seemed as though it would extend into eternity, Nixon decided that this was not the time to enter the political arena. Further, having tasted the faster pace and the intellectual and cultural challenges of New York life and other eastern cities, he was reluctant to return to the provincialism of Whittier. But whatever his decision, he would be graduating the following month and he was now confronted with the problem of employment.

Finding a job in private industry was not going to be easy, he knew. Franklin Delano Roosevelt, convinced that his New Deal programs had banished widespread poverty and unemployment, terminated most of his "alphabet" agencies in 1937, the year Nixon entered the labor market. Home relief and public works were, for the most part, brought to a halt, and the Administration now referred to the depression as a recession—a semantic device that bore little relationship to the state of the nation's economy.*

---

*Although President Roosevelt's confidence, in 1937, led him to stop the flow of Federal funds to such agencies as the Works Progress Administration (WPA), the Public Works Administration (PWA) and other departments whose functions were to bolster the economy, the Bureau of Labor Statistics reported that 11,000,000 people were unemployed in that year as against 12,000,000 who were jobless at the start of the New Deal. The nation's economic recovery did not

The outlook for private employment, especially for someone without prior experience, looked bleak. With few other options available, Nixon turned a scrutinizing eye on the possibility of obtaining a position with the Government, even though many departments had curtailed their hiring, and were in the process of dismissing temporary employees. "The FBI looked very appealing to a young lawyer in need of work that year," Nixon recalled as a Senator.

Flirting With The FBI

Whatever his conscious or subconscious reasons, Nixon took and passed the FBI examination. He also asked his friend and adviser, Dean Horack, to intercede for him. On May 3, 1937, Horack addressed this letter of recommendation to FBI Director J. Edgar Hoover:

> Some time ago you suggested that I might refer to you any exceptional young man who has an interest in the work of the Federal Bureau of Investigation.
>
> I have such a man in mind who is to graduate in June . . . Richard Nixon, one of the finest young men, both in character and ability, that I have ever had in my classes.
>
> He is a superior student, alert, aggressive, a fine speaker and one who can do an exceptionally good piece of research when called on to do so. His position with his fellows is shown by the fact that he is this year president of the Duke Bar Association. . . .

---

begin to show substantial improvement until the Administration changed its policy from one of isolation to one of intervention, a move which resulted in the flood of Government and Allied rearmament orders that once again opened industry's employment gates. In 1941, eight years after Roosevelt had taken office, 14.6% of America's work force was still unemployed.

Hoover was impressed with Nixon's credentials as well as his potential, and in reply promised to consider him for a near-future appointment as an agent. But, by the time four months had passed without an offer of employment, the glamour of working for the FBI had worn thin. He changed his mind and, heeding the advice given him earlier by the dean, decided to practice law in Whittier.

"The FBI has been investigating my character ever since I passed the examination," he was to write to Horack shortly after returning to his home town. "But unless my present plans fail, I will not accept the job even if it is offered to me."*

Final exams were only a few weeks distant when Nixon wrote to his family in what he hoped was his last appeal for money:

> Dear Folks:
> It seems that my letter-writing becomes more and more infrequent. Last night we had our last Bar Association meeting of the year. The speaker was Thurman Arnold, one of the biggest men in law in the country. He is pleading cases before the Supreme Court now.
> The budget for the remainder of the year says that I will need $25. That, I am happy to say, will be the last check I'll be asking for—for good—I hope. It's only two weeks until exams begin and I'm still working on this article. However in about five weeks it will be all over—until the Bax Exam. I'm certainly looking forward to seeing all of you come back here in June. I hope Don will make it as well as the rest of you.
> I'm enclosing a picture so you'll recognize me when you see me.
> That seems to be all for tonight. Write more often.
> Love,
> Dick

---

*As Vice President, Nixon laughingly reminded J. Edgar Hoover of the incident and asked why he had not been appointed. Hoover un-

In June, 1937, the four Spartans of Whippoorwill Manor graduated with honors, with Perdue, Brownfield and Nixon heading the class—in that order.*

As Nixon, in his academic robe, ascended the podium to receive his law degree, his eyes swept the audience and rested on his parents and grandmother Almira Milhous who was then nearing ninety. They had made the long pilgrimage by automobile, spanning a continent so that they might glory in his moment of triumph after years of struggle.

A brief smile passed between them, full of love and understanding.

On balance, there was nothing during Nixon's school years to portend the pivotal roles he would some day play in momentous affairs of state. The impact he made on his fellow students and teachers was neither more nor less than might have been expected from any other socially responsible, highly intelligent youth. His classmates recall him as moral but not straitlaced; as sympathetic but never saccharine; as an industrious, quiet, and rather lonely young man whose rigid self-discipline and capacity for learning gave promise of a bright future in the field of law.

But if there was little or nothing to indicate student Nixon's aptitude for politics, the question logically arises: What are

---

earthed a printed form from the Bureau's files which showed that Nixon had indeed been accepted, but an unexpected reduction in appropriations previously earmarked for the Department of Justice cost him his job. Had the cut in funds been made just a few weeks later, Richard Nixon would have been asked to report for duty as an FBI agent.

*After their graduation and separation into diverse fields, each of Richard Nixon's roommates went on to achieve distinction: William R. Perdue rose to become vice-president of the Ethyl Corporation; Fred S. Albrink, who chose a career in the United States Navy, was commissioned a captain and served as Chairman of the Board of Review in the Judge Advocate General's office, and Lyman Brownfield became an eminent attorney practicing in Columbus, Ohio, and Washington, D.C.

The class of '37 at Duke Law School. Nixon is in the top row (inset).

the intangible reasons which enable a small-town grocer's son to become the elected representative of two hundred million people, while another, born with every advantage of wealth and circumstance, lives out his life in obscurity? Is a man preordained to greatness? Twelve years later, in an analysis of the Hiss case, Whittaker Chambers intimated that Nixon's career was being propelled by the forces of destiny; his guide, a lucky star.

Nixon dismissed the suggestion with characteristic pragmatism: "It appears to me that a man's life in politics is affected to a great extent by chance. History will show that two men may have equal abilities, but opportunity comes to one, not to the other. In my case, a lot of things were factors: geography, age, service in the House and Senate, a chance to be associated with the issues of the day. Certain circumstances developed, and I happened to be tapped on the shoulder."

When Richard Nixon returned to Whittier in 1937, that tap on the shoulder was still nine years away.

3
A Fledgling Spreads His Wings

WHEN RICHARD MILHOUS NIXON returned to Whittier in the summer of 1937, the proud possessor of an impressive looking law diploma, he found himself impeded in several respects as he planned to establish a legal career. He had not applied for permission to take the California Bar examination; moreover, having been out of the state for three years, he was not even eligible. Even worse, the cram course he had planned to take prior to the Bar exam had started earlier, while he was still at Duke Law School.

Once again the name "Gloomy Gus" was in order. Nevertheless, he still held fast to his belief that it was better to lose doing *something*, than to lose doing nothing. Forthwith, he addressed a letter to his old mentor, Dean Claude Horack at Duke University, asking him to intercede on his behalf.

Dependable as ever, Dean Horack followed through with an appeal to Professor E. Brenner of Stanford University, where the Bar examination was to be held. Dean Horack wrote the following: "I would very much appreciate anything you can do which would allow Richard Nixon to take the examination at this time instead of waiting for a future one. He was among our very best students, and I recommend him highly."

After a searching investigation of Nixon's scholastic record, Professor Brenner agreed to intervene, and an exception was made in this one case. Nixon was pronounced eligible, and his name was added to the list of candidates who would be taking the forthcoming examination.

But the bells of hope pealed only in subdued tones for "Gloomy Gus." On July 3, 1937, he wrote to a friend at Duke University:

"The Bar exam cram course I am taking started last March, and here it is July. If I have any hope of passing I will have to double-cram just to catch up with the others. Frankly, I doubt that I can get up the stuff in good enough shape in the two months remaining of this five-month course, but I'm going to try.

"Tell Dean Horack, therefore, that the first Duke graduate to take the California Bar exam has a darn good chance of failing."

"Don't worry," Dean Horack responded. "If they flunk you, none of the others will pass either."

Nixon read the dean's letter while confined to his bed with influenza—another setback. With more time robbed from his study schedule, his chances did indeed look poor. But, as usual, his anxiety was groundless. The final results placed Richard Nixon among the 46 percent who passed the examination. On November 9, 1937, at the State Supreme Court in San Francisco, he was sworn in as a member of the Bar.

Richard Nixon's boyhood dream had been fulfilled.

Nixon Joins Wingert and Bewley

It was a pleasant, warm day, even for Southern California, when on November 18, 1937, Hannah Nixon visited Thomas

W. Bewley, head of Whittier's oldest and busiest law firm, Wingert and Bewley.

"Tom, will you consider taking my son Richard into your office?" she asked.

A fellow Quaker, Bewley knew Mrs. Nixon well and, like everyone else in the community, respected and admired her. His grandfather and Richard's grandfather, Frank Milhous, had been business associates in Indiana, and the thought of once again uniting the two families pleased him.

"Ask him to drop in for an interview," said Bewley.

The timing of Hannah's request could not have been more propitious. His partner was about to retire and Bewley had been quietly seeking a bright young lawyer who was adept at preparing briefs and who could handle the everyday trial work. Since Bewley was also City Attorney in addition to his heavy private practice, he wished to reduce his work load by grooming a new associate as his deputy.

"I clearly recall that first interview," Tom Bewley said. "He impressed me immediately with his mature thinking—despite his youthful appearance. I liked that straightforward manner of his: he was modest but direct. I had the feeling that here was a young fellow who knew what he wanted. He was forceful without being pushy; highly intelligent, but not snobbish. I might add that he also had an engaging personality—a decided asset for a lawyer."

Evelyn Dorn,* Nixon's first secretary, recalled Nixon's first day at Wingert and Bewley:

"We knew he had worked in the law library at Duke University," she said, smiling, "so Mr. Bewley gave Dick his first legal assignment—straightening out the office library. I can still see him, in his sharply-pressed blue serge suit, hauling down from the shelves the several hundred books, dusting them, and cleaning the grimy shelves. Some of those books

---

*Mrs. Evelyn Dorn later served as personal secretary to Hannah Nixon until her death.

hadn't been opened in years and they really needed dusting. As for the shelves, Dick even varnished some of them."

If Nixon had any preconceived notions about starting his career as a defender of the Constitution in the higher courts, he quickly learned that some of Wingert and Bewley's clients had other, more immediate problems.

"Dick started with drunk cases, divorces, and traffic stuff," said Bewley, looking back in time. "He also worked with members of Whittier's City Council, drafting ordinances and so forth. Believe me, some of those councilmen were pretty hard to deal with. He was decisive and thorough, and knew how to get right to the meat of a problem without wasting time. As to his courtroom psychology, he could present his case so that butter wouldn't melt in his mouth, or he could take hold of a cantankerous witness and shake him like a dog."

Working At The Law

Nixon, the apt pupil, and Bewley, the sage mentor, worked well together. Within a year Richard was offered a partnership, and the firm's name was changed to Wingert, Bewley and Nixon.*

Bewley's respect for his young associate was apparent from the very beginning. "We were trying an important fraud case involving heavy-duty oilfield equipment and I decided to introduce Dick to the Superior Court of Los Angeles," said Bewley, chuckling. "Darned if he didn't produce a stop watch and proceed to time each of the opposing lawyers, making notes on how long it took them to question witnesses and present their arguments. When the trial ended he knew more about it than I did—and I was representing the defendant."

As word of his ability spread, Nixon's case load grew cor-

---

*Nixon retained his partnership in the law firm until 1946 when he resigned after his election to Congress, an unprecedented action among lawyer-congressmen.

respondingly heavier. He worked 16 hours a day, begrudging himself even the few minutes necessary for meals.

"He didn't have a regular time to eat," said Mrs. Dorn. "He would send me out at all hours for pineapple malts, hamburgers and, sometimes, Mexican food. He just about lived on them."

Despite his long days, Nixon did not consider his work a grind. On the contrary, he enjoyed it—with the exception of the divorce cases. Raised in the tenets of the Quaker faith, surrounded by fellow adherents since birth, the seamy side of life was abhorrent to him. He actually blushed when his clients discussed their conjugal behavior, and especially when women confessed to him their extra-marital intimacies. His moral convictions bordered on the Victorian, and he became increasingly embarrassed on such occasions. Nevertheless, he seldom failed to attempt a reconciliation between the warring spouses. To him divorce was distasteful; infidelity a sin. It is said that in his efforts to reconcile quarreling wives and husbands, he lost more fees for his firm than he earned.

As a partner, Nixon handled fewer drunk cases, parking ticket offenses, and the distasteful divorces. In his second year with the firm, he performed the legal work he most preferred. He had become the firm's chief trial lawyer and specialist on estate and tax matters, and was understandably proud of his accomplishment.

Branch Office in La Habra

So successful was the young lawyer that in August, 1938, he established a branch office of Wingert, Bewley and Nixon in the neighboring community of La Habra whose population numbered less than 4,000. There was nothing pretentious about his new headquarters—a desk in a real estate office. Here too he quickly made a name for himself, and within months his ability had so impressed the City Council that it appointed him Town Attorney, a position he held while attending to his private practice. Nixon was also appointed Assistant City Attorney under Bewley, as he had promised a year earlier. As an adjunct to this post, he served as the town's prosecutor.* But if all this sounds as though affluence had entered his life, let it also be noted that he was living in a one-room "apartment" over a garage.

Whether or not Nixon believed that his position as police prosecutor was an advancement remains in doubt. Certainly he did not relish many of his duties. The town was dry in those days and it was not until the middle fifties that the Quaker founding fathers permitted the sale of hard liquor within the city limits—and even then in only one cocktail lounge, *La Dolce Vita*, across the street from the Women's Christian Temperance Union.

In the days when Nixon was upholding law and order in Whittier, cafes were allowed to serve light wines with meals. It was inevitable that local imbibers, aided and abetted by eager cafe owners, would try to figure out a way to beat the system—and they did: one sandwich to one quart-bottle of wine. That sort of ratio was not particularly appealing to the good and staid Quakers of Whittier, and after a number of complaints had been lodged, Town Prosecutor Nixon posted his four-man police force at the entrances of the offending cafes and nabbed the "diners" as they staggered from the premises mumbling the words of the then popular song, "Drink to Me Only with Thine Eyes." The *bon vivants* soon learned to do their tippling in the privacy of their homes, and the discouraged cafe owners moved to sinful Los Angeles.**

---

*Should Richard Nixon ever decide to return to his old job, he will be pleased to learn that because he never formally resigned, the records still list him as Assistant City Attorney of Whittier.

**President Nixon drinks little more than an occasional sip of light wine, and then only at official dinners. Privately he will sometimes drink a glass of beer. He does not smoke cigarettes or cigars but, from time to time, will puff a pipe when talking by the fireplace.

Nixon and His Frozen Orange Juice Venture

His early success in the practice of law encouraged him to venture into the world of commerce and industry. Southern California had produced a bumper crop of oranges in 1938 and they threatened to become a glut on the market. For the Whittier area, not yet industrialized and heavily dependent upon its citrus-based economy, prospects were bleak. Characteristically, Gloomy Gus acted like an optimist when he felt most like a pessimist. He decided to enter the frozen orange juice business.

"Among our clients was a wholesaler of oranges who represented a number of growers," recalled Tom Bewley. "They had hit on the idea of marketing their surplus oranges by freezing and packaging the juice, and they convinced Dick that they could all make a fortune in the enterprise. After some discussion, our clients named the new venture the Citra-Frost Company and they invested $10,000 in the firm. Dick was named president."

Nixon was not only Citra-Frost's first and last president, he also served as company attorney and chief orange-juice-squeezer. Modern processing techniques had yet to be invented, and the cost of experimenting with various methods of freezing, preserving and packaging soon began to exhaust their capital.

"You have to remember that Dick and his group were trying to do something that had never been done before, although they were unaware of it at the time," Bewley explained. "They were freezing whole orange juice, not the condensed kind you can buy today. The major problem was packaging—finding a container that would not only hold the frozen juice but preserve it as well. They tried everything: glass jars, metal cans, paper cartons and cellophane bags. None worked."

Nixon's inexperience notwithstanding, the idea was sound.

Two large distributors with substantial accounts throughout the country were ready to contract for all that the little company could produce, but the youthful entrepreneur and his associates were ahead of their time. Their investment capital dwindled and economy became the watchword. After office hours at Wingert, Bewley and Nixon, the president of Citra-Frost would rush to the plant where he squeezed orange juice into whatever containers were in vogue at the moment—a do-it-yourself operation that saved the expense of outside labor. "Dick really worked hard to make a success of the company," said Bewley. "I guess he wasn't destined to be an orange juice magnate."

In spite of Nixon's efforts, Citra-Frost folded in eighteen months. Some of his partners who invested the original $10,000. of working capital believed that the company's failure was due to their young president's lack of business expertise, and they did not hide their disappointment.

Reflecting on the years between 1937 and 1942 when they were actively associated, Bewley could not remember a single occasion when his junior partner was completely relaxed.

"Even when we attended a football game—and that was very infrequently—he'd get so excited you'd hardly call it relaxation," he said. "Another thing, in the five years we worked together I never once went to lunch with him just for the pleasure of it. We weren't formal with each other, you understand; it's just that Dick was always serious. He would either carry on a debate with me and with whoever else might be with us, or he would discuss a case with a client. Working hours? He was on the job night and day. You know, that may be the secret of this guy's success: he never wastes a moment."

For all his 16-hour days, Nixon somehow managed to find spare time where none appeared to exist. Aside from the involvements necessary to his legal career he was active in community affairs—especially those which concerned his alma mater. In 1938 he was elected president of the Whittier

Alumni Association, and in the following year, at the age of 26, he was appointed a trustee of the college—the youngest member of the board. Nor was his participation in school activities confined solely to the executive or administrative levels; he also taught a course in practical law at Whittier College. Apparently, that was not enough to keep him busy, and so he became an active member of the Twenty-Thirty Club, Whittiers' Junior Chamber of Commerce, and utilized his day of rest by teaching a Sunday School class at the Quaker church in East Whittier.

But there was one purely recreational outlet for his surging energies that seemed to afford him the relaxation he could experience nowhere else: the theater. Ever since his high school days, he had nurtured a not-too-secret penchant for performing before appreciative audiences, an ambition which in those earlier days was only partially sated by debating, acting in local plays and, later, through his courtroom histrionics. Perhaps it was his proximity to Hollywood that influenced his liking for the theater, or it might well have been a last attempt to clutch at the waning daydreams he had enjoyed as a child.

Whatever the reason, he joined the Whittier Little Theatre Group, comprised of amateur and professional actors and actresses who were dedicated to the improvement of their skills through appearances in a wide variety of roles. Mostly, they rehearsed after work, during their evening hours, exchanged ideas and suggestions, and coached one another in the many parts they played while dreaming their dreams of stardom.

My Son The Actor

"Richard was 27 when he joined the acting club," recalled Hannah Nixon, searching her memory. "That was in 1940 when he was a struggling young lawyer. It was the only social club with which he ever had time to affiliate. I'm sure my son never seriously contemplated a career on the stage or in films; his whole life was dedicated to his legal work. But he was so busy, he had very little time for social functions of any kind. I knew he had an aptitude for the stage, and he liked the people in show business, so I was glad when he joined the Little Theatre Group."

Nixon's interest in acting was already evident as a Whittier College student when he wrote, directed and starred in *The Trysting Place*. His drama coach and mentor was Dr. Albert Upton, Professor of English, who remembered his former protégé as an undergraduate with a yearning for dramatics. "Like most others who knew him as a college student, I never associated him with high government office," said Dr. Upton, repeating the sentiments of so many others. "But I did detect the ham in him. I rather thought that after graduation he might go on to Hollywood or Broadway as an actor."

Dr. Upton's primary recollection of young Nixon was that of an enthusiast who helped him establish dramatics as a recognized course at Whittier College. "Dick was one of our first successful actors," the drama coach said. "He really loved the stage."

One of the best-authenticated testimonials of Nixon's ability to control his emotions goes back to 1933 when he was 20 years old. The Poet-Campus of Whittier presented an English comedy, *Bird in Hand*, by John Drinkwater.* Nixon's role was that of an anguished father, an elderly proprietor of an inn whose daughter had eloped with a ne'er-do-well. During rehearsals, however, Nixon was unable to express adequately the old man's profound grief.

"I taught him how to cry," said Upton, who directed the play. "I made it plain that the only way he could ever successfully portray the agony of the bereaved old innkeeper

---

Bird in Hand was presented in Whittier College's Founders Hall built by the town's pioneers in 1894. It was here that the President's mother also performed in amateur plays as a student. Founders Hall has since been replaced by a newer and larger structure.

would be to concentrate on getting an actual lump in his throat. Dick practiced the difficult art until I was convinced he had mastered it. But getting a lump in your throat is only a prelude to weeping, and I doubted that he would be able to shed real tears."

On opening night, all the actors in the play were tense, as was Dr. Upton. They need not have been. In the climactic scene Nixon shuffled to the center of the stage, imitating the halting steps of an arthritic old man, sat in his chair, and as he delivered his monologue—the sorrowful story of his daughter's travails—his voice cracked, the elusive lump in his throat developed, and he cried real tears. "That was a *tour de force* for Dick Nixon," said Upton. "I was amazed. I saw his eyes brimming, and then his cheeks were wet. Those tears were genuine—beautiful!"

Thirteen years later Dr. Upton had good reason to remember another weeping scene. Nixon had just made his celebrated speech of 1952 in defense of the accusations about his "secret expense-fund" in which he alluded to his cocker spaniel, Checkers, and to his wife's "respectable Republican cloth coat." The denouement of the crisis took place after Nixon met General Eisenhower at the airport in Wheeling, West Virginia. The nation's press, on its front pages, emblazoned a picture of candidate Richard Nixon weeping on Senator Knowland's shoulder. Where former Vice-President Alben Barkley had been affectionately known as "The Veep," reporters and columnists were now calling Nixon "The Weep."

"That's my boy!" exclaimed Dr. Upton when he saw the photograph. "That's my actor!" But he was quick to add, "There was nothing spurious about that performance. The lump came to his throat and the tears flowed naturally. He really felt it."

It came as no surprise to his family and old friends, therefore, when Richard Nixon sought respite from his heavy work schedule and civic duties by joining the Whittier Little Theatre Group. As it turned out, it was the most important and fortuitous move he had ever made in his life, for it was there that he met the lovely titian-tressed actress, Patricia Ryan.

Love Strikes

In the winter of 1938, Richard Nixon was a striving, ambitious lawyer of twenty-five with a very small bank account, but highly charged and motivated. At this time, the Whittier Little Theatre Group was conducting tryouts for the George S. Kaufman-Alexander Woollcott mystery melodrama, *The Dark Tower*—a play in which the male lead is a district attorney who falls in love with the female star.

Nixon, hearing that a glamorous new teacher was trying out for the romantic lead, was intrigued, and went down to the theatre to find out for himself. What he saw was a poised and charming young woman, her beautiful face framed by flowing red hair.

Immediately, Nixon knew that the role of the district attorney must be his. He tried out for it, and, as planned, got the part. At the same time, the glamorous young teacher won the romantic female lead.

Impulsiveness has never been one of Richard Nixon's characteristics; in fact, it was always his predictable sense of caution that so delighted his admirers and infuriated his detractors. But this time, he permitted caution to take a holiday. He was hopelessly smitten, and on that very first evening, after rehearsal, he proposed.

Who was this lovely, warm, intelligent girl who had been introduced to him as Patricia Ryan, and who, within the first hours of their first meeting, had won the heart of a man destined to become the most powerful figure on earth?

Thelma Catherine Patricia Ryan

To the citizens of Ely, a bleak little mining town in Nevada, the date, March 16, 1912, meant little more than the fact that one day later St. Patrick's Day would be celebrated. For William and Kate Halberstadt Ryan, however, it was a memorable occasion—the daughter they had long hoped for was born on that evening.

The question of a name for the new baby was easily resolved. Mrs. Ryan had selected Thelma Catherine, in honor of two aunts of whom she was especially fond. But her father, coming home from his work in the mines past midnight, and only then learning of his daughter's birth, called her his "St. Patrick's babe in the morn." A compromise of sorts was reached when the child was christened Thelma Catherine Patricia Ryan, but Dad, proud Irishman that he was, ultimately had his way. To him, she was to be "Pat"—then and always—and to posterity as well. So enamored was he of his patron saint that he refused to celebrate her birthday on the 16th, but, instead, insisted on the 17th—St. Patrick's Day. Her mother, however, with predictable German stubbornness, not only observed her daughter's proper birthday, but refused to call her anything but Thelma.

Mrs. Ryan, born in Essen County, near Frankfurt, Germany, had come to the United States as a child of ten to visit an uncle who had no family of his own. Immediately, she fell in love with America, never to return to the land of her birth. Kate Halberstadt Bender was a widow with two children when she married William Ryan in 1909. Pat was the youngest of the three children born to them. Her brothers, William and Thomas Ryan, remain residents of California.

Before Pat was a year old, Kate Ryan, whose first husband had been killed in a mining accident, persuaded William to give up his dangerous job in the local silver mine and, in 1913, the family moved from Nevada to California, settling on a small farm in Artesia, 20 miles southeast of Los Angeles.

Pat's older brother, Tom Ryan, who presently lives in Glendale, California, recalled their early life: "My father planted potatoes, cauliflower, tomatoes and corn. The soil was very rich and we made up for the lack of rain in this area by irrigating the land. We would get two or three crops every year. The pepper tree behind the house was there when we moved in, but Pat planted the walnut tree from seed. She also planted an apricot tree near the tank house. It's gone now, but we got apricots from it for many years. She also had a beautiful flower garden."

Pat's Childhood

Her idyllic early childhood was filled with the contentment and simple pleasures normally enjoyed by rural families of a half-century ago. The family worshipped together, worked together, and played together. These were the luxuries of their lives. The intimacy of a warm and loving family made for a happy life for young Pat, even if much hard work was expected of her. "Pat used to help in the fields," said her brother, Tom. "We all worked; we pitched in from the time we were old enough, the way all early American farm-families did."

When she was very young, Pat just tagged along, but as she grew a little older, she worked right along with her brothers. Along with them she picked corn and tomatoes and even helped pickle the cauliflower and peppers. There were no tractors in those days, so Pat drove the team of work horses.

Whatever measure of fun there was in little Pat's life was usually associated with the farm in one way or another. For example, her father raised peanuts—not commercially, but just for their own pleasure—and often they invited the neighborhood children to old-fashioned peanut-roasts in their front yard. The swimming "hole" was close to the farm and great fun. On summer nights Pat would often go swimming with her brothers.

Mother Ryan loved to bake, and her daughter, Pat, would sometimes help with this delightful task. Pat's favorites were her mother's delicious bread and cinnamon rolls, and she especially enjoyed helping in their preparation. So popular with the children were their mother's goodies that they frequently consumed, in one evening, all that she had baked during that day.

As early as the eighth grade, Pat proved that she had a flair for dramatics. In an Artesia Grammar School program, Thelma Ryan was billed as "The Farmer's Thrifty Wife" (the female lead). The play was called, *Back to the Farm.*

Catastrophe struck the Ryan household, when in 1925 Pat's mother died of cancer. Pat's frolicking, fun-filled days came to an abrupt end. She was only thirteen—but from that time on her girlhood years were devoted to maintaining respectable school grades, and to keeping house for her father and two brothers. Two years later, when she was attending Excelsior High School, her father became seriously ill. She cared for him, as she had earlier cared for her mother. In 1930, he died. Pat was then 18, a recent high school graduate, and completely on her own.

College Years and a Career

Her first ambition was to acquire a college education. She enrolled in Fullerton (California) Junior College, and was able to maintain herself by baby-sitting for the parents of neighborhood children. Later, she worked part-time for a bank in Artesia.

It wasn't long before she was able to fulfill her second ambition: to travel. In 1931, some elderly friends of her father's family were visiting in California. They were going to drive back to Connecticut, which prompted Pat to offer her services as a chauffeur without pay. They accepted her offer, and she drove East with them. Fortunately, she found a job, almost at once, in a hospital near New York City. First she served as a secretary, and later, after a summer course in radiology at Columbia University, she became an X-ray technician, working at this job for two years.

126 A Fledgling Spreads His Wings

In 1934, Pat returned to the West Coast in order to complete her education. She enrolled at the University of Southern California and majored in merchandising. During these college years, she augmented her small savings by working as many as forty hours each week correcting papers for faculty members, and by doing part-time and holiday work in Bullock's Wilshire department store in Los Angeles. In 1937, she was graduated cum laude, the proud possessor of a Bachelor of Science degree in merchandising, and a teacher's certificate to teach in California high schools.

Pat's interest in drama provided her with another source of income while she was still attending USC. She had taken a number of screen tests in nearby Hollywood and, as a result, played two walk-on parts in the films, *Small Town Girl* and *Becky Sharp*.

She had one line in *Becky Sharp* which, ultimately, was cut out in the editing room, but the more important immediate result was that she was paid twenty-five dollars for her work instead of the seven dollars which she had expected. Her other roles were chiefly in mob scenes. "You'd need a magnifying glass to find me," she laughed, "but the pay was very welcome, as it helped me earn my way through college."

After graduation, Pat continued with her acting, mainly for the pleasure it afforded her. She particularly enjoyed the legitimate theatre, especially the stage plays presented by the Whittier Little Theatre group.

Pat's initial hope was to find a career in merchandising—possibly as a buyer for a large department store in Los Angeles, New York or Chicago. But, as it turned out, the first job to come her way after graduation was to teach Business Education courses at Whittier Union High School.

Until she accepted the teaching post, the thought of working in Whittier had never occurred to her. She had studied and enjoyed merchandising, and had already accumulated some experience in that field. She was completely surprised, therefore, when she was offered the position at Union High with a salary of $160 per month. This was excellent remuneration for a teacher in 1937.

Whittier Union High School, with an enrollment of 2,000 students was located on the main street of the quiet Quaker community at the foot of La Puente Hills. In addition to teaching, Miss Ryan quickly became involved in extra-curricular activities, such as a faculty advisor for the "Pep Committee," helping with student rallies, attending all the high school sports events and coaching the cheerleaders, working closely with the PTA, and directing school plays. Off-campus, she dated the handsomest, most eligible bachelors in town, and continued to act in Little Theatre productions.

Sudden Proposal and Marriage

In short, Thelma Catherine Patricia Ryan was having the time of her life when on that winter evening in 1938, at the Whittier Little Theatre, she won the female lead in *The Dark Tower*, and found Richard Nixon onstage, opposite her, playing the leading man in the role of district attorney. Offstage, that same evening, playacting suddenly ceased, as quite unexpectedly she was asked to play the real life role of Mrs. Richard Nixon.

Of course she was surprised and flattered, but, as one reporter put it: "The sudden proposal left her completely *under*whelmed." Pat was in no hurry to settle down, and she made it clear that she cherished her independence. She was a popular, outgoing young lady with an effervescent personality, a good mind, and a zest for living. In her thoughts she had reserved marriage for the indefinite future.

Despite her initial discouraging response to Richard Nixon, he pursued her with dogged persistence, and there were times when his self-effacing stance must have been particularly galling to her. Richard had been squiring a few girls before he met Pat, but thereafter he dated no one else. The pretty redhead, on the other hand, continued to date the eligible bachelors who called on her. Still, Richard was the ultimate in devotion; and when Pat had a date with another fellow, Richard did not hesitate to call for her in his car, drive her to meet her beau for the evening, and sometimes even wait around to take her home.

Whatever reservations there might have been about his unorthodox approach, the result was that it worked. Nixon's courtship game-plan worked. Pat and Richard became engaged on May 1, 1940 when he presented her with a basket of flowers in which he had hidden an engagement ring. The cost of the ring just about exhausted his bank account, and they both agreed that from that day on, their savings would be kept in a joint account.

Seven weeks later, on June 21st of that same year, two years after they first met, they were married.

Their honeymoon was completely unplanned. They had no particular destination in mind as they drove off in the general direction of Mexico City, heading first for Laredo and then driving down the Pan American Highway. This was, undoubtedly, one of the very few times in his life that Richard Nixon dared indulge in the luxury of not being fully rehearsed for what might lie ahead.

Their honeymoon over, the newlyweds settled down in an apartment over a garage. Pat continued to work as a teacher, while Richard struggled to build up his law practice. The young couple joined the young-married set and embarked on what promised to be an uneventful, but satisfying life together in the peaceful environs of Whittier.

In 1938, Nixon registered as a Republican, and made a few speeches locally, for his party's presidential nominee, Wendell Willkie. But these were of small consequence, and the serenity of small-town life remained unspoiled. Politics was of little concern to Whittier's peaceful people, even when Germany had begun to conquer much of Europe, and daily headlines proclaimed the advances being made by Hitler's panzer divisions. Even when the *Luftwaffe* raids began to terrorize London and turned the city into a shambles, the war in Europe continued very remote for tranquil Whittier.

Reluctant Government Employee

December 7, 1941: the Japanese struck at Pearl Harbor; and everything began to change. Life took on a different hue. The young Nixons had been married for a little over a year now, and suddenly everything was different. Along with millions of others gripped by the new national fervor, the Nixons were caught up in the excitement of a nation at war. Richard's work no longer seemed as important as it had been, and he longed to help in some meaningful way. The idea of active military combat, however, conflicted with every tenet of his Quaker faith. "I had to think things through," he said. His thoughts led inevitably to non-military service, even though it meant the sacrifice of his now flourishing legal practice.

In January, 1942, Richard and Pat Nixon gave up their Whittier apartment and journeyed to Washington, D.C. "We had only one objective—to find work in a department of the Government that would enable us to contribute in some way to the war effort," Pat later wrote in a magazine article.

Ironically, Nixon found a job with the Office of Price Administration (OPA), an agency which in just a few years was to come under his own vitriolic attack. It was not a very important job—certainly not for a talented lawyer who had given up a lucrative practice. The OPA could do no better than assign him to the job of drafting resolutions and handling rulings concerned with the rationing of automobile tires. And on his 29th birthday, Richard Nixon found himself a cog in the wheel—an anonymous cipher among other anonymities doing much the same work.

When he had applied for this job, Nixon had been hired by Professor Thomas I. Emerson of Yale Law School who was serving at that time as associate general counsel of the OPA. Professor Emerson had hired Nixon on the spot. An ardent advocate of left-wing philosophies and causes, Emerson later testified as a voluntary witness before the House Un-American Activities Committee (HUAC), expressing vehement opposition to the Mundt-Nixon Anti-Communist bill. Along with Alger Hiss and others who shared their philosophy, he was a member of the International Juridical Association, President of the National Lawyers Guild (another organization of "radical" attorneys to be cited by HUAC) and was also Connecticut State Chairman of Henry Wallace's Progressive Party. However, although it was known that Hiss had been connected with a number of organizations that were called "subversive" by the Attorney General, his first meeting with Nixon (his later nemesis) was pleasant. Undoubtedly, this meeting was the turning point in Nixon's career.

"Dick Nixon came into my office on January 9, 1942, without an appointment," Emerson told a reporter for the Boston *Globe*. "As far as I can recall, he didn't even have a letter of recommendation—he just walked in and said he wanted to help in the war effort. I found he had an excellent record at Duke University, and a good law practice in California which he gave up when he came to Washington. He was a nice looking fellow, clearly intelligent and without doubt a man we could use. I gave him the job right then and there."

Nixon's starting salary was $3,200 per annum, roughly $62 per week—substantially less than he had been earning in Whittier, and hardly a windfall for a talented married man. He was soon given a raise to $4,600 a year and was earning $5,900 when he resigned in August of 1942.

The eight months he spent as a government employee were not particularly happy ones. The pettifoggery of the newly-appointed, as well as the firmly established, bureaucrats angered him. He was especially irked to find that when he would answer routine correspondence, his letters were often "corrected" by a supervisor whose "corrected" version was in turn "corrected" by a still higher authority—and so on up the supervisory treadmill. He was appalled by the scores of inept employees in the higher echelons, who, he was firmly convinced, were using the OPA as a vehicle for the permanent control of profits (an opinion that outraged his sense of individual initiative that was a bedrock belief to this grocer's son). That he would some day exercise his authority as Chief Executive to institute a far stronger program to control wages *and* profits was as inconceivable to pre-political Nixon as it still is to the diehard rightists of today. Yet, anomalous though it may be, it was this short period of employment that shattered his liberal illusions and veered him towards conservatism.

"In OPA," said Nixon in 1956, "I learned respect for the thousands of hard-working government employees, and equal contempt for most of the political appointees at the top who feathered their nests with all kinds of overlapping and empire building. I was also startled by the mediocrity of so many civil servants. And, for the first time, I saw there were people in government who were not satisfied with interpreting the regulations, carrying out the law that Congress passed, but who were actually out to 'get' business, and used their authority to that end. These were, of course, some of the remnants of the old, violent New Deal crowd. They set me to thinking at that point.

"I came out of college more liberal than I am today," Nixon continued; "more liberal in the sense that I thought it was possible for government to do more than I later found it was practical to do. I became more conservative after my first experience with OPA."

There was another overriding reason for Nixon's dissatisfaction with his desk job. The thought of sitting out the war, "fighting the Battle of the Potomac," rankled within him, urging him to action. As a Quaker, he could have applied for exemption from military service, but his pacifist beliefs deeply troubled him: the moral posture inculcated in him since childhood was not easily shaken. For three months he self-counseled with the "Inner Light to illuminate his path," as the Quakers express it. Finally, he came to terms with himself. He applied for a commission in the United States Navy in March, 1942. On September 2nd he was assigned to active duty as a Lieutenant Junior Grade.

The War Years

Nixon's evolution from the Quaker orthodoxy of his early youth to that of *laissez faire* was not as precipitous as it may seem, and came about only after many months of agonized soul-searching. His mother had hoped that he would enter the ministry, but he had not felt the "call." In Prescott, he had even gone so far as to shill for a gambling concession in order to earn the money to save his brother's life. This transition was signalled by a number of precedents, unimportant in themselves, but whose sum total led to his abandonment of the anti-war philosophy that had always been at the core of his Quaker belief. Dr. Upton, his English teacher at Whittier College, described his former student as a "fighting Quaker." The term apparently pleased Nixon.

In his successful bid for a Senate seat in 1950, he alluded to Korea and to America's need to maintain a strong military posture. "It is not easy for me to take this position. It happens that I am a Quaker; all my training has been against displays of strength and recourse to arms.* But I have learned through hard experience that, where you are confronted with a ruthless, dictatorial force that will stop at nothing to destroy you, it is necessary to defend yourself by building your own strength."

---

*This was not mere rhetoric. In the early morning hours of October 15, 1970, when some 100,000 demonstrators converged on Washington, D.C., President Nixon, standing on the steps of the Lincoln Memorial, told a group of war dissenters, "When I was a student at Duke University I believed that Neville Chamberlain was the greatest man living, and Winston Churchill was a madman. It was not until later that I realized my error."

The mileposts that ticked off his increasingly moderating attitude toward the religious concepts held by his forebears brought him to the final confrontation with his "Inner Light."*
When he accepted his commission as a Navy Lieutenant he severed for all time the link that had bound him to the doctrine of nonresistance to physical force.

Of the many thousands who fought in the South Pacific following the attack on Pearl Harbor, two Navy officers were destined to assume the mantle of Chief of State: John Fitzgerald Kennedy, called "Shafty" by his fellow officers, and Richard Milhous Nixon, known as "Nick" to his shipmates.

Lieutenant Junior Grade Nixon's first eight weeks in the military service were spent at Quonset, Rhode Island, where he received his basic training.** It was here, also, that he met William P. Rogers whose political fortunes were to be closely intertwined with his own.*** Lieutenant Nixon had applied for sea duty and, in his naïveté, was confident that he would be assigned to a fighting ship. He was soon to receive his first lesson in military non-science: that the Royal Snafu is not necessarily confined to the Army. Instead of the requested sea duty, he was sent inland and was assigned to a desk job as aide to the executive officer at an unfinished air base in Ottumwa, Iowa.

----

*Nixon's adherence to his Quaker faith continues to this day, his strong belief in military defense notwithstanding (although non-denominational services are held in the White House). His church contributions, since he assumed the Presidency, have not been disclosed. The last public record is contained in his income tax returns for 1952 which showed deductions of $55 in 1949, $40 in 1950 and $50 in 1951, with all contributions made to the East Whittier Friends Church.

**In May, 1943, a year after volunteering for Navy duty, Nixon was promoted to full lieutenant. He was raised to lieutenant commander in October, 1945. In June, 1953, when he had been Vice President for six months, he was given the rank of full commander in the Naval Reserve.

***Nixon was a headline-producing Congressman embroiled in the Hiss case when he again met young William Rogers who, at that time, was serving as counsel for a Senate investigating committee. They renewed their wartime friendship and, in the years that followed, Rogers

Lieutenant Junior Grade Richard Nixon with members of the Quonset Association at the Naval Train-

As usual, Nixon worked out a game-plan—to salvage whatever was worth saving for future use! He learned that the grain grows high in the Middle West; that corn futures are something more than prophecies made in Gypsy tents. Having been reared in the West, he knew its people, its needs, its aspirations. As a student at Duke University, he had familiarized himself with the problems unique to the Eastern seaboard. Unexpectedly, finding himself in the hinterland, he again put the iron butt to work and set about storing up facts about this region—a source of information that he was later to make good use of in both of his campaigns for the Presidency. "Whether it's football, politics or poker—change the rules on Nick and he'll beat you at your own game," was how one of his fellow officers put it. "That guy sees all and forgets nothing."

Nixon's disappointment with his inland post was lessened when his wife joined him soon after he arrived. She worked in a bank during their stay in Ottumwa and, five months later, when her husband's second application for sea duty was successful, she moved to San Franicsco where she was employed as an economist for the Office of Price Administration.

Assigned in May, 1943, to the South Pacific Combat Air Transport Command (SCAT), Nixon's unit moved with the advancing Navy and Marine forces, hopping from island to island in the South Pacific chain. He served as an operations officer while on his home base on Guadalcanal, and also as

---

shared many of Nixon's momentous activities as Congressman, Senator, Vice President and President. It was Rogers' sage advice that persuaded Nixon to remain as Eisenhower's running mate when the "slush fund" crisis exploded during the 1952 campaign. In 1955, when Eisenhower suffered his heart attack, Nixon moved into Rogers' house to better avail himself of his friend's wise counsel at a time when any innocent word might be construed as a sign that he was about to "seize Presidential power." Rogers, who served as Deputy Attorney General during the Eisenhower administration, was appointed Secretary of State by President Nixon.

officer in charge of the SCAT enclaves on Bougainville, Vella Lavella and Green Island. His group was charged with the difficult task of maintaining fluidity along the ever-lengthening lines of supply.

Nixon has often been criticized as one attempting to pass himself off as a veteran who had seen actual combat. In a political speech after the war, Nixon declared: "I believe the returning veterans—and I have talked to many of them in the foxholes—will not be satisfied with a dole or a government handout." While his critics find the statement concerning the attitude of returning veterans quite correct, they consider the reference to foxholes as nothing more than political hyperbole since Nixon's unit was not involved in combat, but travelled in the immediate wake of the widening American perimeter.*

The truth is that Nixon's assignment was not without danger. During one period, he and his men were under intense Japanese bombardment for twenty-eight nights in one month. "We got used to it," was Nixon's laconic reaction. "The only things that really bothered me were the lack of sleep and the centipedes."

Nixon's outfit consisted of about a dozen enlisted men in addition to radio operators, aircraft technicians and base service personnel. Almost completely unequipped except for a few hand tools, they would be landed on a beach and, left to their own ingenuity, were expected to set up a makeshift base to accommodate the DC-3's—or, when positioned in the interior of an island, to hack a landing strip out of the jungle in a matter of days.

However, there was more to the duties of the outfit than just establishing bases for the DC-3's. Planes landing at the remote SCAT outposts had to be loaded and unloaded, and fresh food had to be supplied for the pilots, their crews, and for the litter cases who were returning to American-held ter-

---

*The full context in which this statement was made is detailed in the next chapter.

ritory. Schedules were always tight, with never a minute to spare.

"Things would get a little hectic at times," admitted Edward J. McCaffrey, one of Nixon's wartime buddies who later became Democratic postmaster of Concord, Massachusetts. "We were always in an almighty rush—always under pressure. I recall one instance, in January, 1944, when Nick received a radio alert that thirty planes were arriving at our base on Bougainville. Each plane carried 135,000 pounds of rockets. Nick and his nine-man crew were ordered to unload the rockets and then put them in firing place on the combat planes that were flying the missions in the air strike against Rabaul. The thirty empty planes were then to be immediately flown back to Guadalcanal filled with the men who had been wounded in the enemy attack on Bougainville the night before. The actual loading and unloading was a job for the enlisted men, but Nick peeled off his shirt and sweated through the hard physical labor right along with the rest of the men. The job was finished on schedule."

Non-combat officers in the Pacific theatre of war seldom attracted attention beyond the confines of their individual stations, but Lieutenant Nixon was hardly the man to remain "just another officer." On Green Island, where rations were not exactly gourmet fare, he opened a non-profit venture, "Nixon's Snack Shack," the only hamburger joint in the South Pacific. Located alongside the airstrip, weary pilots and their crews were able to get hot coffee, sandwiches and fruit juices —all free.

"Nick was able to wheedle the supplies for his Snack Shack from other outfits that were better stocked," recalled McCaffrey. "Some of the stuff was, shall we say, 'liberated'—but Nick could swap anything. Just a small trade would set in motion a series of bigger trades that not only had his men well-housed, but kept the hamburger stand operating. If you ever saw Henry Fonda in *Mr. Roberts*, you have a pretty good idea of what Nick was like."

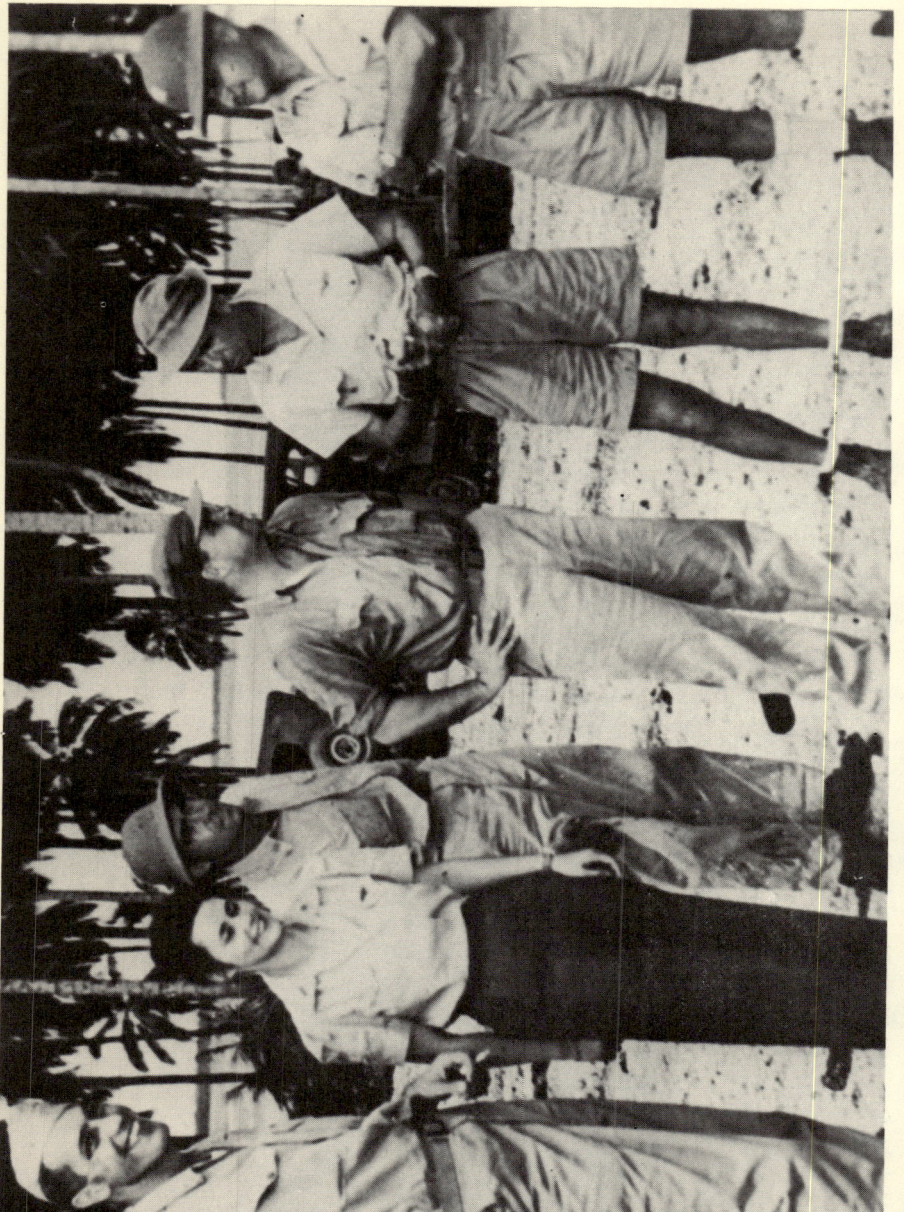

Kay a (third from left) with the SCAT unit on Green Island in 1944.

Lt. Nixon in front of "Nixon's Snack Shack"—the only free hamburger joint in the South Pacific.

Some of the items on the menu were not on the government issue list; an occasional bottle of whiskey, for example—a rare treat which he doled out among the men without regard to their rank. Soon, "Nixon's Snack Shack" became known throughout the area, and the veil of obscurity that had cloaked him since his enlistment (an unthinkable situation for him) was thankfully lifted.

The Broadening War Influence

The war seems to have exerted a broadening influence on Nixon's behavioral pattern, a gradual change that began soon after he was shipped to the South Pacific. Whatever vestiges remained of the "loner" that he had been in his earlier youth, these were now largely dissipated, although he was never to achieve the gregarious nature that characterized Franklin D. Roosevelt, Harry Truman or John F. Kennedy.

Whereas, until now he could not stand anyone who smoked, and characterized this practice as "disgusting," he was now able to tolerate it; and he even found himself enjoying an occasional cigar from time to time. Prior to his enlistment, he would inveigh against the evils of alcohol with all the fervor of a fundamentalist preacher, but those men with whom he served remember him as having joined them in a few drinks. As to profanity, his vocabulary had been limited to such mild expletives as "hell" and "damn" . . . used sparingly. In the Navy, however, his expertise grew and there were times when he could and did hold his own with the sailors and marines who passed through his base. Nevertheless, it should be added, his ingrained propinquity to moderation controlled these lapses and kept them within reasonable limits.

There was one other area of departure from his Quaker mores that illustrates the degree of change in Nixon's worldly outlook. The Society of Friends has always frowned on card playing: when played just for fun it is considered a frivolous waste of time; when played for money, it is gambling and therefore sinful. Nixon, far away from the sheltering influence of the East Whittier Friends Church, managed to make his peace with some of his earlier, confining scruples and to address himself to the national pastime in the Pacific—the art of poker.* With only the scantiest knowledge of the game and well aware of his vulnerability, he decided to put an old theory to work: study and master the problem at hand and *then* play for keeps; a kind of early-day Nixonomics that always worked beautifully.

As in his Whittier football days, he first studied the fundamentals—the rules of the game; analysing, probing, carefully examining whatever constants existed among the variables of poker; weighing the percentages for or against betting on certain hands; learning the advantages and disadvantages of relying on one play or another. He had the best of teachers: James Stewart (not the actor) and Lester Wroble, two officers whose clever playing marked them as poker theoreticians in the classic sense. They played for hours on end during the lull in bombardments, and on quiet days and evenings between the landings of supply and combat planes, as well. It was not very long before Nixon had evolved a game-plan of his own. He felt he had mastered the art to perfection, and he was ready to play for high stakes.

"I doubt that Nick ever lost a cent at poker," commented Lester Wroble. "He had a passion for analysis; he always played it cautious—close to the belt, and there was never a time when he didn't know exactly what he was doing. He thought everything out beforehand and never took chances."

The single-minded concentration with which Nixon pursued the intricacies of poker was well worth the effort. Sometimes the stakes were quite high, especially the games on Green Island where a pot sometimes ran well over $1,000.

---

*I played bridge just once, when I was in law school," says President Nixon. "It was not until I joined the Navy that I knew anything at all about poker. As Vice President I played only once—and broke even."

Estimates of his total winnings vary, but a figure of $3,500 strikes a median average. He was a registered Republican, but he was very democratic about raking in the pots. He took money from enlisted men and officers alike, without the slightest hint of partiality. In any event, it was this money that enabled him to launch his political career.

The day inevitably dawned when nearly all of the Japanese military forces were driven back to their own shores, and the chain of islands, scene of a blood-letting unparalleled in that part of the world, once more returned to their pre-war tranquility. In July of 1944, after 14 months in the South Pacific, Nixon was transferred back to the states where he was assigned to Fleet Air Wing 8, at Alameda, California. There, Pat rejoined him.

At war's end, Nixon found himself in Baltimore, re-assigned to the Navy Bureau of Aeronautics and, for the first time since he donned a uniform, his duties were in his chosen field of law. (This is a familiar little game that the military establishment often plays—putting men with special skills into jobs far removed from their training, until just a few weeks before discharge, when they are finally put into the job that they should have been doing all along.) Now a lieutenant commander, Nixon was busily engaged in renegotiating and terminating contracts with such aircraft companies as Bell and Glenn Martin. The work was important, but it brought him no satisfaction. Mrs. Nixon, who accompanied him to Baltimore, could sense his unrest, and understood the reason for it. "Like millions of others, he longed to be out of uniform and doing something meaningful with his life."

But he had formulated no post-war plans, and this indecision disturbed him greatly.

For a man of Richard Nixon's temperament, the prospect of being isolated in some beehive office building, a faceless worker among thousands of other faceless ones, must have been a frightening vision. His former job at the Office of Price

Lieutenant Commander Richard Nixon.

Administration was still available, but he shrank from the very thought of involving himself in a situation that would place him at a desk along with countless other desk-occupants, all of whom would live in constant mortal terror of a man whose desk was just a little larger than their own.

He still retained his partnership in his Whittier law firm, but the idea of returning to the type of minor cases which he could expect in his home town held little appeal for him. Time was moving along, but his own situation continued to be confused. He was growing increasingly anxious. His wife was expecting their first child. With his release from the Navy due in November—a matter of weeks—he would be left jobless. Greatly worried, he weighed the relative merits of working for the OPA or returning to his Whittier office.

Into this difficult state of affairs stepped providence, and with a generous assist from a group of men in California who were totally unknown to him, all of his doubts were resolved. In September, 1945, Richard Nixon received a telegram that changed his life and plunged him into the eye of the turbulent political tornado that was to change the complexion of American and world history.

4
The Political Arena

CALIFORNIA'S TWELFTH Congressional District encompassed an area that extended from the barren foothills on the southern border of Los Angeles to the San Gabriel mountains on the north. For years a bastion of die-hard Republicanism, the district had nevertheless supported a Democrat, an ardent New Dealer, Horace Jeremiah (Jerry) Voorhis, who had been elected to the House of Representatives ten years earlier. Now seeking his sixth consecutive term, he continued to be the scourge and nemesis of all Republican hopes in his bailiwick.

The popular Congressman was no ordinary politician. The son of a millionaire, he graduated Phi Beta Kappa from Yale, and, spurning his father's wealth, went to work in a factory for 39¢ an hour. A succession of other humble jobs followed, and after several years of footloose wanderings in impoverished areas of Europe and the United States, he married an ordinary working girl. Shortly thereafter, with money borrowed from his father, he founded an orphanage for destitute children.

Voorhis was in his mid-twenties when he decided to pursue an activist role in politics. The capitalist system held little appeal for him. He registered as a Socialist, became an enthusiastic advocate of the socialist political ideology, and supported the "funny money" schemes promulgated by Upton Sinclair's "End Poverty in California" (EPIC) movement. As the years moved on, he matured politically and intellectually, and began to favor the New Deal program of President Roosevelt. Ultimately, he became a Democrat.

The Voorhis Phenomenon

In 1936, Voorhis scored a political upset in the heavily Republican Twelfth District by riding to victory on Franklin D. Roosevelt's coattails. Roosevelt's death in 1945 did not diminish the young Congressman's popularity. He sponsored a number of excellent bills, and, being an astute politician, was always aware of the need to keep the press on his side so that he would receive full and adequate publicity aimed at his constituents back home. His radical inclinations declined as he grew more and more aware of the importance of his position and the consequences of his official actions. The years found him emerging as an articulate foe of communism, one of his major contributions being the Voorhis Act: Public Law 870, which he authored. It stipulated that any organization controlled by a foreign power must register with the Department of Justice. This measure was savagely fought by the liberals and radicals of the day.

Jerry Voorhis was re-elected every two years from 1938 onward, with steadily increasing majorities. He not only captured Democratic votes, but a substantial number of Republican votes as well. To the regular GOP organization in the Twelfth Congressional District, Voorhis was more than just a formidable adversary; he was an invincible adversary.

As early as the summer of 1945, when the Congressional elections were still fifteen months off, the Republican Party's professional stalwarts had already thrown up their hands and were expecting another defeat at the hands of Voorhis. To confront the seeming foregone conclusion, a dispirited group of Republicans assembled on an August evening in San Mateo—one of the smaller towns of the Twelfth District. The gloom was so pervasive that only a handful of GOP regulars bothered to attend. The majority of those in attendance consisted of what many called "amateur politicians." Among them were the district's businessmen, career women, merchants, citrus growers, and a cross-section of other citizens ranging from oilfield workers to bankers—men and women who had always supported Republican candidates at the polls, but had seldom taken an active role in party affairs.

The group was confronted by one paramount and humiliating problem: Where to find a Republican of any stature in the district who was willing to run against the unbeatable Jerry Voorhis. What to do? Which way to turn? Clearly, they could not conduct a campaign without a candidate.

The Committee of One Hundred

The meeting was a stormy one, and out of the welter of rhetoric and schemes that were proposed, a decision was finally reached: to organize a Committee of One Hundred—roughly the number of men and women present. The primary function of the Committee was to find a suitable candidate to oppose Voorhis. They chose a method that shocked some of the staid Old Guard Republicans who were in attendance, but which seemed perfectly acceptable to the neophyte politicians. They decided to *advertise* for a candidate!

The new Committee had not yet established a working fund, so, for the sake of economy, a "Help Wanted" ad was circulated as a political announcement—a shrewd move, as it turned out, because by its very novelty it became newsworthy. The desperate plea was featured on the front pages of twenty-six newspapers in the Twelfth Congressional District. It read:

> WANTED: Congressman candidate with no previous experience to defeat a man who has represented the district in the House for ten years. Any young man, resident of the district, preferably a veteran, fair education, no political strings or obligations, and possessed of a few ideas for betterment of country at large, may apply for the job. Applicants will be reviewed by 100 interested citizens who will guarantee support, but will not obligate the candidate in any way.

To implement the candidate-finding program, the Committee of One Hundred selected from its ranks a small group of knowledgeable amateurs and professionals to conduct the preliminary interviews. The selectees included Stanley Barnes, a brilliant lawyer who was later appointed to the United States Circuit Board of Appeals; Frank E. Jorgensen, a vice-president of the Metropolitan Life Insurance Company; Herman L. Perry, president of the Bank of America branch in Whittier, and longtime friend of the Nixon family; Murray M. Chotiner, a Beverly Hills lawyer whose public relations firm had piloted Earl Warren's successful campaign for Governor of California; and Roy O. Day, Republican district chairman who was named to head the Committee.

Roy Day planned to schedule four meetings during which the smaller committee would assess the merits of the prospective candidates. The advertisement, however, drew hardly more than a disappointing lot of malcontents, bigots, intellectual freaks and others totally unsuited to politics. Only two prospects were interviewed during the first sessions: one was a supernationalist who promised to expel all those not born in the United States, and the other, a smog engineer who had an idea for cutting a vast aperture in the Santa Monica Mountains to facilitate the movement of ocean breezes into the Los Angeles Basin. Six more hopefuls were interviewed at the next meeting, but all were completely inept. Not one candidate responded to the ad and no one showed up at the third session. Nevertheless, this September meeting did yield some positive results, for it was here that Nixon's political career had its inchoate beginning.

The group had come to the unanimous conclusion that advertising for a candidate was a waste of time and energy. They also concluded that their best choice, and the ideal man to oppose Voorhis was former Whittier College president, Walter Dexter, later Superintendent of Schools for the State of California. But Dexter, who would have had to resign his position in order to undertake the Congressional race which his opponent was almost sure to win, could simply not afford to take the risk. It was at this point that Dexter himself suggested to the Committee that they consider the merits of Richard M. Nixon, ". . . one of my former students, and exceptionally qualified in every respect to represent the Twelfth District."

A deputation of three Committee members: Frank Jorgensen, Boyd Gibbons and Rockwood Nelson visited Frank and Hannah Nixon at their grocery store to learn more of their oldest living son's background, his interests, and whether they thought he might be receptive to the idea of running for Congress. Frank and Hannah, bursting with pride and excitement answered all their questions, gave them Richard's address in Baltimore, and then surprised the delegation with the news that Herman L. Perry, or "Uncle Herman," as they called him, had already broached the subject to them.

Perry had known the Nixons for many years. He and his fellow Quaker, Franklin Milhous, Richard's Grandfather, had served together on the Whittier College Board of Trustees, and he had met Richard Nixon many times after the young lawyer joined Wingert and Bewley, whose law firm was located in the Bank of America Building where Perry conducted business. His selection of Nixon as a prospective candidate for Congress, therefore, born of desperation though it may have been, was also his reflective choice of a man who, as he said later, ". . . had the personal appeal and the legal qualifications to mount a successful campaign. To me, he was custom-tailored to the job."

When Herman Perry was asked to act as liaison between the Committee of One Hundred and Richard Nixon, he was glad to accept.

Political Lightning Strikes

Still in uniform, Lieutenant Commander Nixon and his wife, Pat, were entertaining Jacob Beuscher and his wife one afternoon in September of 1945, when a telegram arrived from "Uncle" Herman L. Perry. It was Nixon's first intimation that political lightning had struck.

"I don't recall the exact words of that telegram," stated Perry, "but I did ask him to phone me if he was interested in making the race against Voorhis, and whether he was a Republican or Democrat. None of us really knew what his political affiliations were because of California's cross-filing system which allows candidates to file for both the Democratic and Republican nominations.

The Beuschers and the Nixons re-read the telegram. Richard Nixon could hardly believe he was being asked to be a candidate. The flush of excitement carried through to the next day, and after a long and earnest discussion with Pat, Nixon telephoned Herman Perry. The conversation was short and to the point. Nixon opened the conversation by testifying to his Republican credentials. "I registered as a Republican on June 5, 1938, after returning to Whittier from law school," he assured Perry. "In 1940, I campaigned for Willkie and, in order to support Tom Dewey in 1944, I voted for him by absentee ballot from the South Pacific."

"Fine!" said Perry. "Now then, are you available?"

"In about eight weeks when my Navy discharge comes through."

"All right, Dick. We're sending you an expense check for $300. Can you fly out here to California in about two weeks so I can present you to the Committee?"

For eight weeks Nixon was walking on air. The two-month mustering out period seemed interminable. This was a fight Nixon was eager to engage in. Challenge Voorhis in the coming 1946 campaign! Nixon had not yet learned that his opponent had demolished every "upstart" who had dared oppose him in the past.

In spite of this, Perry exuded confidence. He embarked on a whirlwind campaign of his own, writing personal letters to each of the Committee's members, telephoning the more influential leaders, and buttonholing them personally whenever the opportunity presented itself to enhance Nixon's chances for acceptance. His intensive effort was fruitful.

When Richard Nixon rose to address the select group of Republicans on September 29, 1945, there was not one among them who had not heard a favorable comment about him.

Seventy-seven members attended the meeting in Whittier's William Penn Hotel. There were three opposing candidates, but the entire affair consumed no more than ten minutes. The *Whittier News* of October 3, 1945 recorded Nixon's first speech as a politician. He told the Committee that he recognized that there are two schools of thought within the American political system:

> One, advocated by the New Deal, is government control in regulating our lives. The other calls for

individual freedoms and all that private initiative can produce.

I hold with the latter viewpoint. I believe the returning veterans—and I have talked to many of them in the foxholes—will not be satisfied with a dole or a government handout. They want a respectable job in private industry where they will be recognized for what they produce, or they want an opportunity to start their own business. If the choice of this Committee comes to me, I will be prepared to put on an aggressive campaign on a platform of progressive liberalism designed to return our district to the Republican Party.

The result was almost a foregone conclusion. Of the 77 votes cast on the first ballot, 63 were for Nixon, the remaining 14 votes scattered among the three other candidates. On its second ballot, the Committee of One Hundred made it unanimous. Richard M. Nixon had won his first political victory.

Girding for Political Battle

When he was selected by the Committee to represent the Twelfth Congressional District, Richard Nixon was the epitome of what a candidate should be, but seldom is: personable, filled with youthful enthusiasm, socially gracious, a lawyer with a good local reputation, and a veteran. Moreover, he had a lovely and attractive wife—always a plus factor—and he would soon boast of an infant daughter, another distinct advantage which always appeals to the American electorate. Except for his political inexperience, he was an ideal candidate. Although he was not overly blessed with charisma, perhaps, he was not without attractive and likeable qualities.

Flushed with momentary self-confidence at having been selected by his fellow citizens to run for office, Nixon returned to Baltimore. On December 4, 1945, in a letter to Roy Day, he formally accepted the Committee's endorsement.

On January 4, 1946 he was mustered out of the Navy, ready to confront the civilian world in a new battle, the outcome of which was destined to shape the course of world events for decades to come.

With the confidence and naivete of the young and inexperienced, the youthful politician, Richard Nixon, supported by his wife Pat, faced up to a most devastating prospect: having to do battle with the redoubtable Voorhis, the man who in the past had so thoroughly beaten and demoralized all Republican office-seekers in his district that they were convinced that Voorhis was invincible. If Richard Nixon was in any way affected by the prevailing gloom and despair, he did not yet show it.

Now, completely separated from military service, Richard and Pat flew directly back to California. They lost no time in investing half of their mutual savings of $10,000 as the down payment on a house, reserving the other half for personal living and campaign expenses.

It may have seemed strange to some that the Nixons were purchasing a house in California at a time when, if elected, he would be sent to Washington. Perhaps this reflected an inner uncertainty on the part of the two young Nixons. Richard could hardly have been as confident of winning as he proclaimed.

In the months to come Nixon was to sing many a paean of thanks to his wartime poker-playing buddies on Green Island, who, unknowingly, contributed to his campaign fund. Without that extra money, he would have been hard put to survive the primaries, let alone the general election campaign. As it was, there were times when Pat wept with frustration, because they did not have enough money for postage to mail their political literature.

The Campaign Begins

The 1946 campaign had its inception in a small, rented office in one of Whittier's oldest buildings. Richard's mother contributed an old leather couch that had been stored for years in the garage, and his brother, Don, hauled it to the office in the family's grocery truck. They found a battered old desk in a used furniture store which they bought for five dollars, borrowed a few chairs and tables from friends, and a former schoolmate of Pat's contributed a typewriter that was fairly aged, and would only work spasmodically.

Pat worked in the office and accompanied her husband on his speaking tours for the first two months of the campaign. Their first daughter, Patricia, Jr. (Tricia) was born on February 21, 1946. In a matter of weeks, the new mother was again at her husband's side, while Frank and Hannah Nixon cared for their new grandchild.

Dick and Pat set about their joint campaign efforts with renewed vigor, oblivious to the amused reaction in the Voorhis camp, and the polite but thinly disguised expressions of doubt that emanated from their own Republican ranks. But, if the odds against the possibility of success seemed overwhelming to others, it did not succeed in dampening the spirit within the shabby little office in Whittier where an aura of confidence held sway.

Richard Nixon had heard the sound of a distant trumpet; and he surveyed the political arena with an assurance and a strange exhilaration such as he had never felt before.

The Chotinerization of Nixon

Committee Chairman Roy Day was among those who was impressed with Nixon. However, he was astute enough to realize that this neophyte politician would need professional guidance if he was to challenge Voorhis, the entrenched incumbent, successfully.

Early in January, soon after Dick and Pat had furnished their "cubicle" office, Roy Day contacted Murray M. Chotiner, the Beverly Hills lawyer who had masterminded Earl Warren's victorious campaign for the governorship of California, and the race of publisher J. William Knowland for the Senate. Chotiner was intrigued by the report about the neophyte candidate who seemed to exude so much self-confidence. His public relations firm was conducted separately from his law office, and commanded fees ranging from $5,000. to $30,000 for publicity and management services. He was so taken by the candidate Nixon that he agreed to handle the campaign for a mere $500—a sum which the Committee gladly paid.

Chotiner was not Nixon's manager in the 1946 campaign as some biographers have declared. He served, instead, as Nixon's publicity agent, and as a part-time consultant. Most of Chotiner's time and energy was devoted to Knowland's Senate race. Chotiner's acceptance of Nixon, a raw beginner whose chances for success appeared to be minimal, was simply a favor to the Republican Party leaders. It was a favor neither he nor they ever had cause to regret.

Nixon and Chotiner—here was the perfect symbiosis: two men of widely divergent attitudes and backgrounds harnessed in tandem, working toward a common goal.

Nixon was the fired young candidate, clinging to the ethics and verities of an earlier day, not even realizing that many of his views had long since gone the way of the *McGuffy Reader*. Nixon was still quoting from the speeches of Jefferson, Lincoln and Wilson. He still believed that, somehow, he could topple his opponent with quotations gleaned from the musty galleries of history. He was still under the illusion that he could debate issues "on a lofty plane" as he had done in his high school and college years. He had yet to learn that he was now playing in a new league.

For Murray Chotiner, "lofty planes" were reserved for the Olympian gods; and the only matter of real concern to him was to so guide his client that he would develop a winning strategy. His reasoning was simple: noble deeds cannot be accomplished by those who lack the power to effect them.

Chotiner immediately recognized in Nixon an unquestionably superior mind. He was convinced that Nixon even possessed an element of latent greatness. Most important, because it was evident that the young campaigner was well aware of his inexperience, Chotiner was confident that Nixon would be receptive to guidance.

Chotiner, the wise and able political strategist, had years earlier proven his political genius, but it was not until 1955 that his *modus operandi* for winning became known. In that year, the Republican National Committee was deeply disturbed by the results of the political polls. Depressing statements by a number of pundits in the National Press Club in Washington declared that the Party had no candidate strong enough to succeed Eisenhower. Because of this, Chotiner was urged to visit a number of areas in the United States. His assignment: to give secret lectures to local Republican leadership, in which he would explain his method for winning campaigns. A transcript of the 14,000 word lecture happened to fall into the hands of a newspaper reporter who published it, and caused an uproar in many circles.

The Chotiner Method was immediately and violently denounced by the Democrats as ". . . one of the most cynical political documents since Machiavelli's *The Prince* or Hitler's *Mein Kampf* . . . a textbook on how to hook suckers." What the Democrats did not say, and with good reason, was that some of them had already been aware of Chotiner's system, knew of the text, and had been using it for years. Others, who were unfamiliar with the "secret" transcript until it was published, quickly applied it to their own use, and for good or evil, it has served as a guideline for both parties ever since. Interestingly enough, the CIO, through its Political Action Committee, had not only been using its own version of the

Chotiner Method, but in my instances had improved upon it. Yet, this group was among the most vociferous of Chotiner's denouncers.

The Chotiner Method that helped advance Nixon's early career was indeed a remarkable treatise. It classified, with scholarly detail, the various problems that usually beset the campaigner, and provided the solutions as well. Most of the tenets read like religious dogma:

- *Never let the public know all your opinions, but make sure it knows about selected portions of your opponent's views.*

"We never put out the complete voting record for our candidate, vote by vote, in spite of the demands from people within our organization. The reason is this: Even if your candidate has voted 99 per cent right according to the person who reads the record, the one per cent will often turn the prospect against you."

This supports Chotiner's contention, a view widely held by both Parties, that people often vote *against*, not *for*. The less the public knows about your own stand, the less they have to be against, leaving you free to hammer away at whatever part of your opponent's record the voters are most likely to resent.

- *Start the campaign at least one year before the election.*

"You need that time to deflate your opposition. . . . There are many people who say we don't want that kind of campaign in our state. They say we want to conduct a constructive campaign, and we want to point out the merits of our own candidate. I say to you in all sincerity, if you do not deflate the opposition candidate before your own candidate gets started, the odds are that you are going to be doomed to defeat."

Here, Chotiner expounds on his conviction that the opponent's weak point must be found as early in the campaign as possible, then continue to bear down on it right up to election eve.

The successful campaigner must draw first blood, and while the opposition candidate is defending himself against the accusation, another blow must be struck which will give him something more to explain—and then another blow, and another. While he is explaining accusation number one, accusation two and accusation three should be ready and waiting for release at the correct psychological moment.

- *Advance to the attack, but side-step the smear.*

"What is the difference between legitimate attack and smear?" Chotiner asks. "It is not a smear, if you please, when you point out the record of your opponent. Of course, it is always a smear, naturally, when it is directed to your own candidate."

- *Refuse to be put on the defensive.*

"If your opponent launches an attack, just *don't answer*. If he persists, however, and you find the attack has reached such proportions that it can no longer be avoided in any way, then reply with an attack of your own against the opposition for having launched it in the first place."

- *Let the public think they are selecting the candidate.*

"People want to feel *they* are choosing the candidate," Chotiner confides, "rather than having the candidate tell them 'I am going to run, come hell or high water.'

"It is really simple to let the people select their candidate. All you have to do is to get a number of people talking: 'Now if we can only get so-and-so to run for this office.' "

There was nothing specious about this strategy. Chotiner revealed that in 1941 Knowland started a "talking campaign" that elected the then obscure Earl Warren to the office of Governor of California.

- *Organize a Democratic or Independent "front."*

"At the very beginning of the campaign, Republicans should make sure they have a separate organization of Democrats or Independents or whatever you want to call them."

A separate organization with no *public* connections to the candidate's own Party can be useful on those occasions when the endorsement of non-Republicans are needed for publicity purposes; nor does it hurt when "Democrats" or "Independents" issue unfavorable statements about their own candidates.

- *Create a favorable image with the press.*

"Contact every newspaper in your area at the start of a campaign and ask for their advertising rates. It tells them we are thinking of putting an ad in the newspaper. It may help some of our stories."

"We come to the question of ethics in the campaign," Chotiner concludes. "I cannot overemphasize the fact that truth is the best weapon we can use."

It was a nice touch, that question of ethics so delicately put, and represents the only time it was mentioned in the lecture. The postscript, which he neglected to add, was that stating falsehoods would be unnecessary for those who followed his methodology.

Nixon did not emerge from the campaign as a plastic reflection of Murray Chotiner. He managed to retain his own personality. He adhered to his earlier beliefs, and often reiterated the noble aspirations that had always been his mainstay. But his receptive mind did absorb the hard facts of political reality so that by the time the campaign was over, and possibly without being fully conscious of it, Richard Nixon had been thoroughly Chotinerized.

The Race Against Voorhis

On March 19, 1946, Richard Nixon and Jerry Voorhis filed in both the Democratic and the Republican primaries. This was permissible under California State Law.

Cross-filing, originally intended as a device to eliminate corruption, enabled a candidate to estimate his strength within his own party, and at the same time to gauge his appeal to the voters in the other. If skillful, the candidate could build a large following within the ranks of the opposing party.

Voorhis, as the established incumbent, chose wisely to ignore his rival. He realized that any attention that he might give to his adversary's political attacks would only result in publicity for his opponent. This, he studiously avoided. He chose, rather, to play the role of the elder statesman who was too busy with important affairs in Washington to take note of any comments of the "upstart lieutenant commander." This reference did not escape Chotiner and other Republican professionals who knew that there existed an undercurrent of resentment against officers by many enlisted men. Voorhis wisely made capital of this trend.

Nixon, on the other hand, campaigned energetically, unable to attract large audiences, but carrying his message to the public through newspaper ads, street-corner "rallies" and door-to-door distribution of his political literature.

The primary campaign had just begun when, one afternoon, Chotiner visited Nixon's office. The aspiring politician was elated. A steady stream of "volunteers" had been coming to the office for the past several days asking for batches of the literature which Dick and Pat had printed at their own expense. The volunteers had assured the jubilant Nixon that they were handing out the circulars, flyers and pamphlets to voters throughout the district. Chotiner listened to the enthusiastic young couple. At first, he shared in their delight at the pleasant turn of events. Then, suddenly, he became quiet and sank into reflection. "It can't be!" he said to himself. His political instincts told him that something was awry. After a hasty investigation his suspicions were confirmed. "Dick," he said sympathetically, "you've been taken in by one of the oldest tricks in politics. Those 'volunteers' were from the Voorhis crowd. They've been destroying your literature."

Nixon was furious, frustrated and embarrassed. On top of all that, he was hard-pressed for funds. He picked one of the two suits from his closet, sold it, and used the proceeds to print another, much smaller, supply of circulars. But they didn't give these out without caution. He and Pat passed them out during his speaking "engagements"—often on streetcorners, to "crowds" numbering less than a dozen apathetic listeners.

Voorhis, fully aware of Chotiner in the background, cannily avoided every thrust that might have resulted in a direct challenge. Voorhis was simply not giving up any ground, and it began to look like a lost cause for the unknown, poorly-financed newcomer.

In the August primaries, Voorhis waltzed away with a preponderance of the Democratic vote, and polled well enough among the Republicans to give him a healthy lead of 7,000 over Nixon—a sure sign of the fate that would befall the Republican candidate in the November election.

The Committee of One Hundred was glum. Whatever financial assistance it had given Nixon for his primary race was now drying up, and outside help quickly dwindled to a trickle of coins. His morale was at its lowest point.

"I need an issue—just one good issue!" Pat empathised with him as she watched him pace the floor of their now-deserted office.

Nixon carefully studied and analyzed Chotiner's technique and he began to see the basic problem: Without an issue that would ignite the enthusiasm of the people, he could not win. He had to arouse the people. He had to mount an attack that would force a response from his opponent. Voorhis had to be forced to address himself to what Nixon was saying. He could not allow the elusive Voorhis to ignore him.

Nixon took on more hope and his self-confidence began to soar when he learned that the Voorhis primary vote represented only 53.5 per cent of the total—a substantial drop from the 60 per cent he had polled in 1944. "Keen political observers thought we ran a darn fine race, and this was the best Republican primary showing in years," Nixon wrote to Chairman Roy Day. "Frankly, Roy, I really believe it is time some of the rest of the people began to realize it."

Nixon's letter sounded hopeful and full of enthusiasm, but it hardly told the whole story. What he had neglected to mention in his letter to Day was that the "keen political observers" he was referring to consisted of one isolated Los Angeles reporter who had arrived at his hopeful statistics through his own brand of arithmetic. But it did help Nixon to keep his spirits buoyed up.

Chotiner, reading a copy of Nixon's optimistic letter, smiled to himself sagely. He knew that his protégé would need something more than a "win complex" to achieve victory in the general election. It would not be easy to launch an attack against a popular favorite who completely ignores his opponent. Where was the issue to be found that would draw out the adversary and cause him to make the fatal error? Without it, victory was impossible.

Voorhis simply refused to allow Nixon an opportunity to find the slightest crack in his armour. He was using Chotiner's own technique, and the sagacious Chotiner could not help but admire the five-term Congressman who had obviously learned much from past battles.

An Issue Rears Its Head

The political climate in 1946 was filled with unrest and dissatisfaction. California, like many other parts of the nation, was beset by the problems that followed in the aftermath of World War II.

A growing restlessness could be observed among the rank and file of labor as war contracts were summarily cancelled. Continuing meat shortages added to the public's resentment, and a lack of sufficient housing to accommodate the newly-marrieds among veterans and others increased the feeling that "something was wrong in Washington."

Rightly or wrongly, the target for this pent-up dissatisfaction was the incumbent New Deal Administration which was being continued by President Harry Truman following the death of President Franklin D. Roosevelt. Republicans took up the battle cry: "Had enough?—Had enough?" They threw the slogan at the public at every turn.

The cavalier attitude of the Soviet Union toward the United States and its former wartime allies was another source of mounting anger among the citizenry of this country. Our suspicion that Stalin had planned all along to subjugate Eastern Europe, just as Hitler had planned to conquer all of it, was a bit late in coming. But the International Workers of the World (IWW) was still a potent force, operating openly or clandestinely in most countries of the world, under the direct supervision of the Kremlin.

In the United States, at least during the 1940's when Russia was a military ally against Nazi Germany, and in the early fifties, when America produced such extremists as Senator Joseph P. McCarthy, there were those who were convinced that they could advance the cause of "democracy" by fostering Communism. Some were open advocates, while others supported the Communist philosophy secretly.

Many of these native American communists were indistinguishable from any other average American citizen. They succeeded in infiltrating the labor unions and, in some instances, achieved positions which enabled them to subvert the very policies that insured the well-being of the working membership.

Among the unions most affected by this infiltration was the Congress of Industrial Organizations (CIO); and especially its "public relations" arm, the Political Action Committee (PAC). Although most Democrats, including Voorhis, acknowledged that they were aware of Communist infiltration into this great labor union, the Republicans seized the opportunity to link their Democratic opponents to the CIO-PAC, whose support and endorsements they enjoyed to the near exclusion of Republican candidates. Indirectly, of course, Democratic candidates were being portrayed as tolerant supporters of communism and fellow travelers of the Moscow line. Guilt by association became the dominant theme of the campaign. In some instances the accusations were deserved; in most, they were not.

Voorhis Blunders

The early days of the Nixon-Voorhis contest produced no fireworks. Without a confrontation with his rival, Nixon seemed to flounder in a sea of self-serving clichés that had gone out of style with Theodore Roosevelt's Rough Riders. The one opportunity for which he had prayed finally presented itself through an ironic and rather whimsical turn of fate.

After the birth of Tricia, Voorhis sent the Nixons a government pamphlet entitled *Baby Care*, as he did to all new parents in his district. Tickled at the thought of sending his opponent a booklet, the Democratic congressman scribbled a note on the cover: "Congratulations! I look forward to meeting you in public."

It was the mistake of his life.

Voorhis, who had won his own first campaign in 1936 by luring his better-known opponent into debate, had himself fallen into the trap. Nixon immediately publicized Voorhis' scrawled comment as a firm commitment to formal debate.

The Democrat attempted to ignore the strident demand, but the Independent Voters of South Pasadena, a non-partisan association, joined the Chotiner-inspired hue and cry. The demand spread that the Congressman meet Nixon face-to-face in an open discussion of the issues. The pressure grew, and Voorhis, unable to deny that he had "committed" himself in writing, finally agreed to confront his rival.

Little Tricia had brought about what even Chotiner had been unable to accomplish.

There was a high degree of apprehension within the Nixon camp as the day of the first of five agreed-upon debates approached. Voorhis' overwhelming reputation as a powerful speaker loomed large. He was a great debater, a man who could think on his feet, a politician who had humbled every one of his former opponents on the platform. But Nixon, with Chotiner's hearty approval, would not be moved. "If I don't carry the fight to Voorhis," he argued, "this campaign will never get off the ground. I *must* go on the attack."

Nixon had every reason to maintain his adamant stance and to take advantage of the opportunity. He needed this forum badly. He had to publicize his ideas. He was unafraid because he knew his own worth as a skilled debater, as a master of every twist and turn of verbal confrontation.

Voorhis relied on his ten-year image as a kindly "uncle" to his "nephews" and "nieces" in the district, confident that his "sincerity" would overcome any "logic" offered by his adversary.

But Nixon had done his homework—the old iron-butt philosophy was once again put to practical use. Voorhis, he learned, had been endorsed by the local chapter of the National Citizens' Political Action Committee (NC-PAC). Here at last was the issue he had so desperately sought. Communism!

Within a few days, a series of newspaper ads appeared in every paper of consequence in the Twelfth District. In large, conspicuous type the accusation was emblazoned. Here, for example, is the half-page display ad published on October 18, 1946 in the Covina *Argus-Citizen*:

DON'T BE FOOLED AGAIN!

Five times Jerry Voorhis has had the support of the radical groups because he was at one time a registered Socialist and always supports the radical viewpoint.

Voorhis has the endorsement of the National Political Action Committee because he voted their viewpoint 43 times out of 46 opportunities during the past four years.

On all issues involving Russia, the CIO Political Action Committee looks after the interests of Russia, against the interests of America; and whenever a bill is introduced in Congress that would interfere with the Russian, or Communist (subversive) program in this country, the CIO Political Action Committee gets busy and uses its millions to defeat the measure.

While he has been carrying the Democratic colors in recent years for his political purposes, REMEMBER, Voorhis is a former registered Socialist and his voting record in Congress is more Socialistic and Communistic than Democratic.

Aghast at the attack which impugned his very loyalty, Voorhis called a hurried meeting of his colleagues to determine whether he should issue a denial or continue to ignore the charges. Before they could decide, however, Nixon fired another salvo. This time it was a small announcement which contained the sting of a wasp:*

---

*Voorhis' failure to do his "homework" is well illustrated in his post-election charge that a heavy advertising campaign in Nixon's behalf had been financed by New York bankers. The statement was easily refuted. Voorhis had 296 inches of campaign advertising in the *Alhambra Post-Advocate,* the daily newspaper of the largest city in the 12th District, while Nixon had 162 inches.

A VOTE FOR NIXON
IS A VOTE AGAINST
THE COMMUNIST-DOMINATED PAC
WITH ITS GIGANTIC SLUSH-FUND.

Now, even Voorhis' own supporters were insisting that he make a public statement. His name had been closely linked with the PAC, and by strong inference he was being accused of conspiring with the enemies of America.

Voorhis had been caught in Chotiner's web, with no possibility of escape.

On the day following the Nixon blast, Voorhis heatedly denied any association with the CIO-PAC. Thus, the battle was finally joined, each of the two protagonists determined to flay the other on the public rostrum.

The Voorhis Nixon Debates

The series of debates, which drew audiences of five thousand and more, was a far cry from the handful Nixon had formerly been able to attract.

The first of the debates was held at a junior high school in South Pasadena, and Nixon immediately went on the offensive. Old friends noticed a cold grimness in his manner never before part of his debating style. He was the politicized, poker-playing tenderfoot, his eye on higher stakes than he had ever dreamed possible. He was playing for keeps.

There was no question in Nixon's mind that the first debate would decide the outcome of the remaining four, and that his very election or defeat might well depend on how he acquitted himself in this initial confrontation.

In the audience were the Nixon family, his friends, neighbors and former school chums. All looked on in utter amazement. Even his close supporters, members of the Committee of One Hundred, gasped in astonishment as the aspiring politician launched his attack. What had happened to the quiet, gentle Quaker youth? What had become of the introspective, shy young man who had never been known to offend anyone deliberately in his life?

The time had come to put the Chotiner technique to practical use. Nixon opened with his most powerful guns, three newly-learned objectives that spear-headed his strategy:

1. *Put Voorhis on the defensive at once*—allow him no opportunity to counter-attack with accusations of his own.
2. *Limit the issues*—permit him no chance to discuss anything that he, Nixon, did not *want* discussed.
3. *Deflate his opponent*—make him appear less than trustworthy, sincere or truthful.

In a slashing, hit-and-run assault Nixon accused Voorhis of being a puppet controlled by the two Political Action Committees: 1. the National Citizens' organization (NC-PAC), and 2. the labor union's affiliate, the CIO-PAC, which even Voorhis acknowledged was clearly dominated by Communists and their sympathizers.

Lamely, Voorhis attempted to explain that he had not been endorsed by the CIO-PAC, but only by the NC-PAC—the citizen's committee.

In the audience, Chotiner grinned. He had been expecting Voorhis to make a distinction between the two Political Action Committees, and he could feel how one of his most promising students would pounce upon such rhetoric.

Nixon, a sheaf of papers in hand, leaped upon Voorhis' statement, demanding that his opponent explain why, if the two committees were independent of each other, the letterheads of both contained the same names. When Voorhis insisted once again, that he was not a vassal of the CIO-PAC, Nixon whipped out another paper—a document showing that the *National* Citizens' PAC had been asked by its local chapter to endorse Voorhis. This, of course, was not the CIO group, and it is hard to imagine that Nixon did not know this. But Nixon was not one to forget a rule of the political arena: "Pile chaos on top of confusion, but keep your opponent off balance."

The victim tried to extricate himself, but to no avail. Voorhis made a feeble attempt to explain the difference between the two groups, but Nixon continued to hammer away at every faltering reply.

Voorhis' confusion grew as he flailed out like a man attempting to fend off a swarm of bees.

- No, he had not been endorsed by the CIO, nor did he want their endorsement.
- Yes, he had been endorsed by the local chapter of the National Citizens' PAC, but not the parent organization.
- Yes, he understood that the same names appeared on the stationery of both the NC-PAC and the CIO-PAC, but . . .
- No, he was not refusing the support of organized labor, he just didn't want the endorsement of . . .

Voorhis stopped short, knowing he was on the brink of losing the support of the powerful labor movement.

Completely shaken by the unexpected ferocity of the assault, bewildered by Nixon's buzz-saw technique which ripped into his political armor as no other opponent had ever done before, Voorhis was deflated and humiliated. Slowly, he saw himself being destroyed, as the debate continued to its inexorable end, without even being allowed the opening in which to mention his record as a congressman.

An article in the *Saturday Evening Post,* published soon after the November elections of 1946, described the manner in which Nixon took complete charge of his first encounter with Jerry Voorhis:

Nixon kicked off the debate by asking Voorhis if he was endorsed by the PAC. Voorhis denied this categorically. In long strides the challenger crossed the stage and thrust a paper bearing the list of candidates endorsed by the National Citizen's Political Action Committee under Voorhis' nose, commanding him to read it aloud. After an understandable pause, he replied that he didn't know Nixon meant *that* PAC list. Voorhis said he meant that the CIO-PAC had not endorsed him, but Nixon then pointed out—by reading off the names of the officers of the CIO-PAC and NC-PAC—that in many cases the leaders of the two organizations were the same. Not only was Voorhis doing some fancy hair-splitting, Nixon observed, but this was the first time Voorhis had mentioned in his denials the CIO-PAC, which indeed had not endorsed him, as opposed to the NC-PAC, which had.

Three days after that first debate, Voorhis requested that the National Citizens' Committee withdraw its endorsement, but it was too late.

Nixon continued his relentless cannonade and even used his opponent's tardy rejection of the NC-PAC against him. In a widely publicized speech, Nixon said, in part:

In the last four years, out of forty-six issues sponsored by the CIO and the PAC, my opponent has voted against the CIO and PAC only three times. Whether he wants it or not, my opponent has the PAC endorsement and he has certainly earned it. It is not how a man talks, but how he votes that counts.

Voorhis Falters and Falls

The remaining debates were anti-climactic. The fifth and last, held at the San Gabriel Mission on the outskirts of Los

Angeles, drew an overflow crowd. Amplifiers were installed to accommodate several hundred people who had arrived too late for admittance.

Finances were no longer a pressing problem for Nixon. Contributions, mostly under $100 were now flowing into his political war chest. Very few professionals were in evidence, but his headquarters and frequent rallies teemed with amateurs, their enthusiasm spreading to many others who were promptly converted. Naming Voorhis as "the PAC candidate," they distributed 25,000 plastic thimbles inscribed: *Elect Nixon and Needle the PAC*—a slogan that Chotiner might have rejected as puerile, but one which the amateurs loved. The surge of enthusiasm for Nixon, however, resulted in diminishing space given to Voorhis in the Twelfth District's thirty-two newspapers, while Nixon's speeches and activities were featured in nearly all of them.

In his last speech, a few days before the elections, Nixon did not even mention Voorhis' name. Instead, he bore down on the issue of communism, linking it with federal control and the loss of freedom:

> There are those walking in high official places in our country who would destroy our constitutional principles through socialization of American free institutions. These are the people who front for un-American elements, wittingly or otherwise, by advocating increasing Federal controls over the lives of the people.
>
> These are the people who would lead us into disastrous foreign policies whereby we would be guilty of collusion with other nations in depriving the people of smaller nations of the very freedoms guaranteed ourselves by our Constitution.
>
> Liberty is the very essence of our Constitution. Today the American people are faced with a choice between

two philosophies of government; one of these, supported by the radical PAC and its adherents, would deprive the people of liberty through regimentation; the other would return the government to the people under constitutional guarantee, and, needless to say, that is the philosophy for which I will fight with all my power in Congress. . . .

This is not a campaign between two men, but is one between two divergent fundamental political beliefs. If the people want bureaucratic control and domination, with every phase of human activity regulated from Washington, then they should not vote for me, but for my opponent. If on the other hand, the people want a change so that a man can call his life his own once more, then my election to Congress will help to bring it about.

The issues in this campaign are whether we will have a national administration that will promote a system of free enterprise and whether we will have a Congressman who will represent the views and principles of the people of this district.

Nixon Tastes His First Victory

When the votes were counted on November 5th, Richard Nixon's victory was overwhelming—65,586 to 49,994. In Whittier, he defeated Voorhis 5,727 to 2,678.

Nixon's victorious campaign, while widely praised by his supporters as a feat of genius, has been condemned vigorously by many people. This was not high-level statesmanship, they claimed—it was hitting below the belt. And the Senate race against Helen Gahagan Douglas was to these same detractors but an encore performance.

But, it is well to place the campaign in the context of the

Nixon with his mother celebrating his victory in the November, 1946 Congressional election in California's 12th District.

times. The problems of federal controls, Communist domination of our labor unions, and the whole issue of communism itself were concerns felt by the people in every community in the nation. Republicans and some conservative Democrats recognized this concern and seized upon it as a legitimate vehicle for victory in their political campaigns. Nixon himself recalls the contest simply as one between a conservative Republican and a New Dealer. "Voorhis lost because ours was not a New Deal district," Nixon reflected twelve years later. "Our campaign was a very honest debate on the issues."

Voorhis, although destroyed politically by his opponent's *blitzkrieg,* took his defeat gracefully. He wrote Nixon a long and generous letter in which he offered to give the beginning Congressman "any help that you believe I can render." Said Voorhis:

> I remember most poignantly the time when I first came to Washington as a new Congressman. Little did I realize then all the job entailed, the long hours of very hard and frequently thankless work, the many periods of frustration when one was unable to get the thing done which he believed most necessary for the country, as well as those times of encouragement when something worthwhile seemed to have been accomplished.
>
> During the ten years of my service I came to have a profound respect for the Congress of the United States and to realize the critical importance of its work, not only for the future of our country, but for the future of the whole world. . . .
>
> I sincerely wish you well as you undertake the tremendous responsibilities which will soon be yours. . . . I want you to know that I will be glad to be of any help that you believe I can render.

There was one more paragraph, seldom quoted by Nixon's friends, but one which gives a measure of satisfaction to his enemies. Voorhis, it seems, finally got the last word:

> I have refrained, for reasons which you will understand, from making any references in this letter to the circumstances of the campaign recently conducted in our district. It would only have spoiled the letter.

Apparently, the circumstances that would have "spoiled the letter" were not as terrible or as enduring as Voorhis had thought. In his book, *Confessions of a Congressman*, published in 1947, Voorhis reported:

> A couple of weeks passed and I began to wonder whether Mr. Nixon had received my letter. Then one day when I came back from lunch he was standing there in the outer office. He smiled and so did I. We shook hands and went into the inner office, which by that time was pretty bleak and bare. We talked for more than an hour and parted, I hope and believe, as personal friends. Mr. Nixon will be a Republican Congressman. He will, I imagine, be a conservative one. But I believe he will be a conscientious one. And I know I appreciated his coming to see me very sincerely indeed.

How conscientious he would be as a freshman Congressman no one could foresee. Within the next two years he was to become a national figure, hated by President Harry Truman, the liberal press, the academic community, and the nemesis of one Alger Hiss in a case of intrigue with few equals for drama and suspense.

5
Nixon in Congress

NO FANFARE, NO CHEERING throngs greeted Congressman-Elect Richard M. Nixon when, on December 14, 1946, he arrived in Washington with his wife, his eleven-month-old daughter, and three old, battered suitcases. His total resources consisted of $10,000 in government bonds, a $14,000 life insurance policy, a used Ford car, and $3,000 in savings which was to be used for living expenses until his first salary check as a Congressman would arrive in the latter part of January. Whatever wardrobe the family possessed was mostly Pat's and baby Tricia's; Nixon owned but two suits, and he always wore one of them.

Washington's eternal housing shortage was no less acute than it is now, and the Nixons were compelled to live in a modest hotel room. They had no kitchen, so they ate all their meals in restaurants. After two months they made a $700. down payment on a small house in the Spring Valley section of Washington which touched the outer reaches of the city's Northwest area.

The Lull After the Storm

Unlike Pat, Richard could not adjust immediately to his new environment. The relative tranquility which he was now enjoying, after the excitement of an intensive and heated campaign, brought on an uneasy restlessness. In analyzing himself, he was unable to pinpoint the precise reason for his feeling so adrift even though his two feet were planted solidly in the churning political vortex of the exciting capital city of the nation.

This feeling of isolation did not disappear even after he was sworn in as a member of the Eightieth Congress on January 3, 1947. Neither he nor Pat cared for the cocktail party circuit that often bedazzles newly-elected Congressmen; and they studiously avoided the back-slapping older Representatives who sought to ingratiate themselves with the newcomers. These friendly overtures Nixon could not accept for he knew they were not purely motivated and that they were offered only to win support for legislation in which the older members had an interest. Not feeling at home with this kind of pretending, and finding himself a "nobody" in Washington after just having been the center of attraction in a widely publicized California campaign, Nixon suffered a clammy coldness on the outside and an aching void on the inside. It was difficult, and completely out-of-character for him to exist as a non-entity among his peers. "I had the same lost feeling in those early days that I had when I first went into the military service," he reflected.

Nixon's ego, already deflated, was not helped any when soon after his arrival in Washington, the *Washington Post* dubbed him "the greenest Congressman in town"—a description that was not too far from the truth. He was indeed provincial. His clothing, which had looked so neat and trim in Whittier, lacked the stylish cut to which Washington sophisticates were accustomed. He was unable to discuss the latest Broadway plays with the kind of *savoir-faire* to satisfy

Richard, Pat and ten-month-old Tricia bicycling around the Tidal Basin (Jefferson Memorial in the

the cosmopolitan playboy-types and their wives—with which every session of Congress is afflicted.

But although Richard Nixon may have been somewhat provincial in dress and outlook, he was certainly no rustic. Not taken into account was his education and his high degree of scholarship, his depth of understanding and ambition, and his remarkable aptitude for grasping complex problems. And one additional quality was overlooked: despite his youth, he had earned a reputation as a pragmatic, hardnosed lawyer—one who had defeated a man in the last Congressional election who had been considered unbeatable by every political pundit.

His "lost feeling" was not especially helped when he was assigned an office on freshman row—often called "the attic"—on the fifth floor of the House Office Building where first-termers were placed. The area was as far removed from the center of legislative activity as possible, and succeeded in leaving Congressman Nixon as well as most freshman Congressmen fully frustrated.

The Struggle for Recognition

But Nixon, with his rare instinct for top-level involvement, had no intention of remaining buried in an "attic" in the hinterland of power. Together with California's Republican Congressman Donald Jackson, another freshman whose office was next-door to his, he organized the Chowder and Marching Club—a group comprising fifteen Republican Representatives, all newly-elected and exiled to the fifth-floor Siberia of the House. The club members never got around to sampling chowder, and probably disdained the very thought of marching, but they did accomplish their purpose: to overcome their individual ineffectiveness as rookie Congressmen by acting in concert.

Meeting every Wednesday, the members would plan their activities for the coming week, make exhaustive studies of bills, hearings, reports and amendments, and then descend on other Congressmen with detailed facts and figures to persuade them to vote in accordance with the club's collective judgment. The strategy proved eminently successful. Before long, Nixon was acknowledged as the leader of the group.*

Greenest Congressman indeed! Within eight weeks Nixon, with the strength of his club behind him, had "marched and chowdered" his way into the inner sanctums of the most powerful leaders in the Republican-controlled House. The fifteen members of the ambitious new group had begun to exchange whatever information they were able to glean from the various committees, and with their knowledge multiplied through their very act of sharing, the freshmen were soon among the best-informed newcomers in Congress.

Shrewdly, Nixon kept the group's membership small, realizing that any unusual or untoward growth might tend to arouse the suspicion and hostility of the older Congressmen. As it turned out, this was the right decision. The small but effective bloc won the attention it sought.

With the growing recognition of his leadership in the Club's House-wide activities, Nixon's feeling of being adrift, of floating aimlessly in a strange sea, quickly disappeared as did the depressing thought that he was just another unknown face

---

*The fifteen members (other than Nixon) of the Chowder and Marching Club were: Kenneth B. Keating of New York and Norris Cotton of New Hampshire, both of whom went on to the Senate; Thruston B. Morton of Kentucky, who also was elected to the Senate and eventually became Chairman of the Republican National Committee; John J. Allen of California, later Under-Secretary of Commerce; John Byrnes of Wisconsin, now senior Republican on the House Ways and Means Committee; Donald Jackson of California; Gerald Ford of Michigan, now Minority Leader of the House; Glenn Davis of Wisconsin; Walter Norblad of Oregon; John Lodge of Connecticut, who was appointed Ambassador to Spain; Charles Potter of Michigan, who went into business after his defeat for re-election to the Senate; Claude Bakewell of Missouri, later postmaster of St. Louis; Charles Nelson of Maine, who became a professor in the political science department of the University of Miami; Harold Lovre of South Dakota, who practiced law in Washington, D. C. after leaving Congress; and J. Caleb Boggs, who went on to become Governor of Delaware.

Congressman Nixon on the Speaker's rostrum in the House of Representatives as he presides over a discussion of the War Department appropriations bill. He had been in office only seven months when this photo was taken on July 14, 1947.

among his peers. He had delivered no stentorian speeches on the floor to command the interest of the press; he had made no effort to ingratiate himself with his senior colleagues by fawning; nor did he engage in any of the undignified acts of subservience through which all too many freshmen legislators hope to win favor with their entrenched seniors. But he did deliver the one vital commodity that every Representative and Senator understands and respects: votes!

Richard Nixon, not yet three months in office, had established a power base within the hallowed halls of Congress.

First Committee Assignment

House Minority Leader Joseph W. Martin gave the ambitious young legislator his first important chance in the House. Reading a newspaper one morning while at breakfast with Pat, Nixon learned that Representative Martin had appointed him to membership on the Select Committee to study the tentative Marshall Plan which had recently been proposed to help Europe get back on its feet. He was to prepare and issue a full report to the House. The eighteen-member committee consisted of ten Republicans and eight Democrats, with Congressman Christian A. Herter, later Governor of Massachusetts, as Committee Chairman.

Political analyst Arthur Krock, at that time among the foremost of Washington's correspondents, characterized the Committee in these words:

> The personnel and program of the committee just appointed to make a first-hand survey of the situation in Europe are of primary consequence in molding the shape of the future. The appointees were chosen with care by Speaker Joseph W. Martin, Jr.
>
> . . . Chairman Christian Herter did not know what the personnel would be until Martin informed him.

Herter was pleased. Their colleagues come from the ranks of the hard and serious workers of the House. ... On the whole it is a serious, able group—apparently without a playboy member—that will make a report which is certain to have momentous effects.

Nixon, the only freshman Representative in the group, visited Europe with his fellow members to study economic conditions on the continent. It was an intensive fact-finding tour which brought him to a fuller realization of America's responsibilities towards the rest of the world. He returned firmly convinced of the need for foreign aid, judiciously administered. On the floor of the House, he became an ardent advocate of the Herter program whose report, running to thousands of pages, served as the guide for the Marshall Plan later enacted by Congress, and to which Nixon made an important contribution.

Thereafter, completely convinced that the Marshall Plan would serve as a buttress against further Soviet conquest in Europe, he also supported the North Atlantic Treaty Alliance (NATO), military aid to this country's allies, relief assistance to the people of war-ravaged nations, and (to the consternation of his protectionist-minded colleagues and constituents) the Reciprocal Trade Agreements Act. To many of his more conservative fellow-Congressmen, who were concerned with balancing a budget that was already out of kilter because of World War II, Nixon was considered as something of a maverick Republican. But, their opinion changed when the deluge of foreign orders, admittedly paid for with American dollars, began to flow into the coffers of our industries as a result of the European reconstruction effort.

Polls taken at the time showed that the majority of his own constituency in California's Twelfth District was opposed to the Marshall Plan and the other foreign aid programs which Nixon supported so strongly, but he would not be swayed. Returning to Southern California on a number of occasions,

The Herter Committee arrives in Athens, Greece, during the autumn of 1947, (left to right) Congressmen Carrol U. Mahon (P. Toy.) Bichard M. Nixon (R-Calif.) and Thomas A. Jenkins (R-Ohio). They

he spoke to the people directly and explained his position. Finally, he was able to win the grudging assent of the majority of his largely conservative district.

Legislating Labor Laws

Although Nixon has publicly stated that his work on the Herter Committee was the most important of his tenure in the House of Representatives, his favorite assignment was connected with his membership on the Labor Committee. This committee took part in drafting the Taft-Hartley Law. Nixon assumed a leading role in this effort and in the subsequent battle for its enactment.

The urgent need for revision of the nation's labor laws, as embodied in the old Wagner Act and the Norris-LaGuardia Act, had long been recognized. Both had been passed at a time when flagrant exploitation of labor was widespread. Union members were subjected to vicious beatings by company-owned goon squads, and many labor leaders were murdered. Sweat-shops flourished everywhere; wages and hours were whatever management dictated; child labor was a national disgrace. The Wagner and Norris-LaGuardia Acts changed all this by establishing a legal basis for collective bargaining, the right to strike, and other provisions that would enable the weak, ineffective, and hitherto defenseless unions to challenge their oppressors in open court.

But no one, least of all the workers themselves, envisioned the immense power that would be concentrated in a relatively small clique of union chiefs and their muscle-men who, like George Orwell's pigs, with the help of their watchdog enforcers, eventually took over the farm and walked in their former master's shoes. Nor could the workers foresee the great wealth that their organizations would amass—wealth that could be expended only by their leaders, and without consulting the membership.

"Sweetheart" contracts between big business and big labor,

in which union members were manipulated like pawns, added to the bulging treasuries of organized labor. As a result of their economic strength, and the docility of union members who voted as they were ordered (upon threat of physical assault as well as loss of employment), there grew the inevitable evils which are the by-products of immense, raw power. Union influence was in evidence in the halls of Congress and in the White House itself—and not always to the advantage of the working man.

With the power of union leaders often directed along political paths suited to satisfy their own special interests, management now found itself in the novel position of defending the right of its employees to work without intimidation by the labor bosses. But management was unable to protest. While any accusation by businessmen against unions was deemed an "unfair labor practice," organized labor could and did hurl whatever charges happened to suit their purposes. Communists, and their sympathizers in the policy-making echelons of their national unions, made every effort to retard production at the time when the United States was at war with Nazi Germany and the Soviet Union was unofficially allied with the enemy in a "non-aggression pact." Slowdowns and strikes at such defense plants as Allis Chalmers and Vultee were common. But within twenty-four hours after Germany attacked Russia, these same Red labor bosses who had been proclaiming "the Yanks aren't coming" ordered all members back to work, demanded extra production shifts around the clock, and began screaming for our immediate intervention on a "second front" in Europe.

Such was the climate when Richard Nixon rose to do battle with the Red Mafia. It required courage—a quality he had never lacked—to work with Representative Fred Hartley in drafting corrective legislation. Nixon was well aware of the power exerted by the national unions and knew that they would strive to put an end to his political career. As events were to prove, his precognition was well grounded, even though it was common knowledge that he had modified some of Hartley's more extreme views. Nor was he attacked by labor alone. The Truman Administration charged that the proposed bill would be a "slave labor" law.

"Not so," argued Nixon. "The issue is that this Congress must recognize that this is the time to enact a labor bill which is not class legislation, but which is in the best interests of all the people of America."

On April 16, 1947 he addressed the House of Representatives in a speech that aroused the anger of President Truman:

> The suggestion has been made that this bill was introduced because a few greedy monopolists ordered one which would allow them to wring the last dollar out of the laboring men of this country. But what are the facts? When this Congress convened in January of this year, it looked back on a record of labor-management strife. . . . We know that in the year after V-J Day we had lost six billion dollars in the standard of living in America due to industrial strife. We had seen how a few persons . . . could paralyze the entire country by ordering a strike—by the stroke of a pen. . . .
>
> President Truman recommended that machinery should be set up providing for peaceful settlement of jurisdictional disputes, secondary boycotts arising out of jurisdictional disputes, and disputes over the interpretation of contracts. . . . I wish to point out that if this Congress were to limit its action to carrying out the President's recommendations, we would be acting only on disputes which caused less than five percent of the days lost in strikes in the United States in the past two years. . . .

Are the workers of this country, the members of its unions, objecting to this bill? Or are the objections coming only from a few entrenched leaders of union labor? Do . . . [the workers] object to the fact that [this bill] gives them the right to vote freely in democratic elections for their officers and to organize and bargain collectively? Do they object to the fact that it protects their right to strike over fundamental issues involving wages, hours and working conditions? Do they object to the fact that this bill provides that where two union leaders are fighting between themselves . . . such a dispute shall not be a basis for a strike depriving innocent workers of their jobs . . .?

The workers of America have a great stake in the passage of this bill. It has been said that management suffers from strikes, but we must remember that the man who suffers most, the man who has the greatest stake in industrial peace, is not management, but is the man who goes out on strike. . . . [That man] should make the determination as to whether he should go out. So we have provided that the decision to strike will be made . . . by secret ballot of a majority of all employees in the plant affected.

One month later, in May of 1947, Nixon met an opponent of the Taft-Hartley Act, a Democrat with whom he became friendly despite their political differences. Taking opposing sides of the question, they debated the issue in McKeesport, Pennsylvania, neither knowing, of course, that they would one day engage in a series of debates that would enthrall an entire nation. Nixon's youthful opponent was the freshman Representative from Massachusetts: John Fitzgerald Kennedy.

The Taft-Hartley Act was passed into law by a vote of 308 to 107, the intensive lobbying and public propagandizing by the labor bosses notwithstanding.

"It's not a perfect act, and I have always said I would vote to amend it," said Nixon several months later. "But it hasn't been repealed because the average union leader knows it hasn't hurt his union. And he knows, too, that labor has made great gains in wages and hours under it."

Nixon Loses Labor's Vote

To this day, many leaders of organized labor have been political enemies of Nixon because he dared to assert that neither labor nor management were sacred cows, and that neither was beyond criticism or the reach of the law. "Labor is a legitimate force, serving a legitimate function in the nation's economy," he replied in answer to their accusation that he was a "labor baiter." He reminded them: "In every situation, its demands and its grievances must be judged strictly on the merits of the case. No Congressman can do his job properly if he is dogmatically for or against labor. The same applies to business—big or little. I know this is an unpopular position on labor-management relations, because you catch it from both sides. But it is the only one I can take."

One statement above all others enraged the union leadership. Said Nixon: "When you talk about labor, what do you mean? There is often a big difference between the interests of the labor leader and the man who pays the dues." The overlords of labor, especially those with high incomes, were terribly upset by this, for they could never agree that their interests did not coincide with those of the dues-paying member.

Nixon was quite right when he characterized his stand as an unpopular one. Despite the fact that the Taft-Hartley Act has benefited the working man, Richard Nixon has paid a heavy price for his forthright stand against corrupt labor practices. And to this day he is still paying for it in the loss of union support! Times have not changed the attitudes of the union chief. His support and financial contributions are directed to Nixon's political opponents even though the sympathies of the rank and file of organized labor may be with their benefactor.

The House Un-American Activities Committee

Nixon's accomplishments as the spark-plug of the Chowder and Marching Club had demonstrated that he was a natural leader among his colleagues. His Club activities were, of course, seen for what they were by his politically-sagacious seniors in the House—shrewd moves to gain status among the older and more influential Representatives who were in positions of power and who controlled the choice committee assignments. These were the men who wielded the power and were in a position to effect passage of bills favorable to local constituencies. Few politicians can hope to win re-election if they are unable to produce results beneficial to their own areas.

It was a by-product of all these maneuverings which resulted in Nixon's appointment to the House Un-American Activities Committee (HUAC). Strangely, this assignment which he did not request was the one that catapulted him into national fame.

His decision to accept membership did not come easily. HUAC was regarded with contempt by much of the nation's press, and with some justification. The Committee's most vociferous proponent was Congressman John Rankin of Mississippi, a racist next to whom television's Archie Bunker would come off as the most liberal of liberals. Martin Dies, an earlier HUAC chairman, frequently allowed his zeal to smother his belief in constitutional processes. He was widely regarded as a man who trampled on the rights of the innocent through his witch-hunting expeditions. Moreover, a recent Committee chairman was J. Parnel Thomas of New Jersey

—a man indicted for fraud, then convicted and imprisoned.

Because of the Committee's unsavory reputation, Nixon wrestled with his conscience before accepting the appointment. His friend and fellow Chowder and Marching associate, Representative Donald Jackson, recalled the day Nixon entered his office and nervously paced the floor from one wall to the other. He was concerned with the possible stigma that an association with the tainted Committee would place upon him, but also wondered about his moral obligation to correct the injustices he had heard so much about.

As a practical politician, he also realized that membership on the HUAC could serve as a springboard to front-page headlines, but that, for him, was notoriety, not publicity. In any event, he was not convinced that the Committee was as maladroitly conducted as the liberal press had indicated. "Politically, it could've been the kiss of death," said Nixon to Congressman Jackson, "but I figured it was an opportunity as well as a risk; so I took it."

During World War II, pro-Soviet public opinion was prevalent throughout the United States—a condition that lingered even after the war. Russia was called our "bleeding, heroic ally," and Stalin was referred to as "good old Uncle Joe" by none other than President Truman himself. Anti-Communists were castigated as "fascist Red-baiters."

When Nixon accepted membership on the House Un-American Activities Committee in 1947, a change in sympathies had overtaken the American people. The Soviet Union's bludgeoning of freedom in Eastern Europe, and the exposure of proven Soviet spy rings operating jointly in Canada and the United States, caused a reversal in the thinking of many Americans. Anti-communism, no longer the epithet it had been, became equated in some quarters with loyalty. The fact that Russia succeeded in infiltrating the highest echelons of government, industry, and labor was sufficient cause for the anti-communist attitude to spread.

The attention of America was drawn more and more to the pronouncements of the founders of communism who were dedicated to our destruction "by legal or illegal means," as Lenin had stated. An intensely anti-communist atmosphere began to prevail. And those Communists who chose to ally themselves with the Soviet Union—some for money; others because of their belief in Russian-style communism; and the remainder out of fear for their lives or those of their loved ones—were looked upon as traitors.

Perhaps it was over-zealousness to protect America that propelled HUAC to indulge in some of the excesses for which it gained notoriety. History has borne testimony to the fact that many innocent people were victims of the madness that ensued. But Nixon, who soon became a key member, insisted on proper legal procedures. He refused hearsay testimony, protected the civil rights of witnesses at every turn (often in the face of their scathing insults and arrogant abuse), and together with his fellow committeeman, Representative Karl E. Mundt, changed the direction from Rankin's injudicious outbursts to the calm and orderly procedures of the courtroom.

Fighting International Communism

Nixon had his initial experience with a Communist soon after HUAC began its 1947 session. The first witness to appear before the Committee was Gerhard Eisler, a notorious international Communist who was then in the custody of the United States Immigration Service, being charged with passport fraud.* Eisler was a high-ranking Soviet agent who later jumped bail, escaped on a Polish steamer, and shortly there-

---

*Eisler's visa originally granted him the status of an "alien in transit." In 1943, during the Allied-Soviet wartime alliance, his status was changed to that of "alien for pleasure," which permitted him to travel anywhere in the United States without restriction. Eisler's espionage activities were conducted before, during, and after the war, as a paid spy for the Soviet Union.

after emerged in East Germany where he became a high-ranking Communist *gauleiter*.

Subpoenaed to appear at the HUAC hearing, Eisler made it known at the outset that he had no intention of revealing anything about himself or his Red network affiliations. The Fifth Amendment ploy, to avoid self-incrimination, had not yet come into vogue, but Eisler used the next-best method of evading the truth. Secure in the knowledge that he would soon be safely behind his own side of the Iron Curtain, he deliberately courted a contempt of Congress citation rather than answer the questions put to him by the Committee's chairman or by Robert Stripling, HUAC's chief investigator:

> *Stripling:* Mr. Gerhard Eisler, please take the stand.
> *Eisler:* I will not.
> *The Chairman:* Mr. Eisler, will you raise your right hand?
> *Eisler:* No! Before I take the oath . . .
> *Stripling:* Mr. Chairman . . .
> *Eisler:* Shut up! I have the floor now . . .
> *The Chairman:* Just a minute! Will you please be sworn in?
> *Eisler:* No, not before you hear a few remarks.
> *The Chairman:* There will be no remarks until . . .
> *Eisler:* Then save your breath. There will be no hearing from me.

Nixon, his face dark with suppressed anger, took the floor of the House on February 18, 1947, and, in this, his maiden speech, made a formal request for a contempt of Congress citation against Eisler. The only opposing vote, as might have been expected, was cast by Vito Marcantonio, the blatantly pro-Communist Representative from New York. Also speaking against the contempt citation was Harlem's Congressman

Adam Clayton Powell who then abstained from voting.

Newsweek magazine gave Nixon his first national publicity. It described his maiden speech as "deeply impressive." And it was! Not once, as he unfolded Eisler's background of subversion in Germany and China, did Nixon ever allow his voice to rise. He detailed the murders that this arrogant Communist had ordered in Asia and Europe; the sabotage that he had engineered in various countries of the West; his espionage in the United States. "And this is the man who has the impertinence to question the constitutionality of the Committee's right to question him," Nixon snapped.

Quoting undeniable statistics, naming fact after damning fact, Nixon attracted the rapt attention and approval of Congress and the public as well. Concluded *Newsweek*: "He spoke in calm and measured tones, and with intense sincerity; but there was a quality of steel behind the voice."

A parade of witnesses gave further evidence of the widespread espionage then being conducted by the Communist Party, with much of the testimony freely given by former Communists. Among the principal witnesses was Gerhard Eisler's own sister, Ruth Fischer, once a key member of the Austrian Communist Party. Her exhaustive and scholarly book, *Stalin and German Communism,* was later published by Harvard University. In her testimony, she disclosed the Party's method of perpetrating its criminal acts which ranged from espionage and sabotage to murder. Her allegations were supported by numerous other witnesses including Victor Kravchenko, author of *I Chose Freedom.*

Kravchenko had been part of the Soviet Purchasing Commission in New York during World War II. He produced a mass of evidence to prove that the "purchasing agency" was little more than a nest of Soviet espionage agents whose tentacles reached into the inner-most core of our society. And the crucial problem of those days was that there was no law on the books to deal with this specific problem.

The required action was finally taken when HUAC, late in

1947, appointed its junior member, Richard Nixon, to head a special sub-committee to propose suitable legislation. As chairman, he was immediately deluged with suggestions from the far left and right. Some called for the abolition of "communistic-sounding" speech—whatever that meant. Others demanded complete amnesty for anyone caught in an act of subversion. With the help of Representative Karl E. Mundt, another moderate member of the sub-committee, a preliminary report was delivered to the House in February, 1948. The report, written by Nixon himself, ended with the following paragraph:

> The sub-committee has not attempted to recommend legislation which will deal with so-called theoretical Communists in the United States. We are seeking rather to strike a body blow at the American cadre of the Soviet-directed communist conspiracy. We believe that if its criminal activities are prosecuted, its false fronts exposed, and its foreign assistance and direction cut away, the movement in the United States, standing alone for what it is, will be overwhelmingly defeated.
>
> We are willing to permit the theories of communism and democracy to clash in the open marketsplace of political ideas in America, but we insist that communism not be allowed to have the unfair advantages in this conflict of the unrestricted use of illegal means, the cloak of secrecy and fraud, and the assistance and direction of a foreign communist dictatorship.

The Mundt-Nixon Bill

The Mundt-Nixon Communist-Control Bill which followed —the first legislation to be proposed in the ten years of HUAC's existence—was floor-managed by Nixon on May

18, 1948, and passed in the House of Representatives by a landslide vote of 319 to 56.*

The principal provisions of the bill called for:

1. Registration with the Department of Justice of all Communist Party officials and members;
2. Identification of the source of all printed and broadcast material issued by organizations which are designated as Communist-front groups by the Attorney General;
3. The disclosure of the names of all officers in such front groups—but with the right of these individuals to appeal the Attorney General's classification in the Federal courts;
4. Denial of Federal employment to Communist Party officials;
5. Discontinuing tax-exemptions for Communist-front organizations;
6. Keeping accurate records of all funds received and disbursed by the Communist Party and its front groups, and the disclosure of all sources of such moneys;
7. Deportation of aliens convicted of Communist activity and the denial of passport privileges for American-born officials or members of the Communist Party.

A series of penalties was imposed for violation of the above,

---

*The Mundt-Nixon Communist-Control Bill embodied a composite of conservative and liberal suggestions. Contributors were: John Foster Dulles, later Secretary of State under President Eisenhower; A. A. Berle, who became Chairman of New York's Liberal Party; Louis Waldman, Socialist Party chief; Felix Cohen, former Ambassador to the Soviet Union; Admiral William H. Strandley; Professor William Yandell Elliott of Harvard University; and other Republicans and Democrats.

ranging from heavy fines and imprisonment to loss of citizenship.

Upon passage of the bill in the House, a furious outcry arose from Communist-front organizations, as well as from a number of well-intentioned liberal groups, who were the so-called "intellectual" community. The perennial radical educators and sympathetic labor leaders were all joined by a large segment of the press in their hysterical denunciations. A fearful Senate, its eye on the next elections, pigeon-holed the bill. It was not revived until the next session, by which time the mood of the public, the press and the Senate had changed.

During the passing months, the magnitude of Communist infiltration was revealed in the Hiss case, in the sex-spy affair involving a Justice Department employee named Judith Coplon, and in a series of other disclosures that shocked and alarmed a hitherto lethargic America.

This time, however, Nixon was not as successful in his efforts to hold to a moderate course. Leading the fight for a much stronger bill was the powerful Senator, Pat McCarran, for whom the resultant bill was named when it was finally enacted into law. By that time, Nixon had lost identity with what was once the Mundt-Nixon Bill, especially after Senator Hubert H. Humphrey added an amendment to the McCarran Act that called for the establishment of concentration camps in the United States. Nixon and Mundt were appalled. Five such camps were set up to confine "suspected" Communists in times of "national emergencies," in much the same manner as thousands of Japanese-American citizens were herded into the infamous camps after Pearl Harbor.*

For Congressman Nixon, his first term can hardly be

---

*The amendment did not define the legal meaning of "emergency," nor did it give a legal definition as to what constituted a "suspected" Communist. Nixon, a lifelong "constitutional constructionist," would have none of the Humphrey amendment. The concentration camps were finally, and properly, closed down.

termed an adventure in serendipity. He knew exactly what he was doing and what he was about to do. He made few moves that resulted in accidental windfalls. When he organized the Chowder and Marching Club, he was well aware of the potential clout he would carry as the leader of that small power nexus. He knew, as a novitiate among the high priests of the House, he could not expect to become a member of the respected Herter Committee. He could not have become known as a popular exponent of the Marshall Plan had he not made it known among Congressional leaders that he was a new face who would have to be recognized; that he not only controlled a bloc of votes, but was, in additon, a gifted speaker with an exceptionally astute mind.

It is true that Nixon did not ask for memberhip on the House Un-American Activities Committee, but the impending assignment could not have been made without his prior knowledge. Surely, he knew that he was being considered. The HUAC at that time offered a great opportunity for national publicity unequalled by any other committee in either the House or Senate. Dozens of Republicans with substantial contacts among the more influential members of Congress were vying for a place on this committee. In the face of such strong competition, it would have been next to impossible for an almost unknown freshman to win this coveted plum by sheer happenstance. It had to be the by-product of careful design.

Clearly, Nixon's movement up the ladder of political power was the consequence of forethought and design and planning. Within weeks after his arrival in Washington, he initiated the first steps toward his own advancement. He did it by establishing a power base, referred to as the Chowder and Marching Club. Then he took advantage of each opportunity by applying his well-tested "iron-butt" philosophy of doing his homework, which many other Representatives often neglected.

But even Richard Nixon, with all due regard to his careful and perceptive planning, could not have foreseen that a seemingly insignificant event, that took place on a hot summer's day in 1948, was to be the first of a series that would propel him into the limelight. He could never have imagined that because of this event, within five short months, his name would become a household word, and his actions the topic of conversation everywhere. That fateful day was August 3rd! On that day a deceptively unprepossessing little man, a former member of the Communist Party, appeared before the House Un-American Activities Committee to offer testimony against his erstwhile fellow conspirators.

The name of that man was Whittaker Chambers. Among those whom he accused of passing national secrets to the Soviet Union was the brilliant and highly respected Alger Hiss.

6
The Hiss Case

The Hiss case was the first major crisis of my political life. My name, my reputation and my career were ever to be linked with the decisions I made and the actions I took in that case, as a thirty-five-year-old freshman Congressman in 1948. . . . Had it not been for the Hiss case, I might never have been Vice President of the United States and, thus, a candidate for President.

Richard Nixon
Six Crises, 1962

Who Was Alger Hiss?

THE 1940's PRODUCED a legion of clever men whose talents were recognized in the highest circles within the Democratic and Republican parties. Of these, a few were exceptionally shrewd and resourceful and possessed the superior intellect which we identify with the natural leader who is destined to rise head and shoulders above the others.

Such a man was Alger Hiss.

Just turned forty-three, and looking no more than thirty-five at the outside, Hiss was urbane, witty and articulate; the product of a fine family; an intellectual who was well known in the upper strata of government and international councils, but almost completely unknown to the general public.

A graduate of Johns Hopkins University and the prestigious Harvard Law School, he served for a year as Secretary-Clerk to Supreme Court Justice Oliver Wendell Holmes, a signal honor for any Harvard graduate. He practiced law for three years and, then, in 1933, when twenty-eight years old, became (with Lee Pressman) Assistant General Counsel to the Agricultural Adjustment Administration. A year later, his exceptional ability led him to the position of Counsel to the Senate committee investigating the munitions industry—the Nye Committee. His next appointment was that of assistant to Solicitor General Stanley F. Reed who was later appointed to the Supreme Court.

In September of 1936, Assistant Secretary of State Francis B. Sayre appointed Hiss to the position of Assistant Legal Adviser, and from there he progressed to become Director of the Office of Special Political Affairs. In that capacity, he served as Executive-Secretary to the International Monetary Conference at Dumbarton Oaks and was also given the responsibility of preparing for United States participation in the Yalta Conference, which made him a political adviser to President Roosevelt in his dealings with Churchill and Stalin. Additionally, he was among the key American officials at the international meeting in San Francisco.

Hiss resigned his government post when he was offered the presidency of the Carnegie Endowment, one of the most respected private organizations in the realm of foreign affairs. The chairman of the board was John Foster Dulles who also served at that time as chief foreign policy adviser to the Republican nominee for President, New York Governor Thomas E. Dewey. The man who recommended Alger Hiss to head the Carnegie Endowment was Adlai Stevenson.

This was the man who would soon engage Richard Nixon, the neophyte Congressman, in a battle of wits that was as devastating as it was dramatic. And these were the powerful friends and associates whom Hiss could, and did, call upon in days to come.

The Hush-Hush Policy

The Hiss case need not have happened. Hundreds of United States counter-intelligence agents were aware of the Soviet Union's epionage and sabotage activities; the names of Russian agents and many of their highly-placed contacts in government and industry were known and had been reported to the proper authorities. President Roosevelt, however, feared that widespread arrests, even if executed secretly, might hurt relations between this country and Russia during the war years. Despite the fact that American intelligence had ample evidence that the Soviet Union was secretly conspiring to dominate the world in much the same way as Hitler had done, Roosevelt hesitated to make a move that would create friction between the two allies.

Vice President Truman, realizing that such disclosures would be harmful to the Democratic Party, exercised Executive privilege and used whatever means were at the disposal of the White House to block Congressional hearings and, as we shall see, thereby shielded many men who were security risks. Indeed, even though some of these people were known to be Communist Party members, they were regularly promoted to offices of influence and prominence, and found themselves in such positions that they were able to shape the course of government policy in its domestic and international affairs. Among those whose names had been given directly to the President as suspected espionage agents was Alger Hiss.

It is generally assumed that Richard Nixon never heard of Hiss until he appeared before the House Un-American Activities Committee. The young Congressman, however, did learn of Hiss in February, 1947, soon after he arrived in Washington. Nixon at this time was busily engaged in organizing the Chowder and Marching Club, and in establishing his power base in the House. A colleague, Representative Charles J. Kersten, suggested that he meet with the Reverend John F. Cronin if he was interested in learning the extent of Communist subversion in this country. The meeting took place a few days later.

A Catholic priest, Father Cronin had recently arrived in Washington from Baltimore where he was a professor of philosophy and economics at St. Mary's Seminary and assistant director of the Department of Social Action of the National Catholic Welfare Conference. He had come to Washington to assist in organizing labor unions in the various war plants scattered across the nation. Before long, Father Cronin was made aware of the magnitude of Communist penetration into our most secret manufacturing centers, and of how great was their control, through American-born partisans of the Soviet Union, over many of our labor unions. His investigations produced other frightening details, including revelations concerning a network of espionage in our atomic energy facilities, and of the existing reluctance, or downright refusal, of the authorities to do anything about it.

In a two-hour conference with Father Cronin, Nixon, hitherto unaware of the seriousness of the Communist infiltration, listened with rapt attention as the priest opened his files and began to cite specific instances and names. Among the individuals enumerated, which included Harry Dexter White, Arthur Alexandrovitch Adams, Steve Nelson and

Clarence Hiskey, was a man named Alger Hiss.*

It was clear to Nixon that a Congressman who had been in office for only a few scant weeks might find it next to impossible to document these findings in a manner that might be made to stick. The identities of the spies and saboteurs were already known to the Attorney General. It was he who had refused permission to J. Edgar Hoover to place them in custody. They were also known to the Assistant Secretary of State, and, in the case of Alger Hiss and Harry Dexter White, to the President himself.* The suspects had not only gone

---

*While this chapter must necessarily be confined to the roles played by Richard Nixon, Alger Hiss and Whittaker Chambers, the seriousness and extent of the communist underground movement becomes clear as we examine, very briefly, the known facts about the men named by Father Cronin. Although it will be correctly deduced that the Hiss case was not actually the most important one to be considered by the HUAC, it certainly was the most dramatic. More than any other disclosure, it helped alert the public to this country's internal weakness.

Arthur Alexandrovitch Adams, a Soviet spy, was deported from this country in the 1920's. He returned, illegally, during World War II. Thereupon, he organized a spy ring which succeeded in stealing nuclear secrets from Los Alamos and the Radiation Laboratory of the University of California. He was caught by the FBI, but the Bureau was restrained by the State Department from taking him into custody on the grounds that it would offend Russia.

Steve Nelson, who studied sabotage and espionage at the Lenin School of Military Intelligence in Moscow, was tracked down by the FBI and placed under constant surveillance. Nelson was finally caught in the act of passing atomic secrets to an official of the Soviet Embassy. In this case, too, the State Department would not permit the FBI to make an arrest. Not long after the Hiss-Chambers case ended, and when he could speak without jeopardizing Hiss's constitutional rights, Nixon said indignantly:

"I just can't forget Steve Nelson's answer when I asked him which country he would fight for in the event of a war between the United States and the Soviet Union. You know what that guy said?—'I refuse to answer on the ground of self-incrimination.' "

Clarence Hiskey, an official employed by the top-secret Manhattan Project that developed the atomic bomb, passed along nuclear secrets to Steve Nelson and other members of his underground cell. Security officers, who initially discovered Hiskey's espionage activities, notified the FBI. Once again the Bureau was refused permission to make an arrest.

unpunished, but had regularly been rewarded with successive promotions. These were the early days of Nixon's career, and he had not as yet been appointed to the House Un-American Activities Committee (HUAC) or any other committee. Consequently, he had no investigative facilities at his disposal.

Miss Elizabeth Bentley Appears

Father Cronin's charges became well known in the months to come, and others, taking up the accusations, went so far as to accuse the entire Democratic Administration of being "infested with Red spies"—obviously a patent exaggeration. The recurrent accusations could no longer be ignored. On July 31, 1948, Elizabeth Bentley, a former Communist espionage agent, appeared before the HUAC and made headlines when she named thirty-two government officials as her contacts in the Communist apparatus. These officials, she testified under oath, had supplied her with classified documents which she, in her capacity as courier for a Soviet spy ring, had microfilmed and then passed along to Russian agents who, in turn, transmitted them to Moscow.

Those named by Miss Bentley were called before the Committee, but by this time the artful dodgers had discovered the Fifth Amendment, and most of them refused to testify on

---

*Testifying at an HUAC hearing, Lieutenant General Leslie R. Groves, who was in charge of the entire wartime nuclear project, was questioned by the Committee's chief investigator, Robert Stripling. The exchange brought the question of espionage directly into the White House:

> *Stripling*: General Groves, did you report the efforts of espionage agents to obtain data concerning our atomic development to the President of the United States?
>
> *Groves*: Yes, I gave the report to President Roosevelt who read it in my presence and then discussed it with me. He left for Yalta shortly thereafter. It was also brought to the attention of President Truman immediately after he took office and as soon as the Secretary of War could make his very first appointment. The report was then read in its entirety by President Truman.

the ground that their answers would tend to incriminate them. They not only went scot free, but were welcomed back to their various government posts. The few who did not take the Fifth simply denied any involvement in espionage. It was their word against that of Miss Bentley, and, without the necessary substantiation, they too were excused.

But the hearings produced one significant result: Committee members learned that another man had been a communist functionary in the 1930's, before Elizabeth Bentley had become a spy. That man was David Whittaker Chambers, formerly city editor of the *Daily Worker* and a writer for the *New Masses*, who then became a senior editor of *Time* magazine, earning $25,000. a year.

David Whittaker Chambers Summoned

On August 3, 1948, three days after Miss Bentley completed her testimony, Whittaker Chambers was summoned to appear before the Committee in an effort to determine whether he might be able to corroborate part of the serious charges she had made. He seemed reluctant to answer the questions put to him, but Nixon and his fellow Committee members were patient, knowing he had told his story—or at least part of it—to the Department of Justice and to the Assistant Secretary of State, although nothing had come of it.

Certainly, Chambers was not a witness to inspire confidence. Nixon recalled their first meeting on that hot and humid day: "Both in appearance and in what he had to say, Chambers made very little impression on me or the other Committee members. He was short and pudgy. His clothes were unpressed. His shirt collar was curled up over his jacket. He spoke in a rather bored monotone."

Nixon had been so ill-impressed with the witness that he considered leaving the almost-empty hearing room to return to his office where he might attend to his mail. But, as Chambers droned on, explaining that he had joined the Communist

Party in 1925 and then left it in 1937, Nixon gathered his wandering thoughts and focused all his attention on the witness who was now admitting that he once believed communism to be the "new wave," and that American democratic institutions were doomed.

"I quit the Party because I finally became convinced that Communism was a form of totalitarianism which could only result in slavery to all mankind," said Whittaker Chambers. His voice, low to begin with, now carried overtones of deep regret and a curious sense of despair as he continued: "Yet, so strong is the hold which the insidious evil of Communism secures upon its disciples that I could still say to my wife at the time—'I know that I am leaving the winning side for the losing side, but it is better to die on the losing side than to live under Communism.'"

Nixon scrutinized him intently, sensing that here was a man who was the antithesis of the witnesses who had heretofore paraded before the Committee. "It was not how he spoke; it was, rather, the sheer, almost stark eloquence of his phrases that needed no histrionic embellishment," said Nixon in retrospect. "From that moment I came more and more to realize that despite his unpretentious appearance, Chambers was a man of extraordinary intellectual gifts and one who had inner strength and depth. Here was no headline seeker, but rather a thoughtful, introspective man, careful with his words, speaking with what sounded like the ring of truth."

Chambers went on to tell the House Un-American Activities Committee of the communist cell to which he had belonged. Many of its members, he noted, later transferred to the newer cell about which Miss Bentley had testified. Among those he named as members of his communist group, and whose primary function was to infiltrate the higher echelons of government were: Nathan Witt, former Secretary of the National Labor Relations Board; John Abt, former Labor Department attorney; Lee Pressman, former Assistant General Counsel for the Agricultural Adjustment Administration, later Counsel for the Works Progress Administration (WPA), and still later, General Counsel for the CIO; and Alger Hiss, a State Department official who, Chambers said, had been a Communist and who proved his allegiance to the Soviet Union even during the 1939-41 years when the Communists and Nazis were allies. Chambers concluded his list by naming Donald Hiss, Alger's brother, and Mrs. Alger (Priscilla) Hiss as Communists. Just as positively, he asserted that Mrs. Donald Hiss was not a Communist. Additionally, he named as a "fellow traveller," Harry Dexter White, former Assistant Secretary of the Treasury.

None of these accusations involved espionage; that was to come later. But without documentation, and with nothing more than the word of a confessed ex-Communist, the Committee was prepared to let the matter rest unless and until irrefutable evidence could be produced. What disturbed Nixon, however, was Chambers' testimony that he had told his story to government officials as far back as 1939, when the Hitler-Stalin pact was signed—an act so abhorrent and frightening to Chambers that he was compelled to disclose what he knew of the Soviet-American underground. Yet, the officials had not taken a single positive step to end the subversion.

Fascinated, but obviously skeptical, the Committee members fired questions at Chambers that touched on every aspect of his testimony. But it was Nixon, with his penchant for hard facts, who established the course which the investigation would take:

> *Nixon*: Mr. Chambers, you indicated that nine years ago you came to Washington and reported to the government authorities concerning the Communists who were in the government.
> *Chambers*: Yes.
> *Nixon*: To what agency did you make that report?
> *Chambers*: I went to see Berle and told him much of what I have been telling you.

Here was the first tangible fact that could be checked for authenticity. Adolf A. Berle, Jr., whom Chambers was careful to identify as an anti-Communist, was then Assistant Secretary of State for Intelligence, a highly respected and honorable man. Berle became very distraught, Chambers said, and took extensive notes of his report, but the accusations were simply too unbelievable for Washington's bureaucracy. "The Soviet Union and the United States are entering a new era of friendship," Berle was told in effect. "Don't rock the boat."

Nothing came of his report to Berle, and Chambers was not approached by anyone in government until four more years had elapsed. Then, in 1943, agents from the FBI visited him at his farm in Westminster, Maryland, where he again told his story. He was visited twice more by the FBI, in 1945 and 1947, repeating for the third time the account he had given Berle. Again nothing happened.

It was apparent that J. Edgar Hoover was interested in Chambers' story and was conducting his own investigation, despite the Administration's policy to avoid any offense to Stalin. But Chambers knew that Hoover, however powerful he might be, could only investigate; he could not prosecute or proceed with any other type of action unless granted approval by his superiors in the Department of Justice and in the White House. That approval would not be forthcoming, and Chambers finally realized that his reports had been quietly buried.

The hearings of August 3, which was Chambers' first day on the stand, ended on a note of boredom. The few reporters in attendance yawned and stretched. No sensational spy stories had evolved from the account given by "the drab little man" whom the press considered far less newsworthy than Elizabeth Bentley, and whose testimony had resulted in headlines. Nevertheless, Chambers' story did make the front page. Had it not been published, the case would have died right there.

"I gave very little thought to Chambers or his testimony that evening or the following morning," recalled Nixon. "Then Robert Stripling, the Committee's chief investigator, phoned me. The Committee, Stripling said, had received a telegram from Alger Hiss requesting an opportunity to publicly deny, under oath, each and every accusation made against him by Whittaker Chambers."

The Phone Call That Changed History

Of all those cited by Chambers, only Hiss had volunteered to appear before the HUAC. He demanded an immediate appointment so that he might clear himself, and the Committee was more than glad to comply. His appearance was scheduled for August 5th, the very next day.

If ever one event changed the course of history, it was that one telephone call. It changed Hiss's life as it changed Richard Nixon's whole career. Hiss was supremely confident of his ability to match wits with anyone on the House Un-American Activities Committee. He had heard a few rumors about the hard-working, dynamic new Congressman from "some little village in California"—he could not remember the town's name—but he dismissed Nixon as one might dismiss a bright child.

Hiss, it was clear, did not know Richard Nixon, the man. He knew only of Nixon "the greenest Congressman in Washington." For that matter, even Nixon did not know Nixon. He had no idea how he would react to the case which he termed "the first great crisis of my life."

From the moment that Alger Hiss raised his hand to be sworn in, it was evident to all in the packed caucus room of the Old House Office Building that here was no ordinary figure. The press section was filled to capacity with newsmen, many of whom liked and respected him. Many remembered Hiss from the time when he was chief of the Secretariat at the

San Francisco Conference which established the United Nations organization. One of his duties at that time was to brief the press on UN developments and, in that capacity, as in all others, he had earned their respect for his intelligence and ability. If anything, he was regarded with a touch of awe by the Committee members, the reporters, and his influential friends in the spectators' gallery. Here was no man to plead his case by standing there wringing his hands like a two penny-halfpenny washerwoman. Instead, he wore an expression of wounded innocence that would melt a policeman's badge. His performance, Nixon wrote twelve years later, was as brilliant as Chambers' had been lackluster.

As the official transcript shows, Hiss immediately went on the offensive:

> My name is Alger Hiss. I was born in Baltimore, Maryland, on November 11, 1904. I am here at my own request to deny unqualifiedly various statements about me which were made before this Committee by one Whittaker Chambers the day before yesterday.
>
> I am not, and never have been, a member of the Communist Party. I do not and never have adhered to the tenets of the Communist Party. I am not, and never have been, a member of a Communist front organization. I have never followed the Communist Party line directly or indirectly. To the best of my knowledge none of my friends is a Communist.

Had Alger Hiss concluded his testimony at this point, the affair would have ended then and there. Scores of witnesses had appeared before the Committee and denied communist affiliations. They had all been cleared because it was simply their word against that of their accusers.

Hiss might even have acknowledged knowing Chambers as a casual acquaintance and brushed him off as a harmless eccentric, and that too would have ended the matter. But here, Hiss made what Nixon called his first irreversible mistake. Not satisfied with leaving well enough alone, he stated that he had never heard the name Whittaker Chambers. "The name means absolutely nothing to me," he testified.

At that point the Committee was ready, even anxious to drop the case, realizing that its old reputation as an inquisitor of innocent citizens would again be emblazoned in the press. Whittaker Chambers, it was true, had attained a position of respectability as one of six senior editors of *Time*, and unless he bore a deep, personal grudge about which the Committee knew nothing, there could be no reason why he would jeopardize his $25,000 a year job! But, then again, he was an admitted former Communist—unlike Hiss whose redoubtable credentials were known to everyone at the hearing.

Examining the Fine Print

Nevertheless, Hiss's response had struck a discordant note in Nixon's mind. Consulting his notes, it seemed to him that Hiss had never really denied knowing Chambers; he had stated only that he had never known a man *by that name*! Nixon exchanged a few words with Stripling, the Committee's investigator, who posed the question once again:

> *Stripling*: You say you have never seen Mr. Chambers?
>
> *Hiss*: The name means absolutely nothing to me, Mr. Stripling.

Nixon's lips tightened. Hiss had not answered the question. "I was a lawyer and I knew he was a lawyer . . . As I read the testimony later I became convinced that if Hiss was lying he was lying in such a way as to avoid perjury with a very careful use of phrasing. He would say, 'To the best of my knowledge' over and over again. He had never once said flatly, 'I don't know Whittaker Chambers.' He constantly reiterated when the question was put to him, 'I have never known a man *by the name of* Whittaker Chambers.' In other words, he was too careful in his testimony, too smooth. It was very possibly an act, it seemed to me."

Stripling then handed Hiss a photograph of Chambers and asked if he could now identify him as a man he had known. Hiss studied the picture for long moments and said, "If this is a photo of Mr. Chambers he is not particularly unusual looking." He looked up and directed his gaze to Representative Karl Mundt, the acting Chairman of the Committee. "He looks like a lot of people," he continued, smiling. "I might even mistake him for the Chairman of this Committee."

Richard Nixon is Irish on both sides of his family, and the incident that followed Hiss's sally stirred him to classic, if silent, Gaelic anger. A wave of laughter broke out among the many friends of Hiss who had left their government offices to attend the session; the elite of Washington society, of which he was an honored member, tittered like so many delighted magpies. Hiss responded by turning his back to the Committee and acknowledging the reaction with a graceful Tyrolean bow and a warm smile.

Karl Mundt's face reddened. "I hope you are wrong in that," he retorted.

"I didn't mean to be facetious," Hiss apologized quickly, realizing that his humor was not only inappropriate, but misdirected. "Seriously, I would not want to take an oath that I had never seen that man . . . Is he here today?" He then glanced around the room as though he expected his accuser to step forward and identify himself. "I had hoped he would be present," Hiss concluded with an air of deep disappointment. "I would like to see him."

In his book, *Six Crises*, Nixon recalled Hiss's appearance as a "virtuoso performance." Indeed it was; and it was worthy of a film star. He had not voiced a single word of recrimination against Chambers, yet he had successfully created a self-image of an innocent, harassed public servant who was either being persecuted by a madman for reasons he could not comprehend, or else was the victim of a terrible case of mistaken identity.

As the hearing drew to a close, Nixon searched his mind, seeking a logical answer to the oft-repeated: "I have never known a man by the name of Whittaker Chambers." Suddenly he was struck with a thought. He called Ben Mandel, a staff member, to his side, and in a low voice asked him to telephone Chambers who was in New York at the time. "Find out if he might possibly have been known under another name during the period he was a Communist functionary," Nixon requested.

Chambers was not in his hotel room when Mandel tried to reach him. When he finally returned the call, the question was put to him.

"Yes," Whittaker Chambers said without hesitation. "I was known to Hiss and the other members of our Communist cell by my Party name—Carl!"

It was too late to ask Hiss if he had ever known Chambers as Carl, but whatever Nixon's doubts they were not shared by most of the other members of the Committee; nor were they shared by the spectators and press. As the hearing neared its end, Mundt, certainly an avowed anti-Communist, complimented Hiss on his conduct: "The Chair wishes to express the appreciation of the Committee for your very cooperative attitude, for your forthright statements and for the fact that you were the first among those whose names were mentioned by various witnesses to communicate with us, asking for an opportunity to deny the charges."

Even John Rankin, nemesis of anything smacking of radicalism, to say nothing of communism, was moved to add: "I want to congratulate the witness for not refusing to answer the questions on the ground that it might incriminate him. And he didn't bring a lawyer here to tell him what to say."

As the gavel was rapped, signifying adjournment, Rankin left his seat and led the general rush to shake hands with Hiss. Smiling and bowing, Hiss acknowledged their support with modest murmurs of thanks. Within minutes, he was completely surrounded, not only by his well-wishers from the State Department and other agencies, but also by congratulatory newsmen and members of the Committee—with one exception: Richard Nixon remained in his chair.

When the hubbub quieted down and the room cleared, Nixon went to the House restaurant for lunch, and it was there that he gained his first intimation as to the reaction of the press. A stream of reporters approached his table. "How is the Committee going to dig itself out of this mess?" asked one of the newsmen. Mary Spargo, covering the hearings for the *Washington Post*, asked no questions but made a blunt statement: "This case is going to kill the Committee unless you can prove Chambers' story."

Ed Lahey, of the Chicago *Daily News*, whom Nixon described as "one of the most honest and objective reporters in Washington," stalked over to him and almost snarled, "The Committee on Un-American Activities stands convicted, guilty of calumny in putting Chambers on the stand without first checking on the truth of his testimony."

Truman's "Red Herring" Charge

Nixon had not yet finished his lunch when he learned of Truman's reaction. The President, at his press conference, had called the investigation a "red herring" dreamed up by the Republican-controlled Congress to divert the American people from attending to such vital matters as price controls, inflation and other important legislation. Truman followed up his blast with a presidential order in which all federal agencies were prohibited from releasing information on government personnel to Congressional committees.

Nixon's colleagues were all in favor of washing their hands

of the whole affair. His friend, Congressman Christian Herter, under whose chairmanship he had served a year earlier to study United States foreign aid programs in Europe, sighed: "I'm afraid the Committee has been taken in by Chambers." Another Republican leader lamented, "We're ruined!" Acting Chairman Mundt agreed with the other members that they had been "suckered into a bad deal by a maniac or a nut with a personal grudge of some kind." Congressman F. Edward Hébert, the gentlemanly Louisiana Democrat, suggested that they turn the entire case over to the Department of Justice and be done with it. "Let's get rid of the whole mess," he insisted.

"That appeared to be the majority view," said Nixon. "Had Hébert put his suggestion in the form of a motion it would have been carried overwhelmingly. I was the only member of the Committee who expressed a contrary view, and Bob Stripling backed me up strongly and effectively."

Urging the Committee to continue its pursuit of the truth, Nixon made these arguments:

> 1. Should the case be turned over to the Department of Justice, the Committee's reputation would not be rescued but would probably be destroyed. It would be a public confession that they had been reckless and incompetent in their treatment of Hiss.
>
> 2. The Committee had a responsibility to see the case through to its conclusion in view of Chambers' testimony in which he asserted that he had told his story on four occasions to representatives of government agencies, and that none had made an effort to check the truth or falsity of his charges. That being the case, the investigation would certainly be dropped once again if the Committee's files were turned over to the Department of Justice.
>
> 3. Although Hiss seemed to be a completely forthright and truthful witness, he had never made the cate-

gorical statement that he did not know Whittaker Chambers. He had, instead, qualified his answer each time by saying he did not know a man "by the name of" Chambers. He was too careful in his testimony; too slick. As to his comment that Mundt might be mistaken for Chambers, followed by his searching glance around the room as though he were earnestly seeking his accuser—it was overdone, too contrived, and very possibly an "act."

4. While it might be virtually impossible to prove whether or not Hiss was a Communist, inasmuch as it would be his word agaist Chambers', the Committee should be given the chance to determine whether or not Hiss was lying about knowing Chambers. This, it was reasonable to suppose, they could establish by corroborative testimony. If Chambers had known him intimately for three years, as he claimed, evidence of that association should be adducible.

There was one further sordid note that aroused Nixon's suspicions. Immediately following Chambers' testimony, and even before Hiss had concluded his own, vicious rumors began to circulate. The calculated whispering campaign, Stripling told the Committee, accused Chambers of alcoholism, homosexuality, insanity—and even that he had been confined to a mental institution. All of the allegations were untrue. Hiss, of course, might not have originated the scandalous rumors, but character assassination was an all-too-familiar tactic employed by Communists to destroy the credibility of any witness—especially a former Communist who dared to forget Party discipline to the extent of testifying against the Party and its members.

Nixon Heads HUAC Subcommittee And Puts Career on the Line

Nixon's arguments prevailed. He was appointed to head a special subcommittee to continue the Hiss-Chambers investigation, but thereafter in executive session—behind closed doors, with the press and general public barred.

In his zeal to prevent the Committee from dropping the case prematurely, Richard Nixon, freshman Congressman from Whittier, had unintentionally placed himself in the position of defending the reputation of the widely disliked House Un-American Activities Committee. He deliberately placed himself on a personal, head-on collision course with the President of the United States who had already voiced his contempt of the Committee. Additionally, he knew he was about to antagonize the press corps, most of whom were unswervingly sympathetic to their old friend Hiss who was charming and personable, and had always gotten along well with newsmen.

Finally, from a practical standpoint, Nixon realized that an aroused public opinion could easily end his political career. After all, he was the man solely responsible for continuing a case in which he was indirectly defending a known Communist against one of the most attractive and brilliant young men in public life. "Yet, I could not go against my own conscience," Nixon wrote in his memoirs, "and my conscience told me that in this case the rather unsavory-looking Chambers was telling the truth, and the honest-looking Hiss was lying."

With nothing more to go on than his intuition, Nixon, after assuming the chairmanship of the newly created HUAC subcommittee, issued his first order. He requested Stripling to subpoena Chambers to a hearing on August 7th, just two days later.

Nixon Follows His Hunch

Nixon's hunch that Chambers and Hiss had known each other and had been close friends led to the strategy that was to unravel the imponderables that surrounded this bizarre case. Surely, Nixon reasoned, Chambers would have to be familiar with intimate details of Hiss's life—details which could be known only to someone who had enjoyed his complete confidence. In order to explore this theory fully, the Subcommittee met on August 7th, a Saturday, in the Federal Courthouse in New York's Foley Square. Accompanying Nixon were Congressmen Hébert and John R. McDowell, and several staff investigators headed by Robert Stripling. For three full hours Nixon grilled Chambers without letup, examining and cross-examining his witness about everything that pertained to Hiss's personal life:

> *Nixon*: When did you first meet Alger Hiss?
>
> *Chambers*: In 1935—and I saw him on numerous occasions through 1937.
>
> *Nixon*: Occasions? What sort of occasions?
>
> *Chambers*: I collected Communist Party dues from him.

As Whittaker Chambers went on to describe minute details of Hiss's personal life, Chambers' phenomenal memory seemed to enthrall the Subcommittee members and their investigators. "Even his most bitter enemies had to agree that Chambers was a man of extraordinary intelligence," said Nixon. "As a Communist underground agent, he had to train himself to carry vast amounts of information in his head so that he could reduce to a minimum the risk of ever being apprehended with documents on his person. As a result, his mind's retentive capacities were developed to an astonishing degree."

That power of recall was now ably demonstrated. Chambers told of the several times he had stayed at Hiss's Washington home—once for a whole week. He spoke of the cocker spaniel dog owned by Alger and his wife, Priscilla, and even gave the name and address of the kennel on Wisconsin

Avenue, in Georgetown, where the spaniel was boarded when they vacationed on Maryland's eastern shore. He remembered their nicknames: Priscilla called her husband "Hilly" and he called her "Dilly." Their friends referred to them as "Hilly and Dilly," but never in their presence. He described Mrs. Hiss, gave her maiden name, her birthplace and background; he offered a description of Hiss's stepson, and described the interiors and exteriors of three different houses in which Alger and Priscilla had lived during the time he was associated with them.

Nixon could not help but be impressed. "I realized that all this information might have been obtained by studying Hiss's life without actually knowing him," he reflected. "But some of the answers had a personal ring of truth about them, beyond the bare facts themselves." That "ring of truth" was evident in Chambers' replies to the next two questions:

"Did he have any hobbies?" Nixon asked.

"Yes, he did. In fact, Hiss and his wife both had the same hobby. They were amateur ornithologists—bird watchers. They used to get up early in the morning and go to Glen Echo out on the canal to observe birds. I recall once how excited they became when they spotted a prothonotary warbler."

Congressman McDowell, himself an amateur ornithologist, nodded. "A very rare specimen," he commented.

Chambers smiled for the first time that day as he acknowledged the Congressman's comment. "I never saw one," he replied. "I am also fond of birds."

Hiss's Dilapidated Ford

For possible future use, Nixon filed the information in the recesses of his own retentive memory bank. But the answer to his next question provided the blockbuster of the session:

"Did they have a car?"

"Yes. It was a 1929 Ford roadster, black and dilapidated.

The windshield wipers, I recall, had to be worked by hand. Hiss wanted to give the old Ford to the Communist Party when he bought another car in 1936. It was against all the rules of the underground organization—and I think this investigation proves how right the Communists are in such matters. But Hiss insisted. Much against Peters' better judgment, he finally got us to permit him to do this thing."*

"To whom did he give the car?"

"Hiss turned it over to a Communist in a Washington service station and it was later transferred to another Party member. I should think the records of that transfer would be traceable."

As the hearing drew to a close, Chambers agreed to submit to a lie detector test on any phase of the statements he had made that day.

"I told the truth," he said quietly.

The Probing Begins

During the nine days left before Hiss's scheduled appearance on August 16th, Nixon and his staff worked 'round the clock trying to substantiate or refute the new information Chambers had given them. They checked and double-checked. They spoke to real estate agents about the leases pertaining to the three houses in which, according to Chambers, Hiss had lived from 1935 to 1937. They located the dog kennel on Wisconsin Avenue where Alger and Priscilla Hiss boarded their cocker spaniel when they went on vacation. In these and all other details where they were able to check with third parties, Chambers' story proved to be true. The one vitally important piece of documentation they were unable to find, however, was the Motor Vehicle records which would substantiate Chambers' statement that Hiss had transferred title of his old Ford to the Communist Party.

---

*J. Peters was the head of the Communist underground in the United States.

A Consensus of Guilt Emerges

Still unable to rid himself of his uncertainty as to whether Hiss or Chambers was the liar, Nixon sought out a few trusted men whom he felt would be impartial, though possibly inclined to favor Hiss. He first consulted the late Bert Andrews, chief Washington correspondent of the New York *Herald Tribune*. Andrews, a recent Pulitzer Prize winner, and James Reston of the *New York Times*, had joined Adlai Stevenson in recommending Hiss to John Foster Dulles for the Carnegie presidency. Agreeing to write nothing until the material was released for general publication, Andrews read every word of the testimony, pausing here and there for reflection. When he finished his perusal he looked up from the stack of papers. "I wouldn't have believed it, after hearing Hiss the other day," he said slowly. "But there's no doubt about it. Chambers knew Hiss."

Among others whom Nixon consulted was William P. Rogers, his old friend whom he had met while both were in the Navy, and who was now chief counsel for the Senate Internal Security Subcommittee that was busily engaged in investigating the charges made by Elizabeth Bentley. Rogers also agreed that Chambers had revealed too intimate a knowledge of Hiss's personal life to have fabricated the story.

Congressman Charles Kersten, who had introduced Nixon to Father Cronin the year before, was also convinced of the Hiss-Chambers relationship. Kersten then imparted a bit of information that moved Nixon to decisive action. "I've heard rumors that Hiss is trying to get John Foster Dulles and other members of the Carnegie Board of Directors to issue statements in his support," Kersten said. "If they do that publicly, you might as well quit the investigation now."

Nixon telephoned Dulles at once and they arranged a meeting for that very night at New York's Roosevelt Hotel where he was spearheading the Dewey presidential campaign. Present, besides John Foster Dulles, was his brother Allen—

later head of the CIA. Together, they read Chambers' testimony and, when they finally laid the pages down, they both wore a look of incredulous surprise. "There's no question about it," Foster Dulles said after a long pause. "It's almost impossible to believe, but Chambers indeed knows Hiss." Allen Dulles nodded. "No doubt about it."

Nixon Visits Chambers' Farm

But the sullied background that plagued HUAC continued to encroach on Nixon's thoughts. If Chambers, rather than Hiss, proved to be the liar, the Committee's reputation would be damaged beyond repair and its very existence would be ended, as threatened by President Truman. Moreover, Nixon's own career might well be finished. To assuage his anxieties, he made three trips to Chambers' farm, travelling in his personal car to avoid any publicity.

His first visit was not particularly enlightening. However, as he was leaving, he casually mentioned that he was a member of the Society of Friends. Chambers replied that he and his wife, Esther, attended the Friends meeting in Westminster. Suddenly he snapped his fingers as a thought occurred to him. "That reminds me of something!" he exclaimed. "Priscilla is a Quaker and I believe she converted her husband. She often used the plain speech when talking to Alger at home."

As a Quaker, whose mother, grandmother and other close relatives used the plain speech (e.g. "thee" and "thou") only in the privacy of their homes, Nixon realized that Chambers *had* to know the Hiss family intimately. Yet, the doubt persisted: someone else who knew Priscilla Hiss could have informed Chambers of this habit.

Two days later, Nixon again visited Chambers, this time in the company of Bert Andrews. Taking a shot in the dark, Nixon asked if there was anything in the house that Hiss had given him—some tangible proof that they had known each other. Silently, Chambers produced a volume of Audubon prints, a Christmas present from Hiss. As they glanced through the book, Chambers pointed to the drawing of a hooded warbler. "As I recall, the Hisses had this picture in the dining room of one of the houses they lived in," he said.

On August 14, two days before Hiss was to be questioned, Nixon made his third trip to the Westminster farm. With him was Bob Stripling. The meeting was brief, the questions perfunctory, but as they drove back to Washington, Stripling made an observation: "I'm convinced that Chambers knew Hiss, but I don't think he's given us the whole story. He's holding back something—something important."

When the Subcommittee met again in executive session on August 16, Alger Hiss was no longer the confident, somewhat supercilious figure he had been just ten days earlier. Nixon had exerted every effort to keep Chambers' testimony of August 8th secret, but Hiss, through his powerful connections had, somehow, managed to learn that his accuser had furnished page after page of details that only a very close friend of the family might be expected to know. His attitude of disdainful superiority, his dapper, poised manner was beginning to vanish. He dodged questions, refused to answer directly, and changed the subject when the matter of Chambers' week-long stay in his home was brought up. He altered his story a number of times, adding fuel to Nixon's suspicions. As the hearing neared its end, whatever remaining doubts Nixon may have had were dissipated.

Before concluding the day's hearing, however, Nixon made it clear that he had grown weary of Hiss's feinting and weaving. He showed the witness two photographs of Chambers:

"Mr. Hiss, after looking at these pictures, I ask you if you can remember that person, either as Whittaker Chambers or as Carl or as any other individual you have met."

Hiss made an elaborate show of examining the photos minutely, and then he answered: "In the public session when I was shown another photograph of Whittaker Chambers

I testified that I could not swear that I had never seen the man whose picture was shown me. Actually, the face has a certain familiarity."

As Nixon continued to chip away at this first tiny crack in Hiss's earlier story in which he denied knowing Chambers, Hiss grew increasingly desperate. He turned and twisted—laboring to find logical answers to answer the mass of supporting statements Chambers had given of their past relationship. At bay, he attacked the Committee itself, accusing it of bias and entrapment. Addressing Nixon directly, he declared:

> I have been angered and hurt by the attitude you have been taking today, to the effect that you have a conflict of testimony between two witnesses—one of whom is a confessed former Communist, and the other is me; that you simply have two witnesses saying contradictory things, and that you find it most difficult to decide on credibility. I do not wish to make it easier for anyone who, for whatever motive I cannot understand, is apparently endeavoring to destroy me. I should not be asked to give details which, somehow, he may hear and then may be able to use against me as if he knew them before.

Forgetting, or, in his desperation, ignoring, the fact that he himself had raised the issue as to whether or not he knew Chambers, Hiss continued:

> The question is not whether this man knew me and I don't remember him. The question is whether he had a particular conversation that he said he had with me, and which I have denied; and whether I am a member of the Communist Party or ever was, which he has said, and which I have denied.

Nixon bore in, reminding Hiss that the issue before the

Committee was not his alleged membership in the Communist Party, but only whether he had or had not known Chambers. If it could be shown that Chambers had lied about knowing him, then every other accusation would obviously be false. "However," concluded Nixon, "the relationship can be confirmed by third parties."

George Crosley Enters

After a short recess, Hiss returned to the Committee room in an altered frame of mind. Still insisting that he did not recognize the person shown in the photographs, he offered a new name, a man called George Crosley, to whom he had sublet his apartment and who had spent several nights at his house with his wife and baby. He described Crosley as a deadbeat who had stayed in the apartment throughout the summer of 1935 without paying any rent.

Now the case assumed new dimensions as Nixon and Stripling moved into the hole that Hiss himself had opened:

> *Stripling*: What kind of automobile did this Crosley fellow have?
>
> *Hiss*: He had no automobile at all. I sold him an automobile. I had an old Ford that I threw in with the apartment that I had been trying to trade in and get rid of. A slightly collegiate model. It wasn't very fancy, but it had a sassy little trunk on the back.
>
> *Nixon*: You sold him that car?
>
> *Hiss*: I threw it in. He wanted a way to get around and I said, "Fine. I can't get rid of it. I have another car. We kept it for sentimental reasons—not worth a damn." I let him have it along with the rent.

Hiss then acknowledged Nixon's questions with several answers that brought a gleam to Nixon's eyes. Yes, Alger and

Priscilla had vacationed at Maryland's eastern shore during the summer months. Yes, they had boarded their cocker spaniel at the kennel in Georgetown, not too far from Rock Creek Park. Yes, they had an Audubon print of a bird in one of their houses.

Suddenly Nixon fired an unexpected question at the witness: "What hobbies, if any, do you have?"

"Tennis and amateur ornithology," replied Hiss.

Congressman McDowell asked, "Did you ever see a prothonotary warbler?"

Hiss nodded. "I have, right here on the banks of the Potomac."

Nixon and McDowell exchanged glances as Hiss continued, once again glib and master of himself. He explained that he had not seen Crosley since 1935 when the lease on his apartment expired, and that only one small payment on account was ever paid. He then recalled that Crosley had also given him a rug which he said some wealthy client gave him. "I've still got the damned thing," he added.

Apart from the rug, Hiss claimed that he had received a total of about $15 on the rent, which would have been $225 for the three-month summer period. He concluded by saying that neither he nor Crosley had ever discussed communism and that, to his knowledge, Crosley was not a member of the Communist Party. All he knew about his tenant, Hiss affirmed, was that he was a free-lance writer, although he had never seen any of his writings.

Nixon then pointed out that Chambers had agreed to take a lie detector test and, abruptly, he asked Hiss if he would also be willing to submit to the same test.

Replied Hiss: "I would like to have an opportunity for further consultation as to the accuracy of such tests before I give my answer."

As the session ended, the entire membership of HUAC voted to hold an open hearing on August 25, at which time Chambers and Hiss would meet face-to-face.

The strain of long hours of travel to New York and Westminster, lack of sufficient sleep, and, in general, his preoccupation with the case, were taking their toll of Nixon. The investigation was constantly on his mind, and it was beginning to sap his energies. But he drove himself relentlessly. Upon leaving the August 16 hearings, he returned to his office and telephoned Pat. "Sorry, honey," he apologized, "but I won't be home for dinner this evening. I'll be going over the testimony."

"Oh, no," she protested, worry showing through her disappointment. "Well, at least promise you'll have a decent dinner."

"Sure," he replied cheerfully, and then sent out for a hamburger, an order of French fries, and a milkshake.

Nixon and Stripling spent the evening poring over the day's transcript together, both convinced that Crosley and Chambers were one and the same. But, if that were so, then the rest of Chambers' story might also be true. What was the nature of their relationship? Would a man earning $25,000 a year jeopardize his position and risk a prison term for perjury without reason? Why had Hiss stepped out of character by his explosive use of the word "damn" when referring to the old car? He had also used the same word in anger when he mentioned the rug Chambers had supposedly given him.

Why? Could there be a connection between the two? It was possible, Nixon surmised, that both items were more important to Hiss than he had indicated.

Another question arose in Nixon's mind: Why had Hiss not mentioned the mysterious George Crosley at the outset?

It was close to midnight when Stripling left, but Nixon remained at his desk, pondering the many unanswered questions. As he mulled over the transcript, it gradually dawned on him that the time element was all in Hiss's favor. August 25, the date Hiss was to confront Chambers in person, was still nine days in the future; if he had invented the elusive Crosley, as Nixon believed, he would have ample time to make his story fit the facts. Further, considering his unquestioned prestige in the upper levels of the Administration, and the weight of a friendly press giving him support, Hiss could develop a favorable public opinion that might not only promote his complete vindication, but might also push for the dissolution of the Committee itself.

At two o'clock in the morning, a weary Nixon picked up his telephone and called Stripling at his home. "Bob," he said to the sleepy investigator, "we can't afford to wait until the twenty-fifth of the month. I want you to summon both Chambers and Hiss before the Subcommittee in New York this afternoon."

After only four hours of sleep, Nixon boarded a train from Washington to New York and, en route, read the front page story of Harry Dexter White's heart attack and death. White, when he had appeared before HUAC after being named a Communist by Elizabeth Bentley and Whittaker Chambers, had denied every allegation against him. He had proceeded to insult individual members of the Committee, lectured them on the meaning of civil rights, and brushed aside the obvious fact that he had been the main source of employment and the protector of Communists during his term as Assistant Secretary of the Treasury. He had responded to questions with sarcastic replies as though he were admonishing a group of country bumpkins on the meaning of democracy. He had followed all this by stalking out of the hearing room to the plaudits of his government friends and the Washington corps of newsmen that was present—although, in fairness to them, it should be noted that at that time the documents had not yet been found that linked him to the Soviet-American underground which had been systematically looting the United States of its national secrets.

Medical records ascribed White's death to heart failure, but a strange doctor rather than his own physician had signed the death certificate. He was then hastily cremated.

As might be expected, the Committee was not only accused

of having harassed White to death, but also that Hiss was being summoned to confront Chambers for the sole purpose of diverting public attention from White. "All I can say is that this accusation, like so many others against the Committee, is completely untrue," said Nixon. "I myself had made the decision on the confrontation well before I learned of White's death."

The Chambers-Hiss Confrontation

The session began at 5:35 P.M. on August 17, in room 1400 of the Commodore Hotel. Nixon opened the hearing by informing Hiss that since he himself had raised the possibility of a third party—George Crosley—the Committee had decided that Hiss and Chambers could resolve the question by confronting each other at this meeting.

The transcripts for that day, and Nixon's personal memoranda, vividly captured the scene:

> From the moment Hiss arrived he was edgy, nervous, hostile, and on the defensive. He complained that if the hearing lasted more than fifteen minutes he would be late for a dinner engagement. He implied that the Committee had leaked his secret testimony of the day before to the press. Following that, he pleaded that he was not in the best mood to testify because of his shock upon learning of his friend Harry Dexter White's death.
>
> A staff investigator was then asked to bring in Whittaker Chambers who was waiting in the adjoining room. After a few seconds, they entered through the door at Hiss's rear, and, walking behind him, went to the davenport and sat down. But in all this time, Hiss did not once turn to look at the man he claimed he was so anxious to meet. Instead, he kept his eyes on

the Committee, staring straight ahead in stony silence.

The two men were asked to rise.

Nixon: Mr. Hiss, this man is Whittaker Chambers. Can you tell me now if you have ever known him?

Hiss: Before answering I would first like to hear him speak.

Nixon: Mr. Chambers, will you please state your name?

Chambers: My name is Whittaker Chambers.

Apparently Hiss was not satisfied. He approached the davenport until he was less than a foot from Chambers' face and then requested him to open his mouth wider so he could inspect his teeth. George Crowley's teeth were in poor condition, Hiss explained. He went on to say that this man's teeth seemed to have been improved by considerable dental work. He then addressed Chambers for the first time:

Hiss: Are you George Crosley?

Chambers: No, I am not. But you, I believe, are Alger Hiss.

Hiss took several steps backward as though reeling from a slap in the face. "I certainly am," he snapped.
Chambers nodded pleasantly. "That was my recollection."

Nixon asked Chambers if he had undergone any dental work since he had last seen Hiss. Chambers replied that he had had a few teeth extracted and other minor improvements. Hiss then demanded the name of the dentist who had worked on Chambers' teeth.

The charade had gone far enough. "Mr. Hiss, are you telling this Committee that a dentist will have to tell you the details of his work before you can identify this man?" Nixon asked, his patience wearing thin.

"Well, he looks different in other respects, too—his jowls and so forth," replied Hiss, sounding unsure of his words.

Hiss's Defense Falters

The crack in Hiss's defense widened to a chasm. He refuted his own testimony of the day before, and claimed that he had not been paid a penny on his rental agreement with Crosley, forgetting that he had already stated that he received about fifteen dollars on account. He stubbornly maintained that he gave the "slightly collegiate model Ford with the sassy little trunk on the back" to Crosley, a man he knew only casually and who was a "deadbeat" at that. Moreover, he testified, he had given this "casual acquaintance" several loans even after he was delinquent in his rent and asserted that Crosley had also spent several nights at his home, the unpaid rent on his own apartment notwithstanding. As to Crosley's changed appearance, Hiss protested that "he could have had his face lifted."

Chambers' rebuttal was direct and unequivocal: "Alger and I were both Communist functionaries. I was a member of the Communist Party underground cell of which Mr. Hiss was also a member. We became friends, and it was at his suggestion that I rented his apartment on Twenty-ninth Street in Washington."

Stripling turned to Hiss and pointed out the many inconsistencies in his testimony. Then he reminded him once again of the corroborative evidence the Committee had gathered. "In view of all this," Stripling asked, "are you still prepared to testify under oath that you have never known this man?"

A long silence ensued. Then, his voice filled with cold hatred, Hiss replied: "I am now prepared to identify Whittaker Chambers as the man I knew as George Crosley."

The unexpected answer elicited a long sigh of relief from Chambers, the only sound in the room. McDowell turned to him and posed the key question: "Mr. Chambers, are you prepared to identify this man, Alger Hiss, as the one who was a member of the Communist Party and at whose home you stayed on a number of occasions?"

"He is the man," Chambers replied without hesitation. "He was a Communist when I knew him and he may be one today."

Hiss reacted as though he had been jabbed with an electric needle. He leaped from his chair and strode over to Chambers until their faces were scant inches apart. Shaking his fist under Chambers' nose, his voice dramatic with Shakespearean overtones, he thundered, "I challenge you to repeat that statement outside of this Committee where you can be sued for libel—and I hope you do it damned quickly!"

It appeared that Hiss was about to strike Chambers, and an aide lightly placed a restraining hand on his arm. Hiss's voice rose an octave. "Sir, take your hand off me!" he shrieked.

When order was restored, Hiss again denied that he had ever been a Communist. He insisted that he had not known that George Crosley was a Communist, and again asserted that there was nothing unusual in his gift of a car to a "deadbeat" whom he scarcely knew.

Nixon brought the hearing to a close with, "Thank you, Mr. Hiss."

Snapped Hiss: "I don't reciprocate!"

The open admission by Hiss that he had known Chambers, even under a different name, helped lessen the public outcry against the Committee. But the last hurdle was not yet in sight, as Nixon knew. Chambers had been strangely reluctant to discuss the nature of his conversations at the weekly meetings held by his Communist Party cell, brushing the questions aside with "just recruiting matters and Party politics." Another obstacle loomed before the Committee: the need for proof, other than Chambers' unsupported accusation, that Hiss was a Communist.

Hiss's 1929 Ford

Nixon and his staff had been working ceaselessly to substantiate Chambers' story of the alleged transfer of Hiss's 1929 Ford, for here was the missing link in the chain of evidence that would determine, without question, which of the two men had lied. Late one evening, Nixon was examining the testimony when a wayward thought entered his mind. 'Suppose the transfer had not taken place in 1935 but, instead, a year earlier—or later!' On the following morning, his staff of investigators searched the records of the Department of Motor Vehicles in Washington for all auto transfers in the years 1934 and 1936. They hit paydirt! On August 23, just forty-eight hours before the public confrontation was to take place, they found the documents that, for Hiss, was the beginning of the end.

The Certificate of Transfer was dated, not in 1935, but on July 23, 1936. Notarized by a Marvin Smith, title to the car had been transferred to someone named William Rosen. Neither George Crosley nor Whittaker Chambers was mentioned anywhere. Also found was a Certificate of Title to a new Plymouth in the name of Alger Hiss. The document was dated September 7, 1935.

Within hours, Marvin Smith, the notary, was subpoenaed. "Yes," he swore, "Alger Hiss signed the Certificate of Transfer in my presence."

William Rosen, to whom the old Ford had been transferred, proved to be a hostile witness. A well-known Communist for many years, he invoked the Fifth Amendment, refusing to testify on the ground of self-incrimination.

Recalling that exhausting week prior to the next open

session, Nixon wrote in his memoirs:

> I put in longer hours and worked harder than I had in any time of my life. I stepped up my activity until I was spending eighteen to twenty hours a day at my office, and as August 25 approached, I began to notice the inevitable symptoms of tension. I was "mean" to live with at home. I lost interest in eating and skipped meals without even being aware of it. Getting to sleep became more and more difficult.

Hannah Nixon expressed a mother's anxieties when asked about her son's emotional and physical condition at that time. "The Hiss case, for Richard, was a crusade," explained Mrs. Nixon. "It was part of his nature to be thorough and sure. He despised communism, of course, because it opposed every moral precept he had known since childhood, but he was always careful to avoid any rash accusations. He was just as dedicated to protecting the innocent as he was in exposing the guilty. It is no secret that he is an ambitious man, but it was something more than ambition that drove him to work himself to the point of near collapse. He was convinced of the rightness of his cause."

Nixon agreed with his mother that he had reached a point of fatigue where he might be unable to go on. Recalling the day before the August 25 session, he said: "There is naturally a physical limitation on how long an individual can sustain activity of this intensity. Age has something to do with it. I found, for example, that at thirty-five my capacity for intense mental work was greater than at any time before or since. But even while the body can take such punishment for days, it cannot do so indefinitely."

"I recall the afternoon before the big hearing on the twenty-fifth. Bert Andrews stopped by my office. He exclaimed, 'You look like hell. You need some sleep.' By that time my case had been prepared and, at Andrews' insistence and for the first time in my life, I took a sleeping pill before going to bed. I slept for twelve hours and woke up the next morning physically refreshed, ready for the most important test I had had up to that time."

The revelation of Hiss's admission that he had indeed known Chambers by whatever name, brought out the Washington corps of newsmen in strength. The caucus room, where Hiss had appeared three weeks earlier, was again packed. Although it was a sweltering day, every seat in the spectators gallery was taken.

Hiss fought like a cornered animal, but, in his desperation, he lost whatever vestige of rational thinking he possessed. His denials bordered on foolishness. He contradicted his own earlier testimony. He invoked the names of highly-placed officials in the Democratic Party, accusing the Committee of persecuting him in an effort to discredit the Roosevelt and Truman administrations.

But Nixon would not be dissuaded by Hiss's fulminations. With grim persistence he adhered to the evidence at hand. He quoted source after source to prove that George Crosley had never existed, except in his fertile mind. He grilled Hiss unmercifully about the Ford, proving by the very date of transfer that he still had the car in his possession a year after he swore he had parted company with "Crosley," and that, as the document showed, he had not turned the car over to Chambers *or* Crosley, but instead had given it to a Communist Party organizer—exactly as Chambers had charged.

Hiss made a lame attempt to change his story, implying that the Committee and the recording secretary had misquoted and misunderstood his previous testimony. He now stated that he had not meant to say he had given or sold the car to Crosley, but that he had "only given Crosley the *use* of the car."

"But why would you even lend a car to a man who had welshed on his rent?" Nixon persisted.

"These were housekeeping details which a busy government

official couldn't possibly be expected to remember," Hiss replied loftily.

Hiss had been on the stand for a full five hours before his accuser was called upon for his testimony. Chambers did not change his story one whit. Again he branded Hiss as a Communist, denied he had ever borrowed his car, and denied that he had ever been known as George Crosley—to Hiss or anyone else.

Nixon then delved into Chambers' possible motive for testifying against Hiss:

> *Nixon*: You were quite fond of Mr. Hiss?
>
> *Chambers*: Yes, he was perhaps my closest friend . . . the closest friend I ever had in the Communist Party.
>
> *Nixon*: Mr. Chambers, can you search your memory now to see what motive you can have for accusing Mr. Hiss of being a Communist at the present time?
>
> *Chambers*: What motive I can have?
>
> *Nixon*: Yes. Is there any grudge you have against Mr. Hiss because of something he has done to you?
>
> *Chambers*: The story has spread that in testifying against Mr. Hiss I am working out some old grudge or for motives of revenge or hatred. I do not hate Mr. Hiss. We were close friends, but we are caught in a tragedy of history. Mr. Hiss represents the concealed enemy against which we are all fighting, and I am fighting. I have testified against him with remorse and pity, but in a moment of history in which this nation now stands, so help me God, I could not do otherwise.

Chambers Appears on "Meet the Press"

The "tragedy of history" now rushed toward a climax that

neither Hiss nor Chambers desired, and one which Nixon had not foreseen.

Despite the many implications inherent in the case, Nixon had been able to prove—by corroborative evidence and testimony—that Chambers and Hiss had known each other, and that Hiss had given his car to a Communist. But this was certainly no crime! The entire case might have languished at this point, despite the clear fact that Hiss had committed perjury before a Congressional committee.

But Hiss had issued the one disastrous challenge from which he could not retreat: In their initial confrontation on August 17, Hiss dared Chambers to repeat his accusations outside the protection of Congressional privilege so that he could sue for libel. Ten days later, on August 27, and two days after their public meeting, Chambers obliged. Accepting an invitation from Lawrence Spivak to appear on the radio program "Meet the Press," the question that changed the complexion and direction of the case was posed by Ed Folliard of the *Washington Post*:

"Mr. Chambers, at this time are you willing to publicly repeat your charges against Alger Hiss?"

"Alger Hiss," Chambers replied firmly, "was a Communist and may still be one."

It was ironic that a *Post* reporter would light the fuse that detonated the explosive events which followed. The paper had constantly berated the Committee and supported Hiss from the day he first testified. However, when three weeks had passed since Chambers publicly denounced Hiss with no hint of legal action against him, the formerly sympathetic newspaper admonished Hiss editorially: "Mr. Hiss has created a situation in which he is obliged to put up or shut up. He has left himself no alternative."

In the latter part of September, with much of the press now following the *Post*'s lead, and facing the growing suspicions of many of his colleagues in government, Hiss filed a defamation of character suit in the U.S. District Court in

Baltimore, asking $50,000, a sum which he later increased to $75,000.

Nixon, believing that his participation in the case was now at an end, busied himself with speaking engagements on behalf of the Republican candidate for President, Thomas E. Dewey. His own re-election was assured, having won both the Republican and Democratic primaries in June.

Truman's victory over Dewey gave Nixon ample cause for worry. The President had left little doubt that he would either abolish the House Un-American Activities Committee or strip it of its powers—a relatively easy task now that the November 1948 elections had placed the Democrats in control of the Eighty-first Congress.

Nixon accepted the political change philosophically and decided that he would take his wife on a long-planned vacation, their first since his arrival in Washington almost two years earlier. On several occasions they had been on the verge of leaving the heat and bustle of the nation's capital for a few days of relaxation, but something "important" had always managed to delay their departure. The last "important event" was the Hiss case. Now, they were determined to enjoy the long-sought holiday. Together with a party of other Congressmen and their wives, they booked passage on the *S.S.* Panama for a ten-day cruise through the Canal Zone, sailing on December 2 from New York.

"This time, hon," he assured Pat, showing her the tickets, "I'm not going to let anything interfere with our vacation."

"I hope you're right," she said, smiling dubiously, "but you'll have to show me."

Richard and Pat had completed their packing and were looking forward to ten days of leisure when he was jolted upright by a UP dispatch in the Washington *Daily News*:

> The Justice Department is about ready to drop its investigation of the celebrated Alger Hiss-Whittaker

Chambers controversy, it was learned today . . . Department officials said privately that unless additional evidence is forthcoming they are inclined to forget the whole thing. One Department source said that on the basis of available evidence, officials in charge of the case believe it would be unwise to take it before a Grand Jury.

Another newspaper story, however, suggested that the Department of Justice was not dropping the case because of the lack of evidence, but instead because Chambers had furnished documentary proof that Hiss was not only a Communist, but a spy for the Soviet Union. The revelations, it was further hinted, were too "hot" for public dissemination, and too damaging to the reputation of the Truman and Roosevelt Administrations.

On December 1, only twenty-four hours before sailing time, Nixon telephoned Stripling and together they drove to Westminster to question Chambers. Pat, vastly disappointed, and dreading another postponement of their vacation, prepared sandwiches for them so they would not find it necessary to stop for lunch. She waved them off, dry-eyed, but suspiciously close to tears.

They arrived late in the afternoon, and tried to learn the nature of the documents Chambers had turned over to the court. "The papers document my charge that Hiss was a Communist, but I can't say anything more than that right now," Chambers told them. "I was warned to keep the evidence secret or be found guilty of contempt of court. I can only say that the documents were a real bombshell."

Nixon then learned that the papers were so volatile that Alex Campbell, Chief of the Justice Department's Criminal Division, had flown to Washington and confiscated the documents Chambers had furnished.

"You mean Campbell took the only papers you had?" Nixon demanded.

Chambers guessed the unasked meaning behind the question. "No, I wouldn't be that foolish," he replied. "My attorney has photostatic copies. If the Justice Department attempts to suppress the information I have another bombshell to offer."

"Don't turn that second bombshell over to anyone but the Committee," Nixon urged.

As they drove back to Washington, Nixon and Stripling discussed Chambers' use of the word "bombshell." He was rarely given to flamboyant expressions and Nixon was convinced that Chambers was anxious to convey a sense of urgency without risking retaliation by the courts or the Justice Department.

Before returning home, Nixon stopped off at the Committee's offices and signed a subpoena on Chambers for whatever documents were in his possession relating to the accusations he had made against Hiss during the Committee hearings. Stripling agreed to serve the subpoena the very next day—a move which would forestall the Democratic-controlled Justice Department should it try to bury the evidence and, thus, avoid embarrassment to the Administration.

"I really should have cancelled the vacation," Nixon said later, "but I didn't have the heart to disappoint Pat again." The next afternoon, on schedule, he and Pat boarded the *S.S. Panama* for what they hoped would be a pleasant cruise through the Canal Zone and back.

Pat was radiantly happy. "The best thing I like about this cruise is that we won't be interrupted by telephone calls or mail," she observed. The fact that radiograms were commonplace did not occur to either of them.

The Bombshell Evidence

The first of what was to be a stream of radio messages reached them when they had been at sea for only a day. On December 3, Bert Andrews of the *Herald Tribune* cabled:

> INFORMATION HERE IS THAT HISS-CHAMBERS CASE HAS PRODUCED NEW BOMBSHELL STOP INDICATIONS ARE THAT CHAMBERS HAS OFFERED NEW EVIDENCE STOP ALL CONCERNED SILENT STOP HOWEVER JUSTICE DEPARTMENT PARTIALLY CONFIRMS BY SAYING IT IS TOO HOT FOR COMMENT STOP

There was little in the message that he had not already learned or guessed after speaking with Chambers, but again that word "bombshell" returned to plague his thoughts. That same evening, as he and Pat were having dinner at the Captain's table with a number of other Congressmen, the purser brought another cable, this one from Stripling:

> SECOND BOMBSHELL OBTAINED BY SUBPOENA 1 A.M. FRIDAY STOP HEAT IS ON FROM PRESS AND OTHER PLACES STOP IMMEDIATE ACTION APPEARS NECESSARY STOP CAN YOU POSSIBLY GET BACK?

Nixon read the radiogram aloud and Pat threw up her hands in dismay. "Oh no, she cried. "Here we go again!"

The third cable arrived on Sunday when their ship was just entering the Caribbean area, on their third day out. This message, again from Andrews, could not be ignored:

> DOCUMENTS INCREDIBLY HOT STOP LINK TO HISS SEEMS CERTAIN STOP LINK TO OTHERS INEVITABLE STOP RESULTS SHOULD RESTORE FAITH IN NEED FOR COMMITTEE IF NOT IN SOME MEMBERS STOP NEW YORK JURY MEETS WEDNESDAY STOP COULD YOU ARRIVE TUESDAY AND GET DAY'S JUMP ON GRAND JURY STOP MY LIBERAL FRIENDS

DON'T LOVE ME NO MORE STOP NOR YOU STOP BUT FACTS ARE FACTS AND THESE FACTS ARE DYNAMITE STOP HISS'S WRITING IDENTIFIED ON THREE DOCUMENTS NOT PROOF HE GAVE THEM TO CHAMBERS BUT HIGHLY SIGNIFICANT STOP STRIPLING SAYS CAN PROVE WHO GAVE THEM TO CHAMBERS STOP LOVE TO PAT STOP (SIGNED) VACATION-WRECKER ANDREWS

Exchanging cablegrams with Stripling, Nixon made immediate arrangements to fly back to Washington. Stripling managed to get through to Defense Secretary James Forrestal who ordered a Coast Guard amphibian PBY to pick up the Nixons—who were then in Cuban waters—and to deliver them to Miami.

The Pumpkin Papers

He was greeted by a delegation of newsmen and photographers, all clamoring for an answer to a single question: "What about the pumpkin papers?"

Nixon could only shake his head in bewilderment. "Pumpkin papers? Is this some kind of joke? What are you talking about?"

Piecing the story together from their brief responses, Nixon learned that when Stripling served Chambers with the subpoena on December 2 which required that all pertinent documents be turned over to the Committee, Chambers had led Stripling and other staff investigators to his pumpkin patch at, or close to, midnight. Lifting the top from one of the pumpkins which had been hollowed out, Chambers withdrew five rolls of microfilm containing photographic copies of secret State Department documents.

'So that was why Chambers had been reluctant to discuss the subject of his conversations with Hiss and other Communist Party members,' Nixon thought. 'They had been discussing espionage!'*

Hiss, as it turned out, was himself responsible for the new dilemma in which he found himself. He had committed the cardinal sin of withholding the full truth from his own attorney—a surprising lapse considering that he too was a lawyer. His chief counsel, confident that Chambers' accusations could not be documented, had demanded that Chambers produce written proof of his former relationship with Hiss. To his dumbfounded amazement, Chambers did just that.

The events that led to the disclosure of the stolen documents equal anything that might be concocted by a fiction writer of spy stories. On November 14, Chambers had made a secret trip to the Brooklyn apartment of his wife's nephew, Nathan Levine. There, ten years earlier, immediately following his break with the Communist Party, Chambers had left a large, bulky envelope with instructions that its contents be made public only if he should be murdered. He had good reason to fear assassination; the material had been stolen from the files of the State Department and he, Chambers, had in turn stolen them from his Communist colleagues rather than pass them along to couriers for transmission to Russia. For him, it was a form of "life insurance."

---

*In his book, *Witness,* Whittaker Chambers explained that he had maintained silence about Hiss's role as a spy because his main objective was to expose the Communist underground, not to destroy Hiss. It was his hope that, with the evidence out in the open, Hiss might admit his Communist affiliations and join him in fighting subversion in the United States. But at the pretrial hearings in Baltimore, Hiss's attorneys subjected him to such a merciless third-degree, impugning his character, his honesty and his very manhood, that he began to think of fighting the devil with his own pitchfork. When his wife, Esther, was cross-examined with such ferocity that she was moved to tears, Chambers made up his mind to counterattack in kind. Hiss was determined to destroy Chambers forever. Fighting back, Chambers had no other recourse than to produce the evidence that would indelibly mark Hiss as a Soviet agent.

Congressman Nixon and HUAC investigator Robert Stripling examine the microfilm hidden by Whittaker Chambers in a hollowed-out pumpkin and then replaced in his pumpkin patch. The film-copies of secret government documents were stolen from both the State Department and the Communist Party, and kept by Chambers for ten years as "life insurance." The microfilm changed the case from one of subversion to one of spying.

Levine led Chambers to the actual hiding place—not in his own home but in another apartment occupied by his mother. There, tucked away in a long-unused dumb-waiter, lay the sealed envelope, covered with the dust and cobwebs of ten years' accumulation. Inside, still intact, were sixty-five typewritten pages of secret State Department documents, many of which were later identified as having been typed on Hiss's Woodstock typewriter in 1938. These included, three documents in Hiss's own handwriting, eight pages of classified State Department information in the handwriting of Harry

Dexter White, two strips of developed microfilm on which were reproduced additional State Department classified material, and three cylinders of undeveloped microfilm. Enlarged to their original size, the microfilm represented thousands of pages of copied and original State Department classified documents which, in their original form, would have been stacked four feet high.

On November 17, Chambers gave Hiss's attorneys the documented proof they had demanded; the sixty-five typed pages, the notes in Hiss's handwriting and the ten-year-old envelope which had contained the papers and films. This constituted the first "bombshell" Chambers had mentioned to Nixon. The second was the five rolls of microfilm Chambers had withheld as further "life insurance." It was this photographic evidence that was referred to by the press as the "pumpkin papers."*

Attempts to Quash the Proceedings

As a result of the first "bombshell," Chambers was summoned to appear before the blue-ribbon Grand Jury in New York on December 6—the day Nixon returned from his interrupted vacation. The question now arose as to whether the Committee should turn over the microfilm to the Justice Department and wash its hands of the whole affair. The members decided against it for a number of reasons: strong doubt existed as to the Justice Department's ability to resist the political pressures to drop the case against Hiss; the Depart-

---

*It is popularly believed that the so-called "pumpkin papers," which were not papers at all but microfilm, were kept in the hollowed-out pumpkin for ten years. Actually they were hidden in the same envelope as the other material, and were kept in the old dumb-waiter from 1938 to the year of the Hiss-Chambers trial in 1948. After retrieving the microfilm from the Brooklyn apartment, Chambers kept the five rolls in his own house until the day before he gave them to Stripling. On that last day, fearing that Hiss's investigators might find them, he hid the evidence overnight in the pumpkin and replaced it among the other pumpkins in the patch so that it appeared to be undisturbed.

ment had done absolutely nothing to investigate the disclosures of espionage after Chambers had furnished the court with the typewritten pages and memoranda written in Hiss's own hand; and, finally, in a brazen effort to quash the entire proceedings, a story had been leaked to the press that the Justice Department was about to drop the Hiss-Chambers case "for lack of evidence," two weeks after they took possession of the first "bombshell."

But the "informed report" that clinched Nixon's determination to retain the "pumpkin papers" was the persistent story, attributed to the usual "unimpeachable sources," that the Department was planning to indict not Hiss, but *Chambers*! Other press reports quoted Hiss supporters as declaring that the documents were innocuous, not in the least dangerous to the national security, and that no harm was done by their removal from the State Department files.

Fire flashed in Nixon's eyes. Was there no end to the impudence of Hiss's apologists? On that same day, Monday, December 6, he sought out John Peurifoy, Assistant Secretary of State for security affairs, and Under-Secretary Sumner Welles. Both officials acknowledged (and on the following day testified under oath) that a foreign government who acquired even one of the documents, would have been able to break the secret State Department code. The Soviets, in possession of these papers, would not only be in a position to decipher the secret messages to United States embassies and consulates throughout the world, but also to learn of our confidential dealings with other governments during the time immediately prior to the Stalin-Hitler pact.

William C. Bullitt, United States Ambassador to France and the Soviet Union during that critical period, was aghast at the enormity of the crime. "These coded messages reveal the identities of my best sources," said Bullitt. "They reveal the names of important officials of other governments who were furnishing me with confidential information. These documents killed them off."

The St. Louis *Post-Dispatch*, formerly as staunch a supporter of Hiss as the *Washington Post* had been, editorialized:

> Whatever else President Truman may say in the future about the spy investigation, he cannot again call it a "red herring." It is no longer a red herring after the release of more than two hundred documents which are out of their places in the confidential files of the State Department.

Apparently Truman failed to read the editorial. Three days later, he again castigated Nixon and his staff as "witch-hunters belaboring a red herring."

December 6th continued as the most hectic day in the course of the entire investigation. It was imperative that Nixon query Chambers about the microfilm, but Chambers was testifying in New York and the Justice Department refused to permit him to appear before the Committee in Washington. Left with no alternative, Nixon decided to leave for New York at once.

His sense of urgency was well founded. The term of the Grand Jury in New York would be over in just nine days. Should it fail to return an indictment against Hiss before its expiration on December 14th, the case could not be presented to a new grand jury for many months. In that event, Hiss would have a golden opportunity to muster all his political support—and it was still considerable—to avoid an indictment. Moreover, in January—now only three weeks away—the Chairman of the HUAC would no longer be a Republican, but a Democrat, loyal to Truman who had flatly promised speedy abolition of the Committee.

Authenticity of Pumpkin "Papers"

As Nixon was about to leave for Union Station to board

the noon train for New York, the telephone rang. The caller was Keith Lewis of the Eastman Kodak Company. He had been asked to check the microfilm to determine its age. It was no ilde request. In a desperate attempt to support his denials, Hiss's supporters argued that the "pumpkin papers" had not been filmed ten years ago as Chambers claimed, but only after the Committee hearings had begun. "The films are phony," they cried."It's a frame-up!"

Stripling's face mirrored complete shock as he listened to the caller. Nixon later wrote: "His voice was strained when at last he was able to speak: 'Are you telling me this type of film was not even manufactured until 1945?' Mechanically, Stripling replaced the receiver in its cradle and turned to me. 'It's all over,' he said obviously shaken. 'Eastman Kodak didn't make the kind of film Chambers gave us until 1945. He couldn't possibly have microfilmed those papers in 1938 as he said—not on *this* film.'"

They were too stunned to talk. So it was Chambers who had lied all along! They had maligned Hiss—an innocent man —and almost destroyed his life. All the hard work, the endless hours, the loss of sleep and neglect of their families since the investigation began had been for nothing. "It seemed we had been taken in by a diabolically clever maniac who had finally made a fatal mistake."

Within a few minutes, Nixon had Chambers on the long-distance phone. "I want a few straight answers from you," he said grimly. "Did you or didn't you swear to me that you filmed the documents in 1938?"

"Yes, why?" There was no concern in Chambers' voice— just curiosity.

"I'll tell you why," Nixon snapped. "The Eastman Kodak people just informed us that they did not make the type of film you turned over to us until 1945. What have you got to say about that?"

There was dead silence at the other end of the wire. When Chambers finally answered it was like the despairing cry of a wounded animal: "I don't know what to say. God must be against me."

All the disappointment and frustration that welled from deep inside him now erupted in a burst of rage—an extraordinary surge of fury for the usually self-controlled Nixon. "You're going to need a better answer than that," he grated. "We'll be in New York this evening and we'll expect to see you at the Commodore Hotel. You'd better be there, understand?"

Nixon slammed the receiver down without waiting for a reply. He turned to Stripling and, with a heavy heart, told him to call in the Washington press corps who had been covering the Committee hearings. There was nothing to be gained from postponing a public admission of his terrible mistake. "This will be the biggest crow-eating performance in the history of Capitol Hill," he said glumly.

Five minutes before the press conference was to take place, and with several reporters already waiting in the outer office, another telephone call came in for Stripling. It was Keith Lewis of Eastman Kodak again. Stripling used the phone on Nixon's desk to be out of earshot of the reporters in the reception room. As he listened to the brief message, his expression underwent a transformation from gloom to utter joy. "What? Say that again! You were wrong? You did manufacture that type of film in 1938, but discontinued it during the war?"

Chambers Told the Truth

There was no need for further explanation. Stripling put the receiver down, let out a Texas rebel yell, grabbed Nixon by the arms and together they danced around the room in a frenzy of unadulterated delight. Chambers had told the truth —they would never doubt him again!

The press conference was brief, a short statement that the Eastman Kodak Company had manufactured the film at the time Chambers said he had used it. Nixon then placed a call to Chambers to tell him the good news and to apologize for his churlish manner. But he could not be reached. In any event, Nixon promised himself that he would make amends to Chambers when he met with him at nine o'clock that evening at the Commodore Hotel in New York.

Nixon's message that the film could not possibly have been manufactured in 1938 was a shattering blow to Whittaker Chambers. That one statement, he knew very well, automatically branded everything else that he had said as a lie. He stared at the phone dully after having hung up on Nixon, then put on his topcoat and left his hotel room. For hours, he paced the streets, unseeing, heedless of traffic lights, oblivious to the sights and sounds and smells of crowded New York. Head bowed, he shuffled aimlessly toward the East River, a man whose future was behind him, a man without hope. He gazed at the sluggish, dark water, greasy with oil-slick. He thought of the lovely, clear streams that bubbled so joyously near his Westminster farm. A sob welled up in his aching throat. His thoughts no longer dwelt on the developing Hiss case, but instead on Richard Nixon, the one man who had believed in him—the only real friend he had in the world. And now Nixon had abandoned him. "Oh, Dick, I told the truth!" he cried silently. "I would *never* lie to you, my friend."*

Somehow he managed to find his way back to his hotel. There he learned, from Nixon's secretary, who had been instructed to keep calling him, that a later report had fully exonerated him. But he was unable to rid himself of his black depression, and, for the first time in his life, Chambers bowed

---

*They were indeed friends. In *Witness,* Chambers wrote: "Throughout the most trying phases of the case, Nixon and his family, and sometimes his parents, were at our farm, encouraging me and comforting my family. My children have caught him lovingly in a nickname. To them, he is always 'Nixie,' the kind and the good, about whom they will tolerate no nonsense. His somewhat martial Quakerism sometimes amused and always heartened me."

to the pressures that threatened to engulf him. Late that night he made an unsuccessful attempt at suicide.

Nixon, with rare discernment, perceived the inner torment that wracked Chambers' very soul. In a poignant and sensitive paragraph, he wrote in his memoirs:

> Looking back, I think I can understand how he must have felt. His career was gone. His reputation was ruined. His wife and children had been humiliated. But all this would not have mattered to him if the cause for which he had taken these calculated risks had some chance to prevail. And now it did seem that "God was against him." From the time he testified on August 3, through the months of summer and fall, I had been the one public official who had stood by him, and on whom he thought he could count. And now I was deserting him. Chambers was to go through many crises during Hiss's two trials, but this proved to be his most difficult moment. It seemed the height of irony that I was the one who found it necessary to put him through this ordeal—and all because of a mistaken report.

Nixon arrived in New York at 7:30 that evening (still December 6) and was confronted by representatives of the Justice Department—not at the Commodore Hotel, but at Grand Central Station. Accompanying him back to his hotel, they began a verbal battle. The Justice Department insisted throughout the stormy encounter that Nixon hand over the microfilms to them and that, thereafter, he take no further action on the case.

Nixon clearly understood the motives behind their pleading. He knew that the Justice Department had no alternative but to suppress any evidence that might embarrass the Truman Administration. As long as the Committee retained possession of the microfilms, and as long as they continued to raise the threat of public hearings, the Department could follow no course other than the expeditious prosecution of the case.

They reached a compromise. In return for copies of the microfilmed documents, the Department agreed to allow Nixon and his fellow Committee members to question Chambers even though he was bound to silence by their subpoena.

Chambers' Unbridled Testimony

Chambers was on the stand from nine o'clock until midnight. He finally admitted under oath that he, Hiss and other government officials were something more than just members of the Communist Party; that they, in fact, had been spies for the Soviet Union. Explaining their *modus operandi*, Chambers described the general pattern: Alger Hiss would steal documents and, at the close of the working day, he would smuggle them out in his brief case. He would then turn some of the papers over to Chambers who would have them microfilmed by Communist photographers and return the originals to Hiss the same night. Hiss would replace them in their proper files the next morning. At other times, Alger's wife, Priscilla, would type summaries of the secret papers at home on the family Woodstock typewriter. These copies were then microfilmed and given to Chambers who, in turn, would pass them on to Colonel Bykov, his superior in the espionage ring. Bykov, an officer in Soviet intelligence, would then transmit the data to Moscow.

Having made up his mind to forsake the Communist Party, Chambers began to horde the documents given him by Hiss, White, and other members of the spy apparatus, instead of transmitting them to Colonel Bykov. This was the "life insurance" he had alluded to, should his former Red associates threaten to kill him. It was also the evidence he had turned over to his own and Hiss's lawyers in Baltimore, and to the Subcommittee in Washington—the two "bombshells" that gripped the attention of an entire nation.

A month earlier, during the August 16 hearings, Hiss had used the expletive "damn" when describing the 1929 Ford and the rug which he claimed "Crosley" had obtained from a wealthy patron and then given to him as part payment on his rent. Now the true story was revealed. Chambers had been presented with not one but *six* Bokhara rugs by Colonel Bykov as a token of appreciation for the volume and importance of the classified papers the Hiss-Chambers combine had been furnishing to Soviet intelligence. The rugs were to be distributed to the members of the espionage ring as an expression of gratitude by the Russian government. Chambers dutifully gave one to Harry Dexter White, another to Alger Hiss and those that remained to the other co-conspirators. The rug, according to Chambers' sworn testimony, was a gift pure and simple, and had nothing to do with rental payments.

"Richard looked so tired I thought he would break apart," said his mother anxiously when her son returned to Washington. But the time for relaxation had not yet arrived. Although convinced that the evidence against Hiss was now so overwhelming that the Justice Department would be compelled to seek an indictment, Nixon intuitively felt that the ordeal was not over. He was right. On December 8, the earlier rumors that Chambers, and not Hiss, would be indicted became a reality. Nixon learned that the Department of Justice planned to ask the Grand Jury to indict Chambers for lying. He had committed perjury, said the Department, when he denied any knowledge of espionage. True enough, he had lied to the Grand Jury before he produced the microfilmed and typed documents but he was also the key witness against Hiss. An indictment of Chambers would inevitably result in the complete destruction of the entire case the Committee had so painstakingly developed.

The Nixon Nobody Knows 255

Nixon was now left with only one choice: he would take the issue to the people and, through the weight of public opinion, force the Justice Department to seek an indictment of Hiss. That same evening of August 8, at an open Committee meeting heavily attended by the press, and including the newsmen representing UP, AP and the radio networks, Nixon announced:

> We have learned from unimpeachable sources that the Justice Department now plans to indict Chambers for perjury before any of the other people named by Chambers in this conspiracy are indicted. It is clear that the Justice Department does not want this Committee to hear any witnesses scheduled to go before the Grand Jury, and is bringing pressure on the Committee to drop its investigation.
>
> Chambers has confessed. He is in the open. He is no longer a danger to our security. If Chambers is indicted first, Hiss and the others will go free because the witness against them will have been discredited as a perjurer. The Administration is trying to silence this Committee. But we will not entrust to the Justice Department and to the Administration the sole responsibility for protecting the national security in this case. We intend to do everything we can to see that the Department does not use the device of indicting Chambers as an excuse for not proceeding against Hiss who has continued to decline to tell any of the truth up to this time.

The next day, President Truman brushed aside Nixon's announcement with the monotonous charge that the Hiss-Chambers investigation was a "red herring."*

---

*President Truman's contempt for Hiss equalled Nixon's. When shown copies of the stolen documents by a representative of the Justice

But Nixon had scored. On the following day, the *Washington Post*, among Truman's most ardent supporters, and certainly no Committee partisan, observed:

> The President's attitude suggests a desire to suppress the whole business, and the indictment of Mr. Chambers at this time would certainly be a step in that direction. If this is the Administration's policy, it is incredibly shortsighted.

Nixon, with the cards stacked against him, but always the canny poker player, beat Truman and the upper echelon officials of the Justice Department at their own game. With only six days remaining before the Grand Jury's term was to end, the Department finally gave J. Edgar Hoover permission to complete the investigation his agents had started at least five years before. In a classic case of crime detection, the FBI, on December 13, uncovered evidence that directly pointed to Hiss's guilt—a batch of old letters admittedly typed by Priscilla Hiss on the same Woodstock machine on which Chambers said she typed the incriminating documents. The type, of course, matched.*

Department, Truman thumbed through the pages, muttering, "Why, the son of a bitch—he betrayed his country!" Yet, in his next press conference, on August 9, 1948, the President again called the Committee's investigation a "red herring." Privately, however, he told a friend, "Of course Hiss is guilty. But that damned Committee isn't interested in that. All it cares about is politics, and as long as they try to make politics out of this Communist issue I am going to label their activities for what they are—a 'red herring.' "

*When asked by the prosecutor to explain how, in the face of his denials, his wife's letters and the State Department copies were typed on the same Woodstock, Hiss drew derisive laughter from the spectators and newsmen in the courtroom with his answer: "Until the day I die, I shall wonder how Whittaker Chambers got into my house to use my typewriter."

The Nixon Nobody Kno

Grand Jury Indic

On December 15, all nineteen members of the f Grand Jury voted to indict Hiss on two counts of perjury: first, that he had lied when he stated under oath that he had not illegally removed any secret documents from the State Department and given them to Whittaker Chambers; and second, that he had lied when he testified that he had not seen Chambers after January, 1937.

The first trial, during which time the FBI found the Woodstock typewriter on which the documents were copied by Mrs. Hiss, began May 31, 1949, and ended on July 8, with the jury deadlocked eight to four for conviction. The hung jury came as no surprise to the Committee.

"Federal Judge Samuel H. Kaufman was so completely biased in favor of Hiss, I really didn't expect a different outcome," Nixon stated. "The judge, for political reasons, would not permit two prosecution witnesses to testify. His attitude, throughout the trial, was obviously sympathetic to Hiss. Frankly, I believe that the entire Truman Administration was behind Hiss, because a guilty verdict would have lent credence to the many charges of communist infiltration into the government."

The second trial began on November 17, 1949, and ended January 21, 1950. This time the jury found Hiss guilty on both counts. He was sentenced by Judge Henry W. Goddard to five years in prison, with the verdict and sentence upheld by the U.S. Circuit Court of Appeals on December 7 of the same year. Appeal was then made to the U.S. Supreme Court, but on March 12, 1951, the Court refused to review the case.*
Hiss's libel suit against Chambers in Baltimore was, of course, dismissed following the conviction.

Alger Hiss was confined in the Lewisburg Federal Prison

---

*Hiss had to be indicted and convicted not for espionage, but for perjury—for lying when he denied committing espionage. The statute of limitations, requiring prosecution for espionage within three years after the crime had been committed, had long expired.

in Pennsylvania where he served three years and eight months of his five year sentence, with time off for good behavior. He was released in November, 1954, at the age of fifty, and found employment as a stationery salesman, an occupation he follows to this day.

Whittaker Chambers, who became a lifelong, devoted friend of Nixon, retired to his farm in Maryland where he wrote his autobiography. He died on July 9, 1961, at the age of sixty.

Hiss Case Aftermath

"The Hiss case brought me national fame, but it also left a residue of hatred and hostility toward me," said Nixon in retrospect. "I refer not only to the Communists but to much of the intellectual community as well. This hostility remains even today."

Bert Andrews, the *Herald Tribune* correspondent who had formed a warm friendship with Nixon, summed up the motivation for this continuing attitude: "The surest way to make yourself unpopular with anyone who considers himself an intellectual is to prove him wrong once he has gone out on a limb on an issue so charged with emotion as the Hiss case."

The undisguised hatred of Nixon that followed the Hiss-Chambers case is best illustrated by Nixon's own words:

> As an aftermath of the case, I was subjected to an utterly unprincipled and vicious smear campaign. Bigamy, forgery, drunkenness, insanity, thievery, anti-Semitism, perjury—the whole gamut of misconduct in public office, ranging from unethical to downright criminal activities—all these were among the charges that were hurled against me, some publicly and others through whispering campaigns which were even more difficult to counteract.

Truman, with his usual perspicacity, had correctly foreseen

the political mileage that Nixon and the Republican Party would be able to extract from the Hiss case should an indictment and a conviction be obtained. Five days after Hiss's conviction, on January 26, 1950, Nixon delivered a major address on the floor of Congress in which he quoted the massive evidence that linked communist infiltration, subversion and espionage to the negligent Truman Administration and its predecessors.

The speech, delivered to 150 Congressmen and a packed press gallery, was made the day after the Secretary of State, Dean Acheson, had said, "I do not intend to turn my back on Alger Hiss." No one will ever know what prompted Acheson to issue the statement which was seen by most Americans as an insult to the intelligence of the American people in general and to Nixon and his fellow Committee members in particular.

The *Congressional Record* of January 26, 1950, records Nixon's biting response:

> Why was it that Administration officials persisted in their refusal to act through the years, even when substantial evidence of espionage activities was brought to their attention . . . ? There are some who claim that Administration officials failed to act because they were Communist or pro-Communist. But the great majority of our officials were not in this category, and I cannot accept this accusation as a fair one.
>
> What was happening was that Administration leaders were treating the reports of Communist espionage on a "politics as usual" basis . . . [And] because they treated Communist infiltration into our American institutions like an ordinary petty political scandal, the Administration officials responsible for this failure to act against the Communist conspiracy, rendered the greatest possible disservice to the people of the nation.

> ... The great lesson which should be learned from the Alger Hiss case is that we are not just dealing with espionage agents who get thirty pieces of silver to obtain the blueprint of a new weapon—the Communists, of course, do that too—but this is a far more sinister type of activity because it permits the enemy to guide and shape our policy; it disarms and dooms our diplomats in advance to defeat before they go to conferences; traitors in the high councils of our own government make sure that the deck is stacked on the Soviet side of the diplomatic table.
>
> America today stands almost alone between communism and the free nations of the world. We owe a solemn duty, not only to our own people, but to free people everywhere on both sides of the iron curtain, to expose this sinister conspiracy for what it is, to roll back the Red tide which to date has swept everything before it, and to prove to peoples everywhere that the hope of the world lies not in turning toward totalitarian dictatorship, but in developing a strong, free and intelligent democracy.

Truman's hatred of Nixon grew with the years as the importance of the revelations in the Hiss-Chambers case was superceded by the serious, overall charges of communist influence in government. Indeed, Nixon continued to use the Hiss case and its relationship to communist infiltration until 1956, when he magnanimously "forgave" Adlai Stevenson for recommending Hiss for the presidency of the Carnegie Endowment Fund.

The issue of communism did not end here with Richard Nixon. It continued as a major force as he approached the next rung in his political career—specifically, in the 1950 campaign for a Senate seat in which he faced the formidable Helen Gahagan Douglas.

7
The Nixon-Douglas "Debate"

I have consistently maintained that where the record of an individual indicates how he might approach an international or a national problem, that record should be brought to the attention of the people. I expect mine *to be brought forth.*

Richard Nixon
(From an interview with
Henry Brandon, *The Sunday Times*, London)
January 4, 1959

Communism Issue Lingers On

IN ITS SUCCESSIVE STAGES, a rare fusion of circumstance and talent has continually marked Richard Nixon's rise from the simple days of obscurity in a desert hamlet to the exciting years of Washington. His election to the House of Representatives transformed the impossible into the possible. His legislative record as a first-term Congressman and his triumph in the Hiss case made the possible probable. And his 1950 Senate race against California Congresswoman Helen Gahagan Douglas made the probable inevitable.

The 1950 campaign was a two-way donnybrook that differed very little from scores of other free-swinging contests taking place throughout the nation in that election year. Nor could it have been otherwise, considering the temper of the times.

The complacency with which many Americans had hitherto viewed communism on the domestic as well as the international front had slowly changed to anger. The Soviet Union's conquest of the Balkan countries (at the same time that it was brazenly accusing the United States of imperialism) aroused the ire of nearly everyone. The cold war attempt by Russia to starve the entire population of West Berlin into submission—an aggression that was frustrated by our air lift which brought tons of food, fuel, medicines and other necessities to that city's beleaguered people—added to the wave of indignation that swept the country. This anger was again heightened when Mainland China fell to the Communists—a loss which many people felt, and still feel, could have been prevented. On the domestic scene, there was widespread protest against a Truman administration which refused to prosecute espionage agents even after their activities were known to the authorities.

All of this discontent and resentment, at a time when there was no longer any doubt that the United States was being victimized by known spies, inevitably resulted in the conviction of Alger Hiss in a trial which many liberals, for reasons they have never explained, used as a cloak in which to enshrine Hiss as a martyr. As for Nixon, a combination of talent and timing placed him in the very center of the communism issue and also made him the main target of the left. He had already been castigated by the liberals and their more radical cohorts when, during his campaign against Voorhis, he exposed the presense of Communists in the highest ranks of organized labor. But, now he was labelled ". . . the Fascist who railroaded Hiss to prison." This was one of the milder phrases used to denigrate Nixon. The full litany of abusive charges Nixon was forced to endure was quite extensive.

"Nixon could afford to shrug it off," wrote a columnist in the Los Angeles *Examiner*. "He not only had the truth on his side, he had Murray Chotiner, and you can't beat that combination."

At the very start of the 1950 Senate race, Nixon announced that the issue on which he intended to base his campaign would be "simply the choice between freedom and state socialism." But this central theme quickly became intertwined with the one issue that seemed to permeate the political atmosphere of the day—the issue of communism. What Mrs. Douglas' associates conveniently neglected to mention, however, was that the "Pink Lady" charge was initially leveled against her, not by Nixon or any other Republican, but by her fellow *Democrats* during the primaries of that turbulent year.

Nixon Takes the Plunge

Nixon made up his mind to run for the Senate as early as September, 1949, but mentioned it to no one but his wife until October of that year when he informed his old friend, Herman Perry, of his intentions.

To Nixon's consternation, his former supporters on the "Committee of One Hundred," who had helped launch his race against Voorhis, met his declaration with open hostility. Once again, Nixon met the challenge head-on. He phoned his former law partner, Tom Bewley, and asked if he would be willing to hold a meeting of the most influential Committee members, without fanfare, and in Bewley's own office. Bewley agreed. He put in another call to Republican Chairman Roy

RICHARD M. NIXON
12TH DISTRICT, CALIFORNIA

COMMITTEES:
EDUCATION AND LABOR
UN-AMERICAN ACTIVITIES

Congress of the United States
House of Representatives
Washington, D. C.

October 7, 1949

Air Mail   Confidential

Mr. Herman Perry
424 North Friends Avenue
Whittier, California

Dear Herman:

    After considering all the factors involved, I have definitely decided to file for the Republican nomination for United States Senator in 1950. While I do not believe that this is the time for a public announcement, I wanted you to know what my decision was, and you are at liberty to disclose this information in confidence whenever you feel it would be helpful in furthering the campaign.

    As far as the public announcement is concerned, my present intention is to time it after I have had an opportunity to make a speaking tour through the northern part of the state. The final decision on this matter, of course, will be made after consultation with you and others who are interested in the campaign.

    I shall look forward to seeing you next week.

    With best regards,

                               Sincerely,

                               Richard Nixon, M.C.

RN:vc

In this confidential letter to his old friend and political mentor, Herman Perry, Representative Richard Nixon reveals his decision to run for a seat in the United States Senate.

Day, whom he had heard was favorable to him, and asked that he speak to the others in support of his Senatorial ambitions.

The meeting, never publicized, was a stormy one. Among the holdouts was Frank Jorgensen, a man who had supported Nixon enthusiastically in the 1948 campaign.

"Most of us were against Dick's ambition to run for Senator because it was the first time in a decade that we had been able to put a Republican in Congress. We figured he was firmly entrenched, and we saw no purpose in risking a sure thing for the vague possibility that he might win the Senate race. All we might wind up with could be the loss of a seat in the House and another loss at the polls. After all, statewide, the Democrats outnumbered us three to one."

Roy Day rose to Nixon's defense, arguing that Nixon's record as a Congressman would help him capture votes in both parties. Herman Perry, another holdout despite his many years of friendship with the Nixon family, jumped excitedly to his feet and roared, "Mr. Day, you obviously do not have the best interests of this community at heart. You are nothing but a politician."

"I am not about to ask a young man to sacrifice himself because of our petty fears," Day retorted, his face flushed.

The meeting ended on a note of uncertainty. It was apparent that he would have their individual support but not the collective strength they might have given had they acted together as a "Committee of One Hundred."

Nixon publicly announced his candidacy on November 3, 1949, a full year before the elections. Starting his Senatorial campaign with a tempo that never slowed, he declared:

> The issue is simply the choice between freedom and state socialism. They can call it planned economy, the Fair Deal or social welfare—but it is still the same old Socialist baloney, any way you slice it. Believe me, I am well aware of the Communist threat. I do not

discount it. However, I am convinced that an even greater threat to our free institutions is presented by that group of hypocritical and cynical men who, under the guise of providing political panaceas for certain social and economic problems, are selling the American birthright for a mess of political pottage. Slowly but surely they are chipping away the freedoms which are essential to the survival of a healthy, strong and productive nation.

All this was rather heady stuff for the good people of Pomona who had gathered to hear Nixon's first speech in his try for the Senate. If they had assembled to hear him affirm that he would continue to send free government pamphlets on baby care, home planning, or the latest innovations in citrus culture, they had much to learn about this earnest, maturing politician whose flamboyant rhetoric reminded the oldtimers among them of the thunderous orations given by the still-revered William Jennings Bryan.

"I am convinced beyond the shadow of a doubt that the election of 1950 will be the most crucial election in our nation's history," Nixon warned, his obvious sincerity doing much to soften the outrageous statement. "Of course," he added quickly, "I realize that this has been said before with reference to past elections, but all we need do is survey the situation here and abroad to confirm this conviction. . . . There is only one way we can win, so let me make this perfectly clear: we intend to put on a fighting, rocking, socking campaign."

He was as good as his word. Not for him were the baby-kissing gestures so dear to the hearts of yesteryear's office-seeker. Nor was he given to bear-hugging embraces or the avuncular smiles whose sincerity started and stopped at the lips. Travelling about the state in a borrowed Mercury station wagon, with Pat always by his side, Nixon carried on a two-fisted campaign in which he appealed to the Democrats as well as the Republicans for votes.

"The Democratic Party's record, in the past, has been one of great distinction," he began. "But today, nationally and in our own state of California, it has been captured and is completely controlled by a group of ruthless, cynical seekers after power; men committed to policies and principles completely foreign to those of the Party's founders. If those early, great Democrats could see the phony doctrines and ideologies now being foisted upon the American people, Thomas Jefferson and Andrew Jackson would turn over in their graves." He then appealed to his listeners to regard his candidacy as "a banner of freedom which all people, regardless of party can follow."

Opposing Nixon was Congresswoman Helen Gahagan Douglas, among the first of the Hollywood luminaries to enter politics. A woman of exceptional beauty, with rare talent as an actress and possessing a fine mind, she was the right woman at the wrong time. Had she campaigned for the Senate a few years earlier, or later, there is little question but that she would have enjoyed an outstanding political career. Circumstances were against her from the very outset. She was devoured by her own colleagues who provided much of the ammunition her Republican opponents were to fire back at her. Later, as it turned out, her advisers were simply no match for the Nixon-Chotiner team whose gift for the synecdoche kept her continually on the defensive, defending positions that added little to her campaign efforts, and usually detracted from them.

Floundering and Feuding Democrats

It all started during the pre-primary season when Helen Douglas decided to challenge incumbent Democrat Sheridan Downey for his Senate seat. She came out of her corner with both arms flailing, charging that the Senator was a mouthpiece for big business whose record in Washington was close to zero. Downey retorted that she had thrown in her lot with "extremists." Her personality and the "gut issues" which she expounded, however, soon gave her a decided edge in the public opinion polls, and two months before the primaries Downey withdrew from the race, claiming ill health. Mrs. Douglas might have fared better had she then courted his favor and at least made an attempt to win him over to her side. Instead, she issued a blast in which she termed his "for reasons of ill health," a cheap gimmick, thereby earning his eternal enmity.

Downey's successor in the Democrat primary was Manchester Boddy, publisher of the Los Angeles *Daily News*. His principle supporter, not too surprisingly, was Sheridan Downey.

The change in candidates did not alter the Congresswoman's vigorous style in the least: "It's the same tired plot with a new leading man," she declared.

Boddy had his own ideas as to the best strategy to employ in defeating Mrs. Douglas. Communism as a threat to the United States was an issue that was being used in a number of states with good results—depending on whether it was the accuser or the victim who was making the judgment. In Florida, Claude Pepper had been tagged as "Red Pepper." It was easy enough to label Helen Douglas as "The Pink Lady." Boddy fired his biggest campaign guns with his first speech:

> There is indisputable evidence of a statewide conspiracy on the part of a small subversive clique of red-hots to capture, through stealth and cunning, the nerve centers of our Democratic Party, and by so doing to capture the votes of real Democratic citizens.

Boddy then went on to add that this clique had drawn up "a blueprint for subversive dictatorship that would convert the Democratic Party to serve the twisted purposes of these red-hots."

There was no doubt in anyone's mind that Boddy's reference to the "red-hots" included Mrs. Douglas. But, Sheridan Downey, although out of the race, was not satisfied with subtleties. He proceeded to expand on what had heretofore been indirect insinuations!

"Mrs. Douglas gave comfort to the Soviet tyranny by voting against aid to both Greece and Turkey," declared Senator Downey in a major radio address that was broadcast throughout California. "She voted against the President in a crisis when he most needed her support and most fully merited her confidence. She was one of a small, determined band which fought to the bitter end to keep Henry A. Wallace on the Democratic ticket at the 1944 Democratic convention, and she wept in total collapse when Harry Truman was finally nominated over Wallace."

Downey's statement linking Mrs. Douglas to "the Soviet tyranny" heated the campaign to a temperature that never cooled. But Downey was not yet through. He then charged that, "Mrs. Douglas opposed an appropriation that would enable Congress to uncover treasonable Communist activities," and that she "joined Representative Vito Marcantonio, an admitted friend of the Communist Party, in this effort to prevent an investigation of communism."

Although all these accusations were mouthed by Democrats, these and many other statements have since been ascribed to Nixon. It is a matter of record that Nixon did little more than embellish upon charges initiated by the Democratic candidates who had been attacking each other.

Occasionally, Democratic campaigners would remember that they were being opposed by a Republican and would take a few moments out of their internecine warfare to say something unflattering about Nixon. On one such occasion, Mrs. Douglas stated, "I have nothing but utter scorn for such pipsqueaks as Nixon and [Joseph] McCarthy."

Nixon was tempted to reply in kind, but was restrained by Chotiner. "You can't get into a name-calling contest with a woman," he said tersely. "The cost in votes would be prohibitive. Let the Democrats continue to chew each other up—they're doing our job for us." Nixon not only refused to be needled into a reply, but did not once mention Mrs. Douglas' name throughout the primary campaign—a strategem Voorhis had used against him in his first Congressional race.

Douglas Becomes Candidate

Helen Gahagan Douglas won the Democratic nomination by a healthy margin, with 734,842 votes given her by the Democrats and a bonus of 13 per cent of the Republican vote. Some 830,000 ballots were cast against her, and in favor of Manchester Boddy and lesser known candidates on the Democratic ticket. The Republicans in the state gave Nixon 64 per cent of their vote and the Democrats gave him 22 per cent of theirs—a plurality of about 170,000 votes over those received by Mrs. Douglas.

Viewing the results, Nixon again became the "Gloomy Gus" of his college days. For him it was a Pyrrhic victory. He knew that he could not possibly win the forthcoming general election unless a sizeable number of the 830,000 voters who had cast their ballots against her could be induced to leave the Democratic fold and vote for him. But, for all his characteristic pessimism, Nixon was glad that Mrs. Douglas had emerged triumphant over Boddy and the others.

"Actually, we wanted her to win," explained Chotiner. "I knew it would be easier to defeat the out-and-out liberal she represented than a conservative Democrat. If Boddy had won the primary race he could have cut into Nixon's own Republican vote and held on to nearly all of his regular Democratic support."

Long after the campaign was over, Mrs. Douglas continued

to see the 1950 campaign waged by her opponent as an onslaught on human decency and her own behavior as an exercise in civic righteousness. It was neither. In state after state, political contests reflected the ugly mood of the post-war period, and most campaigns were no better and no worse than the Nixon-Douglas melee and in some instances far more vicious.

Chotiner Takes Charge

The mastermind behind the Nixon campaign was Murray Chotiner—the clever political tactician and strategist who had offered Nixon guidance at the very outset of his political career. Chotiner had already attracted the attention of Washington's highest political circles—the National Republican and Democratic committees—although he had never managed a campaign outside of California.

Chotiner's credentials were impressive. He was known, surprisingly enough, as a quiet, self-effacing man, but, when necessary, a strong and capable leader who knew how to make a decision and see that it was carried out. It was he who had maneuvered Senator William F. Knowland's landslide victory over his Democratic opponent, Will Rogers, Jr.; and it was he who was mainly responsible for swinging the vast Knowland political machine in northern California to Nixon, along with the support of publisher Knowland's *Oakland Tribune*. Chotiner had also won laurels for his management of Earl Warren's campaign during his race for Governor of California.

Nixon, of course, was well aware of Chotiner's demonstrated skill. Whereas the canny vote-getter had served Nixon in the capacity of "public relations adviser" in the race against Voorhis, he was now named manager of the Southern California area, and placed in general charge of the statewide campaign. Nixon and Chotiner genuinely liked and respected each other, although that rapport was not without its initial clashes.

"Nixon was a perfectionist," said Chotiner. "He was like a general who demanded absolute precision and carefully planned coordination in every move, but that is simply not possible in the slugging matches of political campaigns. In the heat of battle there are always situations in which quick, tough decisions have to be made to meet the circumstances. Nixon wanted to do everything himself."

The showdown was inevitable. In their one and only confrontation, Chotiner reminded Nixon that the most serious error an office-seeker can make is to wear two political hats at the same time. Irritated, he told Nixon: "Dick, you can be either the candidate or the manager. But you can't be both. A candidate's job is to make speeches and reach the voters. You go out and do that, and let *us* make the other mistakes."

The advice was heeded. Although Nixon tended to his end of things, it would be naive to assume that he was not fully aware of Chotiner's tactics in the 1950 campaign.

Broadsides and Smears

As he had promised, Nixon unleashed a "rocking, socking campaign" which, combined with the hysterical tactics used by the Douglas forces, resulted in one of the ugliest political contests in California history.

The hysteria which marked the Douglas campaign and the aggressive attacks which marked Nixon's own campaign were inaugurated in their first encounter. Using only the charges made against her by her Democratic rivals in the primaries, Nixon said:

> Mrs. Douglas' record in Congress discloses the truth about her soft attitude toward Communism. . . . If she had had her way, the Communist conspiracy in the United States would never have been exposed. . . . It just so happens that my opponent is a member of a small clique which joins the notorious Communist

Party-liner, Vito Marcantonio of New York, in voting time after time against measures that are for the security of this country. . . . Is she really a Democrat? I challenge her to tell us where she stands. If she doesn't, I'll do it for her.

Had Chotiner been *her* manager, she would have ignored the speech and let fly with a barrage of her own. Instead she beseeched President Truman to affirm that she *was* a Democrat, a move which caused Chotiner to chuckle with delight. She then sent telegrams to more than twenty of her top supporters and contributors:

I HAVE RUN INTO A FRIGHTENING CRISIS. I NEED YOUR HELP, YOUR ADVICE, YOUR SUPPORT. WILL YOU COME TO DINNER AT MY HOUSE, TUESDAY, SEPTEMBER 26, 7 P.M., SO THAT WE CAN TALK OVER THIS TERRIBLE SITUATION AND HOPEFULLY FIND A SOLUTION.

Bernard Brennan, Republican Chairman for Southern California, caused Mrs. Douglas further anguish when he said, "During her five years in Congress Helen Douglas has voted 353 times exactly as has Vito Marcantonio. . . . How can Helen Douglas, capable actress that she is, take up so strange a role as a foe of communism? And why does she, when she has so deservedly earned the title of 'the Pink Lady'?"

It was at this point that Mrs. Douglas adopted the same technique that her opponents were using against her. Indeed, she went a step further, and for the remainder of the campaign added fascism to the communism charge she attempted to lay on Nixon. But hers was a series of emotional outbursts and certainly no match for the devastating skill with which Chotiner prepared his broadsides.

Describing Nixon and his supporters as "a backwash of men in dark shirts," an obvious allusion to fascists, she immediately followed through with the charge that although he was among the most reactionary Congressmen in Washington, it was actually he, not she, who was pro-communist. "On every key vote Nixon stood with Party-liner Marcantonio against America in its fight to defeat communism," Mrs. Douglas declared. She then went on to assert that Nixon had voted with the much-maligned New York Congressman opposing aid to Korea, and had also supported him in his effort to cut European aid in half.

This statement which became known as the "yellow sheet," was easily disproven. Nixon had voted for economic aid to Korea in 1949, but in the following year, he voted against a measure that would have provided aid to Korea, but none to Nationalist China on Formosa. He subsequently supported the bill when it was rewritten to include both countries. As to the charge that he had voted to cut foreign aid in half, he had simply supported a measure that called for a one-year rather than a two-year aid bill, with options for renewal.

Chotiner's response to the "yellow sheet" was a "pink sheet" in which he elaborated on the charges originally made by Democrats Downey and Boddy. The leaflet was packed with dates, Congressional data and semi-legal phrases that convinced thousands of California voters of its "authenticity." It was an imposing document:

IS HELEN DOUGLAS A DEMOCRAT?
THE RECORD SAYS *NO*!

Many persons have requested a comparison of the voting records of Congresswoman Helen Douglas and the notorious Communist Party-liner, Congressman Vito Marcantonio of New York. Mrs. Douglas and Marcantonio have been members of Congress together since January 1, 1945. During that period,

Mrs. Douglas voted the same as Marcantonio 354 times. While it should not be expected that a member of the House of Representatives should always vote in opposition to Marcantonio, it is significant to note, not only the *great number of times* which Mrs. Douglas voted in agreement with him, but also the issues on which almost without exception they always saw eye to eye.

Chotiner ordered more than a half-million copies of the flyer, suggestively colored a bright pink. The document did not mention, of course, that the majority of Democrats frequently voted with Marcantonio on many issues, as did some Republicans, including Nixon who voted with the New York Congressman 112 times.

Mrs. Douglas, of course, was no Communist, nor was she pro-Communist. She had supported a number of anti-Communist measures; refused to join Henry Wallace's Progressive Party when it was evident that Wallace had become a pawn of the Communist Party; and, indeed, was so intensely disliked by Marcantonio because of her support of American security measures that he often referred to her, privately, as "that bitch."

As for Murray Chotiner, his credo never changed. He simply quoted the facts in the pink sheet, knowing that the average voter was in no position to separate fact from border-truth that he had so adroitly woven into the leaflet. "Destroy the opposition" remained his most important maxim. "Political campaigns aren't won by following Marquis of Queensbury rules."

Chotiner's advice was taken, literally, by the *Douglas* forces. A vicious whispering campaign was launched against Nixon, the intent of which was to smear him with the brush of anti-Semitism. The charges of racism reached such a base level that it was no surprise that they boomeranged. Many in the large Jewish community of Los Angeles at whom the rumors were aimed came to Nixon's defense—many of these were individuals who had never supported him politically before. The Anti-Defamation League of B'nai B'rith, incensed at what it recognized as a deliberate slander, issued a public blast against the rumor-mongers and declared its confidence in Nixon.

When the accusations were widened to the point that he was being characterized as violently anti-Negro, Nixon could no longer refrain from replying. Refusing to follow Chotiner's advice, he addressed a statewide rebuttal:

> I have never sought, accepted or would accept the support of any fascist or communist organization. I have been told of attempts by my political opponents to create the impression that I have received and accepted the support of Gerald L. K. Smith—the notorious racist agitator—and his organization. I want to make it clear that I do not want that support and that I repudiate it. I denounce anti-Semitism in whatever form it appears.

The question of adequate finances continued to plague Nixon as it had in his earlier campaign. Obversely, Mrs. Douglas enjoyed the support of organized labor and her treasury was always full. It enabled her, for example, to fly from one speaking engagement to another in a helicopter. Nixon, on the other hand, continued to use his borrowed station wagon, speaking on street corners when he was unable to hire a hall. But money could not get the Douglas campaign off the ground.

The Douglas forces, now desperate, evolved a new "Stop Nixon-at-Any-Cost" technique: they decided to embarrass and outshout him at his street-corner meetings. A Douglas sound-truck followed him from place to place, its loudspeaker blaring forth a volley of questions, interrupting him with insulting comments, drowning him out with ceaseless heckling.

Pat Nixon, who accompanied her husband throughout the campaign, recalled one particular day in San Francisco when he had just started to speak. Standing on the tailgate of the station wagon, he had attracted the attention of only a few pedestrians when the opposition's sound truck appeared. "They simply would not let Dick speak," she said. "Whenever he tried to say something, they would scream questions over their loudspeakers. Even when he tried to answer them, he could not be heard above the din."

But Nixon would not be stopped. He raised his voice and tried to answer the questions above the amplified sound, and, as he did, the few original listeners soon swelled to a curious crowd.

"Please, Dick, don't answer them," his wife pleaded. But he refused to quit.

His determination and courage proved contagious and within minutes he had completely won the sympathy of his audience. Many urged him to pay no attention to the truck. "I won't be silenced," Nixon called out above the clamor. "I'll answer every question they throw at me."

Pat, who had been circulating in the crowd passing out literature, made this observation: "They didn't realize it at the time, but the Douglas people brought a lot of voters over to our side with that sound truck. It was the last time they ever tried to drown us out. They used to send paid pickets to demonstrate wherever Dick was speaking in an attempt to disrupt the meetings, but that stopped, too, because they saw Dick was a fighter; that he wouldn't be intimidated; and that it was costing them votes."

The "Tricky Dick" Pejorative

On September 29, an editorial was published in the *Independent Review* in which the appellation "Tricky Dick" was first used, a peculiar pejorative considering that the opposition was engaged in a whispering campaign that attempted to create a totally false image of Nixon as an anti-Semitic, anti-Negro fascist. The editorial charged that Murray Chotiner had organized a conspiracy, with Nixon's full assent. The purpose of the conspiracy was to defame the character of Mrs. Douglas "by falsely accusing her through infamous insinuations and whispered innuendo of being a Communist." Ignoring the published evidence that Mrs. Douglas had repeatedly attempted to link Nixon with Communists, and also with Senator Joe McCarthy, the editorial went on to say, "Representatives of her Senatorial opponent, Tricky Dick Nixon, are the chief mouthpieces for this partisan effort to crucify Mrs. Douglas."

Nixon was in a dark mood. Too late for immediate rebuttal, he learned that the Douglas camp had issued a statement to the effect that certain wealthy backers had given him so much money that he had used some of the contributions to erect "Nixon For Senator" signs on the other side of the Rio Grande, in Mexico. The charge, of course, was absurd. Organizations supporting Nixon reported campaign expenditures of only $62,899, whereas Mrs. Douglas reported $156,172.

Adding to his indignation was Mrs. Douglas' last desperate act to destroy his credibility. She called on Attorney General J. Howard McGrath, with Harry Truman's blessing, to prove that Nixon was indeed the "pipsqueak" she had earlier called him. In a press conference in Los Angeles, McGrath set out to belittle Nixon's role in the Hiss case: "I can assure you, gentlemen, Alger Hiss would have been prosecuted by the Department of Justice without prodding from Nixon," he stated.

Fortunately, a correspondent for *Newsweek*, Ralph de Toledano, was among the reporters present. On his own, he prepared a detailed analysis of the Justice Department's record in the Hiss-Chambers affair which was given wide publicity. Its patent truth could not be denied.

Nixon's ire remained in full heat, and he would have made an angry reply had it not been for the restraining counsel of

Murray Chotiner. "Dick," he reminded the candidate, "Helen attacked your strength, not your weakness. She's gotten herself into a mess she can't get out of. In any case, Toledano's analysis, coming from a respected third party, undoubtedly helped you. Forget it."

But Nixon could not forget it. Rather than listen to the election returns that were just starting to trickle in from outlying precincts, he decided on a family picnic—although he was really in no mood for it. The weather that day, chilly and cloudy, befitted his pessimism. The beach was cold and a slight drizzle had begun, making their outing even more dreary.

Pat had had enough. "Let's go home," she said. "If we have to be miserable, we can at least be warm."

"How about a movie, instead?" he suggested. "I don't feel like meeting people and hearing about the returns."

After the movie, they drove home, passing *en route* several Douglas sound trucks whose amplifiers were exhorting the public to vote "Thumbs Down for Nixon," and to "Support Helen Douglas, friend of the working man." The trucks were all in the industrial areas between the Pacific Ocean and inland Los Angeles.

"By the time we arrived home, Dick was quite depressed," Pat recalled. "He was sure we had been defeated."

That night, a surprised and delighted Nixon learned that he had won the election by a 680,000 vote margin, running seven percent ahead of the Republican congressional slate. It was the largest plurality received by any senatorial candidate that year. The final tally was 2,183,454 for Nixon; 1,502,507 for Mrs. Douglas.

"We hopped from one victory celebration to another, far into the night," Pat reminisced, smiling at the memory. "Dick was so exuberant. Wherever he found a piano he played 'Happy Days Are Here Again.'"

Those "happy days" were to be marred, however, in the

Just elected to the Senate in November, 1950, Nixon spends a quiet evening at home with Tricia, Julie and Pat.

aftermath of the campaign. The accusations hurled at Mrs. Douglas by her fellow Democrats were soon to be attributed to Nixon; the "Tricky Dick" label was to plague him throughout his career; his enemies, like Abou Ben Adhem's tribe, increased tenfold, and with them grew the myths of Nixon's "reprehensible conduct" during that campaign of 1950—myths and legends which became increasingly enlarged and unfounded with each passing year.

In defeat, Helen Gahagan Douglas, normally a sensitive woman, evidently found the harsh rigors of political campaigning too much to bear, and she retired from political life.

In victory, Nixon, of course, went forward, but carried with him the "Tricky Dick" appellation which was to become his albatross.

8

Senator Nixon Behind the Scenes

The Freshman Senator

AMONG THE POPULAR misconceptions that surround Richard Nixon is the belief that he voted the Republican viewpoint without deviation. Another is that Dwight D. Eisenhower's attention was drawn to the young Senator solely on the basis of his success in exposing Alger Hiss. Neither contention is true.

During his first term as a Representative, to be sure, Nixon did vote almost entirely for Republican-supported legislation, much of which was to constitute the essence of the Eisenhower program. According to the *Congressional Quarterly*, Nixon voted for Republican measures 91 per cent of the time. In his second term as a Congressman, *CQ* reported that he voted for GOP-sponsored bills 74 per cent of the time. During his two years in the Senate, however, he voted the

Republican line 70 per cent of the time—a drop of 21 per cent from his early congressional record.

As a Senator, he continued to work as hard and as long as he had in the past, usually voting moderately conservative on domestic issues, and liberal on foreign policy matters. He was, basically, in the vanguard of the progressive Republicans —the "new breed" born in this century, not shackled to the orthodoxies of the past, but unwilling to surrender the verities that had broadened the nation's geographic, social and economic frontiers.

It has been noted that Nixon's fortunes were the result of talent and circumstance, but given his unique personality, he was psychologically unable to remain in limbo and simply wait for something fortuitous to happen. His political instincts, honed ever finer with each passing year, told him that whatever ambitions he might harbor, they would not be fulfilled by some lucky stroke, but would be the result of concentrated forethought and deliberate and dedicated planning.

As a freshman member of the United States Senate which convened in January, 1951, Nixon found that at age 38, he was the youngest member of that august body. Perhaps such an achievement would have been enough satisfaction for most men, but for Nixon the record seems to indicate otherwise. Acutely aware of his junior status, he looked forward to greater accomplishments—and he was fully aware that they would not result from happenstance. *He* would have to *make* them happen! And make them happen he did.

Nixon had not been in office four full months when he seized his first opportunity and except for a brief note in the *Congressional Record*, the event might have gone completely unnoticed. On May 14, the *Record* discloses, Nixon was excused from attending Senate sessions for one week so that he might, as a member of the United States delegation, attend the World Health Organization meeting in Geneva, Switzerland.

Nixon Meets Eisenhower

The trip itself and the results of the meeting had no effect on whatever secret ambitions Nixon may have set for himself, but the return trip was significant. It was then that he took time out to make an important, unscheduled stopover in Paris. The *Congressional Record* for May 21 shows that Nixon answered the roll call and reported his findings, but made no mention of a stopover. But the June 5 *CR* proves more revealing. In the course of a brief discussion of an obscure bill, he unexpectedly announced:

> I had a very interesting experience two weeks ago when I sat in the office of General Eisenhower in Paris. I was impressed, let me say parenthetically, with the excellent job he is doing against monumental odds, in the position he holds. He pointed out to me that one of the greatest tasks which he has at the present time is to convince our allies abroad of the necessity of putting first things first.

Innocuous? Spoonfed pablum? Of course! Nixon had no intention of saying anything that might be misinterpreted or quoted out of context against him. He had only one point to make in that opening gun: he had met the most popular figure in the country and had made a good impression.

Although still in military service, and prohibited from engaging in partisan politics, General Eisenhower had been engendering wide political appeal and was looming large as a possible presidential candidate. The *Draft Eisenhower for President League*, a group of amateur politicians, mostly newsmen of a conservative bent working in Washington, was launching local clubs in every state of the union over the vociferous objections of the general who, at that time, had no choice but to disavow political ambitions. The slogan, "I Like Ike" had recently been coined by this author who was a co-founder of the League and was serving as its national

Director of Publicity. Eisenhower's growing visibility as a Republican contender in opposition to party stalwart Senator Robert A. Taft could no longer be ignored.

Perhaps it was coincidental—and perhaps it was not—but immediately following Nixon's statement, there began a steady procession of important Republicans to Eisenhower's Paris headquarters. The pilgrimages were clearly declaring that here was a President-in-the-making. If Nixon, not yet more than an embryonic Senator, did not convey the impression that he was aware that he was playing a key role in an irreversible game of destiny, he was, at least, making all the right moves and all the right sounds.

Twice previously he had displayed his talent for creating his own propulsions—the first time, at Whittier College when, within the first few weeks following his matriculation, he became its best known student; the second, when as a very junior Congressman he established his Chowder and Marching Club as a power base from which to jump from obscurity to national recognition.

Now, as a freshman Senator, he repeated himself by ignoring the hoary seniority system and approaching directly what he believed would be the source of power in the forthcoming primary and election campaigns. At the same time, he was careful not to alienate Senator Taft, known everywhere as "Mr. Republican."

Nixon's almost too-casual remarks on the floor of the Senate did not go unheeded by the press. The Scripps-Howard *Daily News* in Washington picked up the story in which Murray Chotiner's fine hand was clearly visible between the lines (although the item was not attributed to him): "Senator Nixon stopped off at General Eisenhower's headquarters, not to talk politics, but to learn about NATO and SHAPE."[*] Other news reports affirm that the General complimented the new Senator on his anti-Communist activities and was favor-

---

[*] NATO was the North Atlantic Treaty Organization and SHAPE was the Supreme Headquarters, Allied Powers in Europe.

ably impressed with him as a "young man with a bright future."

Nixon's May 1951 visit with Eisenhower and his stature within the Republican Party as the man who had twice defeated heavily-financed, Administration-backed liberal Democrats led to another meeting during that same month of May. Harold Stassen, another GOP presidential aspirant, invited Nixon to a conclave held at a New Jersey private estate. The strategy conference, attended by forty-five distinguished Republicans, was the first tangible evidence that Nixon's political star was rising. Stassen took him aside and offered him the vice-presidential nomination if he, in return, would swing the California delegation to his support. Nixon, third man in the triumvirate—along with Governor Earl Warren and Senator Bill Knowland—could have exerted pressure in Stassen's behalf, but he refused to commit himself. "I'll think about it," he replied.

Whether or not Nixon could have influenced Warren is problematical. By this time they despised each other. Warren, like Stassen, was a candidate for the presidency, and Nixon lost no time in tarnishing his "favorite son" image. This was not done for petty, personal reasons, of course, but rather to fortify his own position as California's strongest Republican with the lone exception of Senator William Knowland. Nixon mailed twenty-five thousand form letters to GOP registered voters within the state in which he stated:

> As a result of the primary election of June 3, I am to be one of the delegates to the Republican National Convention. This delegation is pledged to support Governor Warren for President. As you know, Mr. Warren has assured us that he would release the California delegation in favor of Eisenhower if he should find that his chances for winning the nomination at the convention were not possible.*

---

*In April 1952, when entering the Wisconsin primary, Warren did indeed promise that he would release his delegates to Eisenhower if

In that context, it would be appreciated if you would fill in the blank in the following statement:

From my conversations with other voters and my analysis of all the factors involved, I believe that .... is the strongest candidate that Republicans could nominate for President.

Hell hath no fury like a politician scorned. When the results were tabulated, Eisenhower proved to be the overwhelming choice of the electorate, and Warren was left speechless with rage. Nixon, as might now be expected, not only publicized the returns, but saw to it that Eisenhower also received a copy of the results.

Nixon to the Hustings

A few days later, "the man with no further political ambitions," as one reporter described him, took to the hustings. On June 28, 1951, Nixon addressed the Young Republican National Federation in Boston in a keynote speech that might well have served as the battle cry of his own campaign to win friends and influence delegates.

Calling his speech, "The Challenge of 1952," he began with the observation that the Republican Party could not win the national election unless it could win the support of Democrats:

---

it should become obvious that he could not win at the convention. When his lopsided defeat in that state by Senator Taft showed that he was no longer a contender and could not possibly win, he nevertheless insisted upon remaining in the race, refused to release his delegates, and clung to the hope that Taft and Eisenhower would be deadlocked. In that event, he planned to emerge as the dark horse candidate and capture the nomination. For that reason, he ran in the California primary and won the state's full slate of delegates to the national convention, all pledged to him by law until he released them to vote "as their consciences dictated."

I say we Republicans have been talking to please ourselves for the past twenty years, and we have found out that there aren't enough of us to win.

Then he threw out a Chotinerized call for political activism:

I believe there is only one sure-fire formula for victory. We have to work, we have to fight, we have to stand for something. . . . Let's see that the Republican Party in 1952 puts on the kind of a fighting, rocking, socking campaign that will bring home to the people the merits of our candidate and our program.

And then he outlined the program:

We must pledge ourselves to cut all non-defense expenditures right down to the bone. We must attack inflation at its source. . . . In the final analysis a balanced budget and high production are the only effective answers to inflation. . . . We shall not allow this emergency to be used to socialize any basic American institution.

He reviewed the Hiss case and warned of its implications:

The tragedy is that our top administration officials have refused time and time again to recognize the existence of the fifth column in this country and to take effective action to clean subversives out of the administrative branch of the government.

Using the same arithmetic that had proven so successful in his campaign against Helen Douglas, he attacked the Truman administration's most vulnerable weakness—its foreign policy:

Six years ago the United States was the most powerful nation on the face of the globe. We had the strongest army, the strongest navy and the strongest air force in the world. We had a monopoly on the atomic bomb. As far as people in the world were concerned, there were approximately 1,760,000,000 on our side and only 180,000,000 on the Communist side . . .

Six years have passed—six years of conferences, of little wars like the one in Korea, of lack of leadership in Washington. And what is the situation today? Today we are no longer stronger on the ground. We are stronger strategically in the air, but weaker tactically. We're stronger on the sea, but weaker beneath the sea. We no longer have a monopoly on the atomic bomb, though we believe that we have more than our potential enemy. And when we analyze the breakdown in peoples in the world, what do we find? Today there are only 540,000,000 people that can be counted on the side of the free nations—our side. There are 800,000,000 people on the Communist side, and there are 600,000,000 that will have to be classified as neutral—countries like India and Pakistan. In other words, six years ago the odds in people in the world were nine to one in our favor, and today they are five to three against us. . . . We have lost 600,000,000 people to the Communists in six years—100,000,000 a year.

Party Policy Spokesman

The Boston speech established Nixon, junior Senator though he was, as a leader around whom other Republicans could rally. He soon became one of the most popular spokesmen for Party policy in the country, carrying his ringing defiance of the Democratic administration to the voters in eleven states in just five months.

But something was happening to Richard Nixon that might be called a retrogression of personality. Throughout his early life he had almost universally been known as a moody, remote young man, a man lost in his own thoughts and unable to communicate the sense of warmth that was actually deeply ingrained in his character and so seldom revealed. His early reticence was probably little more than a defense mechanism —a fear of rejection. He wanted love, he yearned for the respect of his community, he longed for the approval of his friends, neighbors and associates. The thought of a possible rebuff to his overtures, however, was something he would not or could not endure. His remoteness became a way of life. But his truly human feelings, held captive for so long, emerged to a degree during his college days and finally blossomed after he met and married Pat.

Now, in the year 1951, with a family to love and be loved by, with the adulation of large responsive audiences ringing in his ears, and with the mounting respect of his seniors in the Party structure, one might have expected that Nixon's relationship with others would have become warmer and closer. Yet, his aloofness seemed to grow and keep pace with his increasing popularity. Possibly, he could not believe that the public actually liked him, or that they respected his opinions, or that they saw in him the makings of a leader. Perhaps he feared that their surge of approval was transitory and would vanish with the first winds of discontent.

Going beyond anything even Chotiner espoused, he regarded his adversaries as his enemies, a trait shared by other national figures, notably Harry Truman and Lyndon Johnson. His speeches dwelled less and less on purely local matters, even when addressing his own constituents. His penchant for foreign affairs began to absorb much of his time; his outlook became national rather than regional; and his perorations were statesmanlike, whether one agreed with him or not. He was clearly headed for an important role in the coming elections, although no one, possibly not even he, could foresee in the early months of 1951 how important a part he was destined to play.

His social life suffered. He found himself away from home and family more often than he wished, and far more frequently than he had anticipated. Yet, whatever aloofness about him the public may have sensed, his closeness with his wife and family remained unaffected.

He was completely devoted to the family. Sometimes, in the course of his extended speaking tours which now numbered as many as fourteen every month, his longing to see his daughters, Tricia, at that time age 5, and Julie, born on July 5, 1948, in Washington, D.C., and then 3 years old, was so intense that he would fly home if only to have a few precious unpublicized hours with them. His evolving aloofness as a public figure was not reflected in his home life.

Was Nixon indeed so naive as to discount the portending events that began to assume definable images? The record says yes, but our native intelligence is compelled to say no. On May 8, 1952, only two months before the national convention, and a year after he made the keynote address to the Young Republican National Federation in Boston, which launched him as one of the most sought-after speakers in the Republican party, he was invited to speak before a blue-ribbon audience of GOP moguls. The event, a fund-raising dinner in New York, was not significant because of the speech he made, but rather for what occurred after his usual dynamic presentation.

Governor Dewey, titular head of the Republican Party, approached him after the banquet and invited him to his hotel suite where, in scarcely veiled terms, he advised Nixon that he was his choice for the vice-presidential nomination on the Eisenhower ticket. Moreover, Dewey said, he would have the backing of Herbert Brownell, Jr., Dewey's campaign manager in both his unsuccessful runs for the presidency. (Brownell was later a central figure in Eisenhower's presidential campaign, and, still later, Attorney General in Eisenhower's cabinet.)

Julie (left), four, and Tricia, six, with Julie's doll, Tiny, peer out the window of their Washington home in 1952.

Nixon could not brush these sentiments aside. He had already received a communication from Brownell in which he complimented Nixon as a "brilliant campaigner whose victory in California served as a basis for Republican victories nationally." As for Dewey, Nixon realized that the tacit commitment, coming as it did from the top GOP kingmaker, was not to be taken as mere idle chatter.

Nixon's assumed role of coy bride hoping for a proposal by a personable swain who was too circumspect to force the issue was probably the only one he could take. As a newly elected Senator, and as the youngest member of the Senate, he was competing for power with others who had long since served their apprenticeship. A few had been elected to office before he was born.

Again, he reverted to the wily poker player he had been, playing the cards close to his chest, careful not to offend party leaders by what would have been considered a presumptuous grab for power by an upstart. Deftly, he parried questions that related to his ambitions, continued with his hectic speaking schedule, and waited for the opportune moment when he could cash in on his mounting acceptability. He addressed civic groups, bar associations, trade associations, labor groups, and appeared as principal speaker at many Republican Party rallies and fund-raising dinners. As convention time approached, Richard Nixon was one of the most popular speakers in the Republican ranks.

The 1952 GOP Convention

Although Nixon, as a convention delegate, was committed by law to Earl Warren, the Governor of California, he used every means to withhold his support in every other way. When asked, bluntly, if he was "for" Warren, his reply was evasive: "I am for the man who can best sell the Republican program to the people. I challenge you to name any one of the prominently mentioned Republican candidates who wouldn't be a tremendous improvement over what we have in the White House now. . . ."

Nixon was convinced that the fight for the presidential nomination would be a contest between Eisenhower and Taft; that Warren's intrusion was futile; and that, in the event of a deadlock, Warren could not win as a dark horse compromise. There was also the fact—an opinion Nixon never publicly articulated—that Governor Warren did not represent the Republican thinking of the times; that his liberalism would only be construed as a kind of "me-tooism;" that he was no more than a carbon copy of his Democratic opponent. In addition, Nixon felt no obligation to support the man who had refused to endorse him in his campaign against Voorhis and Mrs. Douglas.

The Eisenhower-Taft forces met head-on on July 7. It was the opening day of the convention in Chicago. Four days earlier Nixon had condemned the Republican National Committee which was dominated by Taft supporters for granting temporary recognition to the Georgia delegation, and for also giving it permission to vote on its own eligibility as the regular delegation. It was an audacious move from the standpoint of backroom politics, but the first day of the convention revealed that the Taft managers had additional surprises in store. The Credentials Committee, under Taft's tight control, had voted to seat two sets of temporary delegations from Texas and Georgia. Now, in a gamble that out-Chotinerized Chotiner, the Committee voted to unseat the delegations supporting Eisenhower and to give permanent status to its own people. Had the loss of these sixty-eight delegates been allowed to stand, Taft's strength would have reached the point where a bandwagon might have been set into motion in his behalf.

The furor that resulted was predictable. Eisenhower heatedly accused the Credentials Committee of "cattle rustling." Harold Stassen denounced the Committee as being the private property of Senator Taft. Henry Cabot Lodge who, along with Stassen, was a contender for the second spot on Eisenhower's ticket, prepared a leaflet which carried the heading, "Thou Shalt Not Steal." The printed admonition was distributed to every delegate prior to the all-important vote. In an effort to out-flank the opposition, Eisenhower's backers introduced the Langlie "Fair Play" resolution which would have denied the contested seats to the Taft delegations of Georgia, Texas and Louisiana on the grounds that Taft's Credentials Committee had gained control of these delegations by dishonest means.

Prelude to a Nomination

Nixon's moment had finally arrived. He recognized it immediately and intuitively. The right time, the right place and the right circumstance had come together all at once. The California delegation had caucused to obtain a consensus on the "Fair Play" resolution, a meeting that was torn by dissension from the outset. They realized the implications behind the proposed amendment. If it were adopted, Taft's chances of attaining enough delegate strength to capture the necessary votes to win the nomination would be crippled. In that event, Warren's hopes for a deadlock would be destroyed and his dark horse aspirations would come to an end. Senator Knowland, always loyal to his Warren commitment, urged that California's delegates be split, with half of the votes going to each of the candidates. That suggestion, which would in effect have cancelled out the gain by either Eisenhower or Taft, and would have given Warren the deadlock he was seeking, was well received.

It was at this crucial juncture that Nixon made his dramatic move. Leaping to his feet, he strode to the microphone. Calling up his considerable talent as an orator, he pleaded the cause of morality. "You must not and cannot accept a compromise," he told his fellow delegates. "I urge you to vote your conscience."

This was pure rhetoric. Every delegate to the convention knew that turning the problem into a moral issue was a screen. What they were dealing with was a struggle for power that involved two strong men. Which of them would be the convention's candidate?—that was the question. Addressing the caucus, but with his eyes on Knowland and Warren, Nixon exhorted them to yield. "I feel that any candidate who is nominated for President of the United States would have far greater difficulty in winning in November with those contested Taft delegations than otherwise," he asserted.

Nixon was then reminded that the convention was bound to accept the majority opinion of the Credentials Committee. But he objected to this contention and said: "I submit to you that if we were to feel that we were bound automatically to accept the decisions of our committees, there would be no reason for us to come to the convention at all. We could leave the nomination entirely up to the committees."

Eisenhower: Republican Nominee

The response was enthusiastic agreement. Warren and Knowland succumbed, and released the state delegation to "vote its conscience." When the vote was tallied, fifty-seven were in favor of the "Fair Play" amendment, giving Eisenhower the momentum he needed to start his own bandwagon rolling and the margin he needed for victory.

On July 11, 1952, Dwight David Eisenhower was nominated on the first ballot.

The presidential nomination had taken place in the forenoon, and the convention recessed until 6:30 that evening so that the new standard-bearer and his advisers could decide on a running mate for the new nominee.

Two separate meetings were held. The first took place in Eisenhower's suite at the Blackstone Hotel. In attendance were the five men who comprised his unofficial political cabinet: Governor Dewey, Senator Lodge, Herbert Brownell, Arthur Summerfield and Senator Carlson. Much to their surprise, they learned that the nominee had no idea that he could virtually name his own Vice-President. He asked his counselors for suggestions, but when they demurred, explaining that it was his prerogative, he reluctantly surprised them with his list of favorites. "Any one of these seven men will be acceptable to me," he said.

Richard Nixon's name headed the list. Also named, in about this order, were: Senator Lodge, Governor Thornton, Governor Langlie, Governor Driscoll, Senator Knowland and Governor Stassen.

The group then hurried across the street to the Conrad Hilton Hotel where the second caucus was held.* Here a number of possible vice-presidential possibilities were suggested, including Taft—a suggestion that was quickly shot down by national committeeman J. Russell Sprague of New York who said flatly that the GOP could not carry his state with Taft on the Eisenhower ticket. As they were discussing him, Taft himself telephoned to plead the case of Senator Dirksen, to whom he owed a political debt. But since Dirksen, only a day earlier, had made some remarks which Dewey felt were personally disparaging, his chances were practically nil.

It was Dewey who brought the deliberations to a close. "I would like to propose as the only logical candidate for the vice-presidency—Richard Nixon." The governor had not once mentioned the list prepared by Eisenhower, but his stature as the former standard-bearer, and his obvious esteem for the new presidential candidate, left no one with any doubt that Dewey was expressing Eisenhower's wishes. Former Economic

---

*Among those present at the second caucus were: J. Russell Sprague, former Senator Sinclair Weeks of Massachusetts, Senator James H. Duff and Governor John S. Fine of Pennsylvania, Arthur Summerfield, Sherman Adams, Governor John Lodge of Connecticut, Paul Hoffman, Herbert Brownell, Barak T. Mattingly of St. Louis, and Roy Roberts, president of the *Kansas City Star*.

Cooperation Administration (ECA) chief, Paul Hoffman, rose in support: "Everything in Senator Nixon's background is a plus for the party," he said to his colleagues. "He is one of the Republicans who has an enlightened view on foreign affairs, and I am convinced that a man of his views would be an asset for General Eisenhower."

No mention was made of Nixon's efforts that broke the California delegation's stand for Warren, or that he had, single-handedly, swung that state's sixty-eight votes to Eisenhower, but the message came through loud and clear. The committee vote was unanimous for Nixon.

Brownell lost no time and picked up two phones and arranged a conference call; one to Eisenhower on the other side of the street, and the other to Nixon.

To Be or Not to Be a Candidate

Immediately after Eisenhower was nominated, Nixon had left the convention hall with Chotiner and Bernard Brennan, an old friend who was also a Republican trouble shooter, and went to the nearby Stockyards Inn where the California delegation was headquartered.

In their room at the Inn, Dick and Pat discussed the possibility of his being offered the vice-presidential nomination. She questioned him about rumors that had begun to circulate at the start of the convention, but he dismissed them with a wave of his hand. "Those things just don't happen," he said. Nevertheless, Pat continued to express concern. She was quite content being a Senator's wife. But if his senatorial duties occupied so much of his time, how would he ever manage to lead a normal family life as a Vice-President?

Nixon insisted that the rumors were without foundation. However, when Jack Knight, the highly knowledgeable editor and publisher of the Chicago *Daily News* made the blunt prediction two days before the balloting began that second place on the ticket would go to Nixon, he confessed to Pat that he had already been approached by both the Taft and Eisenhower factions. Pat, of course, would never stand in her husband's way. He knew that she did not share his passionate affinity for politics despite the fact that she had served faithfully at his side during his House and Senate campaigns. Now, there was no avoiding the issue. She was deeply troubled, and they talked far into the night as she continued to verbalize her doubts. "I want to be a wife and mother, not a public figure," she argued.

At four o'clock in the morning Nixon telephoned Chotiner who was also occupying a room at the Stockyards Inn. "Murray, I'd like to talk with you," he said. "Can you come down?"

The moment Chotiner entered the room he detected the constraint that filled the air.

"Tell me something," Nixon began, "if the vice-presidency is offered to me, do you think I should take it?"

"Yes, I do," Chotiner replied.

"Why?"

"Because it's in your best interests."

Chotiner knew that Pat was opposed to her husband's getting involved in still another political campaign, and that she hoped he would refuse the nomination if it were offered. But Chotiner was—and still is—a man who speaks his mind. "Dick," he went on, "right now you're a junior Senator from California, and unless something happens to Bill Knowland—and he's young and healthy—you'll never even be a *senior* Senator. He holds all the power in the state, so you'll always be second string—and you know as well as I that a junior Senator doesn't amount to much in politics.

"What you have to face is that the time has come for you to go up or out—there's no other way. All right, suppose you run for Vice-President and lose the election? So what! You'll still be the junior Senator and you haven't lost a thing. But if you win, you'll be the Vice-President of the United States, and at the end of four years, if you're not re-elected you can always go back to practicing law in Whittier. As a former

Vice-President, and as young as you are, you'd be the most successful lawyer in town."

Pat recalled the incident. "I knew in my heart that I would do what was best for Dick," she said. "But the surprising thing is that when I finally agreed that he should accept the nomination, he himself was still not certain. . . . He was still debating it, turning it over in his mind, when I left at 5 A.M. to go back to bed."

Nixon spent the following day, July 11, at the convention that nominated Eisenhower. In the evening, he returned to his room at the Stockyards Inn. He was bone-weary, having been up almost all through the previous night. He noticed that he needed a shave but he was too tired. Instead, he took off his shirt and lay down to rest, and in a moment was sound asleep.

The telephone awakened him.

He lifted the receiver without even being aware of it, and the caller's magic words brought him to instant wakefulness. It was Herbert Brownell, and he was speaking, not to Nixon, but on another telephone to Eisenhower:

"Hello, General, I wanted to tell you that the committee has unanimously agreed on Nixon."

Nixon had a moment to sit down and catch his breath before Brownell spoke again—this time on Nixon's line. He repeated the statement, and then added, "Can you hurry over here, Dick? The General wants to see you right away."

Moving faster than he ever had in his life, Nixon put on a freshly-laundered shirt. Still needing a shave and with clothes rumpled, he and Chotiner rushed out of the Stockyards Inn in search of a taxi. None was in sight. But Chotiner quickly borrowed a car from the Inn's parking lot attendant, and then triumphantly produced a motorcycle escort. To the tune of a screaming siren, they made the trip to the Blackstone Hotel in record time.

The Eisenhower-Nixon Team

In his suite, Eisenhower greeted Nixon with a warm smile and a handclasp. He was presented to Mrs. Eisenhower, and they exchanged a few cordial comments. Then Eisenhower proceeded with the formality of offer and acceptance:

"This will be more than just another campaign," he said. "I want this to be a *crusade*. Will you join me?"

"I'd be proud and happy to join your crusade, sir," replied Nixon. Again they shook hands.

Then Nixon turned to Knowland: "And I'd be grateful if you made the nomination." Knowland, who had backed Warren up until the time that Nixon swayed the California delegates to back Eisenhower, smiled and nodded. This was the great game of politics he understood so well. "Glad to, Dick," said Knowland.

Everyone seemed to know about Nixon's approaching nomination even before it was announced. While he was closeted with Eisenhower, Chotiner phoned the glad tidings to Nixon's parents in Whittier. "Oh, we know all about it," they exclaimed. "In fact we're listening to a news broadcast right now."

Pat Nixon had not been in their room when the call came from Brownell asking that her husband meet with Eisenhower as soon as possible. She thought he was still at the Inn catching up on his sleep.

"I guess I was one of the last to learn that he had accepted," Pat reminisced. "I was in a restaurant, eating a lettuce and tomato sandwich. They were showing an old movie on television, and I had just taken my first bite when the movie was interrupted for a news bulletin announcing that General Eisenhower had chosen Dick as his running mate. Was I surprised! I never did get to finish that sandwich. I paid the check as fast as I could and caught a cab to the convention hall."

The vice-presidential candidate arrived at the hall at 5:30

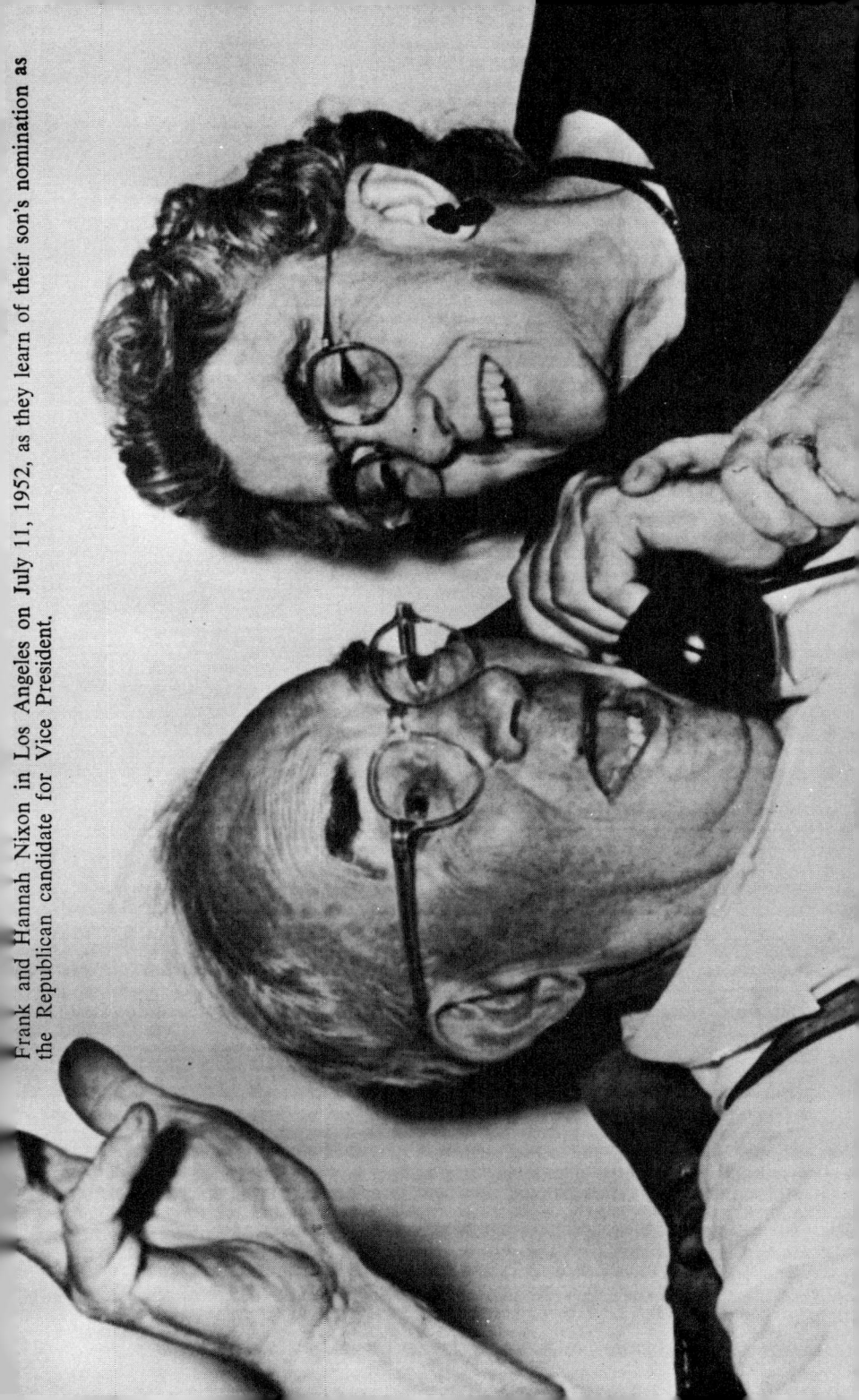

Frank and Hannah Nixon in Los Angeles on July 11, 1952, as they learn of their son's nomination as the Republican candidate for Vice President.

to the chant of "We Want Nixon." Pat, who was waiting for him at the edge of the platform, waved to him as he approached. "We want Nixon," she called gaily. On the other side of the continent, in Whittier, Tricia, Julie and their grandparents were watching the proceedings on television. "We want Nixon," shouted Frank and Hannah, their laughter filling the room. "We want Nixon," Tricia joined in. Julie was the only holdout. "I want Mommy," she cried.

Knowland made the nominating speech and Governor Alfred E. Driscoll of New Jersey seconded the nomination. At this point, Governor John S. Fine of Pennsylvania rose to ask that the roll call be dispensed with. A motion to that effect was carried amidst a roar of approval.

Nixon was nominated by acclamation!

Still needing a shave, his clothes even more rumpled than they had been, he stood before the wildly cheering delegates with Pat at his side, as she had always been. And as millions watched on television, he raised both arms high in his now familiar "V for Victory" sign. He was smiling and laughing and bubbling over in a sea of uninhibited joy.

Richard Nixon had come a long way since those days when he sorted spoiled fruit and vegetables in his father's market. And only five years had passed since he was called "the greenest Congressman in town." Now he was campaigning, in tandem, with a man whose incredible popularity was at its height —a person whom the opposition dared not attack personally. It did not occur to Nixon that he was to become Eisenhower's Achilles' heel; that he would be the natural target at whom the slings and arrows of the opposition would be aimed.

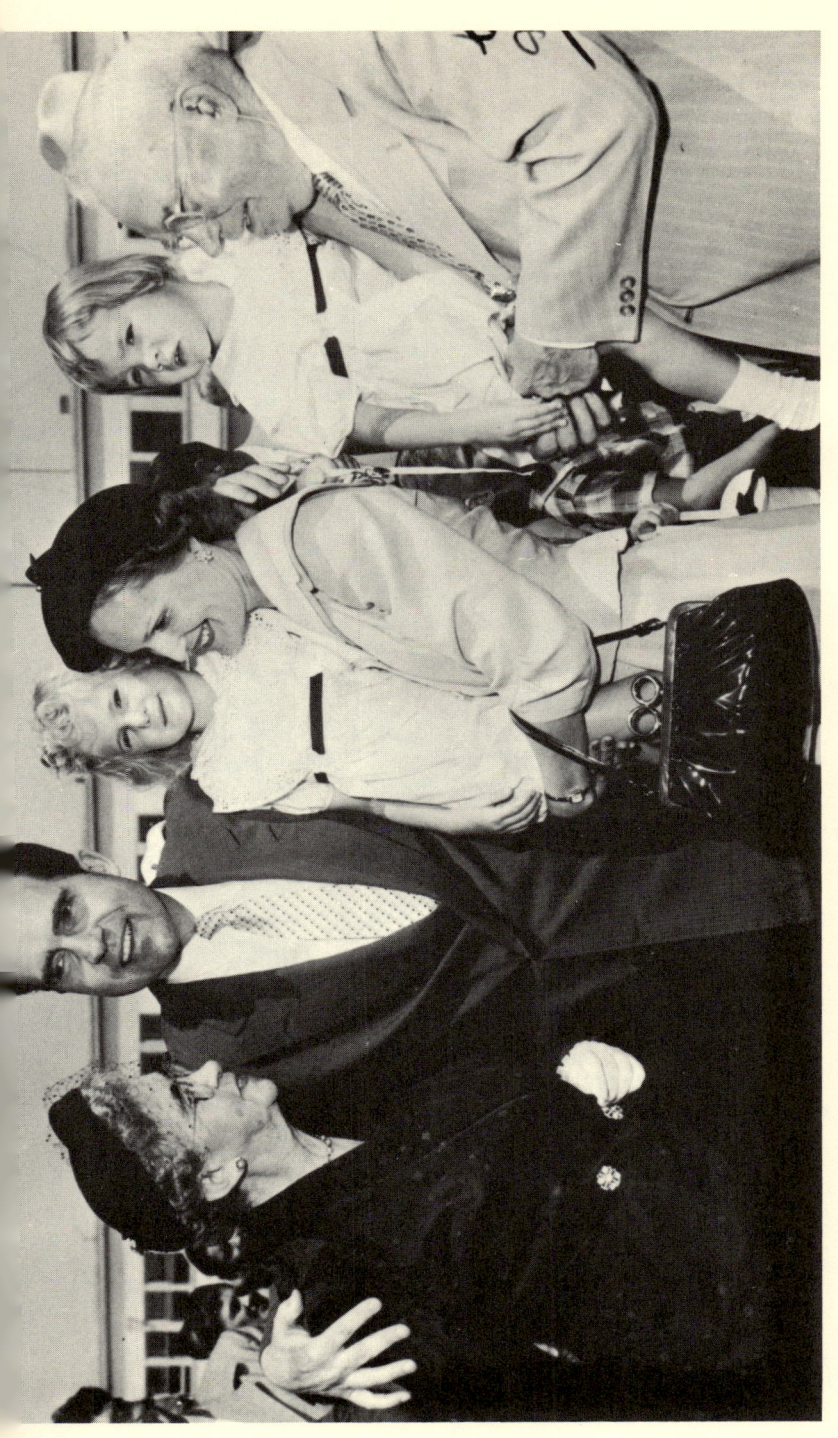

Vice-presidential nominee Richard Nixon and his family are greeted by his parents at the Los Angeles airport on July 28, 1952.

9
The Fund

It isn't easy to come before a nationwide audience and bare your life as I have done.
                    Richard Nixon
            from "The Checkers Speech"

Six Fateful Days

IN THE BRIEF SPAN of just six days, beginning on September 18, 1952, Richard Nixon was transformed, in Stewart Alsop's words, "from a youthful would-be Throttlebottom into the really major political figure he has been ever since." The crisis was precipitated by the accusation that a group of wealthy California oilmen, bankers, and others representing statewide (and in some instances national) business interests had contributed $18,235 to defray political expenses that Nixon would otherwise have had to pay out of his own personal funds. The implication was clear: a candidate for the vice-presidency had been "bought and paid for" by a shadow group who expected favors in return for their largesse.

Deserted by many he had thought were his staunch friends and backed only by Chotiner, Summerfield, Knowland and a few others, Nixon was under pressure from party chiefs to write a letter of resignation to a vacillating, indecisive Eisenhower. Forced to make a lone stand in his own defense before the eyes of millions of television viewers, he displayed a raw, dogged courage that has yet to be equalled in the annals of American politics. Before the "fund" episode, Nixon, like Arthur Miller's Willy Loman in *Death of a Salesman,* had been traveling on a shoeshine and a smile. In its aftermath, he became a candidate in his own right. Still overshadowed by Eisenhower's reputation and charisma, he nevertheless developed into a man of stature and, as it turned out, a man of destiny.

Those fateful six days also supplied his opponents with additional accusations to increase the collection of pejoratives they had been fathering since his political debut in 1946. Following his nationally televised rebuttal in the so-called "Checkers" speech, he was accused of mawkishness and deceit; of shameless sycophancy to the General; and of withholding important facts that would have branded him a liar and a cheat had he made a full disclosure. The "Tricky Dick" label was again fastened upon him, and he was subjected to a series of new smears which, like the "secret" fund, boomeranged when they were proven false. All of this had its effect upon Pat Nixon, already disenchanted with politics.

"The crisis of the fund left a deep scar which was never to heal completely," Richard Nixon said. "From that time on, Pat was to go through campaign after campaign as a good trouper, but never again with the same feeling toward political life. She had lost the zest for it."

The Story Behind the Fund

The first cloud apeared on September 14—a cloud no

bigger than a wisp of cigar smoke, and even less threatening. Thirty-nine year-old Richard Nixon had just concluded a half-hour interview on "Meet the Press," televised from coast to coast. Joining host Larry Spivack and two other reporters was Peter Edson, the highly respected veteran Washington correspondent who represented the Newspaper Enterprise Association, a division of the pro-Eisenhower Scripps-Howard syndicate. After the program, Edson took Nixon aside.

"Senator, I would have asked you this question on the air, but I hadn't time to check out the facts," he said. "There's a rumor making the rounds ever since the convention that you have a supplementary salary of about $20,000 a year—a fund contributed by a hundred California businessmen. Any truth to the story?"

Nixon made no effort to sidestep the question. Indeed, he had nothing to hide! He explained that the rumors might refer to a political fund that had been established by his California supporters to help defray the usual expenses—for travel, printing, postage and clerical help. All of these expenses, he went on to say, were strictly political, and not personal. He then suggested that Edson contact Dana Smith, a lawyer in Pasadena, who was Chairman of Southern California Citizens for Eisenhower-Nixon, if he wanted further information. They parted with a friendly handshake.

Acting on Nixon's suggestion, Peter Edson telephoned Smith in Pasadena who answered all questions in a straightforward manner. There was nothing secret about the fund, Edson learned. Smith, Chotiner and others had stumped California, making personal calls, writing letters and telephoning registered Republicans in an effort to raise the money which would enable their Senator to make periodic return trips so that he might report to his constituents. Contributions from any single source were limited to $500 in a given year. The fund had no effect on his Senatorial campaign—the money was raised *after* Nixon's election to the Senate. A full accounting, including the names of contributors, was available at any time and, in fact, as the fund's trustee, Smith was responsible for all receipts and expenditures. The bank account was in his name. Not a penny had ever passed through Nixon's hands. Bills were paid by Smith only when regular and proper invoices were submitted to him. That, in substance, was the story behind the fund. Most Representatives and Senators had, or hoped to have, a similar fund, and Edson knew that this story hardly merited a feature writeup. He reported it factually in a short news item. As far as Nixon was concerned, when Edson's account was published, it would put an end to the silly rumors.

On September 15, Nixon visited Eisenhower at his headquarters at the Brown Palace in Denver where they reviewed campaign strategy. Eisenhower would conduct his activities on a high moral plane, concentrating on "cleaning up the mess in Washington." He would sound the clarion for a nationwide crusade to drive the "crooks and cronies" out of Washington. Nixon, on the other hand, was assigned the wheelhorse role of dealing with party politicians and attacking the Democrats wherever he might find a weak point. Chotiner himself could not have originated a strategy as sweeping and populist as this: the GOP would cover the entire spectrum of appeal, ranging from Eisenhower's image as the keeper of civic virtue to Nixon's as the "hatchet man"—an appellation which his adversaries claimed he had applied to himself.*

On September 18, the presidential and vice-presidential candidates, each with his own advisers, managers, press agents and newsmen, took to their special trains; Eisenhower's "Look Ahead, Neighbor" caravan heading east and Nixon's special train heading west. Campaigning in Iowa, Eisenhower opened

---

*Actually, this was a distorted allusion to a speech Nixon had made on September 2, in Bangor, Maine. His exact words were: "I intend to make Communist subversion and corruption the theme of every speech from now until the election. If the record itself smears, then let it smear. If the dry rot of corruption and Communism, which has eaten deep into our body politic during the past seven years, can only be chopped out with a hatchet—then let's call for a hatchet."

his bid for the presidency with a ringing pronouncement: "I give you my solemn promise that I will spare no effort to drive the crooks and cronies from their seats of entrenched power. The Democratic so-called Fair Deal will be replaced with an Honest Deal. When we are through, the experts in shady and shoddy government operations will be on their way back to the shadowy haunts in the subcellars of American politics from which they came."

Aboard Nixon's train, all was placid and serene. His "crime-a-day" references to the scandal-ridden Truman Administration; his ceaseless attacks on the Democrats for their "softness" toward Communists and fellow travelers; his repeated references to the Hiss case and the sponsorship and support of Hiss by Adlai Stevenson, the Democratic presidential candidate; his reminders to the public that the Republican Party was the party of four-square probity; all these served further to enrage the Democrats who fervently hoped that they might "get" Nixon for some indiscretion of his own. For Nixon, there were no gray areas: the Democrats were the villains; the Republicans were knights in shining armor.

Meanwhile, the Democrats bade their time: digging deeply into Nixon's past, examining the minutiae that other investigative reporters might have missed. In Los Angeles, three newsmen tipped off about Edson's forthcoming story began their own investigation. They traced the fund to the bank in which it was kept. They examined some of the canceled checks and then visited Dana Smith, the fund's administrator, who had telephoned Nixon after his talk with Edson. He had been assured that it was perfectly safe, even wise, to answer all questions openly.

Three Reporters Begin Digging

The three newsmen, Ernest Brashear of the *Los Angeles Daily News,* Leo Katcher, a correspondent for the *New York Post* who was also a Hollywood script writer, and Richard

Donovan of *Reporter* magazine plied Smith with questions that he, as a lawyer, should have suspected might lead to an unfavorable conclusion. Like Nixon, however, he had no reason to be anything but candid.

"The contributors to the fund were convinced that Richard Nixon had a fine voting record in the House and that he had a wide grasp of American political and economic principles," Smith told the reporters. "After his election to the Senate, we decided to insure his re-election, even though two years' distant, by setting up a fund that would help him keep in touch with his constituents. We realized that his salary was pitifully inadequate to do a real job for his people back home, and we took the position that we had gotten Dick into this and that we were going to see him through."

"What did he need the money for?" asked one of the reporters.

"He needed it for such things as long-distance telephone calls, the thousands of Christmas cards that every Congressman sends out to his constituents, for postage, for radio and TV appearances, and for trips to California. He ought to report back here to the people at least three times a year," Smith went on. "Between the time he was elected to the Senate and his nomination as Vice-President, we spent between $16,000 and $18,000—which I disbursed."

Donovan wrote an accurate report for his publication. Brashear, anticipating a feature byline in his anti-Nixon *Daily News,* prepared a lurid, distorted account and submitted it to his editor, who, in turn, asked the paper's general manager, Robert Smith, for an opinion. Smith, who had been checking out the details of the fund on his own, refused to publish Brashear's version: "Our paper was opposed to Nixon, but we were convinced that he had not diverted the political campaign funds to his own pocket—it was no supplemental salary."

But James A. Wechsler, editor of the *Post,* had no such scruples. When Katcher's report was handed to him, he welcomed it as manna from a Democratic heaven. Here was the "get Nixon" story the Democrats had been praying for.

Euphoric Twilight

Completely unaware of the impending scandal, Senator and Mrs. Nixon relaxed aboard the ten-car special that chugged peacefully from Denver to the West Coast on the first lap of a campaign tour that would take them through California, north to Oregon, and into the state of Washington. *En route,* they made an unscheduled stop at Ely, Nevada, a predominantly Democratic mining town and the birthplace of Pat Nixon. The populace turned out to give a rousing welcome to its native daughter, adding to the sense of security which she and her husband felt in the euphoric twilight that preceded the crisis. Their train then rolled toward Riverside, California where the Nixons, both romanticists, spent the night at the Mission Inn where they had been married twelve years before.

Richard Nixon is no more and no less superstitious than the average citizen, but he felt there was no point in tempting fate. He decided to kick off his vice-presidential campaign in the thriving little town of Pomona, a few miles from the metropolis of Los Angeles—the same community in which he had launched his previous campaigns. "Why interfere with Lady Luck?" he asked rhetorically. "If Pomona was the town where the gods of fortune were ready to smile, then Pomona it would be."

The rally, televised nationally, was a triumph for "the hometown boy who made good," but as the Nixon Special pulled out of the railroad station, Nixon was approached by his press secretary, Jim Bassett, who was on leave from his job as political editor of the Los Angeles *Mirror*. "Dick," Bassett began worriedly, "one of the reporters on the train just told me that his paper is planning a story involving some kind of Nixon fund. It's scheduled for tomorrow's editions."

"Don't let it bother you," Nixon assured him, smiling. "That's probably the Pete Edson story. I know all about it."

They had not yet reached their first scheduled stop in Bakersfield, the heart of California's agricultural belt, when a message was received from Republican headquarters in Los Angeles. They, too, had learned that a Nixon fund story would be published the next day, September 18, and they feared it might have repercussions.

It was now one o'clock in the morning and, although he felt no concern whatever, Nixon decided to review the matter in detail with four of his advisers: William P. Rogers, Murray Chotiner, Pat Hillings (who had succeeded Nixon in the House when he was elected to the Senate) and Jack Drown, one of his oldest and closest friends. Also present was Miss Rose Mary Woods, his executive secretary. Rogers had heard nothing of the fund, and he listened attentively as Nixon reviewed the matter in detail. When Nixon finished, he asked Rogers for an honest opinion.

"The way I see it," Rogers answered after some thought, "the only difference between this fund and other political funds is that yours was openly solicited, the amount of individual contributions was limited, and none of the money passed through your hands. You had a trustee to disburse the funds. The fact that every dime was so scrupulously accounted for, it seems to me, leaves no room for an unfavorable story. There's nothing illegal, unethical or even embarrassing about this fund, and if the opposition tries to build it into some sort of scandal they'll never do it on the facts of the case. Frankly," Rogers concluded, "you haven't anything to worry about."

Chotiner, the political bloodhound who could usually scent a trouble-spot when no one else knew it existed, dismissed it as of no consequence. "Hell, there's nothing to this silly thing; it's ridiculous, a tempest in a teapot," he snorted.

The Nixon Special was scheduled to make ten whistle-stops a day on the tour up the Central Valley of California into the state of Washington. Satisfied that the fund story presented no real problems and could be explained with a brief statement of fact, Nixon and his aides went to bed knowing they would need all the rest they could get in readiness for the campaign rigors which awaited them.

But as the morning of September 18 dawned, tension on the train was growing with ominous rapidity. The press corps aboard had learned of the fund and was clamoring for details. Jim Bassett entered Nixon's private car and silently handed him a copy of the *New York Post*.

The Mounting Tension

Nixon was rocked to his very toes. This was not Edson's objective report but the brass-knuckled attack which had been written by Leo Katcher. The *Post* headline, which dominated the front page, screamed:

SECRET NIXON FUND

The story itself was published on the second page under a two-banner subhead that proclaimed:

SECRET RICH MEN'S TRUST FUND KEEPS NIXON IN STYLE FAR BEYOND HIS SALARY

"The existence of a 'millionaire's club' devoted exclusively to the financial comfort of Senator Nixon, GOP vice-presidential candidate, was revealed today," said the opening paragraph. The headline and the lead paragraph contained the only reference to a "secret" fund or a "millionaire's club." Nowhere else in Katcher's wily story did he actually say, or even indicate, what most readers were calculated to, and did infer—that Nixon was receiving a supplementary salary from a group of millionaires.

"It was a clever example of the half-truth," wrote Nixon. "In fact, more than half the story was true, with substantially the same information that Dana Smith had told all the reporters—but that was the bottom half."

Edson's straight news account was picked up by United Press and Associated Press, as was the *New York Post* version, with the latter receiving most of the headlines. Sensational stories help sell papers, of course, but a number of papers and periodicals refused to carry Katcher's report at all, recognizing it as a smear by the most violently anti-Republican paper in the country.

Because of the time difference between the east and west coasts, the California papers had not yet appeared, and the crowds of people who met the Nixon Special that morning were friendly. At his first stop in Bakersfield, Nixon, standing on the rear platform of the train, called out, "Who can clean up the mess in Washington?" Knowing the expected answer, the crowd jubilantly responded, "Ike can."

The whistle-stops continued throughout that Thursday, September 18, with Nixon speaking from the rear of the train to throngs in Tulare, Fresno, Madera, Merced, Stockton and Sacramento. And at each stop another contingent of reporters would board the Nixon Special, besieging Jim Bassett for a statement about the "secret" fund.

Nixon, finally facing the gravity of the accusation, barred newsmen from his private car from Fresno onward while he, together with Chotiner and Rogers, prepared a brief statement —a 200-word fact-sheet with regard to the fund—and handed it to Bassett. "This should satisfy the reporters," he said confidently. Bassett, however, knew the reporters had scented blood.

The Attack Begins

Taking advantage of what appeared to be the luckiest break of the campaign, Democratic National Chairman Stephen Mitchell, in a mimeographed handout, demanded that Eisenhower call for Nixon's withdrawal as a candidate. On that same day, just hours after Nixon had issued his reply, Mitchell followed up his press release with radio and television appearances in which he exhorted the Republican candidate for President to force Nixon to resign or else stop prattling about "morality in government."

Chotiner recognized the Democratic offensive for what it was: a tactical move to take advantage of what promised to be a political harvest of immeasurable value. "You've issued your statement, and that's enough," he told Nixon. "We have to ignore the attacks. Answering them would play into their hands by giving them even more publicity. So far, the crowds along our route have been favorable, so why raise unnecessary issues?" The advice made sense to Nixon. "All right, let's wait and see what they do," he said.

By the time Nixon's train arrived in Marysville the next morning, the story had boiled into headlines everywhere. The *Sacramento Bee* observed:

> The man who the people of the sovereign state of California believed was actually representing them is the pet and protege of a special interest group of rich Southern Californians. To put it more bluntly, Nixon is their subsidized front man if not, indeed, their lobbyist.

Marysville, a small mining town in northern California, was considered pro-Republican, and was no cause for concern to Nixon. Despite its small population, a rather large crowd had gathered to see and hear him, and he delivered his speech with the usual gusto and enthusiasm that had been winning him new converts along his whistle-stop route. The people of this small town had heard about the "secret" fund but apparently had not been too impressed.

In Sacramento, however, the Stevenson forces had made up their minds to confront Nixon directly, if for no other reason than to disrupt his highly successful itinerary. Under the supervision of Glen Wilson, a group of Young Democrats bundled into a car and speeded off for Marysville where they planned to heckle him about the fund. Just as the Nixon Special was leaving the station, the car screeched to a stop, the group of young men ran toward the train and, drowning out the cheers of the local citizens, yelled: "How about that $16,000!"

Nixon's patience—his resolve to ignore his accusers—reached the breaking point. Forgotten was Chotiner's advice that he simply ignore the attacks. "I could not see myself running away from a bunch of hecklers," he recounted grimly. The train began to leave the station when Nixon wheeled around and shouted, "Hold the train!"

One hundred yards down the tracks, it ground to a stop. His eyes narrowed. He was scarcely able to suppress his anger. Face white, he pointed a finger at one of the men who had called out, and let the heckler have it with both barrels:

"You folks know the work that I did investigating Communists in the United States. Ever since I have done that work the Communists and the left-wingers have been fighting me with every possible smear. When I received the nomination for the vice-presidency, I was warned that if I continued to attack the Communists in this government they would continue to smear me. And believe me, you can expect that they will continue to do so. They started it yesterday. They have tried to say that I had taken $16,000 for my personal use.

"What they didn't point out is that rather than charging the American taxpayer with the expenses of my office, which were in excess of the amounts which were allowed under the law, what I did was to have those expenses paid by the people back home who were interested in seeing that information concerning what was going on in Washington was spread among the people of this state."

The young hecklers tried to interrupt, but they were immediately shouted down by the rapt audience who divined that this was an extemporaneous speech—that of a man defending his integrity without written notes or even a forewarning that he would be called upon to explain his actions. They applauded, and Nixon continued:

"I will tell you what some of the others do. They put their wives on the payroll, taking your money and using it for that purpose. Pat Nixon has worked in my office night after night, and I can say this proudly—she has never been on the government payroll since I have been in Washington."

"Tricky Dick!" screamed one of the teenage hecklers. Several persons advanced threateningly toward the youngster, and he ran toward the car that had brought him and his cronies to Marysville. But a peculiar change of mood had transpired. The other Young Democrats who had been listening intently turned to their young colleague and muttered, "Shut up! Let's hear what the man has to say."

"Do you want me to do what some others are doing?" Nixon continued. "Take fat legal fees on the side! During the time I have been in Washington I have never taken a legal fee, although as a lawyer I could legally have done so; and I am never going to in the future. I do not intend to violate the trust which my office . . ."

Nixon was prevented from finishing his remarks. The crowd was cheering itself hoarse. He had touched a responsive chord and they believed him. Anything else he might have added would have been superfluous.

Had he been believed as quickly and as enthusiastically by his own Republican associates, Nixon's problems would have been at an end. But that was not the way it happened.

The Nixon-Eisenhower Secret War

Although the Democrats gleefully seized upon the scandal-ridden "secret" fund story and took advantage of it, it was the Republicans themselves who kept it alive. Supporters of Governor Warren during the primaries, for example, could not forgive Nixon for straying from the "favorite son" path —although, technically, he remained loyal to Warren until the delegation was released from its commitment. Their bitterness was exacerbated when Nixon was nominated Vice-President. When they, along with other California Republicans, were solicited for contributions for Nixon's fund, their resentment boiled over.

In the normal course of frenzied political charges and countercharges, all this would have faded from the news, and other more important and legitimate issues would have crowded it off the front pages and off the airwaves. Adlai Stevenson himself made no direct reference to the fund, confining himself instead to a call for "ethics in high places." The story kept growing as a subject of national interest, because the overly-cautious General Eisenhower, by his refusal to speak out in support of his running mate, was giving tacit approval to the growing "dump Nixon" conspiracy.

When late on Friday, the day following the *Post* account, the General had still not phoned or wired Nixon to express belief in his honesty, the Senator's puzzlement slowly gave way to irritation and concern. It finally dawned on him that political panic was spreading in the Republican hierarchy.

Meanwhile, in Washington, telegrams, telephone calls and hastily called conferences sent the National Committee into a frenzy as it attempted to placate reporters and party workers. But in the absence of any communication from Nixon, other than this 200-word press release of the day before, and in view of Eisenhower's wall of silence, they could do little to stem the mounting suspicions. By nightfall, the gloomy prediction in Nixon's own Washington headquarters was that his resignation was imminent.

Recalling his feelings ten years later, Nixon wrote: "The handwriting on the wall seemed to say: Dick Nixon is through."

Counter-Attack

Never a man to accept defeat without a struggle, the embattled Senator decided to counter-attack with "the plain, unvarnished truth." After consulting with Murray Chotiner and William Rogers, he phoned Dana Smith and instructed him to make public the entire list of contributors. "I also want you to prepare an audit of every penny taken in, and how the money was spent, so I can release that too," he ordered. That, he believed, would put an end to the report of a "millionaire's club" and the gossip of a "supplemental salary."

It was ten o'clock on Friday night when the Nixon Special rolled into southern Oregon. After the vice-presidential candidate made three more rear-platform speeches, the train pulled into a siding for the night. It was here that Nixon learned for the first time that up until then word of the scandal had been withheld from General Eisenhower. His campaign train, Look Ahead Neighbor, had crossed Iowa and passed through Omaha before his staff had informed him of the fund affair. They had withheld the news so that his mind would be clear and free to concentrate on his "Morality in Government" and "Clean Up the Mess in Washington" speeches. That evening, Eisenhower issued a brief statement to the press in which he said "Dick Nixon is an honest man . . . The facts will show that he would not compromise with what is right." But he did not call Nixon.

Within the space of some forty-eight hours, the Democrats' initial insistence that Nixon be forced off the ticket by his chief had risen to a shrill cacophony that played on the nerves of Eisenhower's advisers. A number of them privately agreed that Nixon should offer to resign for "the good of the party." Telephone calls to the train were now running three to one in favor of immediate resignation.

Governor Sherman Adams, Eisenhower's top political adviser, reminded his chief that a vice-presidential candidate could be forced to resign only by the National Committee, although it was a certainty that a demand by the General would be heeded. Adams, convinced that the truth would exonerate Nixon, phoned Paul Hoffman in Pasadena and requested that he begin an immediate and comprehensive investigation of the fund. Hoffman, then recuperating from a slight injury suffered while playing golf, made the arrangements from his hospital bed. He retained the Los Angeles law firm, Gibson, Dunn and Crutcher, and the accounting firm, Price, Waterhouse & Co. Fifty men: lawyers and accountants, all worked around the clock and through the weekend to arrive at the facts which would prove or disprove Nixon's innocence.

Adams then placed another call, this time to Hawaii, where he spoke with the vacationing Senator Knowland. Explaining the circumstances, he asked the Californian to fly back at once. Should the investigation of the fund go against Nixon, Eisenhower would want Knowland at his side—the party would be needing a new vice-presidential candidate.

Tensions on both the Nixon and Eisenhower trains continued to mount that Friday night. Aboard the Look Ahead Neighbor Special, the reporters had taken a private poll in which they voted overwhelmingly—forty-to-two—for dumping Nixon. They also reached a conclusion that Eisenhower's refusal to discuss the problem was an expediency to allow him sufficient time in which to arrange a whitewash.

The results of the poll were handed to the General's press secretary, Jim Hagerty, who brought it to the attention of his chief. Eisenhower read the report and then, red-faced with suppressed anger, ordered an off-the-record press conference. He could see nothing more in the poll than a breach of journalistic ethics. Reporters were supposed to report the news, not make it. They had not only found Nixon guilty before the verdict was in, but their opinion that the General was about to whitewash a guilty man gave rise to the question of his own sense of ethics and honesty.

Clean as a Hound's Tooth

The assembled reporters soon leaked Eisenhower's off-the-record lecture to their respective papers: "I don't care if you fellows are forty-to-two against me, I'm taking my time on this. Nothing's decided, contrary to your idea that this is all a setup for a whitewash. Of what avail is it for us to carry on this crusade against this business of what has been going on in Washington if we, ourselves, aren't as clean as a hound's tooth?"

Nixon had checked into the Benson Hotel in Portland when news of Eisenhower's "hound's tooth" judgment was relayed to him. He read the statement, at first with disbelief and then with incredulity. So it had come to this! His agony of suspense, the long hours of waiting for a direct communication from Eisenhower to him had resulted in this indirect order from on high. He would have to prove his innocence.

Nixon's mastery of politics was superior to Eisenhower's. His chagrin, therefore, was twofold. First, on purely moral grounds, the General should have accepted his brief statement of Thursday in which he outlined the concept and details of the fund. Additionally, from the moral and legal viewpoint, no American need prove his innocence: he is considered guiltless unless proved otherwise. Secondly, it is fundamental to politics—a fundamental he had learned well from Chotiner—that a party must close ranks against opposition attacks upon its members, especially when they are plainly motivated by political gain.

When referring to his predicament years later Nixon refrained from condemning Eisenhower for his expression of naiveté and apparent distrust. Instead, he gave the reaction of his advisers, Bassett, Chotiner and Rogers: "Bassett told me that the press was reading into Eisenhower's statement the implication that Nixon would have to prove himself 'clean as a hound's tooth' if he hoped to stay on the ticket with Eisenhower. Our little group was somewhat dismayed by reports of Eisenhower's attitude. I must admit that it made me feel like the little boy caught with jam on his face."

In their hotel room, Pat Nixon faced her husband and asked point-blank, "Why do we have to submit to this sort of tactic?"

"Because I'm not a quitter, that's why."

Pat Nixon had good reason for her growing resentment. Upon their arrival in Eugene, Oregon, they were met by a hostile crowd of about a thousand people. Among them was a large contingent of Young Democrats from the University of Oregon, many of them carrying signs which read:

SSH: ANYONE WHO MENTIONS
$16,000 IS A COMMUNIST
and
NO MINK COATS FOR NIXON,
JUST COLD CASH

A tussle soon erupted between the pickets and those who wished to hear what the candidate had to say. In the melee, the signs were torn to shreds and a number of people were slightly injured. But Nixon would not be silenced. He delivered his speech exactly as planned, and then tore into the hecklers. "Your pickets say 'No mink coats for Nixon,'" he shouted, his voice rising in anger. "Well, you're absolutely right. There are no mink coats for the Nixons. I'm proud to say my wife, Pat, wears a good Republican cloth coat."

His reception in Portland was even worse, this time almost resulting in physical assault.

"The pickets and hecklers were out in full force," Nixon recalled. "They threw pennies into the car as we motorcaded to our hotel. Some of them were thrown so hard we were forced to duck. When we reached the Benson Hotel we were met by a jeering crowd blocking the entrance. Pat and I were shoved and jostled as we got out of the car, and only with the help of Bob Hamilton, who had taken leave from his job with the FBI in San Francisco to serve as my aide, were we able to force our way into the lobby."

Eisenhower, of course, had been given Nixon's itinerary and knew that his running mate would be at the Benson Hotel for the weekend. But when the vice-presidential candidate asked for his messages, either phoned or wired, he was told that only Sherman Adams had called. He wheeled around and handed the message to Chotiner. "I've had it, Murray. You call Adams back and tell him that I refuse to talk to anyone but the General."

Chotiner called Sherman Adams, but his politically-oriented mind was already on another matter. While Eisenhower was ignoring Nixon or issuing enigmatic statements, one voice spoke out in cautious support of Nixon—the voice of Adlai Stevenson himself. "I am sure the great Republican Party will ascertain the facts and will act in accordance with our best tradition," he said. "Condemnation without all the evidence, a practice all too familiar among us, would be wrong. I hope you will forgive me if I do not cut Mr. Nixon to ribbons."

Chotiner mulled over the statement. "Why?" he kept asking himself. "Why had the Democratic candidate for President said what Eisenhower should have said? Why was he, of all people, urging restraint? Did he have something to hide? Could it be possible—just possible—that Stevenson had a fund of his own—a *really* secret fund that could destroy his chances for victory in the coming election? Chotiner decided that it might be a good idea to look into the matter.

"I'll lay money against odds that Stevenson is afraid of something," he told Nixon. "He doesn't want these attacks to continue."

Anti-Nixon Sentiment Mounts

The hammerblows continued far into the night. A number of reporters on the Eisenhower train, sensing that big news would be made on the Nixon Special, had flown to Portland to cover the vice-presidential candidate. Bassett sounded them out and gave the discouraging report to Nixon. Editorials in the nation's press were running two-to-one for Nixon's resignation. More than 90 per cent of the newsmen aboard the Eisenhower train believed that Nixon was a liability, and that he should quit the ticket. They were convinced that if he did not resign voluntarily, he should be forced to quit. The overwhelming consensus among radio and television commentators agreed with their newspaper colleagues.

But there were also a few reporters and commentators who were beginning to see Nixon's predicament in a different light, and were putting the blame where it belonged. Eisenhower, they said, could have stopped the burgeoning scandal if he had made a decision, one way or the other. He still could, they maintained, if he would break his silence and say something —anything!

Wherever Nixon had been able to tell his side of the fund story, the crowds had reacted with enthusiastic approval. But Eisenhower's closest advisers, aides and friends had either taken little notice of the public's response or ignored it. The sentiment among the members of his staff was that Nixon "owed it to the party—and to the General—to resign." One of them had gone so far as to call key figures on the National Committee urging them to demand Nixon's resignation.

To Resign Or Not Resign

Should he take the initiative and resign? Nixon posed the question to his little group of strategists.

"That depends on whether you can get your side of the story across to the press," said Bassett.

Rogers was of the opinion that he would be forced to resign if Eisenhower demanded that he quit. "But," he added, "unless and until he does, you should fight it out."

Chotiner was convinced that Nixon could not win his battle by fighting it out on the front pages of the country's newspapers. The press was almost unanimously against him. He would have to go directly to the people.

"This is what politics is all about," Chotiner reminded his former pupil. "The prize is the White House. The Democrats attacked you and they'll continue to attack you because they're afraid to take on Eisenhower. You're the lightning rod. If they weren't taking you on in this way, they'd be after you on something else, because they don't know how to get at Eisenhower —they're afraid he's too popular for a frontal assault. If you get off the ticket because Eisenhower forces you off, or even if you quit of your own volition, he will have as much chance as a snowball in hell to win in November. He'll never be forgiven by Republicans who supported you or those who supported Taft, and the Democrats will beat him over the head for his lack of judgment in selecting you in the first place. This whole story has been blown up out of all proportion because of the delay and indecision of the amateurs around Eisenhower.* Every time you go before an audience, you win them. What we have to do is to get you before the biggest possible audience so that you can talk over the heads of the press to the people. They, the people, I'm absolutely convinced, are for you, but the press is killing you."

When the conference ended after three in the morning, they had agreed that the only way Nixon could speak directly to millions of people, rather than only to the thousands that he customarily addressed, would be to appear on a national television broadcast. And the belated conclusion was reached that Nixon could expect no help or assurance from Eisenhower.

There was no letup in the crushing hammerblows. Nixon learned that on the following day editorials would appear in the New York *Herald Tribune* and the *Washington Post* calling for his resignation. He was stunned. He could understand the *Washington Post's* demand for his resignation—that paper had been against him ever since he had been elected to Con-

---

*Although Nixon claims that Chotiner placed the blame of delay and indecision on "the amateurs around Eisenhower," other reports state that Chotiner did not mention "amateurs," but Eisenhower himself.

gress. But the *Herald Tribune,* the most influential Republican newspaper in the east, had been the base of his support! He knew that Bert Andrews, the chief Washington correspondent for the *Tribune,* a man who had been one of his closest friends ever since they had worked together in their investigation of Alger Hiss, was aboard Eisenhower's Look Ahead Neighbor Special. He also was well aware that the "Trib's" publishers were very close to Eisenhower and were among his most influential supporters. Once again he read the all-important sentences: "The proper course of Senator Nixon in the circumstances is to make a formal offer of withdrawal from the ticket. How this offer is acted on will be determined by an appraisal of all the facts in the light of General Eisenhower's unsurpassed fairness of mind."

This was no mere editorial; it was an official demand.

Nixon may not have been as politically astute as Chotiner, but he did have a razor-sharp mind. He recognized that he was being *ordered* to resign before his guilt or innocence had been established. He was to rely on his chief's "unsurpassed fairness of mind," although his chief had made no attempt to ascertain just what the facts were! Considering the stature and high Republican connections of the paper, there could be no other conclusion.

"I knew now that the fat was in the fire," Nixon recounted. "That sounded like the official word from Eisenhower himself."

Chotiner was furious. "How stupid can they be? If those so-called 'advisers' around Eisenhower just had the sense they were born with, they would recognize that this is a purely political attack and they wouldn't pop off like this."

For Nixon, in his despair, it seemed like the end of the world; an inglorious finish to a career that had been so bright with promise. Was there no one, other than Pat and his close circle of friends, who believed in him? As he brooded, Pat Hillings, his twenty-nine-year-old adviser, handed him a telegram. The message, dated September 20, read:

GIRLS ARE OKAY. THIS IS TO TELL YOU WE ARE THINKING OF YOU AND KNOW EVERYTHING WILL BE FINE. LOVE ALWAYS, MOTHER.

This had been her Quaker way, through the years, of saying that she would be praying for him.

For a few silent moments he fought to retain his composure. All the unwarranted abuse he had taken, the continued silence of the one man who could have served as the character witness he needed so badly, the mushrooming desertions of those he had considered his friends and allies, and now this, contrasting, wholly unexpected, expression of love and trust was simply too much for him to contain.

"He broke down and cried," said Hillings. "I left the room and closed the door softly behind me."

Nixon's mood wavered between despondency and determination. Then he received another bulletin, and once again he was filled with anger. Democratic Chairman Mitchell, seeing that Nixon was getting no support from Eisenhower, called the Senator "a Holy Joe that's been talking pretty big . . . Now let him put up some facts."

"I Will Not Resign!"

The turmoil that seethed in Nixon's head prevented him from sleeping. He reviewed the events of that long Saturday and analyzed his options. If he resigned from the ticket it would be considered an admission of guilt, and should the Republicans lose the election as a result, he would forever afterward be castigated as the man who cost Eisenhower the presidency, "No," he decided, "I will not resign. I'll fight it out."

The decision was final. For the next seventy-two hours he

would prepare himself for the ordeal that would follow—he would take his case before the people in a half-hour nationwide television speech. His mind was made up. He went to bed at five in the morning and, as he put it, "slept better than I had since the night the train pulled out of Pomona four days before."

Nixon had expected Sunday to be a quiet day, a period in which he would prepare some notes for his broadcast, answer a few of the avalanche of letters and telegrams he had received since the start of his campaign a week earlier, and spend some time with his wife. But this was to be no day of rest.

Richard and Pat had just finished a ten o'clock breakfast when Pat Hillings wordlessly placed a telegram before him. Harold Stassen, in a three-hundred-word message, urged him to resign. Helpfully, he even suggested the text for the withdrawal announcement. As the telegram continued, Stassen waxed encouraging. "This will strengthen you and aid you in your career," he said, although he neglected to mention how this happy consequence would be achieved. He then proceeded to nominate a new vice-presidential candidate. "Should your resignation be accepted," he concluded, "I believe Earl Warren should be your replacement."

"I'll think about it," Nixon wired back. He could be forgiven the shade of bitterness he now felt. Only eight months had elapsed since Stassen, himself a candidate for President, had offered Nixon the vice-presidency in return for swinging all or part of the California delegation behind him.

Word soon spread that Nixon had decided on a national television broadcast. Several sponsors offered to back the program to be carried without interruption for the usual commercials. It was Chotiner who advised against it. How could Nixon accept a free donation of valuable television time from the very corporations who had supposedly "bought" him?

Nixon agreed. The program would have to be sponsored by the Republican Party itself.

Dewey's Proposal

That Sunday afternoon Tom Dewey telephoned. He concurred with the idea of a presentation of the vice-presidential candidate's views on television, and felt that it might serve to break the deadlock occasioned by Nixon's determination to stay on the ticket and Eisenhower's refusal to support his running mate.

Dewey's proposition was loaded with dynamite.

"I don't think Eisenhower should make the decision as to whether you resign or not," Dewey began. "Let the American people decide. At the end of your program, ask people to wire their verdict as to your guilt or innocence. They can wire you in Los Angeles. You'll probably get over a million replies, and that will give you three or four days to think it over. At the end of that time, if sixty per cent are for you and forty per cent against you, then you can say you are quitting because that is *not enough* of a majority. But if it is ninety per cent to ten, stay on the ticket. If you do stay on, it isn't blamed on Ike; and if you get off, it isn't blamed on Ike. All the fellows here in New York agree with me."

Chotiner's immediate reaction was explosive and unprintable. He and Nixon knew that Dewey's reference to "all the fellows" probably included Eisenhower's staff, or most of it, and might well express the opinion of the General himself. Not once during the fund crisis had Nixon ever attacked Eisenhower himself for his long silence and refusal to support him publicly. He had always referred to "the General's staff" or "the chief's advisers." Chotiner, we know, had labeled them as "that bunch of amateurs around Eisenhower." Now, as they examined Dewey's proposal, they were struck by its full import.

"Some of the members of my staff feared a concerted campaign might be started to stack the replies against me," recalled Nixon in mild understatement of the problem. In reality, his chances of meeting Dewey's ninety-to-ten majority was about equal to winning the Irish Sweepstakes. He would begin his speech as a guilty man asking forgiveness, begging the public to send him telegrams which he would abjectly turn over to his boss for final approval. But even with a sixty-forty vote of confidence, he would still have to resign! In effect, he had been told to either resign or get lost.

Nixon was well aware that the General's advisers—and no doubt Eisenhower himself—were waiting for him to respond to Dewey's telephoned "deal." But the battle was joined as far as Nixon was concerned. Finally, he understood that this was not a conflict between himself and the press, or even with the Democrats. It was a struggle between Eisenhower and himself.

"Are you going to return Governor Dewey's call?" asked Pat.

"No," he replied stubbornly. "I'm not crawling for anyone."

That evening, Richard and Pat went to the Portland Temple Club where he had a speaking engagement. He hoped he would have an opportunity to forget the fund turmoil for a while and discuss other aspects of his program. But, as though he did not have enough problems on his mind, that evening he found himself facing a new one. One of the most malicious smears which had been leveled against him since the Hiss case was the old slander that he was anti-Semitic. This was brought up at the meeting. As usual, his answers were forthright; his matter earnest and sincere. Fortunately, he was able to lay the accusation to rest, and his spirits were lifted as the large audience rose to give him a standing ovation.

They returned to the hotel at nine o'clock, and Nixon called his staff into conference to continue the discussion of plans for the coming broadcast. Chotiner insisted that the National Committee in Washington should sponsor the program, and he reminded the others that the Committee had already scheduled two nationwide broadcasts for the vice-presidential candidate.

Nixon was sitting on a couch, his feet propped up on a coffee table, when their discussion was interrupted by his private secretary, Rose Mary Woods.

"Senator, you have a phone call," she announced crisply. "It's General Eisenhower."

Eisenhower was calling from St. Louis, it was the first and last call he would make during the fund crisis. Nixon's refusal to answer Dewey's proposal had finally moved Ike to break the now mutual silence.

"Hello Dick. You've been taking a lot of heat these last few days. I imagine its been pretty rough."

"It has," Nixon replied briefly.

"You know, this is an awfully hard thing for me to decide," Eisenhower went on. "I have come to the conclusion that you are the one who has to decide what to do."

Nixon, at this point, could have reminded Ike that it was the presidential candidate's obligation to make the decision, not his, and that the decision should have been made last Thursday when the *Post* headline first appeared. However, he maintained a discreet silence.

"After all," the General continued, "you've got a big following, and if the impression got around that you got off the ticket because I forced you off, it will be very bad."

"On the other hand," Eisenhower explained with sweet reasonableness, "if I issue a statement now backing you up, in effect people will accuse me of condoning wrongdoing."

They had been fencing long enough. Both men knew that the results of the fifty-man survey of Nixon's finances being conducted by the accounting firm of Price, Waterhouse and the legal firm of Gibson, Dunn and Crutcher would be in Eisenhower's hands within a matter of hours. There was nothing to prevent the General from issuing a statement of confidence *after* he had studied the report which Nixon, of course, knew would completely exonerate him. But no! Eisenhower had refused to make a decision based on the report. If the people who would not know the results of the report, were to decide that Nixon was honest, then, and only then, would he tender his blessing.

"I don't want to be in the position of condemning an innocent man," Eisenhower said. "I think you ought to go on a television program and tell them everything there is to tell, everything you can remember since the day you entered public life. Tell them about any money you have ever received."

Nixon thought about Dewey's statement that three or four days would be required after the program was finished to evaluate the people's reaction. During that interval his campaign would be at a complete standstill. He would be stranded in Los Angeles, unable to make a single speech, and, with Ike withholding his approval until the votes were counted, his opponents could mount another attack against him.

"General," asked Nixon, attempting a compromise, "after the television program, could you then make an announcement one way or the other?"

Eisenhower was not in a compromising mood. "I'm hoping that no announcement will be necessary," he said evasively. "But maybe after the program we could tell what ought to be done."

The steam that had been building inside Nixon finally blew a valve. "General," he said slowly and carefully, "there comes a time when you either have to fish or cut bait . . . I'll get off the ticket if you think my staying on it would be harmful. You let me know and I'll get off, and I'll take the heat. But this thing has got to be decided at the earliest possible time. After the television program, if you think I should stay on or get off, I think you should say so either way. The great trouble here is the indecision."

"No," insisted Eisenhower, "we will have to wait three or four days after the television program." The fifteen-minute conversation ended with Ike wishing Dick "good luck and keep your chin up."

Nixon did indeed keep his chin up—higher than Eisenhower had thought he would. Now that the General had placed on him the responsibility of deciding his own fate by way of television, he would assume that responsibility without any compromise. Forgotten now was Dewey's warning that he would need a ninety-to-ten majority to stay on the ticket. Political candidates in the United States simply do not receive ninety per cent of a vote, and everyone knew it. He now made his decision: If he, *personally,* considered the broadcast a success, he would remain on the ticket. If he thought it was a failure, he'd resign. He, alone, would be the judge. If they still called for his resignation, they would have to force the issue.

For the next several hours his staff worked feverishly to alter their plans and schedules. At eleven o'clock, Jim Bassett announced that a press conference would be held shortly—Nixon's first since the fund crisis erupted. Chotiner, on the phone with Sherman Adams and Arthur Summerfield at Eisenhower's headquarters, convinced them of the necessity of receiving a guarantee that the $75,000 would be provided for the television program.

At one o'clock, Nixon finally was able to meet with the newsmen, nearly all of whom were expecting him to announce his resignation. Paradoxically, at a time when he had never been more serious in his life, he thought he might as well have a little fun with them, and, in the meantime, increase the suspense. "I have come here to announce that I am breaking off . . ." he paused deliberately as an audible gasp filled the room, "my campaign trip tomorrow for the purpose of going to Los Angeles to make a nationwide television and radio broadcast."

By the time he and Pat checked into the Ambassador Hotel in Los Angeles, he knew that his deliberate attempt to build suspense was succeeding. A swarm of reporters met him at International Airport and asked if he would or would not resign while on the air. Morning papers everywhere carried banner headlines announcing the forthcoming broadcast.

"The speech was to be the most important of my life," Nixon wrote later. "The public reaction would determine whether or not I was a liability to the Republican Party. This broadcast could not be just good—it had to be a smash hit. I knew I had to go for broke."

Preparing for the Broadcast

Nixon had much to occupy his mind as he flew on his chartered plane from Portland to Los Angeles.

"Dick," William Rogers said as they boarded the DC-6, "it isn't just a question of your honesty that's at stake; it's much more than that. If you resign under pressure, and in the middle of a campaign, it will be the first time in our history a calamity like that ever happened. And you can bet your bottom dollar that if the Republican Party loses, you're going to be the scapegoat."

But Nixon's resolve to remain on the ticket was firm. He knew that his battle for political survival depended on his broadcast and he lost no time planning his speech. It would not be enough to quote dull facts to the millions of people he expected as an audience. He would have to inspire them to enthusiastic and active support.

The first requirement would then be to explain the fund and to defend his position in as forthright and convincing a manner as possible so as to hurdle the present impasse. The second requirement would be to establish his integrity so that never again, in the future, would he be plagued by the charge that he had in any way profited financially from his Government service. Third, and thanks to Chotiner's admonition, he planned to use whatever time he had left to launch a counter-attack—to rally the public around the Eisenhower-Nixon banner.

Unable to sleep on the plane, Nixon began to jot down his first notes for the speech, using some picture post cards he found in the pocket of the seat in front of him. He recalled his statement about Pat's cloth coat, and wrote it down as a reminder of the mink coat scandals of the Truman Administration. He thought of Franklin D. Roosevelt's reference to his dog and the satirical comment, "Now the Republicans are attacking poor Fala." Nixon smiled to himself as he decided to mention his own dog, Checkers. The Democrats, he reflected whimsically, could hardly attack him for using the same ploy their own revered leader had done.

He made another note to remind himself of Democratic National Chairman Stephen Mitchell's observation, "If a fellow can't afford to be a Senator, he shouldn't seek the office." Mitchell had implied, indirectly, that only rich men should seek high office, and Nixon chuckled as he thought of the fun he could have with that inadvertent remark.

But, for the greater part of the flight, Nixon was preoccupied with the best way to carry out Eisenhower's suggestion: "Tell them about everything you have ever received from the time you entered public life." It wasn't a pleasant prospect for a man who relished his privacy. But it had to be done. He explained it to Pat who was seated beside him. He would have to expose their personal lives before millions of strangers. In their twelve years of married life they had never acquired much in the way of material things, but neither of them had ever found reason to complain.

"Perhaps we didn't have the latest model car," Nixon recalled, "or the most stylish clothes, or, the biggest house on the block, but neither of us were ever embarrassed by, or even envious of, our neighbors. All we ever asked was that our privacy be respected. We had worked hard to earn what we had and what we owned; and what we owed was our business and nobody else's."

Pat demurred at once. "Why do we have to parade how little we have and how much we owe in front of all those millions of people?"

He shrugged. "All candidates' lives are public."

"Well, it seems to me that we're entitled to at least some privacy."

"Hon, you've got to understand this: these are not normal circumstances. Right now we're living in a fishbowl. If I don't itemize everything we've earned and everything we've spent, the broadcast won't convince the public. I just don't have a choice."

It was almost three in the morning when their plane touched down in Los Angeles. Less than twenty-four hours remained in which to finish preparations for the most important speech he had ever made.

At the Ambassador that Monday, Nixon worked away on his forthcoming speech. He prepared a number of rough drafts on sheets of yellow, lined paper, polishing each successive draft until the final draft which he would use as a guide for his presentation was completed. As was his custom, he would not appear before an audience with a prepared speech, but would rely only on his notes. Ordinarily, he would have allotted a week's time for reflection and writing a speech of such importance, but the deadline was only hours away!

Arrangements for the broadcast had been completed. It would emanate, he learned, from NBC's television studio in the El Capitan theater, not too distant from the intersection of Hollywood Boulevard and Vine Street. Ted Rogers, the Senator's adviser (no relation to William Rogers), wanted a prime-time spot with an assured large audience, preferably the half-hour following a highly popular program. The time which followed the "I Love Lucy" show was available, but Nixon needed all the extra time he could get, so, instead, they took the later spot—immediately following the Milton Berle show. The national hookup, arranged by the Republican National Committee's advertising agency, Batten, Barton, Durstine and Osborn, involved 64 NBC television stations, 194 CBS radio stations, and the entire 560-station Mutual Broadcasting System radio network. Broadcast time was set for Tuesday evening at 6:30 in Los Angeles; 9:30 on the east coast.

The Stevenson Fund

Nixon, isolated in his room where he was putting the final touches on his outline, had just finished reviewing his explanation of the defense of the fund. He was now wondering how he would handle the counter-attack, when, suddenly, the problem solved itself. Chotiner, a wide smile on his face, entered the room and held up a copy of that day's *Chicago Tribune*. There, on the front page, was a report of a Stevenson fund! "I *told* you Stevenson was hiding something!" Chotiner declared excitedly. "This is why he was charitable toward you and the fund. If he hadn't had one of his own, he'd have been at your throat like the rest of the pack."

The "Trib" story revealed that Stevenson had an $18,000 fund. This money, left over from his gubernatorial campaign, was used by him as Governor of Illinois to augment the salaries of deserving state employees. Further, the report disclosed, an official of a mimeograph machine company doing business with the state of Illinois had charged that Stevenson had personally solicited contributions from private businessmen while he was Governor of the state. Stevenson immediately confirmed the story, claiming that he had augmented the salaries of a few members of his administration because they had left higher-paying jobs in private enterprise.

Obviously, there was a vast difference between the Stevenson fund and the Nixon fund. Stevenson's was indeed secret, while Nixon's had been solicited openly and its contributors named. The money had been paid directly to Stevenson and he had disbursed it, while Nixon's had been received and disbursed by a trustee. Stevenson had not offered an accounting of his fund, while the disposition of the Nixon fund had been fully revealed. But the most important difference was that Stevenson's fund had been used for supplemental salaries to his associates, while Nixon's had been used solely for the purpose for which it was created: mailing, printing, travel and other political expenses, with not a penny diverted to any individual.

Chotiner was all for giving it to Stevenson with both barrels, but Nixon thought otherwise. Nothing had been proved against the Democratic candidate; his fund might be proper and above suspicion. He, too, must be judged innocent until proved guilty. But, Nixon thought as he reviewed another paragraph of notes, he did have the right to insist that there must not be two sets of standards—one for the Democrats and the other for the Republicans. Like himself, Stevenson must also be held accountable for all monies received, and must make known the identities of the contributors, and all favors contributors may have received in return.*

On Tuesday, at 4:30, a little more than an hour before he was scheduled to leave for the television studio, Nixon discussed with Rogers and Chotiner the best way for the public to express their opinions—whether he should ask the audience to wire or write to him directly, to Eisenhower, or to the National Committee in Washington. Then the telephone rang. Dewey was on the line with a most devastating message: "There's been a meeting of Eisenhower's top advisers. They asked me to tell you that it is their opinion that at the conclusion of the broadcast tonight you should submit your resignation to Eisenhower."

The Eisenhower camp had made its decision. Nixon was out, regardless of the public's response to the broadcast. Shocked, Nixon was unable to speak for several long moments. Finally, he asked Dewey if his statement represented

---

*Soon after the Nixon broadcast, the New York *World Telegram* broke the story of a new Stevenson fund, this one brought to light by William J. McKinney, former chief of the Illinois Department of Purchases under Governor Stevenson. This second fund involved $100,000 or more, contributed by individuals and companies doing $35,000,000 worth of business with the state. Although Stevenson never denied the existence of fund number two or explained its purpose, sources close to him declared that some of the $100,000 was donated by him to charitable institutions. He felt that "such contributions to worthy causes were expected of a man in his high position."

Eisenhower's judgment.

Dewey couched his reply in careful phrases, avoiding anything that might be directly attributed to Eisenhower, the panjandrum of political probity. "I don't want to imply that the General approves of the decision, but our group would not have asked me to make this call unless we all felt we represented his view."

"It's a little late for instructions like that," Nixon told him. "My notes for the speech are about completed. I don't see how I can possibly change my presentation at this last hour."

"Why not go ahead and explain the fund as you planned?" said Dewey. "After that you can tell the people that although you feel you have done nothing wrong, you don't want to be a liability to Eisenhower, so you are making this formal resignation to him. You can tack the statement on at the end of your speech."

Nixon's fist clenched at this expression of unmitigated impertinence. He had not only been told to go peddle his papers, but was being instructed precisely how to do it.

Dewey's voice, blunt and insistent, came to life again. "Well, can I tell them you've accepted our advice?"

Nixon's nerves were as taut as violin strings. "You can tell them this," he exploded, "their advice doesn't mean a damn thing to me right now. I haven't the vaguest notion about what I am going to do or say, and if your people want to find out, they can watch the show. And tell them I know something about politics too!" he added, slamming down the receiver.

Nixon called his staff to inform them of the verdict which had been handed down even before the case was heard; of the virtual ultimatum to surrender without regard to the public's reaction. He then shaved, showered, dressed hurriedly, and, with less than ten minutes left before leaving for the telecast, went back to his notes. But it was too late for revisions. He had barely started his third outline; he would now have to use his second. Dewey's call had not only upset his carefully planned schedule and shaken the psychological plateau of tension with which he always approached a crisis, but had robbed him of the last few moments to get a firm grasp on the outline he had hoped to commit to memory, based on his notes. At that last moment, and not before then, he made his decision: He would defy Dewey, and indirectly Eisenhower, by demanding the right that is accorded every American—to be judged *after* and not before all the evidence had been heard. He would ask the public to direct their telephone calls and telegrams to the Republican National Committee.

He was jotting down these last few thoughts when Chotiner walked into his room. Nixon looked up in surprise, and with some irritation. He had given strict orders that he was not to be disturbed.

"Dick," Chotiner began, "a good campaign manager must never be seen or heard. But if you're kicked off the ticket I'll break every rule in the book. I'll call the biggest damn press conference you ever heard of and I'll tell everything I know about who called you, what was said, the broken promises, everything; I'll name names, dates and places. The whole bit."

"You'd do that?" Nixon said.

"Sure I would," Chotiner answered. "Hell, we'd be through in politics anyway. What difference would it make?"

This expression of loyalty gave Nixon the lift he needed. Acompanied by Pat, Chotiner and Hillings, Nixon left for the El Capitan theater in Hollywood, making the drive in silence as he pored over his notes. The group arrived twenty-five minutes before broadcast time.

At Nixon's request, the 750-seat theater was empty. There were no on-camera rehearsals. Newsmen had been assigned a press room where a bank of television sets had been installed. With them, also, were the stenographers who would record the speech as it was delivered. Chotiner, Bill Rogers and Hillings were sequestered in another room. So unplanned were the technical details that when the program director asked what movements he intended to make, Nixon answered,

"I haven't the slightest idea. Just keep the camera on me."

"Have you timed your speech, Senator Nixon?" the director asked again.

"No, I'll be talking from notes. I don't have a prepared speech."

He made only one demand: his wife was to be with him throughout the program—within camera range.

In the studio, Pat occupied one of the armchairs while Nixon sat behind a desk. Five pages of handwritten notes lay in front of him. It was two minutes until broadcast time. Overcome by last minute jitters, he turned to Pat, and with faltering voice said: "I just don't think I can go through with it."

"Of course you can," she responded firmly.

Nixon's eyes were on the big clock alongside the camera. He watched the second hand as it swept time into eternity. The camera's red light came to life and began to blink.

He was on the air!

The Checkers Speech

My fellow Americans:

I come before you tonight as a candidate for the vice-presidency and as a man whose honesty and integrity have been questioned. I am sure that you have read the charge and you've heard it, that I, Senator Nixon, took $18,000 from a group of my supporters.

Now, was that wrong? It isn't a question of whether it was legal or illegal; that isn't enough. The question is, was it morally wrong? I say it was morally wrong if any of that $18,000 went to Senator Nixon for my personal use. I say it was morally wrong if it was secretly given and secretly handled. And I say that it was morally wrong if any of the contributors got special favors for the contributions that they made.

And now to answer those questions, let me say this: Not one cent of the $18,000 or any other money of that type ever went to my personal use. Every penny of it was used to pay for political expenses that I did not think should be charged to the taxpayers of the United States.

It was not a secret fund. As a matter of fact, when I was on "Meet the Press"—some of you may have seen it last Sunday—Peter Edson came up to me after the program and he said, "Dick, what about this fund?" And I said: "Well, there's no secret about it. Go out and see Dana Smith who was the administrator of the fund." I gave him Smith's address, and I said: "You will find that the purpose of the fund simply was to defray political expenses that I did not feel should be charged to the government."

And, third, let me point out—and I want to make this particularly clear—that no contributor to this fund, no contributor to any of my campaigns, has ever received any consideration that he would not have received as an ordinary constituent . . .

Well, then, some of you will say—and rightly: "Just what did you use the fund for, Senator? Why did you have to have it?"

Let me tell you in a word or two how a Senate office operates. First of all, the Senator gets $15,000 a year in salary. He gets enough money for one trip a year—a round trip, that is—for himself and his family between his home and Washington, D.C.; and then he gets an allowance to handle the people that work in his office. And the allowance for my state of California is enough to hire thirteen people.

And let me say, incidentally, that the allowance is not paid to the Senator; it's paid directly to the individuals the Senator puts on his payroll—and all of these people and all of these allowances are for strictly official business . . . . But there are other expenses which are not covered by the government; and I think I can best discuss these expenses by asking you some questions.

Do you think that when I or any other Senator makes a political speech, and has it printed, he should charge the printing of that speech and the mailing of that speech to the taxpayers?

Do you think, for example, when I or any other Senator makes a trip to his home state to make a purely political speech that the cost of that trip should be charged to the taxpayers?

Do you think that, when a Senator makes a political broadcast on radio or television, the expense of those broadcasts should be charged to the taxpayers? . . .

The answer is No! The taxpayers shouldn't be required to finance items which are not official business, but which are primarily political business.

You may ask, "Well, how do you pay for these, and how can you do it legally?"

There are several ways that it can be done, and is done, legally in the United States Senate and in the Congress.

The first way is to be a rich man. I don't happen to be a rich man; so I couldn't use that one.

Another way is to put your wife on the payroll. Let me say, incidentally, that my opponent, my opposite number for the vice-presidency of the Democratic ticket does have his wife on the payroll and has had her on his payroll for the past ten years.

Now just let me say this: that's his business and I am not critical of him for doing that. You will have to pass judgment on that particular point. But I have never done that, for this reason: I have found that there are so many deserving stenographers and secretaries in Washington that needed to work that I just didn't feel it was right to put my wife on the payroll. My wife is sitting over here. She is a wonderful stenographer. She used to teach stenography and she used to teach shorthand in high school. That was when I met her. And I can tell you folks that she has worked many hours at night and many hours on Saturdays and Sundays in my office, and she has done a fine job; and I am proud to say tonight that in the six years I have been in the House and Senate of the United States, Pat Nixon has never been on the government payroll.

There are other ways these finances can be taken care of. Some who are lawyers—and I happen to be a lawyer—continue to practice law. But I haven't been able to do that. I am so far away from California, and I have been so busy with my Senatorial work that I have not engaged in any legal practice. And also, as far as my law practice is concerned, it seems to me that the relationship between an attorney and client was so personal that you couldn't possibly represent a man as an attorney and then have an unbiased view when he presented his case to you in the event that he had one before the Government.

And so I felt that the best way to handle these necessary political expenses of getting my message to the American people . . . of exposing this administration, the Communism in it, the corruption . . . was to accept the aid which people in my home state of California who contributed to my campaign, and who continued to make these contributions after I was elected, were glad to make.

I am proud of the fact that not one of them has ever asked me for a special favor. I'm proud that not one of them has ever asked me to vote on a bill other than as my own conscience would dictate. And I am proud of the fact that the taxpayers by subterfuge or otherwise have never paid one dime for expenses which I thought were political and shouldn't be charged to the taxpayers.

Some of you may say: "Well, that's all right, Senator; that's your explanation, but have you got any proof?"

I would like to tell you this evening that just an hour ago we received an independent audit of this entire fund . . . . I have that audit here in my hand. It's an audit made by Price, Waterhouse and Company, and the legal opinion is by Gibson, Dunn and Crutcher, lawyers of Los Angeles, the biggest law firm, and incidentally one of the best ones in Los Angeles . . . . I would like to quote to you the opinion that was prepared by Gibson, Dunn and Crutcher, and based on all the pertinent laws and statutes, together with the audit prepared by the certified public accountants:

It is our conclusion that Senator Nixon did not obtain any financial gain from the collection and disbursement of the fund by Dana Smith; that Senator Nixon did not violate any federal or state law by reason of the operation of the fund; and that neither the portion of the fund paid by Dana Smith directly to third persons, nor the portion paid to Senator Nixon to reimburse him for designated office expenses, constituted income to the Senator which was either reportable or taxable as income under applicable tax laws. (Signed) Gibson, Dunn & Crutcher, by Elmo H. Connor.

Now that, my friends, is not Nixon speaking. That is an independent audit which was requested because I want the American people to know all the facts and I'm not afraid of having independent people go in and check the facts, and that is exactly what they did.

There are some who will say, well, maybe you were able, Senator, to fake this thing. How can we believe what you say? After all there is a possibility that maybe you got some sums in cold cash. Is there a possibility that you might have feathered your own nest?

So now, what I am going to do—and, incidentally, this is unprecedented in the history of American politics— I am going at this time to give to this television and radio audience a complete financial history, everything I have earned, everything I have spent, everything I owe. I want you to know the facts, so I'll have to start early.

I was born in 1913. Our family was one of moderate circumstances, and most of my early life was spent in our store in East Whittier. It was a grocery store—

one of those family enterprises. The only reason we were able to make it go was that my mother and dad had five boys and we all worked in the store.

I worked my way through college, and, to a great extent, through law school. And then, in 1940, probably the best thing that ever happened to me happened—I married Pat. We had a rather difficult time after we were married—like so many of the young couples who may be listening to me. I practiced law; she continued to teach school. I went into the service.

My service record was not a particularly unusual one. I went to the South Pacific. I guess I'm entitled to a couple of battle stars. I got a couple of letters of commendation, but I was just there when the bombs were falling, and then I returned . . . and in 1946 I ran for Congress.

During the war, Pat had worked as a stenographer, and in a bank, and as an economist for a government agency. The total of our savings from both my law practice, her teaching and all the time I was in the war was a little less than $10,000. Every cent of that, incidentally, was in government bonds.

That is where we started when I went into politics. Now, what have I earned since? Well, here it is—I jotted it down—let me read the notes.

First of all, I've had my salary as a Congressman and as a Senator. Second, I have received a total in this past six years of $1,600 from estates which were in my law firm at the time that I severed my connection with it.

I have not engaged in any legal practice and have not accepted any fees from business that came into the firm after I went into politics. I have made an average of approximately $1,500 a year from non-political speaking engagements and lectures. And then, fortunately, we have inherited a little money. Pat sold her interest in her father's estate for $3,000, and I inherited $1,500 from my grandfather.

We lived rather modestly. For four years we lived in an apartment in Park Fairfax in Alexandria, Virginia. The rent was $80 a month. And we saved for the time that we could buy a house.

Now, that was what we took in.

What did we do with this money What do we have today to show for it? This will surprise you because it is so little, I suppose, as standards generally go for those in public life.

First of all, we've got a house in Washington which cost $41,000, and on which we owe $20,000. We have a house in Whittier, California, which costs $13,000, and on which we owe $10,000. My folks are living there at the present time.

I have just $4,000 in life insurance, plus my GI policy, which I have never been able to convert, and which will run out in two years. I have no life insurance whatever on Pat; I have no life insurance on our two youngsters, Patricia and Julie.

I own a 1950 Oldsmobile car. We have our furniture. We have no stocks and bonds of any type. We have no interest of any kind, direct or indirect, in any business.

Now, that's what we have.

What do we owe? Well, in addition to the mortgages, the $20,000 on the house in Washington and the $10,000 one on the house in Whittier, I owe $4,500 to the Riggs Bank in Washington, D.C., with interest at four and one-half per cent. I owe $3,500 to my parents and the interest on that loan, which I pay regularly because it is part of the savings they made through the years they were working so hard. I pay four per cent interest. And then I have a $500 loan which I have on my life insurance.

Well, that's about it. That's what we have. And that's what we owe. It isn't very much, but Pat and I have the satisfaction of knowing that every dime that we've got is honestly ours.

I should say this, that Pat doesn't have a mink coat, but she does have a respectable Republican cloth coat, and I always tell her that she would look good in anything.

One other thing I probably should tell you, because if I don't they'll probably be saying this about me, too. We did get something, a gift, after the nomination. A man down in Texas heard Pat on the radio mention the fact that our two youngsters would like to have a dog; and, believe it or not, the day before we left on this campaign trip we got a message from Union Station in Baltimore saying they had a package for us.

The Nixon Nobody Knows 349

We went down to get it. You know what it was? It was a little cocker spaniel dog, in a crate that he'd sent all the way from Texas—black and white, spotted, and our little girl, Tricia, the six-year-old, named it Checkers. And you know, the kids, like all kids, loved the dog; and I just want to say this, right now, that regardless of what they say about it, we are going to keep him.

Julie and Tricia play with Checkers, the family dog who figured in Nixon's rebuttal to the charge that he maintained a secret slush fund. The emotional reply, broadcast on September 2, 1952, was thereafter dubbed "The Checkers Speech."

At this juncture in his speech, Nixon cast a quick glance at the clock and noted that he had used only half of the thirty minutes allotted to him. His eyes went back to the camera, and in a soft voice, told his listeners and viewers, "It isn't easy to come before a nationwide audience and bare your life as I have done."

It was the understatement of the campaign, and as he himself had said, an unprecedented act in the annals of American politics. His voice had ranged from hoarsely challenging to near pleading. At times he had seemed on the verge of tears. But these were not histrionics; he was a man falsely accused, being tried before the bar of public opinion on charges that any impartial judge would have immediately dismissed for lack of evidence; a man deserted by those he had fully expected would rise to his defense. And he was fighting back—against his opponents and his own Republican Party—fighting with more nerve than anyone would have suspected. He showed himself to be a man with guts.

He stepped around the desk and stood before the camera. The close-up view revealed every expression in his face as he launched into a slashing attack against his adversaries. A shout of pure joy came from Chotiner who was watching the presentation in an adjoining room.

> Mr. Mitchell, the Chairman of the Democratic National Committee, made the statement that if a man couldn't afford to be in the United States Senate, he shouldn't run for the Senate. I want to make my position clear. I don't agree with Mr. Mitchell when he says that only a rich man should serve the Government in the Senate or in the Congress. I don't think that represents the thinking of the Democratic Party, and I know it doesn't represent the thinking of the Republican Party.
>
> I believe it's fine that a man like Governor Stevenson,

who inherited a fortune from his father, can run for President. But I also feel that it's essential in this country of ours that a man of modest means can also run for President, because you remember what Lincoln said—"God must have loved the common people, he made so many of them."

Now I'm going to suggest some courses of conduct.

First of all, you've read in the papers about other funds. Now, Mr. Stevenson, apparently had a couple —one of them in which a group of business people paid and helped to supplement the salaries of state employees. Here is where the money went directly into their pockets.

I think Mr. Stevenson should come before the American people who have contributed to that fund, and give the names of the people who put this money into their pockets at the same time they were receiving money from their state government, and see what favors, if any, they gave out for that.

I don't condemn Mr. Stevenson for what he did. But, until the facts are in, a doubt will be raised.

As far as Mr. Sparkman is concerned, I would suggest the same thing. He's had his wife on the payroll. I don't condemn him for that. But I think he should come before the American people and indicate what outside sources of income he has had.

I would suggest that under the circumstances both Mr. Sparkman and Mr. Stevenson should come before the people, as I have, and make a complete financial statement as to their financial history. And if they don't, it will be an admission that they have something to hide.

Ten minutes still remained in which to conclude his speech. Until now he had been consulting his notes. He had explained and defended his fund; he had laid bare every facet of his and Pat's financial condition; he had counter-attacked and disposed of Stevenson and Sparkman. Now he placed the sheaf of notes on the desk behind him and talked directly into the camera, in the aggressive, free-swinging style that characterized his campaign speeches.

I know this isn't the last of the smears. In spite of my explanation tonight, other smears will be made; others have been made in the past. And the purpose of the smears, I know, is this: to silence me, to make me let up.

Well, they just don't know who they are dealing with. I remember in the dark days of the Hiss case some of the same columnists, some of the same radio commentators who are attacking me now and misrepresenting my position, were violently opposing me when I was after Alger Hiss. But I continued to fight because I knew I was right . . .

The director began to signal that Nixon's time was running out, but the embattled Senator was so engrossed in his subject that he did not notice.

And now, finally, I know that you wonder whether or not I am going to stay on the Republican ticket or resign. Let me say this: I don't believe that I ought to quit, because I am not a quitter. And Pat is not a quitter. After all, her name was Patricia Ryan, and she was born on St. Patrick's Day—and you know the Irish never quit.

> But the decision, my friends, is not mine. I would do nothing that would harm the possibilities of Dwight Eisenhower to become President of the United States. And for that reason I am submitting to the Republican National Committee tonight through this television broadcast the decision which it is theirs to make. Let them decide whether my position on the ticket will help or hurt. And I am going to ask you to help them decide. Wire and write the Republican National Committee whether you think I should stay on or whether I should get off. And whatever their decision is, I will abide by it.

Ted Rogers slipped into the studio and waved frantically to attract Nixon's attention. The director had raised his arm to give the last-minute cutoff signal. But Nixon, a man possessed, had lost all sense of time. "The half-hour's up!" Rogers hissed *sotto voce*. Nixon looked his way but he neither heard nor saw him. Pat, her eyes glued to her husband, sat in frozen immobility as he continued.

> Just let me say this last word: Regardless of what happens, I am going to continue this fight. I am going to campaign up and down America until we drive the crooks and the Communists and those that defend them out of Washington.
>
> And remember, folks, Eisenhower is a great man. Believe me, he is a great man . . .

There, in mid-sentence, the camera light blinked off. Nixon's time had run out just as he was about to give the address of the National Committee where the telegrams and letters were to be sent. Pat Hillings and Bill Rogers, their faces glowing with elation, strode into the studio to offer their congratulations. To their surprise, Nixon was downcast.

"I botched it," he muttered. "I didn't tell them where the National Committee is located. My timing was off."

Chotiner approached. "What are you looking so depressed about? You were marvelous, Dick," he enthused.

Nixon was terse. "I loused it up. I was a flop."

He had gambled everything on the public's response, and now, because he had failed to note the countdown toward sign-off, whatever letters and telegrams the people might send in would be scattered among hundreds of hometown campaign offices and local radio and TV stations, with perhaps the remainder directed to the National Committee in Washington, to Eisenhower and to him. He had hoped for a large flow of responses all going to a single point where they could be counted and checked. Now, he thought disconsolately, he had failed to achieve the one goal that had prompted him to make the broadcast in the first place.

The Public Responds

As Nixon and Pat started out of El Capitan's parking lot, a large Irish setter bounded up to their car wagging its tail. He turned to his wife. "Well," he said with more bitterness than humor, "at least we got the dog vote tonight." For a moment she just stared at him. Then, the corners of her mouth turned up, her eyes twinkled, and she burst into laughter. As they reached the exit to the street, Jim Bassett ran to them with the news that the theater's switchboard was "lit up like a Christmas tree." Similar news greeted them when they arrived at the Ambassador Hotel; its switchboard too was jammed with incoming phone calls.

The response was immediate and breathtaking. Approximately sixty million people saw or heard him deliver the speech, making it the largest audience, to that time, in television history. Thousands of people left their homes at the conclusion of the telecast to form lines at their local Western Union offices. Letters poured in from every area—and they contained enough small contributions to more than cover the $75,000 cost of air time. In Washington, Republican headquarters received 300,000 letters, cards, telegrams, and petitions signed by more than a million people.

Altogether, including those which were dispatched to Nixon, Eisenhower, local radio and television stations, and city and state Republican offices everywhere, the unofficial count was almost two million letters and telegrams containing over three million signatures.

The verdict was an overwhelming 350 to 1 to "keep Nixon on the ticket."

The emotion in Nixon's voice, his manner, and his facial expressions probably accounted for as many favorable votes from the public as did the content of his speech. The audience sensed that this, the first real-life political drama to appear on television, was more than an effort by an accused Senator to vindicate himself politically, it was also a desperate struggle by one man battling against the power structure that was determined to ruin his personal career. After all, in the future —if the accusation stood—who would want to retain a lawyer who had been forced to resign because of cheating? And there was the realization, too, that the outcome of the speech might well decide whether the Republican Party itself would win or go down to defeat in the November elections.

Within a matter of hours it was evident that Nixon had triumphed. But along with victory came an expression of derision, even disgust, which is still voiced today wherever the speech is discussed. He was greeted in the hostile press as "that soap opera performer." His speech was condemned by liberal sophisticates as "the most maudlin half-hour of corn in political history." His reference to his wife's "good Republican cloth coat," followed by "I always tell her she'd look good in anything," became, for reasons unknown, a focal point for anti-Nixon jeers and jibes. And, although he had given a full and painstaking account of the fund, and revealed all of the financial details of his private life, his detractors seized upon his few comments about the family dog, and soon dubbed his entire address as "The Checkers Speech"—a title, incidentally that is not at all displeasing to him.

But the intellectual snobs and "dump Nixon" zealots were in a minority. He had circumvented them and had spoken directly to the people. The very absence of sophistication for which he had been ridiculed by his enemies, the candor with which he disclosed the intimacies of his financial problems touched a responsive chord in the hearts of the American people. Two decades later, Nixon was to label them "the great silent majority." He had good reason to use the phrase with affection.

Eisenhower Reacts

In Cleveland, Ike and Mamie Eisenhower watched Nixon's telecast in the manager's office of the Cleveland Public Auditorium where he was scheduled to address a rally of some 17,000 people after the broadcast. With the Eisenhowers were about thirty others who comprised his staff and their subordinates. As Nixon spoke, it was apparent that he was winning the sympathies of everyone in the room. Mamie (and several of the men present) dabbed their eyes with their handkerchiefs. The General, who had a memo pad before him, intermittently jabbed at it with his pencil, although his face betrayed no emotion. When Nixon challenged Stevenson and his running mate, Sparkman, to follow his own example, saying that a candidate who did not make a public disclosure of his finances must have something to hide, Eisenhower brought his pencil down on the yellow pad with such force he broke its point. He, too, was a candidate, and, while Nixon had not said so directly, the implication—at least to the General—was clear. "All" candidates could mean the General too! (Later, Eisenhower did issue a financial statement—and with good grace.)

Earlier, Eisenhower had informed Nixon, through Tom

Dewey, that the decision as to whether or not a resignation should be tendered would be Nixon's alone. Again, he stabbed at his memo pad as he heard Nixon declare, "I am submitting to the Republican National Committee tonight, through this television broadcast that the decision is *theirs* to make . . . Wire or write the Republican National Committee whether you think I should stay on or get off; and whatever *their* decision is, I will abide by it."

Eisenhower grasped Nixon's strategy at once. He had gone on the offensive; talking not so much to the sixty million people in his nationwide audience, but to *him*. Both were perfectly aware of the fact that Nixon would stand little chance of remaining on the ticket should the presidential nominee ask for his resignation, but how would such a peremptory action affect the people—or the Committee members themselves who had been largely ignored by Eisenhower's staff? The General had been outflanked.

He turned to Summerfield who had watched the Checkers Speech with him and the others. "Well, Arthur, you really got your $75,000 worth." Then Eisenhower fired off a telegram to Nixon:

> CONGRATULATIONS. YOUR PRESENTATION WAS MAGNIFICENT. WHILE TECHNICALLY NO DECISION RESTS WITH ME, YOU AND I KNOW THE REALITIES OF THE SITUATION REQUIRE A PRONOUNCEMENT WHICH THE PUBLIC CONSIDERS DECISIVE. MY PERSONAL DECISION IS GOING TO BE BASED ON PERSONAL CONCLUSIONS. I WOULD MOST APPRECIATE IT IF YOU CAN FLY TO SEE ME AT ONCE. TOMORROW EVENING I WILL BE AT WHEELING, W. VA.

To many observers, the telegram was a series of messages within a message. Fortunately, or unfortunately, depending on one's viewpoint, it was buried in the avalanche of mail that inundated Nixon's headquarters. But one thing was clear: Eisenhower had been deeply impressed with Nixon's display of nerve.

The broadcast had been shown on a huge screen in the Cleveland Auditorium, and as Eisenhower walked to the podium to deliver his address, the crowd struck up a rhythmic "We want Dick." Ike turned to the auditorium's manager: "I would rather go down in defeat fighting with a brave man," he said, "than to win with a bunch of cowards."
Jim Hagerty, who was at the General's side, listened to the shouts of the vast throng and nodded agreement. "General," he said, "you might as well forget your speech on inflation. This crowd wants to hear about your decision." Ike smiled: "I would say that's pretty evident."
The crowd roared itself hoarse as Eisenhower opened with praise for his running mate. "I have been a warrior and I like courage," he began. "I have seen brave men in tough situations, but I have never seen any come through in better fashion than Senator Nixon did tonight." Again the audience reacted with mighty shouts of agreement when Eisenhower declared, "I happen to be one of those people who, when I get into a fight would rather have a courageous and honest man by my side than a whole boxcar of pussyfooters."

The audience in Cleveland now sat back in keen anticipation of Eisenhower's remarks. The moment of great decision had arrived. But, instead of giving his blessing and bringing the entire controversy to an end, Eisenhower hesitated, cleared his throat, and then read the telegram he had just sent to Nixon.
"Obviously," the General explained to the now silent, disappointed audience, "I must have something more than one single presentation—limited to thirty minutes—the time allowed Senator Nixon."

Even now he had not made up his mind. What more he hoped to learn from Nixon, in addition to the facts that had been bared in his broadcast, the General did not say. Quite possibly, even he did not know. Although to Ike the Checkers Speech was "a magnificent performance," suspicions remained, and they would have to be resolved in a face-to-face meeting.

The Battle Is Over

Back in Los Angeles, Dick and Pat were radiant. The long, lonely battle was over. Reports from everywhere in the country indicated that his speech had vindicated him. The Ambassador Hotel reverberated to the strains of "Happy Days Are Here Again." They knew nothing of the lost telegram Eisenhower had sent until a reporter handed Nixon a brief summary of the wire which focused on the General's statement that he could not make a decision until they met face-to-face.

The smiles of elation were erased, the happy song ended. Never a gradualist, Nixon plummetted once again from the pinnacle of joy to the valley of despair. He had expected a definite answer—a conclusion to this six-day nightmare of temporizing. But instead of a definite verdict—whether to quit or stay on—Eisenhower had again vaccilated. And now, suppose he did meet with the General and there was still no decision! Was there to be no end to this state of limbo in which he and Pat were being suspended?

"What more can he possibly want from me!" Nixon's voice rang out in anguish. "I've said everything—I've done everything a man can be expected to do without groveling on his knees. I just can't take any more!"

It was a true reflection of his feelings. He simply could not bring himself to crawl to Wheeling and implore Eisenhower to retain him as his running mate. Finally, and at long last, he succumbed. In the presence of his staff, he called in Rose Mary Woods and dictated a telegram of resignation addressed to National Committee Chairman Arthur Summerfield.

Rose left the room and Chotiner hurried after her.

"I'll take that, Rose," he said.

She watched him as he tore her notes to shreds.

He turned to leave, and she laid a hand on his arm: "I could have saved you the trouble, Murray," she said smiling. "I had no intention of sending it."

Expressions of support were still pouring in, but not a word had been received from Eisenhower. They had not yet discovered his telegram in the jam-packed mailroom, and, consequently, were aware only of Ike's brief statement that came via the newswire.

"Seems to me we should continue our campaign schedule until the General makes up his mind," said Nixon. "He can then either give me his public support or accept my resignation."

"I tore it up," Chotiner broke in. "If you want to resign, do it with flair. Let the whole country know about it; but on your own terms. Yes, continue your planned schedule until Ike makes up his mind one way or the other.

"One thing is sure: I don't think you should allow yourself to be put in the position of going to Eisenhower like a little boy to be taken to the woodshed, properly spanked, and then restored to society thoroughly rehabilitated. You'd never live it down. And why should you? You haven't done anything wrong!"

Nixon nodded. "Very well. Let's go on to Missoula, Montana, as we planned. We'll fly there tonight and resume the schedule from that point."

Reconciliation

The Nixon camp was about to leave for Montana when a call came from the Eisenhower train. Chotiner picked up the phone. Arthur Summerfield was on the line.

"Hello, Murray," Summerfield began affably enough, "everything okay in Los Angeles?"

"Lousy," Chotiner replied tersely.

"Lousy? What the hell are you talking about?"

"Dick just wrote a telegram of resignation. He's had it."

"My God, Murray, tear it up!"

"I did, but don't ask me how long it's going to stay torn."

"Look, everything will turn out fine tomorrow. Dick is flying to Wheeling to see the General, isn't he?"

"No. In fact we're just about to leave for Missoula. We're flying there tonight."

"For chrissake, Murray, you've got to persuade him to go to Wheeling instead."

"All right, Art, we trust you. All I want is your personal assurance, direct from Eisenhower, that Dick will stay on the ticket with the General's blessing. It's the only way I know to persuade him."

The next morning, September 24, at dawn, Chotiner received the assurance he had requested. They were now in Missoula, and he awakened Nixon to convey the message. If Nixon would fly to Wheeling at once, his place on the ticket was guaranteed, and Ike would use the occasion to announce his blessing publicly.

Nixon, without rest for several nights, fell asleep on the last leg of the flight from Missoula to Wheeling. It was late afternoon when the plane touched down. He arose, straightened his tie, put on his jacket, and was helping Pat with her coat when he heard a familiar voice ask, "Where's the boss of this outfit?"

Chotiner rushed up to them. "The General's coming in," he shouted.

Eisenhower, setting protocol aside, had detached himself from his entourage, bounded up the ramp and entered the plane.

"General, you didn't have to come here—to do this," the surprised Nixon gasped.

"Why not?" countered Ike, beaming. "You're my boy."

They exchanged pleasantries for a few moments, then set off together for the Wheeling stadium where Eisenhower spoke first to the enthusiastic crowd. The General, always adept at cutting losses and turning defeats into victory, broke into his captivating grin, and launched into his benediction by first reading a telegram from Nixon's mother:

> DEAR GENERAL: I AM TRUSTING THAT THE ABSOLUTE TRUTH MAY COME OUT CONCERNING THIS ATTACK ON RICHARD. WHEN IT DOES, I AM SURE YOU WILL BE GUIDED ARIGHT IN YOUR DECISION TO PLACE IMPLICIT FAITH IN HIS INTEGRITY AND HONESTY. BEST OF WISHES FROM ONE WHO HAS KNOWN RICHARD LONGER THAN ANYONE, HIS MOTHER.
>
> HANNAH NIXON*

The time of indecision was over. Eisenhower was giving his full and unqualified support to his running mate. "Senator Nixon has completely vindicated his position," he declared after reading the telegram. "I am proud to have him on the ticket with me." Then he presented Nixon to the ecstatic crowd.

For Nixon the ordeal had come to an end, and his happy, confident phrases with which he addressed the audience emphasized his joy. But the emotional strain of the past seven days intruded into his speech, and he had to stop, from time to time, to regain his composure. When the rally was over, he was besieged by well-wishers seeking to shake his hand and offer their congratulations.

Suddenly, he found himself facing his friend and senior colleague in the Senate, Bill Knowland. "You were great,

---

*Frank Nixon's comment, after his son's broadcast, was typical: "It looks to me as if the Democrats have given themselves a good kick in the pants."

Dick," Knowland said warmly. "Everything will be fine from now on."

Nixon, who had fought the Establishment with courage, who had defied the most popular presidential candidate in history, who had faced a nation to clear his name at a time when only a few close friends and associates believed in him, lost his grip. His emotional reserve was exhausted. He tried to say something to Knowland, but his throat was tight. Tears filled his eyes. Knowland moved closer and curled a sym-

> *I am trusting that the absolute truth may come out concerning this attack on Richard when it does. I am sure you will be guided aright in your decision to place implicit faith in his integrity and honesty. Best of wishes from one who has known Richard longer than anyone else his mother*
>
> *Hannah Nixon*

The original rough draft of Hannah Nixon's telegram to Presidential candidate Eisenhower in which she expressed a mother's concern for her son who was fighting for his political life. Eisenhower was so impressed with the message he read it to the nation in his televised avowal of confidence in Nixon, following the "Checkers speech."

pathetic arm around him, and Nixon buried his face in his friend's shoulder. The scene was captured by a news photographer, and the picture of Nixon weeping on Knowland's shoulder, the most poignant of the entire campaign, became the headstone of the fund smear which Republicans and Democrats alike hoped would be buried forever.

I Don't Trust Nixon!

An old British quatrain declares:

> I do not love thee, Doctor Fell,
> The reason why I cannot tell;
> But this alone I know full well,
> I do not love thee, Doctor Fell.

The rhyme has its modern counterpart in the expression: "I don't know why, but I don't trust Nixon." The statement began to circulate in 1952, at the height of the fund incident. One would think that in the aftermath of the scandal, when all accusations had been proven false, the "I don't know why" misgivings would have died a natural death. But, surprisingly enough, the distrust gathered new converts as additional smears against Nixon continued to be voiced throughout that same year.

Nixon expected the new attacks, although he could not have anticipated how vicious they would be. In his Checkers Speech, he said, "I know this isn't the last of the smears. . . . Other smears will be made. And the purpose of the smears, I know, is to silence me." The lesson his enemies should have derived from that comment was that he meant every word of it—he would *not* be silenced, and he *would* counter-attack.

The new smears began at once—in fact while Nixon was still with Eisenhower in Wheeling, West Virginia. Straight from the "horse's mouth"—from the Democratic National Committee—came the charge that Dick and Pat spent

$10,000 with an interior decorator to furnish their home in Washington. The truth: Hannah Nixon had sent her son and daughter-in-law some draperies from their house in Whittier. The "interior decorator" was Pat. Her compensation was not $10,000, but a rare trip to the movies with Dick.

A week after the broadcast, the *St. Louis Post-Dispatch* questioned whether Nixon had really used the proceeds of his fund for political purposes. The paper accused him of having accompanied the fund's trustee, Dana Smith, to Havana where they were seen together in a gambling casino. He had been with Smith as his guest, the paper stated, in April, 1952, when Smith lost $42,000.

Nixon at once branded the story a lie. The truth, however, was unearthed by a cub reporter on the same paper. Nixon, he learned, was five thousand miles from Havana at the time. From the middle of March until May 1, he was in Hawaii where he was making a series of speeches. All dates and places were corroborated. The *Post-Dispatch* retracted the story a few days later in an obscure item on the back pages.*

Drew Pearson, an avowed enemy of Nixon ever since the Hiss case, published an attack in his column which accused the Nixons of making a false statement to the state of California in order to avoid paying their due share of property taxes. Pearson charged that Richard and Pat Nixon had signed a pauper's oath in 1951. This was only a few months before they made their down payment on their Washington home. "If Nixon was a pauper in March, then where did he get the money for his new house in July?"

Nixon, thoroughly incensed with this palpable lie, threatened to sue. Pearson, who had not checked the story for accuracy, probed further and found that another Richard and Pat Nixon had filed the application. He printed a retraction five days *after* the election—at the very bottom of his column.

The Democratic National Committee, not satisfied with the

---

*Two days before the November elections, Drew Pearson repeated the charge in his column; but not the retraction.

paltry smears invented by Nixon's less-imaginative enemies, hurled a newer and bigger charge which, at first, seemed quite serious. Democratic spokesmen accused Nixon of having used his office improperly by acquiring real estate valued at $250,000. In addition, they charged, there existed a "second Nixon fund" involving $52,000.

The "scandal" of Nixon's $250,000 worth of property, improperly acquired, simply fell apart upon investigation, and the Democratic National Committee hastily dropped the matter. Instead, it concentrated on putting Nixon through the rigors of another fund episode. One of the Committee's chief spokesmen was Harry Truman. Truman had never forgotten that it was Nixon who had embarrassed his Administration during the Hiss investigation.

"I have documentary evidence that Richard Nixon has been linked to another fund," Truman told a group of Democratic leaders in San Francisco. "He won't get off so easy this time." The "documentation" to which Truman alluded was a forged letter purporting to show that Nixon had sold his honor and his soul to the oil industry. "Signed" by H. W. Sanders, vice-president of the Union Oil Company, the missive was addressed to Franklyn Waltman, publicity chief of the Sun Oil Company. It read:

> To be certain there is no misunderstanding, let me explain that when I said we would be paying Dick Nixon more than $52,000 in the course of this year, I did not mean that all of it would come from our side. The balance comes from all other segments of the oil industry.
>
> Feel free to call on Nixon for anything you need in Washington. He regards himself as a servant of our entire industry.

The letter was so obviously fraudulent that even Drew

Pearson, at first, refused to publish it, as did Nixon's old nemesis, the *New York Post*. After the election, however, Pearson, who cared little where the daggers came from as long as he could stab an enemy, intimated that a certain letter in the files of the Sun Oil Company would destroy Nixon if it were ever published.

Nixon demanded and got an investigation by the FBI and the Democratic-controlled Senate Elections Committee, both of whom found that the letter was an out-and-out forgery, instigated by his opponents from the far left.

These and other fabrications, all proclaimed with pious genuflections to the Statue of Liberty and the Constitution, were proved false. Nevertheless, the "Tricky Dick" legend persisted. Each new smear against Nixon added to his army of detractors who continued to mouth the slogan: "I don't trust him, but don't ask me why!"

In November, his enemies, who had tried so unsuccessfully to tarnish him with every kind of corruption, were put to rout. The ballot count, on that November 4th in 1952, gave the Eisenhower-Nixon ticket 33,936,234 votes, representing 55.1 per cent of the total vote, as compared with Stevenson's 27,314,922.

Eleven days after his fortieth birthday, and six years from the time he arrived in Washington with a battered suitcase and an old car, Richard Nixon was sworn in as Vice-President of the United States. With the exception of pre-Civil War Democrat John C. Breckenridge, he was the youngest to hold that office, and the first Vice-President born in the twentieth century. "The crisis of the fund was the hardest and briefest of my public life," Nixon recalled. "Yet, if it hadn't been for that broadcast I would never have been around to run for the presidency."

Nixon might also have recalled that he had dared to cross swords with the redoubtable Dwight Eisenhower, thereby earning the General's respect and admiration. But, more than that, he had converted the fund attack from a liability to an

368 The Fund

asset. As a result, he was able to emerge from under Eisenhower's shadow and become a national political figure in his own right.

Richard, with his brothers Edward (l.) and Donald (r.) at Richard Nixon's Washington home on the occasion of his first inauguration to the Vice-Presidency, January 20, 1953, which made him the second youngest Vice-President at forty.

10
Vice-President Richard M. Nixon

Mr. and Mrs. Vice-President: At Home

RICHARD AND PAT, both gifted with active imaginations, could not have foreseen the whirlwind social life they would inherit with the vice-presidency. When they were first married, and even during their courting days, Pat realized that her husband was no social lion. However, she mused, if she had wanted a *bon vivant*, she would have married one.

As a Congressman, and then as a Senator, their social life had consisted of little more than an occasional movie or concert. When he was not away on speech-making tours, his evenings at home were devoted to catching up with his office work. But now, as Mr. and Mrs. Vice-President, their home life was completely altered.

Ike and Mamie Eisenhower avoided the social functions

Family portrait taken at Richard Nixon's Washington home three days after his first inauguration as Vice President on January 20, 1953. Left to right, brother Donald, parents Frank and Hannah,

Richard Nixon had just been inaugurated as Vice President, in January, 1953, but Julie, left and Tricia, right seem unimpressed.

expected of the Chief Executive and his family, and it fell to the Nixons to assume that role, quite often as official representatives of the President. They attended formal social functions on an average of five nights a week, some starting so early in the evening that Nixon bought an electric razor for a last-minute shave at his office. He also kept two suits of dinner clothes in an office closet for quick changes. So adept had he become at speedy preparations, that he could whisk off his formidable five-o'clock shadow in five minutes, get into a black tie in ten, and into a white tie in fifteen. At parties,

Richard and Pat were good mixers, pleasant and, quite naturally for them, examples of moderation. Neither of them smoked, and, while he would occasionally sip a highball, she did not drink at all. Between ten-thirty and eleven o'clock they would leave for home so that they could retire by midnight.

The Nixons lived in a picture-book, four-bedroom white brick colonial house on a corner lot at 4801 Tilden Street, N.W. in Spring Valley, a suburb of Washington. This was the house which Nixon had described in his Checkers Speech. It was always immaculate: "I'm as fussy as an old maid," Pat told a reporter, "and so is Dick."

Nixon began his day in a manner no different from that of many other men who go to work every morning. He ate his breakfast at the kitchen table beside a window that overlooked the back yard. His menu seldom varied: two kinds of fruit, light toast and one cup of coffee with a half-teaspoon of sugar and a touch of cream. He always had a copy of the morning paper on the right side of the table next to his coffee, but found little time to go deeply into the reported events—Julie and Tricia absorbing most of his attention. By 8 A.M. a driver would appear with the Vice-President's official car and he would leave for Capitol Hill, reading the *New York Times* en route.

He rarely left his office for lunch. Instead he usually sent out for a sandwich, milk and some fruit, and ate at his desk while discussing Government affairs with someone. Late at night, even after formal dinners, he enjoyed foraging in the kitchen for a bowl of chile or a hamburger and a glass of milk before going to bed.

When her husband began his second term as Vice-President, Pat Nixon was a chic and attractive strawberry blonde of thirty-four. Her hours were almost as completely occupied as were Richard's. She employed a maid five days a week, helping with a good deal of the housework on the maid's two days off.

Pat, Julie and Tricia make fudge for a church social.

Speaking of her husband's domestic skills, Pat said, "He wasn't exactly handy around the house . . . I learned to drive nails straight, to put up hooks, fix squeaky stairs and sticky doors, put new washers in leaky faucets and new plugs on electric cords."

A proud mama is flanked by her daughters, Julie (l.) age 9, and Tricia (r.) 11, at their Washington, D. C. home in 1957.

Referring to Nixon's mechanical dexterity, a witty reporter once observed, "He had all he could do to operate a paper clip." Pat, herself, laughingly agreed.

Pat did her own shopping at a supermarket a few blocks from their house, always making an effort to be home when Julie and Tricia arrived from school. In addition to these mundane chores as a wife and mother, she devoted much time to the duties expected of a Vice-President's wife, answer-

With Vice-President Nixon off to Africa and Italy as Eisenhower's personal envoy, the ladies of the family attempt a reconciliation between Nicky, their cat, and Checkers, their dog.

ing hundreds of letters and attending countless luncheons, teas, bazaars and benefits.

Tricia and Julie could not remember a time when their father had not been Vice-President. As he began his second term, Tricia was ten and Julie eight. Both attended the Horace Mann Elementary School in Washington. Sunday was their favorite day. It was family day, and their parents would take them to Sunday school at the Westmoreland Congregational

Church, a short walk from home. Tricia and Julie were as happy and active as children can be—and unspoiled. Neither Pat nor Dick were strict disciplinarians, but there were rules of conduct for the two girls, and those rules meant exactly what they said—Pat saw to that.

Like any other father, Nixon enjoyed spending Sunday afternoons with his children. Often he played the piano while they sang, and his heart was warmed; and he could forget for a while the problems of his office. The piano was, and still remains, his chief source of relaxation. There were times, after the children were asleep, when in reverie he would play the Baldwin spinet for an hour or more improvising on Brahms and Bach, his favorite composers.

Pat and Richard had few intimate friends, perhaps the closest being Assistant United States Attorney General William Rogers. And Julie had a brand new "boy friend"— Dwight David Eisenhower II, who was all of eight years old. Occasionally the family's weekends were brightened by a visit from Don or Edward Nixon, the Vice-President's brothers, or, best of all, from his parents. They were loving and indulgent grandparents, and Julie and Tricia were always ecstatically happy to be with them.

On the wall in the kitchen of their home was a plaque which read: *Bless this house.*

It was blessed!

The Office of Vice-President

Alexander Throttlebottom, referring to himself in the musical comedy, *Of Thee I Sing,* titillated his audience with the funny and perceptive observation: "He sits around in the park and feeds the pigeons, and takes walks and goes to the movies. The other day he was going to join the library, but he had to have two references, so he couldn't get in."

The observation was shared by an illustrious group of Vice-Presidents going all the way back to John Adams who de-

Inauguration Day, January 20, 1957. President Eisenhower and his grandchildren Barbara Ann and David Eisenhower, with Vice-President Nixon and his children Julie (l.) and Tricia (r.) in the reviewing stands. Here nine-year-old David casts an admiring look at Julie (also nine).

Julie returns David's glance in what might have been the start of a budding romance, much to the amusement of Eisenhower and Nixon. David and Julie were married eleven years later in New York.

scribed his office as "the most insignificant that ever the invention of man contrived or his imagination conceived." John C. Calhoun made his actions suit his words: in disgust, he simply resigned. Theodore Roosevelt likened his vice-presidential years to "taking the veil." Thomas Marshall, Vice-President under Woodrow Wilson, regarded the holder of the position as being in "a cataleptic fit: he is conscious of all that goes on, but has no part of it." When asked his opinion of the nation's greatest need, Marshall replied with a straight face, "What this country needs is a really good five-cent cigar"—a safe statement that would appeal to Republicans and Democrats alike, and not be offensive to the Boss. But it took peppery Harry Truman to voice the sentiments of his predecessors in earthy language. When offered the second highest post in the land at the 1944 Democratic convention in Chicago, he commented: "Every Vice-President in history was about as useful as a cow's fifth teat."*

Richard Nixon was acutely aware of the gracelessness and irrelevancies of the office which had caused each of his predecessors to smart. In *Six Crises,* he quotes the summation of Charles G. Dawes (who described his term under Calvin Coolidge as the easiest in the world), "A Vice-President has only two functions: to sit and listen to Senators give speeches, and to check the morning's newspapers as to the President's health."

But Nixon had no intention of permitting the vice-presidency to become for him the dead-end street to which it had been assigned by tradition. In this, he was firmly backed by President Eisenhower who reasoned that a General and a President shared a similar problem of replacement. "I don't want a figurehead on my team," he said to Nixon imme-

---

*Upon assuming the presidency following the death of Franklin D. Roosevelt, Truman learned for the first time of the existence of the atomic bomb, although several influential Senators, as well as a number of high government officials knew of it. (In Roosevelt's opinion the Vice-President was considered too unimportant to be burdened with this secret.)

diately after his inauguration. "I want a Vice-President who is trained and ready to step into the presidency smoothly in case the Grim Reaper should remove me from the scene."

President Eisenhower was as good as his word. In addition to his constitutional duty of presiding over the Senate, Nixon and Eisenhower consulted with each other at least three times a week, inaugurating a historical "first" for a President and Vice-President.*

Another break with tradition occurred when Eisenhower announced that during his absences from Washington—and they were many—Nixon would preside over the National Security Council, an assignment which until this time had been reserved for the Secretary of State. Eisenhower also decreed that Nixon would henceforth preside over all Cabinet meetings when the President was away from the capital. Moreover, the President unloaded on Nixon most of the ceremonial functions and appearances that were normally assumed by the Chief Executive.

From the very first week of the Eisenhower Administration, Nixon immersed himself in the greatly expanded duties which had never before been assigned to a Vice-President. Almost at once, he became Ike's liaison between the White House and the Congress. He helped high Administration officers in their efforts to push needed legislation through the House and Senate, arranged military briefings for the various committee chairmen and other Congressional leaders, and personally represented the President in both Houses where his knowledge and experience proved to be valuable assets.

At one point, it was Nixon who broke a deadlock in Eisenhower's own Cabinet—a deadlock which involved United States participation in the St. Lawrence Seaway. The Cabi-

---

*The Eisenhower-Nixon thrice-weekly meetings may be compared with the usual twice-a-month consultations held by many of their predecessors. Others met perhaps four times a year. Franklin D. Roosevelt did not invite his Vice-President, John Nance Garner, to a single meeting for three years.

net was split; half of the members were of the opinion that the U.S. should not participate in building the seaway. Nixon argued that the immense project would probably benefit this country to an even greater degree than it would Canada, and that, from an economic, military and social view, the seaway was a national necessity, and the U.S. should have a stake in it. "If we don't participate in its construction," he warned, "Canada will build it without us." He won his point.

Nixon's hard work, his unassuming but effective leadership, his ability to oil the cogs and cams of government, gradually made an impression upon Washington. In August, 1953, the dean of Capitol Hill's newsmen, Arthur Krock, wrote in the *New York Times:* "Persons familiar with the Vice-President's helpful activities have told this correspondent that they consider him unique in the records of his high office." Five months later, Robert Coughlan reported in *Life* magazine: "Richard Nixon has made the vice-presidency, hitherto the butt of ridicule, an important office, and has established himself as an 'Assistant President,' a mover and shaper of national and world affairs."

Among the important roles assigned to Nixon by Eisenhower was his unofficial designation as international goodwill ambassador. As the President's personal representative, Nixon made nine memorable trips to some fifty foreign countries, from 1953 to 1959, covering almost 160,000 miles. It was ideal training for a man who was only six years removed from the provincialism of little Whittier, California.

In later years, with the full weight of the White House experience behind him, Nixon was to prove himself an iconoclast, as well as a social and political innovator. Those who knew him well were to profess astonishment at the progressive drive and maturity of the "new Nixon." The gradual awareness of the world around him are clearly traceable to this intensive period of travel that Nixon undertook while Vice-President, and to the innumerable hours of fastidious preparation that he devoted to each trip.

It was during this tenure, under Eisenhower, that Richard Nixon realized the world was changing and that he, too, must change with it. He listened as the politicians and diplomats spoke, and he became aware of their attitudes and aspirations; he paid attention to the expectations of labor and industry and placed them in perspective in his mind's eye. He drew on the experience of people in the professions and in government and gained in stature from his new knowledge.

Other Vice-Presidents did not find the vice-presidency an exhilarating experience, but for Richard Nixon it was a stepping-stone to an even brighter future. And of all the events of the years of his vice-presidency, undoubtedly, the McCarthy hearings were the most exciting. It was the McCarthy saga that helped keep the Nixon name in the headlines on a more sustained level than anything else.

The McCarthy Years

Nixon first met Joseph R. McCarthy, the notorious Senator from Wisconsin, in 1947, at a party given by Wisconsin backers of the Stassen for President movement. During the Hiss investigation, he had allowed McCarthy the use of his files on Communist suspects, in much the same way as the chairmen of other Congressional committees were allowed this privilege.

It was McCarthy's sordid use of the material in these files that had been opened to him that aroused the ire of the public. They could not stomach his tactics. The manner in which he conducted his hearings was demeaning. But since the Truman Administration had done nothing to eliminate known subversives from government employment, it became easy for McCarthy to capitalize on this issue, to milk it for all it was worth, and to keep a large segment of the populace on his side.

Before 1950, Nixon and McCarthy met only sporadically. At the outset, the Republicans—Nixon among them—welcomed McCarthy's rough-and-tumble attacks on the Democrats. After all, he was making no specific charges against individuals, nor was he, as a freshman Senator, a spokesman for the GOP.

McCarthy vaulted into national prominence with a speech in Wheeling, West Virginia, on February 9, 1950, in which he said, "While I cannot take the time to name all the men in the State Department who have been named as active members of the Communist Party and members of a spy ring, I have here in my hand a list of over two hundred names that were made known to the Secretary of State as being members of the Communist Party and who, nevertheless, are still working and shaping policy in the State Department."

The furor that ensued, in which demands were made for the disclosure of the alleged Communists, made McCarthy go to the one man who, he was convinced, could furnish the proof—Richard Nixon. It was at that point that the rambunctious Senator from Wisconsin began to understand the Nixon ethic.

"Joe," Nixon began, "try to understand this: you just can't go around calling these people Communists. You'd have been better off if you had referred to them as fellow travelers, or stated that they have Communist-front ties. You might have called them sympathetic to Communist ideas. There's one rule you have to learn—never to make a charge unless you can back it up. Always understate, never overstate your case."

Nixon did not see McCarthy again until the end of that year. On the evening of December 12, 1950, Nixon and other Congressmen, government officials and diplomats, attended a party at the posh Sulgrave Club in Washington. Among those present were Drew Pearson and Joe McCarthy. The columnist and the Senator, who had been at each other's throats in the press and on the floor of the Senate, soon were trading insults. As the argument progressed, their anger grew.

"You'd better read the *Congressional Record* for tomorrow," McCarthy said ominously. "I'll have some things to say about you the public ought to know about."

"I suggest you read what I have to say about *you*," Pearson retorted. "My column is read by a hell of a lot more people than read the *Congressional Record.*"

The party was almost over, and they drifted toward the cloakroom, still arguing. Inside, Pearson turned to McCarthy, "Why not tell the Senate about your income tax? They'd be interested in knowing how you keep out of jail."

For a moment or two McCarthy stared at him in utter disbelief. Then, with a profane growl he lunged at Pearson, grabbed him by the neck and threw him to the floor. Congressman Charles Bennett, lame from a childhood polio attack, attempted to separate the two embroiled men, but fell to the floor. McCarthy helped Bennett to his feet while Pearson put on his coat. "You won't get away with this," muttered Pearson.

"Aw, forget it, Drew, this wasn't such a bad evening after all," McCarthy said, slapping him vigorously on the back.

Again Pearson stumbled, but did not fall. He thrust a hand into his coat pocket, but whether he meant to draw a gun, or even had one, has never been told.

"Take your hand out of that pocket," McCarthy roared, reaching for the columnist's arm. Again they grappled.

At that moment Nixon walked into the cloakroom for his hat and coat. He took in the situation at a glance. "All right, that'll be enough of this nonsense," he snapped. "Break it up."

Instead, McCarthy reached back and, with his open palm, slapped Pearson's face. "That one was for you, Dick," he yelled. As Nixon moved forward to separate them, McCarthy swung at the columnist once more—a roundhouse slap that caught Pearson full on the cheek and sent him reeling. Nixon grabbed the enraged Senator, held him tight in his arms, then pulled him away.

"Come on, Joe," he said grimly, "you're going home."

"He'll have to go first," McCarthy snarled. "I'm not turning my back on that son of a bitch."

Pearson slipped away and Nixon led McCarthy outside

where the fresh air cleared some of the scotch from the Senator's brain. McCarthy had forgotten where he had parked his car and Nixon spent the next half hour searching for it.

In a flash, word of the "battle royal" was out. It was being bruted about that McCarthy *and* Nixon had attacked Pearson, and that a dozen officials were witnesses to the fracas.

But the feared reaction did not take place. Newsmen made only brief reference to the brawl. One of the reports said that "some twenty-five Senators congratulated McCarthy for giving that muckraker the lesson he deserved."

The junior Senator from Wisconsin continued his attacks on the State Department during the remaining years of the Truman Administration, and remained a much talked about personality throughout the country. For the most part, he confined his efforts to castigating the Department for its support of the Chinese Communists whom it termed "agrarian reformers" bent only on an equitable redistribution of land. Their opponents were labeled "fascists under the iron regime of dictator Chiang Kai-shek." To McCarthy, there was no question that a conspiracy existed in the State Department, and the goal was the destruction of the Nationalists and the victory of the Communists in China. Fearing the Communist threat, people from many walks of life backed McCarthy, and the hubbub grew so great that Secretary of State Dean Acheson was at last forced to discharge a few of the more obvious security risks in his Department.

Riding high, McCarthy felt that his activities had helped the Republicans win the 1952 elections. When the Eisenhower-Nixon ticket was swept into office, he concluded, he would henceforth enjoy the prestige of the White House in his continuing campaign against "subversives."

In this he was mistaken. Politics being what it is, it was one thing to attack the Truman Administration for being "soft on Communism," but it was another matter when the administration was in Republican hands. Nixon, the loyal party man, foresaw the difficulties that would result if the GOP, rather than McCarthy himself, were to be accused of "red baiting." It was also clear to him that McCarthy could, and would, claim the personal loyalty of tens of thousands of Americans as an excuse for going it alone, without consulting the Republican leaders.

Division within Republican ranks was already threatening to split the party over the McCarthy issue. This was instigated, to a large degree, by Eisenhower's top adviser, Paul Hoffman. If allowed to develop, the schism might well prove disastrous to the GOP at the next elections. Eisenhower continued to hold himself aloof from intra-factional party disputes, and it soon devolved upon Nixon to maintain the outward appearance of harmony between McCarthy and worried Republicans.

In the spring of 1953, McCarthy lashed out in all directions. Although some of his accusations seemed justified to many of his political friends, without proof he was fast becoming a detriment to the party. Furthermore, now that Republicans were beginning to look askance at what they considered his unwarranted and unhealthy interference in governmental matters, he had no compunctions about working with Democrats.

In one instance, McCarthy decided that President Eisenhower should issue a strong condemnation of allies who trade with Communist countries. Nixon warned that such an announcement would inevitably be regarded as arrogant meddling in the sovereign affairs of our allies; that they had a right to trade with whomever they pleased. Ignoring Nixon's urgings that he drop the matter, McCarthy sent Eisenhower a letter (almost an ultimatum) which was drafted by Robert Kennedy, an ardent supporter and associate of McCarthy. Eisenhower did not see the letter, nor did he learn of it until much later. Nixon saw to it that it was intercepted while still in the White House mail room. A few days later, he managed to persuade the volatile Senator to drop his demands.

Nixon's friendly feelings for McCarthy began to cool as

each week brought with it new crises. Time after time he intervened, not to silence the Senator in his anti-Communist disclosures, but to urge restraint. The Vice-President knew there was much that was true in McCarthy's accusations, but he correctly viewed the Senator as a two-fisted barroom brawler who recognized a pernicious evil and who was always ready to charge in, flailing away at his country's enemies without regard for the niceties of courtroom etiquette or adherence to a code of ethics.*

As late as November, 1953, Nixon still harbored a somewhat forelorn hope that he could restrain the obstreperous Senator, but McCarthy could no more be restrained than could a belching volcano. At a meeting in Florida, the Vice-President reminded the Wisconsin Senator that his reputation as a one-issue politician could hurt his chances for re-election, and suggested that he lower his voice on the problem of Communists in government and concentrate more on other matters of direct concern to his own constituents. McCarthy nodded and thought it might be a good idea. But when Nixon announced to the press that the Senator planned to give his attention to other governmental problems, he was branded a "damn liar" by McCarthy.

When McCarthy accused the military establishment of harboring subversives, President Eisenhower had had it up to his eyeballs. The Senator would have to be chopped down to

---

*Nixon's code of ethics: (1) No witness shall be called unless substantive evidence has been presented that his testimony is imperative. (2) Wherever charges have been made against a witness, he shall be permitted to offer a list of the names of prospective witnesses who will testify in his own behalf, and in rebuttal to statements made by all accusers. (3) The witness shall be allowed to submit a list of questions which should be asked of all accusers. (4) Televising of committee hearings shall be prohibited because it places an unreasonable burden on the average witness. (5) All witnesses are presumed to be innocent, whatever the charges against them, and shall be treated with respect and dignity. (6) All witnesses are entitled to every measure of protection afforded them under the Constitution and its attendant Bill of Rights.

size. No one, Ike fumed, would be permitted to smear his beloved Army. McCarthy had charged that the Army promoted a dentist, Dr. Irving Peress, from captain to major, and had then given him an honorable discharge, even though Army Intelligence had learned that he was a Communist.

Called to explain the circumstances before the Committee, Brigadier General Ralph W. Zwicker, Commandant of Camp Kilmer, New Jersey, lamely explained that proof against Dr. Peress was inconclusive, and that the officer could not be considered a subversive with the scanty documentation in its possession. Nor, he testified, did he know who promoted Peress.

McCarthy exploded with anger, and accused him of being "unfit to wear the uniform." General Zwicker, an officer with an impeccable reputation and a tough soldier, left the hearing-room ramrod stiff, but with tears in his eyes.

A week later, on February 24, 1954, at the famous "fried-chicken and talk" meeting in Nixon's office, a compromise was reached, and the Senator agreed not to pursue the subject. The Army had capitulated in humiliation to McCarthy.

Perhaps it was Adlai Stevenson's widely publicized address that served as the straw that broke the camel's back. He declared that the Republican Party was now a house "divided against itself; half McCarthy, half Eisenhower." The statement seemed justified; the GOP had been badly split, as the next Congressional elections proved. Independent polls supported the press in their conclusions that McCarthy had torn the party apart, and that a voice of unity was desperately needed.

On March 13, Nixon took to the air to reply to Stevenson's assertions. Without mentioning McCarthy's name, he made the final break with McCarthyism:

> Men who have in the past done effective work exposing Communism in this country have, by reckless talk

and questionable methods, made themselves the issue, rather than the cause they believe in so deeply. When they have done this they have not only diverted attention from the danger of Communism, but they have diverted that attention to themselves. Also, they have allowed those whose primary objective is to defeat the Eisenhower Administration to divert attention from its great program to these individuals who followed those methods. Let us remember that the extremes of those who ignored the Communist danger or who covered it up when it was exposed have led to the extremes of those who exaggerate it today.

Nixon then turned to the question frequently asked by McCarthy: "Who cares about fairness when you are out shooting rats?" The Vice-President answered with the same verbiage used by the Senator:

"I agree that the Communists are a bunch of rats. But just remember this: when you go out to shoot rats you have to shoot straight because when you shoot wildly it not only means that the rats may get away more easily, but you make it easier on the rats. Also, you might hit someone else who is trying to shoot rats, too."

When a select committee of the Senate was appointed in April, 1954, to consider a motion of censure against McCarthy, it was Nixon who chose its members. McCarthy was cleared of the counter-charge made by the Army that he had attacked the military because one of his staff researchers, G. David Schine, was drafted. However, in December of the same year, the Senate voted to "condemn" him. After this rebuke, and with the Democrats again in control of Congress after the 1954 elections, McCarthy's influence steadily diminished until his death three years later, in 1957, at age forty-nine.

"Dump Nix in '56"

For the Eisenhower Administration, 1956 was a banner year. The Republican-controlled Congress enacted a large tax cut in 1954, and an over-all revision of the whole tax structure—a move which impressed most people as favorably as did the construction of the St. Lawrence Seaway. Many Americans gave Eisenhower credit for ending the Korean War; and his appeal to the Soviet Union in December, 1953, to join the United States in contributing part of its atomic stockpile for peaceful uses was widely heralded. His popularity throughout the country seemed to increase, and in the presidential race of 1956 he was re-elected over Adlai Stevenson by an even wider margin than in 1952.

For Nixon, as for the President, the second-term campaign provided no serious challenges. But his effort to win the nomination again was another matter. Considering the Vice-President's considerable success during his first term in office, it seems inconceivable, in retrospect, that Eisenhower should have entertained any doubts about having Nixon as his running mate. But that is exactly what happened. On February 29, in that leap year of 1956, Eisenhower announced that he would again be a candidate, making no mention of his proposed running mate. When pressed by Washington's newsmen, he declared that he had suggested to Nixon that he "chart his own course."

It was hardly an endorsement, and it came as a shock to most observers who had noted the increasing respect and affection with which Eisenhower had regarded Nixon in the past four years. Indeed, so fond had Ike grown of his Vice-President that he would permit no attacks against Nixon in his presence. In spite of this, a combination of disturbing rumors, gossip and comments by self-seeking party wheelhorses and Government officials began to reach Eisenhower—not from the Democrats, but from members of his own Republican party. Chief among these was Harold Stassen, a member of Ike's inner circle of advisers. Stassen had decided that it would be best if Nixon were to be denied the re-nomination, and he proceeded to act accordingly.

Knowing Eisenhower's aversion to anything that smacked of dictating policy to party conventions, Stassen reminded him that an endorsement of Nixon at this time, before the delegates had convened, would certainly appear to be a case of nomination by presidential edict. The convention, he emphasized, should remain open. Moreover, he continued, the vice-presidency was a dead end; and Nixon's future would be greatly enhanced if he were given a Cabinet post instead. Stassen then attempted to clinch his argument by producing the results of several polls that showed Nixon as a detriment to the ticket, and that he might well be the cause of Eisenhower's losing in his bid for re-election.

Stassen's view had its desired effect on the always-cautious President. He requested that Nixon come to his office for a confidential discussion, and the Vice-President, happily expecting Eisenhower's delayed approval, told Pat he would return home soon with the "good news." But, instead of a second term, he was offered a Cabinet post—that of Secretary of Defense. Astonished, Nixon listened without a word as Eisenhower reminded him that no Vice-President had been elected to the presidency, directly, in over a century. "On the other hand," Ike said earnestly, "with the broad administrative experience that you would gain as a Cabinet member, you would be in a much better position to run for President."

Ike had expected a response at this juncture—perhaps an eager acceptance—but when Nixon simply maintained his stony-faced silence, Eisenhower continued: "It isn't that I don't want you on the ticket, Dick. I do. But I want this to be a free convention—to leave the selection of the Vice-President to the delegates. I'd rather not give the appearance of dictating to them."

For Nixon this was an acute emotional shock. Once again

he could envision an ordeal similar to his state of limbo when Eisenhower's indecision had almost forced him to resign during the fund crisis in September, 1952. While the President was too politically naive to recognize that his Vice-President was the target of a not-too-subtle Stassen scheme, Nixon himself was well aware of the maneuvering that was taking place.

Nixon's reaction was one of deep chagrin—coupled with a feeling of utter disgust. If this were to be his reward, if he had to suffer another long night of suspense while Eisenhower weighed the advantages and disadvantages of withholding his endorsement, he might as well quit. Certainly he could earn far more money if he retired from public life! He had already been offered a partnership in a New York law firm that would assure him a minimum of $100,000 a year.

Convinced that his only recourse was to leave Government service, he called a press conference for the following day to make the announcement. But the meeting was called off when Leonard Hall, chairman of the Republican National Committee, heard of the planned resignation. He rushed to the White House where he alerted Major General Wilton B. Persons, and together they finally urged Nixon to delay his announcement.*

What changed Nixon's mind was a peculiar occurrence in New Hampshire. Largely through the efforts of Senator Styles Bridges and other Republican leaders, a campaign was conducted in that state, without fanfare, to demonstrate that Stassen was wrong, and that Nixon's appeal to the voters remained as high as ever. When the New Hampshire presidential primary was over, there were more than 22,000 write-in votes for Nixon as Vice-President. At no other time in New Hampshire's history had a vice-presidential candidate ever received more than a few dozen votes in a primary contest. As far as Nixon was concerned this was his mandate to remain

---

*Major General Persons, at that time, was Eisenhower's Deputy for Legislative Affairs. He succeeded Sherman Adams as Chief of Staff.

on the team.

On April 26, he reminded Eisenhower of his suggestion that the Vice-President would be wise to chart his own course. "I've decided to run again," he said. His tone was mild, but it contained the same hint of steel Ike recalled Nixon using when he seemed cornered by his enemies four years earlier. More than anything, the President admired a fighter. Again he surprised Nixon. Smiling, he extended his hand and offered his good wishes. Within minutes he instructed his press secretary, James Hagerty, to follow Nixon's public announcement with a statement of his own. "Jim, after he concludes his announcement to the press, I want you to tell the reporters that I was delighted to hear the news."

It still wasn't a positive endorsement, but it was far better than the silent treatment he had received until then. Eisenhower was determined to maintain his moral posture, Nixon perceived. He had not deviated from the Stassen-inspired "hands-off policy" attitude.

Meanwhile, Stassen, who had visited Eisenhower a number of times to discuss what was now openly called the "Dump Nixon Movement," carried his opposition all the way to the Convention in San Francisco. There, he buttonholed as many leaders as he could, and pushed the nomination of Christian Herter for the vice-presidency, knowing full well that Herter had agreed to make the nominating speech for Nixon. Stassen produced the results of a private poll which showed that Governor Herter was catching up to the front-runner, and that he would soon surpass him. This was, indeed, surprising since the latest Gallup poll gave Nixon 74 percent and Herter only 14.

Eisenhower arrived in San Francisco on August 21, one day before the balloting was to take place. Checking in at the St. Francis Hotel, he summoned Committee Chairman Hall to his sixth floor suite to question him about Stassen's "Dump Nixon" efforts.

"He hasn't gotten anywhere," Hall told the President.

"Herter has absolutely refused to allow his name to be placed in nomination, and all Stassen is accomplishing is supplying the Democrats with a few more adjectives to use against Nixon in the election campaign."

Eisenhower listened intently. Stassen had adroitly warped some of Ike's pronouncements to make it appear that he was encouraging an open convention for the sole purpose of advocating Herter's (or someone else's) nomination. While Eisenhower now realized that he may have brought it upon himself by not issuing a flat statement of support for Nixon at the outset, he was, at this moment, more nettled by Stassen's audacity than by his own error in judgment.

On August 22, nomination day, Hall and Stassen locked horns. Meeting in Sherman Adams' room, Stassen asked coldly, "When are the vice-presidential nominations scheduled to start?"

"Today, of course," answered Hall. "Right after the President is re-nominated. Why?"

"I need more time for canvassing. The vice-presidential nominations will have to be postponed until tomorrow."

Hall fought to retain his composure. "You aren't running this convention," he snapped. "There will be no postponements."

"Then I want to see the President," Stassen insisted.

"Look, I'm going to give it to you straight," Hall said, his voice rising. "The only way you can get to see Eisenhower is to agree, right now, that you will second Nixon's nomination. You can tell him you'll do it in the interest of party unity. If you don't, Nixon will be nominated without you. Take your choice."

Stassen's balloon collapsed, and he followed Hall's ultimatum to the letter. A few hours later, as he watched a TV newscaster announce the decision he had so reluctantly made, he went to his desk and composed a telegram to Nixon:

I HAVE CONCLUDED THAT I WOULD LIKE TO SECOND YOUR NOMINATION FOR VICE-PRESIDENT AT THE CONVENTION AND JOIN WHOLE-HEARTEDLY IN SUPPORT OF THE NOMINEES OF THE CONVENTION—PRESIDENT EISENHOWER AND YOURSELF—FOR NOVEMBER, URGING THE VOTERS WHO HAD FELT AS I HAD, TO JOIN WITH ME IN THIS RESULT. I HAVE SO ADVISED THE PRESIDENT. BEST WISHES TO YOU.

HAROLD E. STASSEN

Additional Highlights of the Vice Presidency

During Richard Nixon's years as Vice President, few events could compete with the McCarthy episodes, from the point of view of newsworthiness or suspenseful excitement.

A number of events, however, are worth recalling, even briefly, for they helped sustain the Nixon image, albeit to a lesser degree.

1. On April 24, 1955, Eisenhower sustained a serious heart attack. He appeared to be at death's door. Besieged by the press and by hundreds of concerned government officials and members of Congress, Nixon moved from his house and sought refuge at the home of his closest personal friend, William Rogers, at that time Assistant United States Attorney General. Within twenty-four hours, the "Tricky Dick" syndrome was again in full sway, as hostile columnists began to whisper about a possible "takeover of the Government" by "that man."

2. On May 13, 1958, during a visit to Venezuela, a Communist riot in Caracas ensued, and Vice-President Nixon and Mrs. Nixon were spat upon and almost killed.

3. In July, 1958, the famous "kitchen debate" with Nikita Khrushchev took place in Moscow. Nixon, always the re-

Richard Nixon and Nikita Khrushchev stroll the grounds of the Premier's summer home on the outskirts of Moscow, following their famed "kitchen debate."

strained gentleman, turned back the Soviet Premier's scatological assaults on American doctrines and institutions with an aplomb that won him the plaudits of the free world.

A Wife Looks At Her Husband

The vice-presidency turned the domestic lives of Richard and Pat topsy-turvy. She recalled him as he had been only a few short years earlier, before he had taken to the hustings in behalf of the Eisenhower-Nixon candidacies. And her heart ached for him.

Poised on the platform in those yesterdays, he was the embodiment of youthful, passionate sincerity. His hair was black and had not yet begun to recede. His beetling eyebrows and heavy jaws were pronounced. His voice was beautifully modulated and (at least to her) "well . . . kind of thrilling. And when he smiled, he looked positively boyish." Yet, she recalled, when he railed against an injustice, "that same loving voice could get as hard as any prosecutor's."

Her natural bias aside, Pat's evaluation was rather accurate. The young Richard Nixon had, indeed, presented a picture of masculine vigor. Although just under six feet tall, he had the body of an athlete, well proportioned and muscular. But now she could see weary lines forming in his face, and the first signs of the jowls that were to become so familiar to the nation. He was a tired man.

Finding him in his favorite chair one evening, reading the editorial page of the Washington *Evening Star,* she approached him from behind, encircled him with her arms, and, bending over, placed her cheek against his. "Promise me something, Dick," she said softly.

"Sure, anything you say," he replied absently, absorbed in the newspaper.

"Promise that you'll leave politics when your term is over."

He looked up at her and saw that she was dead serious. "I promise," he assured her. "I really mean it."

She brought him a pen and a sheet of paper. "I haven't been a lawyer's wife all these years for nothing," she announced with an impish grin. "Any objections to writing it down?"

Solemnly he wrote: "I promise to Patricia Ryan Nixon that I will not again seek public office."

11
1960
The Nixon-Kennedy Campaign

THIRTEEN YEARS had passed since the spring of 1947 when, in McKeesport, Pennsylvania, Richard Nixon and John Fitzgerald Kennedy held their first public debate, with Nixon arguing the pros and Kennedy the cons of the Taft-Hartley Act. As members of the Education and Labor Committee, they were the most junior representatives of their opposing parties, or, as Nixon smilingly put it, "We were low men on the totem pole."

Now, in the year 1960, they were to become locked in a crucial struggle for the presidency of the United States.

The idea of running for the office of President certainly did not spring full-blown in Nixon's mind during the latter part of the Eisenhower Administration. As far back as 1952 he had begun to consider the White House as his goal, but at that time his only major political assets were his success in the Hiss case, his election to the Senate, and his growing reputation as an excellent speaker. These attributes, while valuable for a junior Senator, were hardly imposing enough to claim the office of Chief Executive.

However, on May 8 of that year, at a fund-raising dinner in New York, Governor Dewey said to him, "Make me a promise: don't get fat; don't lose your zeal. You can be President some day."

"I was somewhat embarrassed," Nixon reminisced. "I assumed Dewey just wanted to say something encouraging to a political colleague. However, as I was to learn when I began to know him better, he isn't given to idle praise. He had seen something in me that I had not seen myself."

Nixon's candidacy began on Friday, November 7, 1958, which he himself describes as "a bleak day at the start of a long, cold winter in Washington." The fortunes of the Republican Party had sunk to a low point following its defeat in the 1958 Congressional elections. Heading into the 1960 campaign, the GOP was once again in the minority. In the Senate, there were only 35 Republican Senators. Nationally, only 14 Governors were Republicans, and only seven state legislatures were in GOP hands. It was not only the weather that was bleak that winter, but Republican prospects as well.

Richard Nixon, who had stumped the entire nation in behalf of party candidates, found his popularity among the voters as depressingly low as that of other Republican leaders. One Republican exception was Governor Nelson Rockefeller of New York who had won a decisive victory in his state. The press, with some justification, predicted that Nixon was on the way out and that Rockefeller was the most likely candidate to succeed Ike. What the columnists and editorial writers had not been aware of, however, was Nixon's continuous and assiduous cultivation of the power-units of his party—from small-town mayors and local district leaders in scores of cities, to the policy-making hierarchy in Washington. Rockefeller, for all his ability, and for all his popularity with the liberal establishment, had made no effort to mend his political fences, and his chances of beating Nixon were about as probable as flagging down the Twentieth Century Limited with a candle.

There was little question as to whom the Democrats would nominate as their presidential candidate. Senator John F. Kennedy had won an overwhelming victory in Massachusetts, adding impetus to the political machine which he and his lieutenants had kept intact after his narrow defeat for the vice-presidency in 1956. Now, according to a Gallup poll, the Republican candidate, whoever he might be, would have to hold almost all of the Republican votes, persuade over fifty per cent of the independent voters to support the GOP ticket and, as if that were not difficult enough, would have to win the votes of six million Democrats.

1958: The 1960 Campaign Begins

On that "bleak day" in November, Nixon received a telephone call from Leonard Hall, former Chairman of the Republican National Committee, suggesting that they meet to discuss the coming campaign. After dinner that evening at Nixon's home, they and Clifford Folger, U.S. Ambassador to Belgium, brought the conversation around to the real purpose of the meeting.

"Dick," Hall began, "it's time for you to decide what you are going to do in 1960. If you expect to be a candidate, you'll have to start now."

Nixon, who had been expecting the approach, carefully weighed the odds against himself, and his analysis offered a gloomy prospect. After discussing each of the obstacles, Nixon terminated the conjecturing with a blunt question: "Considering all of these problems, what are the odds against my winning the nomination and the election?"

"I'm sure you can get the nomination," Hall answered slowly, "but I would say that the odds on winning the election are about five to one against you—or any other Republican."

"That's some offer," reflected Nixon thoughtfully.

"But the odds can change drastically if we put on a fighting campaign," countered Hall. "You know that better than I. We still have two years before Election Day in 1960."

Nixon agreed. And that very night they laid the initial plans to line up delegates for the National Convention, with Hall directing that phase of the campaign. Ambassador Folger, in private life a Washington investment banker, agreed to head up the Finance Committee. Others whom Nixon added to his staff in key positions were Robert H. Finch, a California lawyer (subsequently Lieutenant Governor of his state) who was to serve as campaign director; Herbert G. Klein, a San Diego editor, and the most able press representative Nixon ever had; and a number of others who joined later as the campaign took on the brick and mortar of a tangible entity. Two years of hard work followed.

By July 27, 1959, Nixon had finally mollified the liberals and conservatives within his party, and on that day was unanimously nominated for President. For his running mate he selected Henry Cabot Lodge.

Campaign Planning

Four debates between Richard Nixon and John F. Kennedy were the highlights of the campaign, and many observers believe they determined its outcome.

Prior to the Democratic and Republican conventions, Congress had passed a resolution which provided that the radio-television networks could give free time to major political candidates without being required to furnish free time to candidates of minor parties. Forthwith, Thruston Morton, Republican National Chairman, stated publicly that the Republican nominee, whoever he might be, would agree to debate his Democratic counterpart. Kennedy, of course, lost no time in demanding that Nixon fulfill his party's "solemn promise."

The lesser-known Kennedy, Nixon realized, would benefit

enormously from the gratuitous publicity while he in turn, would gain little or nothing. Further, the Massachusetts Senator, as the challenger, would be on the offensive while he would be forced into defending his record in whatever areas his opponent thought most vulnerable. It was the very trap against which Chotiner had warned him, and the one which he had used in reverse to defeat Congressman Jerry Voorhis in 1946. Yet, he felt that he could not refuse Kennedy, whose taunts were beginning to make front page news. Moreover, public pressure, whipped to fever heat by the press and all three networks, was resulting in a clamor which he could not ignore. In addition, stories were being circulated that he was afraid to defend his record against a man who was as adept as he in the art of public speaking.

Thus, with a sigh, and fully aware of his risk, Nixon agreed to debate Kennedy on national television.

Although Bob Finch was his nominal campaign manager, Nixon soon took control of almost every facet of the race against his Democratic opponent. Apparently, he had forgotten Murray Chotiner's stern admonition of almost fourteen years earlier: "You can be a manager or you can be a candidate, but you can't be both."

Indeed, had Chotiner served as Nixon's campaign manager, the results might have been quite different. Certainly, Chotiner would not have allowed his candidate to become embroiled in a series of debates in which there was nothing to gain and so much to lose. He could have easily circumvented Chairman Morton's commitment by insisting that no one can commit the nominee in advance; that he is his own man and makes his own deals.

But unfortunately for both Nixon and Chotiner, Chotiner was back in Beverly Hills, California, having been summoned to appear before the Senate Permanent Investigating Subcommittee in what was described as an effort to destroy him, and remove him from the political scene. The charge was influence-peddling. The Subcommittee's counsel, Robert Kennedy, subjected him to a merciless ordeal, but because of his obvious innocence the charge could not be proved. Nevertheless, the adverse publicity had its desired effect: Chotiner's withdrawal to California.*

Following his nomination, Nixon had promised to visit every state in the Union, not only on his own behalf, but to bolster the election chances of local Republican office-seekers. Lyndon Johnson quickly moved to upset Nixon's itinerary. Instead of adjourning Congress before the Democratic Convention as is customary, he merely called for a recess which would require Congress to reconvene during the Republican Convention.

"This was one of the shrewdest maneuvers of the 1960 campaign," said Nixon. "It meant that while the Senate was in session, I would again be held down in Washington because of the possibility of a tie vote." Kennedy, and Johnson, his running mate, would, of course, be free to campaign anywhere, at any time. Should their votes in the Senate be needed, they could front for each other as a "live pair." The scheme to delay Nixon's nationwide trek was eminently successful, leaving only his weekends for short jaunts when there was no possibility of a sudden vote, while Kennedy, always within reach of Johnson, swung into action.

Nevertheless, Nixon managed to fly to Detroit, Birmingham, and Atlanta. But he was not yet through with campaign delays. On August 17, in Greensboro, North Carolina, he struck his knee on a car door—a painful crack that made him wince. However, he had been given such a tumultuous ovation at the conclusion of his speech that he promptly forgot the injury. But at home that Friday night, the pain grew intense. Pat applied hot compresses in an effort to bring

---

*Back in his own state, Chotiner ran for Congresss but was defeated because, among other reasons, he ignored the sage advice he had given Nixon—he served as his own campaign manager. But, in time, he would reappear at Nixon's side.

relief so that he could sleep. When the pain had not subsided on the following day, Dr. Walter Tkach, the assistant White House physician, advised that he go to Walter Reed Hospital for a fluid tap to test for infection.

For the next two weeks he was busy with plans for his next campaign swing through the New England states and then to Alaska when, on a Monday, August 29, his work was disrupted by a telephone call from Dr. Tkach. "You'll have to get right over to the hospital," the physician told him.

"But I have a heavy schedule coming up," Nixon protested. "I just don't have the time."

"Well, you'd better *make* time," the doctor said bluntly.

"But my schedule...."

"I know all about your schedule," Dr. Tkach interrupted, "but if you don't get out here to the hospital you'll be campaigning on one leg."

At Walter Reed Hospital, Dr. Tkach gave him the bad news. His knee was infected with hemolyptic *staphylococcus aureus*. The infection was under the kneecap, and would require at least two weeks of hospitalization for treatment. Immediately hospitalized, with his leg in traction, he was given massive shots of penicillin and antibiotics.

The Catholic Issue

But bad luck continued to plague him even during his confinement at Walter Reed. On September 8, he opened the morning paper to find that the prominent clergyman, Dr. Norman Vincent Peale, had joined other Protestant signers of a statement which expressed concern as to whether a Catholic President (Kennedy was a Catholic) could resist the "extreme pressure" from the hierarchy of his church.

Nixon realized at once that he was in for some real trouble. And, before the day was over, cries of "religious bigotry" were being heard everywhere.

Dr. Peale, who had signed the statement without realizing

its full import, was heartbroken not only because of the embarrassment he had brought to Nixon (who with Pat had attended his church when they lived in New York at the end of World War II, thus starting a friendship which had continued through the years), but because he had meant to convey nothing more than the message that a President's duty was to continue the concept of separation of church and state.

Nixon, considerably weakened by the antibiotics he had received, and considerably underweight, was released from the hospital the next day, September 9. The following Sunday, just three days later, he responded to the religious question on "Meet the Press."

"I have no doubt whatever about Senator Kennedy's loyalty to his country," Nixon stated in answer to a direct question by NBC's Herb Kaplow. ". . . If he were elected President, he would put the Constitution of the United States above any other consideration. I don't believe there is a religious issue as far as Senator Kennedy is concerned . . . It would be tragic for this election to be determined primarily, or even substantially, on religious grounds . . . I have issued orders to all the people in my campaign not to discuss religion, not to raise it, not to allow anybody to participate in the campaign who does so on that ground, and as far as I am concerned, I will decline to discuss it."

Unfortunately, the issue remained alive, much of it due to the usual bigots who infest both parties, and to some leading Democrats who used it to discredit Nixon and woo Republican votes. For himself, Nixon thought that he had settled the controversy once and for all on his "Meet the Press" appearance, but of course he had no control over the strategists in the Democratic camp.

On the very next day following Nixon's "Meet the Press" TV statement, John F. Kennedy made his famous and laudable speech before the Houston Ministerial Association. With eloquent passion he appealed to the good conscience of the American electorate not to deny him the presidency solely because of his religion. He reminded his audience that he had fought in the South Pacific and that he had lost a brother in World War II—and that no one had then questioned their religion or their loyalty. In a ringing voice he declared, "I believe in an America where the separation of church and state is absolute . . ."

If thereafter the Massachusetts Senator remained silent on the religious issue, he apparently had given no such instructions to his associates. As Nixon put it, "It was not what JFK was saying, but what Lyndon Johnson, Adlai Stevenson, Robert Kennedy, Walther Reuther and other leaders in the Kennedy campaign were saying and doing on the religious issue."

Robert Kennedy seized on his brother's statement to the Houston ministers and, on every possible occasion, raised the question, "Did they ask my brother Joe whether he was a Catholic before he was shot down?" The fact that no one was raising the question was immaterial. These and other statements by Democratic campaigners resulted in scare headlines which alienated many Catholic voters whom Nixon might otherwise have been able to count on.

Nixon, who had never in his life questioned a man's religion, now became the target of every mean and disgraceful assault in the lexicon of uninhibited politics.

The Democratic strategy was clear. While Kennedy's staff and other top leaders in the party were accusing Nixon of religious bigotry, they were doing everything possible to keep the issue alive, insisting all the while that to do so was proof of religious prejudice. For Kennedy, it was a "heads I win, tails you lose" proposition. Republican Catholics were urged to vote for Kennedy because he was of their religion; Republican Protestants and Jews were exhorted to vote for him to prove that they were not prejudiced against Catholics.

Most outraged were the Catholics on Nixon's staff who held a meeting and collectively entreated him to address the nation on TV and denounce what they termed "reverse bigotry."*

But Nixon remained adamant in his refusal to recognize religion as a legitimate issue.

"I could not dismiss from my mind the persistent thought that, in fact, Kennedy was a member of a minority religion to which the presidency had been denied throughout the history of our nation," he said, "and that I, perhaps, as a Protestant who had never felt the slings of discrimination, could not understand his feeling—that, in short, he had every right to speak out against even possible and potential bigotry. I felt a responsibility to keep the lid on the boiling cauldron of embittered anti-Catholicism."

Was his decision to stifle the religious issue a correct one, even to the point of remaining silent when he himself was being attacked as a bigot or worse? Said Nixon: "I can think of many things I should have done or might have done differently, but on this key decision I have never had a moment's regret."

The Debates

The first of the Nixon-Kennedy debates was held on September 26, 1960, in Chicago, and was covered by CBS, NBC and ABC.

Nixon, gaunt and tired, arrived in the Windy City at 10:30 on the night before the broadcast, hoping to get a full night's sleep. Although still suffering from the effects of his knee infection, he had been able to prepare for the debate during the previous week, arising early every morning and continu-

---

*Among the Catholics on Nixon's staff and the top officials of the Administration who urged that he fight back against the charges of religious bigotry were: Don Hughes, Nixon's aide; Rose Mary Woods, his personal secretary; Betty McVey, his receptionist; Rita and her sister, Jane Dannenhauer, and Mary Fenton, three of his top secretaries; Jim Mitchell, then Secretary of Labor; Bill Miller, Chairman of the Republican Congressional Campaign Committee; and Peter Flanigan, executive director of the Volunteers for Nixon-Lodge.

ing until late at night when he would fall into bed exhausted. As his plane touched down in Chicago, he was greeted by some 5,000 enthusiasts. His hopes for rest vanished. City Republican leaders had planned five rallies in separate parts of the city, and, when Pat and he arrived at the Pick-Congress Hotel, dawn was approaching. Nevertheless, he arose early, addressed the annual convention of the Carpenters Union at eleven o'clock, and spent the rest of the day working on his mountain of notes.

At the studio that evening, Nixon refused Ted Rogers' suggestion that he use makeup, agreeing only to an application of beard lipstick to lighten the perpetual "five o'clock shadow" which is noticeable on his face within five minutes after he shaves. The powder made him look even paler and more hollow-cheeked than he was. In contrast, Kennedy was deeply tanned, relaxed and brimming with charm.

As Nixon stood before the cameras, he recalled the discussion he had had with his staff regarding the proposed content of the four debates. He had contended that one confrontation should be devoted to domestic issues and another exclusively to foreign affairs. It was in the latter category that Nixon felt he had Kennedy at a disadvantage, and his intense desire was to debate that issue when the largest audience would be watching the program. His opinion was that the first debate would attract the most viewers and that thereafter the audiences would dwindle. The majority of his staff, however, felt that public interest would increase, and that the fourth and final debate would attract the largest audience. Against his better judgment, he yielded to the majority; domestic policy would be discussed in the first debate, foreign affairs in the fourth.

The opening argument was Kennedy's and he did exactly what Nixon would have done had he been in his opponent's place: he attacked. For eight full minutes, without seeming to draw a breath, Kennedy blamed the Eisenhower Administration for the depressed areas in the nation (the so-called "poverty pockets"), the unemployment situation, racial discrimination, the plight of the farmers, the underpaid teachers, rising costs of food and medicine . . . the gamut of dereliction whose syntax has been passed on by each generation of politicians to the next. The Republicans cared nothing about these problems; he did . . .

Nixon recognized his presentation as an exceptionally clever, psychologically sound appeal that would have great impact upon his audience. More importantly, his manner eclipsed the content of his speech: he exuded confidence, radiated good health, and was forceful without giving the appearance of arrogance.

In contrast, Nixon's physical appearance was gaunt, pale and haggard. True enough, he answered Kennedy point by point with facts and figures which ordinarily would have demolished his opponent's stand. "How do you propose to do all these things?" he asked Kennedy. "How much will it cost, and whose money will pay for the panaceas?" . . . Here he encountered another difference in their styles: Kennedy, completely aware of the fact that he need not prove his statements, appealed with a nuance of emotion directly to the viewers. Nixon, on the other hand, seemed to forget his all-important audience and spoke only to Kennedy.

The question period that followed delivered a kidney blow:

"Mr. Nixon, would you comment on President Eisenhower's statement about your usefulness to the Administration?" asked Sander Vanocur of NBC.

Nixon had expected and probably dreaded this moment. On August 24, during a press conference, a newsman had asked Eisenhower, "What major decisions of your Administration has the Vice-President participated in?" Ike had replied: "If you give me a week I might think of one."*

---

*Later, that same day, Eisenhower telephoned the publicly-humiliated Nixon to express his regrets, explaining that he had only meant to be facetious.

Nixon made a forlorn effort to laugh off the incident as a joke, but it was painful to watch.

In their verbal exchange in that first debate, Nixon clearly had the edge over Kennedy. Again he had applied his "iron butt" principle and had done his homework. Those who had not seen the confrontation on television, but had read the texts in the newspapers, or had heard the exchange by radio, leaned toward Nixon. The vast majority who had watched via television not only gave Kennedy extra points, but were appalled at the contrast between the virile-looking Massachusetts Senator and the haggard Vice-President. Too late, Nixon recalled one of Chotiner's sayings, "Appearance often counts more than substance."

A portent of the public's reaction occurred when Nixon returned to his suite at the Pick-Congress Hotel. Rose Mary Woods worriedly told him that her parents had called her from Ohio to ask if he were ill. "Did I look sick to you?" he asked. She nodded, "I'm afraid so."

Dr. Malcolm Todd, Nixon's physician at the time, entered the suite. He too had watched the debate. "How much do you weigh?" he asked gruffly, his concern superceding his usual mild bedside manner. Nixon stepped on the bathroom scales. He was down to 160 pounds, ten below normal, and five less than he had weighed in the past thirty years. His size 16 shirt-collar fit loosely for the first time since his college days.

"You looked like hell on TV tonight," Dr. Todd said. "You looked weak and pale and tired because, in fact, that's exactly what you are." He prescribed: "Ease up on the campaign and drink a rich chocolate milkshake with every meal."

Easing up on the campaign was something Nixon felt he could not do, but drinking milkshakes, his passion since boyhood, was an order he could follow with the greatest of pleasure.

After his initial confrontation with Kennedy, Nixon hoped that the foreign affairs question, which he was saving for their fourth and final debate, would more than compensate for the lackluster presentation he had made on the domestic issues. But here too he was to suffer keen disappointment as a result of following his staff's prognosis that the last debate would outdraw the prior three. His own instincts had been correct: more viewers listened to and saw the first debate than the subsequent ones. Thus, he had delivered his best presentation too late, to the smallest audience.*

On Election Day, Richard and Pat voted in their old hometown of Whittier. But Nixon, too keyed up to face the many people who swarmed about the Ambassador Hotel in Los Angeles hoping to talk to him, needed a few hours to himself. Pat drove back to the hotel while he, driven by John DeBetta of the Los Angeles Police Department, and accompanied by his aides, Don Hughes and Jack Sherwood, headed south in the direction of San Diego. Only once was he recognized, when they stopped for gas in Oceanside. In San Diego, Hughes mentioned that he had never been to Tijuana and, as Nixon himself had not been there for twenty-five years, Election Day found a candidate for President of the United States in Mexico. They returned to the Ambassador Hotel at five o'clock, slipped in through a back entrance and climbed the stairs to Nixon's fourth-floor suite.

The first election returns were mixed. As the polls closed, Nixon was ahead in a few states, but Kennedy was beginning to pull even in the popular vote. Nevertheless, the mood was bright, with hopes high.

A little after five o'clock Herb Klein brought in the Connecticut returns. Kennedy had carried the state by a plurality of 90,000 votes. True enough, Nixon had conceded the state to the Democrats, but not by such an unexpected margin. By 5:30 the network computers at NBC showed the odds in

---

*According to the trade journals associated with the television industry, the first debate was seen by 75,000,000 people; the second by 62,500,000; the third by 60,000,000, and the fourth by 48,000,000.

favor of a Kennedy victory at 7 to 1. At 6:00, NBC lengthened the odds to 15 to 1, and CBS predicted a Kennedy victory with 52% of the popular vote. At this time, only eight per cent of the votes had been tabulated, with Kennedy leading by some three million.

By 7:30, NBC reported the odds on a Kennedy victory at 250 to 1, but, as the returns began to come in from the big states, Kennedy's popular vote began to dwindle. Shortly after 9:30, his lead over Nixon was down to 1.6 million.

"It's going to be a real squeaker," Len Hall told Nixon as the gap between the two candidates continued to narrow. Slight though it was, Kennedy's lead seemed durable enough to put him over the top, and at 12:30 A.M., Nixon decided to talk to the crowd at the Ambassador Hotel that had been waiting for him. He sent for his wife and daughters.

Pat and Tricia were wearing new dresses for the occasion: Pat's a gray-green floral print, Tricia's a blue. The children had gone to bed early and, now that they had been awakened, they wanted reassurance from their father. Pat had been telling them that "the news is bound to get better toward morning."

"Hi, Daddy," Tricia greeted him. "How's the election doing?"

He took her hand in his. "I'm afraid we lost, honey," he told her.

Pat, Tricia and Julie did not accompany him as he made his way to the ballroom where his supporters had gathered. They were in tears. There, he thanked the crowd and told them, "There are still some results to come in, but if the present trend continues Senator Kennedy will be the next President of the United States."

On the following day Nixon dictated a telegram of formal concession to Kennedy:

> I WANT TO REPEAT THROUGH THIS WIRE THE CONGRATULATIONS AND BEST WISHES I EXTENDED TO YOU ON TELEVISION LAST

Vice-President Nixon with a group of political interns from Yale University, in Washington, in 1960. One of the men has just asked, "Mr. Vice-President, do you think the Democratic Party is here to stay?"

NIGHT. I KNOW THAT YOU WILL HAVE THE UNITED SUPPORT OF ALL AMERICANS AS YOU LEAD THE NATION IN THE CAUSE OF PEACE AND FREEDOM DURING THE NEXT FOUR YEARS.

But, even as he dictated the wire, he was troubled by the mounting evidence of fraud which, in a sworn statement, he later charged was evident from a study of the voting procedures in three Texas counties (Fannin County, Angelia County and Fort Bend County), as well as in Chicago's 2nd and 6th Wards.

Nixon was urged by his friends and associates to demand a recount. President Eisenhower himself telephoned to suggest that possibility. But he refused. In the first place, he reasoned, it would take more than a year to get a recount in Chicago's Cook County (Mayor Richard Daley's bailiwick) where much of the chicanery had taken place. In Texas, there was no legal procedure whatever for a recount.

"A call for a recount would have delayed the orderly transfer of responsibility from the old Administration to the new, perhaps for months," said Nixon. "Officials in the old Administration, and those appointed by Kennedy, would not know what clear powers and responsibilities they had, and neither side could make any plans. A Constitutional crisis might have developed. Consequently I made the decision not to support the recount charges."

There were other factors, of course, that contributed to Nixon's defeat. One incident cost him many black votes. On October 19, 1960, the Reverend Martin Luther King had been arrested in Atlanta, along with some fifty others, while engaged in a restaurant sit-in. All were quickly released on bail, but Dr. King was held. A week later, on October 26, he was given a four-month sentence on an old charge of driving without a valid license. The nation's press (outside of the Deep South) viewed this as the rawest kind of racial persecution, and Robert Kennedy, sensing the political mileage to be extracted from the case, immediately telephoned Dr. King's wife to offer his sympathy, making sure that his publicity staff informed the press of his concern for the civil rights leader. He then telephoned the judge in the case in an effort to have Dr. King released on bail. This, too, he quickly and dramatically announced to the press.

Meanwhile, Washington newsmen were inquiring as to Nixon's reaction to the King episode. "You'll have to tell them something," Herb Klein counseled. "I can't hold them off much longer."

"It's my opinion that Dr. King is getting a bum rap," Nixon told his press secretary. "But it would be completely improper for me or any other lawyer to call the judge. And Bobby Kennedy knows that as well as I."

Klein had no alternative other than to issue a "No comment" to the press. One of the reporters in the room who had covered Nixon ever since his first campaign against Congressman Voorhis was heard to remark: "Ah Chotiner! Wherefore art thou, Chotiner?"

For his part, immediately after Klein brought the case to his attention, Nixon asked Attorney General Bill Rogers to determine whether Dr. King's constitutional rights had been infringed upon, thus making it a Federal matter. Rogers at once contacted the White House, strongly recommending that Jim Hagerty issue a statement that the Department of Justice had been instructed to investigate the case. But Eisenhower maintained a "hands-off" policy and Rogers was unable to secure the Chief Executive's approval to issue a press release.

Nixon, who had been a member of, and a contributor to, the NAACP for ten years, and who had been one of the most consistent and effective proponents of civil rights legislation, now appeared to have abandoned Dr. King to his fate without a word of sympathy or encouragement. His attempts to bring practical help through the intercession of the Justice Department and the White House itself were unpublicized; moreover, he did not permit his staff to notify the press of his actions. "I don't care what Bobby Kennedy does," he said stubbornly, "we're not going to use Dr. King to gain some political advantage."

What does a man think about when he has just lost a chance to become President of the United States? The frauds that deprived him of needed votes? The debates that he might have won? The religious issues? . . .

As Nixon went through the painful motions of emptying his desk of his personal effects, his thoughts embraced his family. There was Pat's smiling face looking out at him from a favorite photo; and there, beside it, was a picture of their children. He placed the photographs in a large separate envelope, and took them home that night. And here was a letter he cherished . . . It had been composed by the reporters who had covered him during the campaign up to the day he had eluded them on Election Day—when he disappeared into Mexico. He recalled the smile on Herb Klein's face as he handed him the letter. It read:

> Dear Friend:
>
> You shook us on the Tijuana trail. (But it wouldn't have happened if we had had a Washington newsman and not a Young Republican at the wheel of our car.)
>
> You made us stand for an hour and a half in the grim fog in Lima, Ohio, while your train rumbled back onto the main line.
>
> You told us in Chicago that you never delivered the same speech twice, but some sense we've heard the same phrases once or twice in the course of the campaign.

> You took us from St. Louis to Atlantic City to Roanoke to Omaha in one nightmarish day, and confined us to Convairs for the last two legs of the journey. And if that weren't enough, you sent Fred Seaton down at 3 A.M. to explain your farm program to us.
>
> Your entourage in all these travels was a mixed breed. But as this plane wings eastward, it was the majority opinion of the regulars in the press corps that we have toured the land with a champ. And we double it in spades for Pat.
>
> (signed) *Your Camp Followers*

On January 6, 1961, there remained but one last official duty in his capacity as Vice-President—to announce the results of the Electoral College. Only once previously in United States history had a defeated candidate presided over his own "funeral" by announcing his loss in a joint session of Congress—that gentleman was John C. Breckinridge who in defeat announced the election of Abraham Lincoln.

Speaker Sam Rayburn announced the final electoral tally: 303 to 219, with 15 votes cast for Harry Byrd. Then, Vice-President Richard Nixon approached the lectern to make it official:

> Mr. Speaker . . . This is the first time in 100 years that a candidate for the presidency has announced the results of an election in which he was defeated, and announced the victory of his opponent. I do not think we could have a more striking and eloquent example of the stability of our Constitutional system and of the proud tradition of the American people of developing, respecting and honoring institutions of self-government.

In our campaigns, no matter how hard fought they may be, no matter how close the election may turn out to be, those who lose accept the verdict, and support those who win. And I would like to add that, having served now in Government for 14 years . . . as I complete that period, it is indeed a great honor to me to extend to my colleagues in the House and Senate on both sides of the aisle who have been elected—to extend to John F. Kennedy and Lyndon Johnson, who have been elected President and Vice-President of the United States—my hearfelt best wishes, as all of you work in a cause that is bigger than any man's ambition, greater than any party. It is the cause of freedom, of justice, and peace for all mankind.

It is in that spirit that I now declare that John F. Kennedy has been elected President of the United States, and Lyndon B. Johnson, Vice-President of the United States.

With that, private citizen Richard Milhous Nixon went home to his wife and children—defeated, but still a champ!

12
The Waiting Years

PRIVATE CITIZEN Richard Nixon, following the 1960 presidential contest, faced a dilemma: he was 48 years old, and unemployed. After four years as a Congressman, two as a Senator, and eight as Vice-President, all that he and Pat could claim in a material sense was the equity in their Washington house. They had no stocks or bonds, and they were drawing on their savings to cover their current expenses. He did have a life insurance policy, but it had been acquired too recently to have a cash value. He had set aside nothing for his old age except for the Congressional retirement plan to which he had contributed, but he would not be eligible for its modest benefits until age 62.

There was also the girls' education to consider. It was now 1961: Tricia was fifteen and Julie, thirteen. If they were to have a college education, he would have to begin making money and saving it. In short, he needed a job.

His home state of California held a special allure. He had started his career there; perhaps he could begin anew in what had been his power base. Speculation that he would run for the Governorship was already being heard in political circles, and several newspaper editorials had weighed that possibility.

In February, a month after he left office, Nixon received a letter from his old friend, Whittaker Chambers. Nixon had corresponded with him ever since the Hiss case, and this was to be the last letter Nixon received from him. Chambers wrote:

> It seems possible that we may not meet again—I mean at all. Forgive me if I say a few things which, otherwise, I should not presume to say.
>
> You have decades ahead of you. Almost from the first day we met (I think it is already twelve years), I sensed in you some quality, deep-going, difficult to identify in the world's glib way, but good, and meaningful for you and multitudes of others. I do not believe for a moment that because you have been cruelly checked in the employment of what is best in you, what is most yourself, that that check is final. It cannot be.
>
> On the other hand, speaking in wholly different (and, by contrast, superficial) terms, it seems to me that [the] executive office [of the presidency] has passed to the other party for a long time to come. I should find it hard to believe that you have not drawn the same conclusion. It is true, that changes your routing and precise destination. It does not change the nature of your journey. You have years in which to serve. Service is your life. You must serve. You must, therefore, have a base from which to serve.

Some tell me that there are reasons why you should not presently run for Governor of California. Others tell me that you would almost certainly carry the state. I simply do not know the facts. But, if it is at all feasible, I, for what it is worth, strongly urge you to consider this. There would be a sense and an impression of political come-down. Great character always precludes a sense of come-down, greatly yielding to match the altered circumstances. The public impression will then take care of itself—may, indeed, become an asset. I believe you to be, rather uniquely a man who can do this.

Chambers' letter showed an acute perception of Nixon—the self-styled political animal who had left political life involuntarily, but was irresistibly drawn to return to it. However, Nixon was not yet ready to make a decision; his immediate need was employment.

Offers poured in from everywhere. A number of colleges and universities sought him as their president. A commercial firm in New York wanted him on its board of directors, holding forth the lure of a high salary and a half-million dollars in stocks. And the law firm of Adams, Duque and Hazeltine, through its senior partner, Earl Adams, who had offered him a position fifteen years previously, now invited him to accept a partnership. This was the firm he joined, not as a partner, but simply as counsel, because it permitted him the most freedom.

It was a fortuitous move. Among the firm's prestigious clients were the American Express Company, the Rexall Drug Chain, the Metropolitan Life Insurance Company, and the Prudential Life Insurance Company. His income soared.

A few weeks later, in May, Nixon signed a contract with the *Los Angeles Times Mirror* syndicate to write a series of ten articles for which he received $40,000. (He wrote an eleventh article as a "thank you" gesture.) In June, columnist

Nixon branched out and authored a book. At the suggestion of novelist Adela Rogers St. John, a friend and loyal supporter ever since he had been her grocery delivery boy in Whittier, he applied himself to the writing of his *Six Crises*. The book, a best seller, earned him royalties of over $200,000. The income derived from his legal fees, his political articles, his book, and lecture tours yielded him more money than he had ever hoped for. He earned more in his first year as a private citizen than all the fourteen years as a Congressman, Senator and Vice-President combined!

The family now made its home in fashionable Trousdale Estates overlooking Beverly Hills. Tricia and Julie loved to frolic in the luxurious swimming pool, and to beat their father whenever he dared race them. And their automobile was a spanking new Starfire Oldsmobile convertible.

Summing up his financial circumstances, on November 8, 1961, he wrote, "Materially, private life has been good to me, far beyond anything I had ever expected. My income tax alone this year will be twice as great as my salary as Vice-President last year."

Gubernatorial Contest: 1962

What could possibly motivate a man to surrender the advantages of a successful private life to return to the uncertainties of the political jungle? For Nixon, there were several pressures. Primarily it was because his blood still burned with political fever. Perhaps it was a superstitious feeling, but conceivably the mystic public service destiny which Whittaker Chambers had prophesied for him influenced him even more than he knew: they turned out to be the last political words of a dying man. And undoubtedly of great importance was the encouragement of such Republican stalwarts as Chairman Len Hall, Senator Barry Goldwater, Senator Hugh Scott, and his faithful mentor, Murray Chotiner—all of them quietly and privately assuring him that he could win the governorship from the incumbent Edmund (Pat) Brown.

At home, Tricia and Julie were enthusiastic, but a disturbing deterrent was Pat. She was enjoying the tranquility of their new home and private life, and was reluctant to return to what she called "the rat race."

Eisenhower added his voice to the others. "I believe you have a duty to run," he told Nixon. "The rank and file voters, as well as the officials of our party, want you to lead them in battle. The polls clearly indicate that the majority of the people of California prefer you over Governor Brown."

The polls to which Eisenhower referred did, indeed, show Nixon ahead of Brown, 53 to 37. Nixon was well aware of the survey, but he was also aware of the wide variances published during his race against Kennedy. He grinned, as he always does, when he thinks of the analyses made in 1948. Every major pollster, including George Gallup, Archibald Crossley and Elmo Roper had stated flatly that based on sample surveys representing a cross section of public opinion Tom Dewey would defeat Harry Truman for President. The wildly inaccurate polls inspired L. S. Briggs of the *Berkshire Evening Eagle* to write a quatrain that still delights Nixon:

> *O, section, cross section, and sample,*
> *O, postcard and phone call and bell;*
> *O, Crossley, Roper and Gallup,*
> *O, George! O, Elmo! O, Hell!*

On the evening of September 26, 1961, he held a family conference. "Whether I decide to make the run against Brown depends upon how you feel about it," he told his wife and daughters. "We're the four musketeers."

Pat, the loyal wife whose first thought was always of her husband, gracefully conceded: "I'll go along with anything you think will make you happy—you know that. And by the way," she added, "I haven't forgotten a certain promise you made—and even wrote down—but I'm not holding you to it." She was smiling now as she recalled his earlier promise to retire from public life. He returned the smile. He, too, had not forgotten.

The girls were delighted. "Let's fight those old Democrats," Tricia cried happily. "I just know we'll win."

"Sure you will," echoed Julie, leaping into her father's lap and encircling his neck with her arms. "Everybody loves my daddy."

Nixon announced his candidacy the next day, saying, in part:

"I shall be a candidate for Governor in the state of California in 1962. . . .

"I often hear it said that it is a sacrifice for men or women to serve in public life. For me, I have found it to be the other way around. On my return to private life my income has grown beyond anything I could ever have dreamed, and I have found, of course, other things in private life which are very attractive.

"But after fourteen years as a Congressman, as a Senator and as Vice-President of the United States, I find my heart is not there: it is in public service . . .

"I have concluded that as far as my present opportunities are concerned, the most challenging, the most exciting position that I can seek, and in which I can serve, next to being President of the United States, is to be Governor of what will be the first state in the nation."

As he spoke into the televised cameras and radio amplifiers his face glowed with excitement and his eyes shone. Soon he would be exhorting the voters to enlist under his banner. Once again, as an active candidate for office, he would be surrounded by reporters seeking a story for the next editions. For the first time since his defeat for the presidency, he was truly happy. The old warhorse had returned to battle.

Again Nixon threw himself into the campaign with all his old fervor. Pat Brown also fought hard. It was the usual stiff contest with charges made and denied by both sides. There was one difference, however. Brown always referred to Nixon with undisguised contempt. Nixon invariably accorded Governor Brown courteous respect.

For the former Vice-President, it was an uphill fight all the way. His opponent, with some justification, repeated the popular contention that Nixon planned to use the Governorship as a stepping-stone to the White House, an argument that was widely believed by Republicans and Democrats.

Another hurdle in his path to the state Capitol was the charge that he, of all people, was "soft on communism." The silly accusation had its genesis during the nomination campaign when his rival, Joseph Shell, Republican leader of the State Assembly, had the strong support of California's right wing forces and the John Birch organization within the state. Nixon issued a ringing denunciation of the Birch Society and referred to the Society's founder, Robert Welch, as "a would-be dictator."

He further incurred the wrath of his fellow-Republicans when he made a statement in support of President Kennedy at the time of the missile crisis in Cuba, and, throughout the campaign, the press hammered away at his every statement while, at the same time, they referred to his opponent in glowing terms.

On November 5, the people of California rejected Nixon's bid for the Governorship, giving him only 47.7% of the vote—a loss which he told a few intimates he had expected. On the morning after the elections, Herb Klein, his press secretary, had just conceded the election before a battery of television cameras in the Beverly Hilton Hotel in Los Angeles, when Nixon strode to the microphone. As always, his wife was at his side. Grimly, he faced the cameras, but he addressed himself to the more than one hundred newsmen who were present. This is what he told the astonished reporters:

> Good morning, gentlemen. Now that Mr. Klein has

made his statement, and now that all the members of the press are so delighted that I have lost, I'd like to make a statement of my own:

I appreciate the press coverage in this campaign. I think each of you covered it the way you saw it . . . I don't believe publishers should tell reporters to write one way or another . . .

I congratulate Governor Brown, as Herb Klein has already indicated, for his victory. He has, I think, the greatest honor and the greatest responsibility of any Governor in the United States . . . I wish him well.

I believe Governor Brown has a heart, even though he believes I do not.

I believe he is a good American, even though he feels I am not.

I am proud of the fact that I defended my opponent's patriotism. You gentlemen, didn't report it, but I am proud that I did that. I am proud also that I defended the fact that he was a man of good motives; a man who I disagreed with very strongly, but a man of good intentions.

I want that—for once, gentlemen—I would appreciate if you would write what I say in that respect. I think it's very important that you write it in the lead—in the lead! . . .

One last thing. At the outset I said a couple of things with regard to the press that I noticed some of you looked a little irritated about. And my philosophy with regard to the press has never really gotten through—and I want it to get through. . . . Never in my sixteen years of campaigning have I complained to a publisher, to an editor, about the coverage of a reporter. I believe that a reporter has got a right to write it as he feels it . . . I will say to the reporter sometimes that I think, well, look, I wish you'd give my opponent the same going over that you gave me.

And as I leave the press, all I can say is this: for 16 years, ever since the Hiss case, you've had a lot of fun—that you've had an opportunity to attack me and that I think I've given as much as I've taken. It was carried right up to the last day.

I made a talk on television, a talk in which I made a flub, in which I said I was running for Governor of the United States. The *Los Angeles Times* dutifully reported that.

Mr. Brown, the last day, made a flub in which he said, "I hope everybody wins. You vote the straight Democratic ticket, including Senator Kuchel." I was glad to hear him say it, because I was for Kuchel, a Republican, all the way. The *Los Angeles Times* did not report it. I leave you gentlemen now, and just think how much you're going to be missing. You won't have Nixon to kick around anymore because, gentlemen, this is my last press conference. . .

I hope what I have said today will at least make television, radio and the press first recognize the great responsibility that they have to report all the news and second—if they're against a candidate, to give him the shaft, but also to recognize if they give him the shaft, put one lonely reporter on the campaign who will report what the candidate says now and then.

Thank you, gentlemen, and good day.

Governor Brown, who was watching his defeated opponent on television, leaned back in his chair and grinned. "Nixon will regret making that speech all his life," he declared. "The press will never let him forget it."

Richard and Pat did not forget it. Vividly they recalled that evening when they stood there under the merciless bright lights with the eyes of the national television cameras zeroing in on them to capture every nuance of emotion and expression.

As Nixon, broken and bitter delivered his swan song to the press, Pat was a pitiful picture of dejection struggling to hold back her tears. Both realized that he was a two-time loser.

Mr. Nixon Goes to Wall Street

The promise Nixon once made to his wife was reiterated. He was through with politics, he assured her, and he meant every word of it. If, in the future, it would be of some help to the party, he would make a few speeches, but he would not again consider running for elective office. It was a firm promise that Pat elicited from him with very little prodding.

Nixon now turned to new horizons. "From the standpoint of a place to live, there is no other place that can surpass California for climate, for cleanliness, and for a gracious way of life," he had said. But as he reflected on his comment, he realized that the most important magnet which had irresistibly drawn him back to his home state was its function as a power base. If he were to sever the umbilical cord that bound him to politics, he would have to remove himself from California where his every move and statement was seen in a political context. But where to go? What to do?

For a man of Nixon's hyperactive temperament, he could not long endure the mental and emotional vacuum that resulted from his retirement from politics. The void had to be filled with another equally stimulating pursuit. For him, the signs pointed in only one direction—New York. It was there that a lawyer could find the kind of excitement, the challenges, which might satisfy a restless spirit.

"New York is very cold and very ruthless and very exciting and therefore an interesting place in which to live," he remarked to Robert J. Donovan of the *Los Angeles Times* during an interview. "It has many great disadvantages but also many advantages. The main thing, it is a place where you can't slow down; a fast track. Any person tends to vegetate unless he is moving on a fast track. New York is a very challenging place . . . you have to bone up to keep alive in the competition."

The fast track idea appealed to Elmer H. Bobst, the college drop-out who was Chairman of the Board at Warner-Lambert Pharmaceutical Company. He was a self-made millionaire. Bobst, then in his seventies, had often played golf with Nixon, and for some time had taken a fatherly interest in his younger friend. Following a discussion with Nixon, he paved the way for him to affiliate with a law firm which handled Bobst's legal affairs—Mudge, Stern, Baldwin & Todd. The century old firm, located at 20 Broad Street, in the heart of New York's financial district, had 22 partners and 35 associates, and acted as legal counsel for many of the largest commercial and industrial companies in the United States.

On June 1, 1963, Nixon joined Mudge and Stern. His first personal client was the Pepsi Cola company. Soon he was handling the legal affairs of other giant entities, including a number of railroads: Mutual of New York, General Cigar, the Irving Trust Company (and other banking institutions), Eversharp-Schick, and many others. Before the year came to a close, the name of Mudge, Stern, Baldwin & Todd was changed to Nixon, Mudge, Rose, Guthrie & Alexander. Later, another name was added: John Mitchell—who was to become

Nixon's close friend and political associate.

The life style of the Nixons in New York underwent a dramatic change. They now lived in a twelve-room apartment that comprised the entire fifth floor of 810 Fifth Avenue which overlooked Central Park at 62nd Street. It was not a rented apartment. It was a cooperative which they purchased for $135,000, paying $10,000 a year extra for maintenance. Nixon's neighbors included such luminaries as Governor Nelson Rockefeller and publisher William Randolph Hearst. Oddly, there was not a Democrat in the building—a situation which Nixon described as "very un-Democratic."

Nixon joined all of the in-town clubs: Metropolitan, Links, Recess, and such fashionable country clubs as Blind Brook in Westchester and Baltusrol in New Jersey. Tricia and Julie were enrolled in the Chapin School, Tricia graduating in June, 1964, and Julie in 1966. The girls then went on to higher education—Tricia to Finch College—a four-year liberal arts institution in New York City, graduating in 1968. Julie attended Smith College in Northhampton, Massachusetts, also a liberal arts school, where she majored in history with a double minor in English and religion. She earned a Bachelor of Arts degree in 1970.

Tricia and Julie were presented to society at the International Debutante Ball. At Julie's coming-out, she was escorted by David Eisenhower. The late President's only grandson was attending Amherst only a few miles from Julie's college, but love laughs at short distances. He visited her frequently, and with marked success. They were married in November, 1967.

But, as Nixon's net worth climbed to the half-million dollar mark, and his position as one of New York's most successful lawyers grew even more secure, the old restlessness seized him once again. He grew moody and unhappy. Pat, watching him with an anxious eye, recognized the symptoms for what they were. A healthy bankroll and a "fast track" were pale substitutes for the longings that burned within him. There could be no peace until he returned to the one field which held him in its unyielding grip—politics!

The Incredible Comeback

It has been said that Pat Nixon, in a tearful confrontation with her husband sometime in March of 1963, invoked his promise to forsake elective office forever. Pat denies that the argument reached that stage of intensity. Her denial can be believed.

She had, in the past, often demonstrated her willingness to sublimate her own desire for Richard's happiness. More than anyone else, she understood how unquenchable was his political thirst—and she withdrew her objection. Her acquiescence made an immediate and perceptible change in Richard's attitude. He became more relaxed. His moodiness disappeared. It was as if he had been touched by a magic wand. The "new" Nixon even shed his austerity, becoming downright playful on occasion.

As an example, in that same month of March, he appeared on the Jack Paar television show where he was impishly greeted with the question: "Should I address you as Dick or Mr. Nixon?"

"I wouldn't worry about that," Nixon responded. "I've been called everything."

"Can Kennedy be defeated in '64?" Paar asked.

"Which one?" countered Nixon.

"Boy," muttered Paar to the laughing audience, "I hate a smart-alec Vice-President."

Later in the program Nixon gave a piano recital—an opus he had composed, backed by violins, and surprisingly professional.

"If the California election didn't finish him, this will," observed Paar. But, his quip was lost in the ovation from the audience. Nixon glowed. This too was music—the happy notes he had yearned for and were so sorely missing from his new life.

The Goldwater Debacle: 1964

In June of 1964 Nixon and his family left for a summer vacation in Europe. Ostensibly, he wanted to avoid the blandishments of the Goldwater and Rockefeller camps jockeying for position at the GOP's forthcoming nominating convention. Each had privately sought his support, aware that he still retained a large and loyal following among party regulars. And both had suggested that, in the event of a deadlock, he might emerge as a dark horse candidate. The proferred bait made Nixon smile. "After what happened to me in California," he said, "the odds against my becoming a candidate are about a thousand to one. What sane man bets against odds like that?"

In Europe, however, there was some question whether he was running away from politics or building a new reputation as a statesman. For the next two months, photographs in American newspapers began to appear regularly depicting Nixon at the Aswan Dam, at an audience with the Pope, lunching with Charles de Gaulle, conferring with Adenauer, and visiting Budapest, Venice, Rome, Madrid and other Continental and Middle Eastern cities.

Like some latter day political Lazarus, Nixon once again came to life in the nation's press. Columnists and editorial writers began to speculate on his chances for winning the nomination. But he took their analyses coolly and in stride. For the time being, he was back in contention inside the arena, and that was enough.

He was realist enough to know that Rockefeller, because of his recent divorce and remarriage, and his liberal viewpoints, could not stem the conservative trend which was even then gaining ascendancy among party leaders. Barry Goldwater, although backed by ultra-rightists, had also captured the imagination of many orthodox conservatives. But Nixon was convinced that his nomination would be catastrophic in the general elections. The tragic death of President Kennedy on November 22, and the elevation of Lyndon Johnson to the presidency caused no changes in Goldwater's approach to the electorate. The late President had imbued the average American with a sense of progress, and Goldwater's philosophy seemed anachronistic.

Unlike Rockefeller who denounced Goldwater, Nixon sprang to his support after the nomination. He campaigned on a grueling schedule during the six weeks preceding the election, covering thirty-six states in a 50,000 mile swing around the country—a record that Goldwater himself did not equal. Nixon knew that the party was badly divided, and that many, if not most, Republicans would switch their allegiance on Election Day. But he was fighting mainly to hold a splintered GOP together. There would be other elections, and without a united party there would be little chance of future victories.

Goldwater, as expected, was inundated in the tide of votes that swept Lyndon Johnson into his first elected term. Nixon, however, emerged as a basic source of strength to the Republican leaders who counted most—the men who controlled the purse strings; those who directed the party's destiny in good times as well as in bad; those who were ultimately responsible for keeping the party alive. Almost singlehandedly he had fought to bring together the tattered remains of a disunited Republican party while other, well-known Republicans, refused to associate themselves with the Goldwater campaign.

The year 1964 ended with Nixon emerging as the most important Republican in the country, and, as he continued to speak out with a new confidence, his influence grew even greater.

The 1966 Congressional campaign should have produced a landslide for the Democrats, judging by their victory two years earlier. Once more the pundits were wrong. Nixon campaigned in 35 states in support of 86 Republican candidates, and raised more than five million dollars for the party. His efforts helped the GOP pick up 47 seats in the House, three in the Senate, eight Governorships and 540 seats in various state legislatures.

By contrast, Senator Robert Kennedy launched his national political machine for the 1968 presidential campaign in that same year. But his efforts were minimal. Of 11 gubernatorial candidates he supported, only three won; and of the ten senatorial aspirants for whom he spoke, only four were successful. Politically, he was no match for Nixon, but his name was a tremendous political plus.

The Last Hurrah: 1968

There was no dearth of Republican candidates for the 1968 convention. Potential nominees included Governor George Romney of Michigan, Governor Ronald Reagan of California, Governor Rockefeller of New York—who again proved his mettle as a vote getter—and Senator Charles Percy of Illinois. There was also Richard Nixon who refused to join the free-for-all melee. Instead, he again travelled the world, assuming the role of statesman in a private capacity. As such, he conferred with leaders in England, France, Germany and Italy, and in the Communist bloc with officials in Rumania and Czechoslovakia. In the Soviet Union, officials refused to meet with him, but undismayed, he entered Russia as a tourist. In April, 1967, Nixon arrived in Vietnam where he was closeted with Ambassador Henry Cabot Lodge.*

As a result of his journeys, and the highly quotable statements he was able to send home, Nixon began to draw more attention and to receive more publicity than his rivals, most

---

*When asked by reporters what Lodge and he had talked about during their meeting in Vietnam, Nixon replied with a grin, "Ambassador Lodge and I made a deal. He's going to put a Pepsi-Cola cooler in the embassy of Saigon."

of whom had not yet left their home states to embark on the campaign trail. Meanwhile, time began to take its toll among the presidential hopefuls.

In September, 1967, Romney lowered the curtain on his own chances by confessing that he had been "brainwashed" into supporting the war in Vietnam. Reagan, who had hoped that he would be chosen in the event of a deadlock between Nixon and Rockefeller, simply waited too long to snare the delegate strength he would need in addition to the favorite son bloc he took with him to the convention. Further, when Strom Thurmond of Kentucky, the most important political voice in the south, threw his support to Nixon, whatever hopes Reagan had of capturing the delegates of the solid south disappeared. Percy was running far behind in the polls—his liberal stand had hurt him too severely for a hurried recuperation by convention time. The ubiquitous Governor Rockefeller represented little more than a pesky nuisance. His denunciation of Barry Goldwater, and the entire sorry spectacle of the 1964 Republican Convention left its scars. Nixon was the only viable candidate whom the Republicans could turn to, and at the convention in Miami he was presented with the nomination on the very first ballot. Acting upon a motion offered by Reagan, the delegates made it unanimous.

As his running mate, Nixon's first choice was Robert Finch, an old political ally from California. For political reasons, Finch was compelled to refuse the honor. Nixon's second choice was Governor Spiro Agnew of Maryland, little known to the public, but acceptable to the south. Supporters of Romney placed the name of Michigan's Governor before the convention, and when the votes were tabulated, 168 delegates were for Romney and 1,128 for Agnew. Interestingly enough, the nominating speech for Agnew was made by John Lindsay, a liberal from New York.

The two-time loser, the man who had bitterly held his "last press conference" and who had "retired" from politics with the assertion that now the newsmen would no longer

The Nixon Nobody Knows 435

"have Nixon to kick around any more," had risen from the ashes of defeat, and, like the legendary phoenix, came to life as his party's 1968 presidential candidate.

President Johnson had announced that he would not be a candidate in the coming elections. Feeling certain that he would suffer a humiliating defeat, he bowed out of contention for the nomination. Vice-President Hubert Horatio Humphrey, a decent man with an excellent record for humanitarian legislation, became the Democratic candidate after Senator Eugene McCarthy was eliminated as a possible nominee and after Robert Kennedy's efforts to win the nomination were ended by the bullets of a mad assassin. Senator George McGovern's last minute attempt to woo the votes pledged to the slain Senator Kennedy fell flat. Hubert Humphrey was left without competition.

Humphrey had two things going for him: his wise choice of Senator Edmund Muskie as his vice-presidential candidate, and the wide support of organized labor. Mitigating against him were the riots which stained the Democratic Convention in Chicago. On the one hand, he bitterly criticized Nixon's demand for "law and order" legislation, claiming that first, social legislation should be attempted. On the other hand, when the hippies and yippies ran beserk in Chicago, his own party took up the "law and order" cry.

Perhaps the greatest impediment to victory was the ghost-like image of President Johnson whose presence hovered, phantom-like, over his head, and for whose record Humphrey was being held accountable.

Murray Chotiner, not yet visible, but once again playing a vital role in Republican party strategy, urged caution. True enough the polls showed Nixon far ahead, but Chotiner knew the Democrats would wage a battle royal up until the last voting booth closed. His real worry, as was Nixon's, was the inroads George Wallace was making in the south. As the campaign progressed, Humphrey's prospects rose. Millions of

With the successful campaign over, Tricia poses with Julie and David Eisenhower who were to be married in a few days. Photo taken December 18, 1968.

Democrats and independents, initially aroused by the "law and order" issue in the wake of black rioting in major cities everywhere, as well as by the radicals who had made a shambles of the Democratic Convention, were beginning to wonder if, by some peculiar twist of logic, social action in the Congress and White House might not be more salutary than police protection after all. Further, Humphrey was beginning to sound like "his own man," as he stated at every conceivable opportunity. But the one issue which he could not explain away without offending Johnson was the Vietnam war.

As the campaign neared its end, President Johnson, who could deal Chotiner cards and spades as the resourceful politician, made a spectacular attempt to rescue Humphrey. He announced that he had ordered a halt to the bombing of North Vietnam.

The Nixon camp was a portrait in consternation. Its members could visualize millions of Americans joining the Democratic fold hoping that Johnson, despite his record, had made a tangible move to support peace. Suspicions were rampant, of course, that the President had timed the executive order to infuse a last minute surge of strength into his protege's campaign. But Nixon would permit no such comment to be used in his entourage. He publicly congratulated Johnson. It was a gracious gesture; not only because it could conceivably cost him the election, but because the President had recently questioned his patriotism. The result was that Nixon appeared the gentleman and Johnson the boor.

On Election Day, 1968, a massive turnout of voters decided the issue. Nixon was swept into office with 302 electoral votes as against Humphrey's 191—winning 32 states to his opponent's 13. The popular vote count in round numbers was 31,785,000 for Nixon and 31,275,000 for Humphrey.

For President-elect Richard Nixon the years of frustration had come to an end. The successful campaigner had been counted out more times than any other presidential aspirant

President Nixon delivering his Inaugural Address. Front row, left to right, Mrs. Spiro Agnew, Mrs. Pat Nixon, Chief Justice Earl Warren, former President Lyndon B. Johnson, President Nixon, Vice-President Spiro Agnew, Hubert Humphrey, Senator Mike Mansfield. January 29, 1969.

Pat and Richard Nixon following his Inaugural Address, January 20, 1969.

in American history. But he had believed in himself—often when no one else shared that belief.

He had dared to dream the impossible dream, and that dream had come true. And now, a small town grocer's son would occupy the White House!

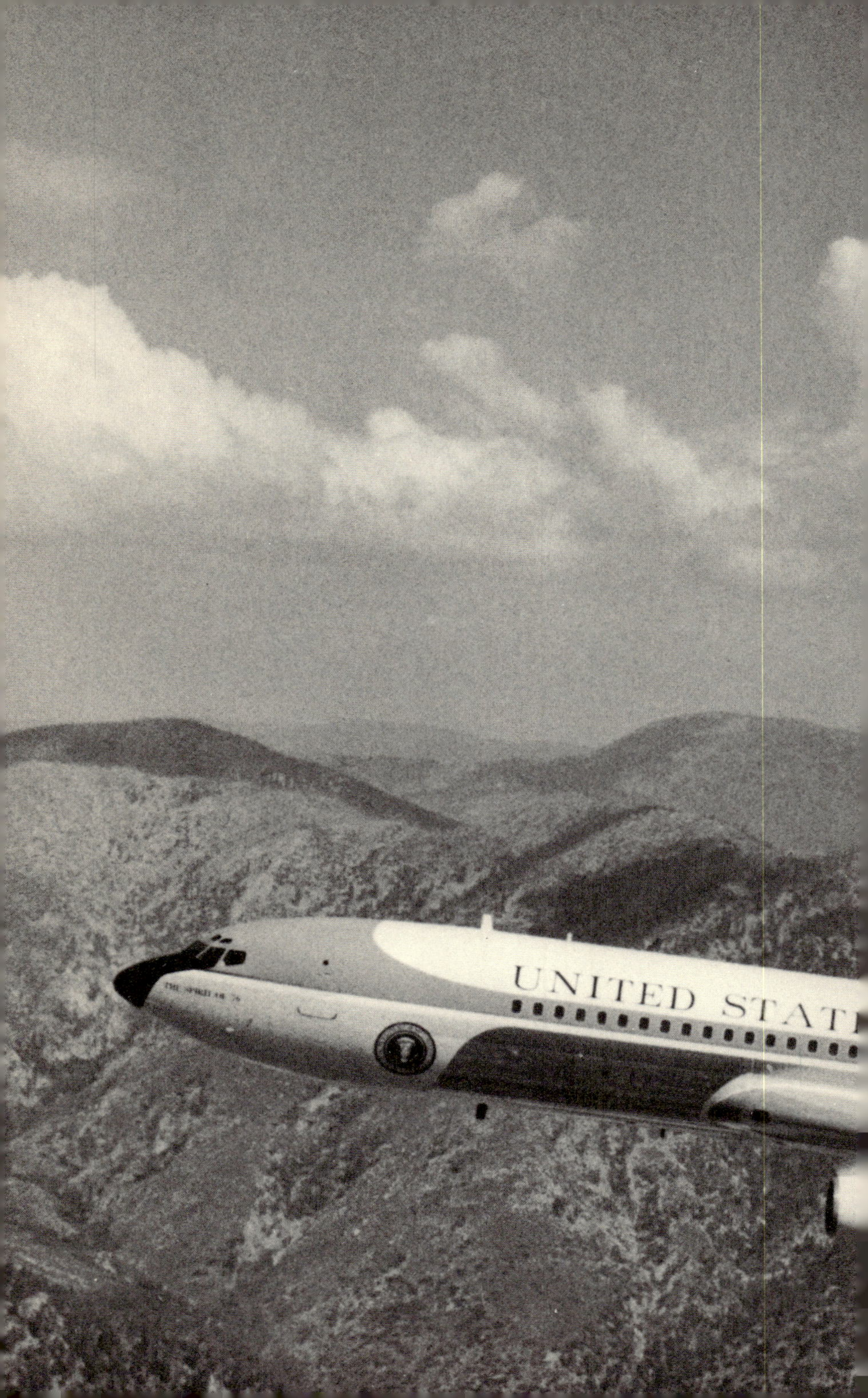
UNITED STAT

13 Fulfillment

Sophocles, the Greek poet, aptly characterized his own situation by saying: "One must wait until the evening to see how splendid the day has been." For me, the evening of my life has not yet come. But for the boy who used to lie in bed in Yorba Linda, California, and dream of traveling to far-off places when he heard the train whistle in the night, I can say even now that the day has indeed been splendid.

Richard Nixon
Six Crises

TRAVELING TO FAR-OFF places was no longer a dream. 'As President, I have traveled to more far-off places than any of my predecessors,' thought Richard Nixon as he was returning from one of his satisfying missions abroad. He looked out of the window of his presidential jet, The Spirit of '76; then cast a glance at Pat. She was exhausted from the long visit abroad, and she was dozing.

Approaching his 60th birthday, he was, perhaps, too young to be indulging in a review of his life; yet he could not suppress the thoughts that kept intruding. The plane was quiet, and he was in a pensive mood.

Physically, the years had been kind to him. His skin was a bit more leathery and his hair discernibly grayer at the temples. His jowls were more pronounced. At the insistence of his old friend and White House physician, Brigadier General Walter Tkach of the Air Force Medical Corps, he was now using glasses for reading (although he is never seen with them in public).

"President Nixon is a very healthy man, the healthiest U.S. President in twenty years," said Dr. Tkach, the White House physician. When Mr. Nixon was Vice-President, back in 1959, Dr. Tkach had accompanied him to the Soviet Union. At that time, recalled the doctor, Nixon had a sore throat. "Since then, I've never given him even aspirin," he said.

Oddly enough, the President has never had a headache in his life. His blood pressure, which Dr. Tkach takes once a week, runs about 124 over 76, up or down about four points. "That's very good for someone his age," the physician said. "An average man of his age would have 140 over 80 or 90."

The doctor's only concern is his patient's limited exercise. With each succeeding year in office, the President spends less time golfing, bowling, walking and swimming. "At first he bowled twice a week; now he doesn't bowl at all," said Dr. Tkach. "And he used to swim, but he stopped after the White House swimming pool was made over into an expanded press area. The only swimming he does now is when he's at

Key Biscayne or San Clemente—and that's not enough!"

But for all his lack of exercise, the President is in excellent condition. He maintains an unvarying weight of 173 pounds, and sleeps soundly for about six hours every night. "He looks younger than he is," Dr. Tkach concluded. "His hair, his eyes, his skin and muscle tone don't show his age. He inherited a good set of genes. His mother was 82 when she died; his father was 78."

Lost in thought, the President suddenly grinned as he remembered the one and only time that Dr. Tkach had been called for an "emergency."

The incident had occurred in the city of Kiev, during the President's 1972 visit to the Soviet Union. Mr. Nixon decided on the spur of the moment to have his picture taken with some Ukrainian folk entertainers. But the offiical photographers had been sent on another assignment two hours earlier. Dr. Tkach, always alert, rushed to his car and returned with his camera. The President, pleased, turned to pose for the picture, and Tkach snapped the shutter. "I think you'd better take another one, Walter," the President said. "You've been traveling with me for three and a half years, waiting for an emergency. Well, that was it."

His thoughts went to his father. . . . It was in San Francisco. The Vice-President was moving from delegation to delegation, working to head off Harold Stassen's campaign to prevent his winning the renomination for a second term. A telegram arrived from his mother with bad news that could not keep. His father had a partially ruptured artery, and could not last much longer. Richard did not wait. He left the pre-convention meetings and hurried to La Habra, where his parents lived.

He found his father weak and deathly pale—but just as absorbed in politics as ever and ready for a good fight. "Promise me something," Frank Nixon said. "I know you're going to be nominated, so do me a personal favor and make

A recent picture of Pat.

your acceptance speech here in California—in San Francisco. I intend to be there."

Richard's spirits rose. Believing that his father had passed his crisis, and reassured by the attending physician, he returned to San Francisco to resume his campaign.

Richard Nixon was renominated for his second term as Vice-President on August 22, 1956. His father died on September 4. "I always believed that your father held on to life that long just so he could see you re-elected," Hannah Nixon said.

Other images and faces and happenings began to press in on his mind.... He thought of good friends. There were only a few. He and Pat used the word "friend" sparingly. Jack and Helene Drown of Rolling Hills were friends.

Pat and Helene had first met when both were high school teachers in Whittier, and when they married, the two couples enjoyed many happy times together. They shared "pot luck" suppers at each other's homes and visited frequently, this being the only "entertainment" they could afford in those early years. When Tricia was born in Whittier, the Drowns were at the hospital with Pat, sharing the joy and excitement. The night Nixon was re-elected to Congress, in 1948, the Drowns and Nixons celebrated together at the Coconut Grove in Los Angeles. That was also the night when they celebrated Tom Dewey's premature "victory" over Harry Truman. And they still laugh when they recall how mistaken they were and how badly the Republican candidate had been trounced.

A truly devoted friend, Jack Drown has worked in every Nixon campaign since 1950. Helene and Jack visit the White House occasionally, and spend time with President and Mrs. Nixon whenever they are in residence at their San Clemente estate.

Almost as old a friend as the Drowns is Bill Rogers. The friendship of William P. Rogers, now the President's Secretary of State, dates back to 1942 when, as Lieutenants Junior

Grade they met at the Quonset Training Station in Rhode Island. They met again in the fall of 1948, when Nixon was involved in the Hiss case, and young Bill Rogers was counsel for a Senate investigating committee. Their friendship deepened.

In 1952, in an almost off-hand manner, Nixon invited Rogers to travel with him on his vice-presidential campaign train. It was William Rogers' calm and shrewd counsel that kept his friend on the ticket in the wake of the "fund" charges that threatened Nixon's political career. Again, in 1955 when President Eisenhower suffered a heart attack, Rogers, then assistant to Herbert Brownell, came to Nixon's rescue. Rogers shielded him from the press, and offered valuable advice so that Nixon would not leave anyone with the impression that he was about to usurp the powers of the ailing president.

Dick cast another glance to his left. . . . Pat was still dozing. How dear she was, how good a person, how understanding a wife. He turned back and saw the friendly full moon in the distance. The moon felt much closer now that our astronauts had trod its surface.

He thought of Bebe Rebozo—his good friend. "Beeb" was blessed with a special intuition which told him when to come close and when to stay at a distance. He knew, instinctively just where to stand. "Dick is comfortable with Beeb," Mrs. Nixon had said. "He's almost like a brother to me, and Julie and Tricia look upon him as an uncle."

Called "Beeb" by the first family, Richard Nixon met Charles Gregory Rebozo in 1951. Born in Tampa, Florida, the son of Cuban immigrants, Bebe made his fortune in the real estate business. His assets are reported in the neighborhood of $5,000,000.

Acting on Rebozo's suggestion in 1962, Nixon began buying stock in Fisher Island, which is on Biscayne Bay, after he was defeated for Governor. He paid $1.00 per share. In 1968, he bought an additional block of stock. In that year,

Nixon released a financial statement showing that his Fisher Island stock was his biggest single asset. He valued it at $350,000 at the time. Shortly after taking office as President in February, 1969, Rebozo engineered the sale of his stock, bringing Nixon a windfall of $180,000.

An associate of Rebozo, in explaining the deep friendship between Richard Nixon and Bebe Rebozo, remarked, "Bebe has everything he wants," and will never make a demand on the President. Mr. Nixon knows this. He can let his hair down, relax, say what he pleases, and be sure that it will never end up in a book."

Like Bebe Rebozo, the two Nixon brothers, Donald and Edward, are fiercely loyal to their illustrious older brother. They do not see each other too often, but keep in communication through letters and occasional phone calls.

"It burns me up when I read about the President being cold and aloof, as though he didn't have a heart," exploded the outspoken Don. "Believe me, if all the people in the United States could just meet him personally, he'd get 85 per cent of the vote next time. People don't look behind the headlines—they don't know that he's a warm, nice guy."

Ed, thirteen years the President's junior, shares Don's opinion, although he expresses himself in milder terms. "I read a lot," he said, "and after a while, I wonder how much influence the press has, and whether people believe it. Because I know better than what I read about Dick. He's not cold and aloof. He's serious and thoughtful. He doesn't snub people—in fact, he goes out of his way to be good to them. Anyone who really knows him will tell you that."

The President recalled Don's proclivity for becoming involved in politically inspired imbroglios that have provided meaty stories over the years.

As early as the 1950's, when Richard was probably the most controversial public figure in the United States, Don also became a target.

The loan Don received from the Hughes Tool Company became a minor issue in the 1962 campaign and has been cropping up ever since. The later versions are little more than embellishments of the original accusations made by the late Drew Pearson. Pearson had charged that the loan was made with the understanding that certain governmental favors would be expected in return.

Don had decided to open a chain of restaurants in Southern California, to be called, "Home of the Nixonburger." He applied for, and received a loan of $250,000 from billionaire Howard Hughes. But Don was no businessman. Two months after the loan was granted, Hughes sent his representatives to Don's office to conduct a routine audit. The accounts, they found, were in disarray. Important creditors had not been paid, and whatever funds remained were being spent without thought to priorities.

There was nothing unethical or illegal in Donald's conduct of business; he was guilty only of poor management. Noah Dietrich, then in charge of the Hughes Tool Company operations, cancelled all future financing of the Nixonburger venture, and Donald Nixon was forced into bankruptcy.

Don joined the Marriott Corporation, an international catering company, in January, 1970. The head of the firm, a friend of the President, had also served as chairman of the Nixon inaugural. In a private meeting, Marriott assured President Nixon that his brother would have no business dealings with the Federal Government and that he would be given no assignments that might cause embarrassment to the White House.

Edward Nixon is a model of propriety. He has the same "ski-jump" nose as the President, and refers to it as "my campaign button." Ed was guided into Duke University by Richard, an alumnus, and received his master's degree in geological engineering at North Carolina State College. He is a self-employed consultant on ecology problems and conducts

Thanksgiving, 1971, the Nixons pose with their daughters and sons-in-law. At the time, David Eisenhower was an Ensign in the Navy, and Ed Cox was completing his studies at Harvard Law School.

an oceanographic clearing house in the Seattle area.

The President noticed that his wife was beginning to stir—a sleepy smile spreading over her face. Pat had entered her sixties, but was still slender and vibrant. She had blossomed during the White House years; and had outdone everyone in tact and diplomacy during the memorable trips to the People's Republic of China and Soviet Russia, just by being her own thoughtful self. Many had called her "America's Ambassadress to the World." But most important, she was a perfect wife and mother.

The President thought of their two daughters. . . . They were now young women: Golden-haired Tricia and her lawyer-husband, Ed Cox; and Julie, darkhaired and goodnatured, who had married President Eisenhower's grandson, David. Yes, their daughters were children they could be proud of, and he and Pat were well aware of their good fortune. That they had married two fine young men made them doubly grateful. They were all serious, sophisticated and concerned citizens; and what more could parents ask. Pat had done a super job with his girls.

Come to think of it, there was a great deal of Grandmother Hannah Nixon in both of them.

Hannah Nixon was gone a number of years now, but her memory still stirred the President. He recalled his mother's use of biblical phraseology, speaking such words as "thou," "thee," "unto" and "thine." Hannah Nixon used these words only when talking with her sisters or fellow Quakers. When her son had asked why, she replied, "Because it might cause others to feel ill at ease. We do not embarrass people—not only because we are Quakers, but because we are human beings."

Faith, for Hannah Nixon was more than belief—it was a way of life. It was his mother, the President realized, who had imbued him with the inner strength to move forward when others had written him off as a loser.

Hannah Milhous Nixon died in 1967, with the firm conviction that her son, Richard, would soon be elected Chief Executive. He remembered the day, shortly after he had been defeated for the office of Governor of California, when he told her he was "through with politics." She took his hand in hers. "That is your thought for the hour, Richard, but there will be other hours. Just hold good thoughts. Good thoughts inspire good actions, and good actions must bring good ends."

And when she saw the bitterness in his face, she added gently, "How can you fail when you have the most wonderful, most understanding Partner imaginable? Do you really think He would abandon one of His children?"

INDEX

Abel, John 207
Acheson, Dean 259, 384
Adams, Arthur Alexandrovich 203, 204
Adams, Earl 420
Adams, Sherman 296, 318, 319, 322, 332, 391, 393
Adenauer, Konrad 431
Agnew, Spiro 434
Albertson, O. C. 64
Albrink, Fred S. 97, 99, 194, 108
Allen, George 92
Allen, John J. 180
Alsop, Stewart 304
Andrews, Bert 222, 223, 235, 241, 258
Arnold, Thurman 107
Aunt Ollie 50

Bakewell, Claude 180
Barkley, Alben 121
Barnes, Stanley 148
Bassett, Jim 310, 312, 313, 320, 322, 323, 332, 354
Bender, Kate Halberstadt 123
Bennett, Charles 383
Bentley, Elizabeth 205, 206, 207, 209, 222
Berle, Adolf A. 196, 209
Beuscher, Jacob 150
Bewley, Thomas W. 113, 114, 117, 118, 263
Bobst, Elmer H. 428
Boddy, Manchester 268, 269, 270, 274
Boggs, J. Caleb 180
Brandeis, Justice 104
Brashear, Ernest 308, 309
Breckenridge, John C. 367, 415
Brennan, Bernard 8, 273, 297
Brenner, E. 111
Bridges, Styles 391
Briggs, L. S. 422
Brock, William 87
Brown, Edmund (Pat) 422-427
Brown, Les 100
Brownell, Herbert Jr. 290, 292, 296, 297, 299, 446
Brownfield, Lyman 54, 97, 98, 99, 104
Bryan, William Jennings 266
Bullitt, William C. 247
Buren, Martin Van 1
Bykov (Col.) 253

Byrd, Harry 415
Byrnes, John 180

Calhoun, John C. 378
Campbell, Alex 240
Cardozo, Justice 104
Carlson, Senator 296
Carl (Chambers' pseudonym) 214, 224
Chamberlain, Neville 132
Chambers, Whittaker 110, 199, 206-260, 419-421
Chiang Kai-shek 384
Chotiner, Murray M. 148, 154-171, 263, 267, 270-5, 278, 279, 284, 289, 298-300, 305, 311, 313-315, 318, 320, 322-325, 327-329, 332, 333, 336, 337, 339, 350, 354, 360, 361, 401, 413, 421, 435, 437
Churchill, Winston 132
Cohen, Felix 196
Coolidge, Calvin, 378
Coplon, Judith 197
Cotton, Norris 180
Coughlan, Robert 380
Cox, Ed 450
Cronin, John F. 203, 204, 222
Crosley, George 226-228, 231-234, 236, 237, 254
Crossley, Archibald 422

Daley, Richard 412
Dannenhauer, Jane 406
Dannenhauer, Rita 406
Davis, Glenn 180
Dawes, Charles 378
Day, Roy O. 148, 154, 155, 162, 263, 264
De Betta, John 410
de Gaulle, Charles 431
de Toledano, Ralph 278, 279
Dewey, Thomas (Tom) 151, 202, 239, 290, 292, 296, 328, 329, 330, 331, 337-339, 357, 398, 422, 445
Dexter, Walter F. 94, 149
Dies, Martin 190
Dietrich, Noah 448
Dilly, See Hilly
Dirksen, Senator 296
Dodson, Leonidas 84
Doheny, Edward L. 52, 53
Donovan, Richard 309
Donovan, Robert J. 428
Dorn, Evelyn 46, 48, 50, 113, 115

453

Index

Douglas, Helen Gahagan 260, 261-280, 287, 293
Downey, Sheridan 267, 268, 269, 274
Driscoll, Governor Alfred E. 296, 302
Drown, Helene 445
Drown, Jack 311, 445
Duff, James 296
Duke, James Buchanan 94
Dulles, Allen 223
Dulles, John Foster 103, 196, 202, 222, 223

Edson, Peter 306, 307, 308, 311, 313, 341
Eisenhower, Barbara Ann 377
Eisenhower, Dwight David (Ike) 6, 53, 121, 156, 281, 283, 284, 286, 294-300, 305-307, 313, 317, 318, 320, 321-326, 328-334, 338, 353, 356-361, 365-381, 385-394, 422, 446
Eisenhower, Dwight David II 376, 377, 429, 450
Eisenhower, Mamie (Mrs. Dwight) 45, 299, 356, 369
Eisler, Gerhard 192, 193, 194
Elliott, William Yandell 196
Emerson, Thomas I. 129, 130

Fall, Albert F. 52
Fenton, Mary 406
Finch, Robert H. 400, 401, 434
Fine, John S. 296, 302
Fischer, Ruth 194
Flanigan, Peter 406
Folger, Clifford 399, 400
Folliard, Ed 238
Ford, Gerald 180
Forrestal, James 243

Gaines, Alan 29
Gallup, George 422
Garner, John Nance 379
Gibbons, Boyd 149
Gloomy Gus 99, 100, 111, 112, 117
Goldwater, Barry 421, 431, 432, 434
Graham, Billy 65
Groves, Leslie R. 205

Haggerty, Jim 319
Hall, Leonard 391-393, 399, 400, 421
Hamilton, Bob 321
Harding, Warren G. 52, 90

Hearst, William Randolph 429
Henderson, Rose 97
Herter, Christian A. 182, 183, 392
Hillings, Pat 311, 325, 327, 339, 353
Hilly and Dilly 220
Hiskey, Clarence 204
Hiss, Alger 130, 133, 175, 197, 199-260, 281, 325, 352, 419, 426, 446
Hiss, Donald 208
Hiss, Mrs. Alger (Priscilla) 208, 219, 220, 221, 223, 253, 256, 257
Hoffman, Paul 296, 297, 319
Holmes, Oliver Wendell 201
Hoover, J. Edgar 106, 107, 209, 256
Horack, H. Claude 94, 95, 104, 111
Hughes, Don 406, 410
Hughes, Howard 448
Hughes, Justice 104
Humphrey, Hubert H. 197, 435, 437

Jackson, Andrew 267
Jackson, Donald 179, 180, 190
Jefferson, Thomas 267
Jobe, Gail 95
Johnson, Lyndon B. 289, 402, 405, 416, 432, 435, 437
Jorgensen, Frank E. 148, 149, 265

Kaplow, Herb 404
Katcher, Leo 308, 309, 312, 313
Kaufman, Judge Samuel H. 257
Keating, Kenneth B. 180
Kennedy, John F. 85, 133, 188, 397-416, 422, 424, 430, 432
Kennedy, Robert (Bobby) 385, 401, 405, 414, 433, 435
Kersten, Charles J. 203, 222
Khrushchev, Nikita S. 394, 395
King, Martin Luther 412-414
Klein, Herbert G. 400, 410, 413, 414, 424, 425
Knight, Jack 297
Knighton, Marjorie Hildreth 54
Knowland, J. William 121, 155, 271, 285, 294-296, 298, 300, 305, 319, 362-364
Kravchenko, Victor 194
Krock, Arthur 182, 380
Kuchel, Senator 426

LaFollette, Robert 81
Lahey, Ed 215
Langlie, Governor 296
Leathers, Harlan 101

Levine, Nathan 244, 245
Lewis, Keith 250
Lincoln, Abraham 415
Lindsay, John 434
Lodge, Henry Cabot 293, 296, 400, 433
Lodge, John 296
Long, Johnny 100
Lovre, Harold 180

McCaffrey, Edward J. 137
McCarran, Pat 197
McCarthy, Eugene 435
McCarthy, Joseph P. 163, 270, 278, 381-388
McDowell, Hebert 219, 227
McDowell, John 219
McGovern, George 435
McGrath, J. Howard 278
McKinley, William 20
McKinney, William J. 337
McVey, Betty 406
Mandel, Ben 214
Marcantonio, Vito 193, 269, 273-5
Marshall, Thomas 378
Marshburn, Rose Olive 50, 51
Martin, Joseph W. 182
Mattingly, Barak T. 296
Melhausen 88
Milhous, Almira 9, 15, 28, 82, 108
Milhous, Elizabeth 9
Milhous, Franklin 9, 113, 149
Milhous, Hannah 9
Milhous, Joshua 40
Milhous, Thomas 8
Miller, Bill 406
Miller, Justin 94
Mitchell, Jim 406
Mitchell, John 428
Mitchell, Stephen 313, 326, 334, 350
Morton, Thruston B. 180, 400
Mundt, Karl E. 192, 195, 213, 214, 216
Muskie, Edmund 435

Nelson, Charles 180
Nelson, Rockwood 149
Nelson, Steve 203, 204
Newman, "Chief" Wallace 88, 90
Nixon, Arthur 6, 26, 64, 65, 66, 71
Nixon, Donald 3, 20, 26, 36, 42, 44, 45, 46, 65, 154, 370, 376, 447, 448
Nixon, Edward 26, 370, 376, 447-450
Nixon, Ernest Leland 18

Nixon, Francis Anthony (Frank) 3, 6, 9, 18, 22, 26, 36, 44, 46, 48, 52, 53, 71, 72, 73, 93, 149, 154, 362, 370, 443, 444
Nixon, George 4, 5
Nixon, George II 5
Nixon, George III 6
Nixon, Hannah 18, 22, 26, 36, 42, 44, 46, 71, 72, 73, 93, 112, 113, 119, 149, 154, 235, 362, 365, 370, 445, 450, 451
Nixon, Harold 6, 26, 40, 64, 65, 71, 73, 74
Nixon, James 4, 5
Nixon, John 4, 5
Nixon, Julie 290, 347, 371, 373-377, 411, 418, 421-423, 429, 446, 450
Nixon, Mary 5
Nixon-Milhous 5
Nixon, Patricia (Pat) 128, 142, 150, 153, 154, 160, 177, 228, 239, 240, 242, 266, 277, 279, 289, 297, 298, 305, 310, 316, 321, 325, 327, 329, 334, 340, 343, 347, 348, 352, 354, 359, 365, 369, 371-376, 395, 396, 402, 404, 410, 411, 418, 422, 423, 427, 429, 430, 446, 450
Nixon, Patricia Jr. (Tricia) 154, 164, 176, 290, 347, 348, 371, 373, 374-377, 411, 418, 421-423, 429, 445, 446, 450
Nixon, Samuel Brady 6
Norblad, Walter 189

Paar, Jack 430
Peale, Norman Vincent 403
Pearson, Drew 365-367, 382, 383, 448
Percy, Charles 433, 434
Perdue, William R. 97, 99, 101, 104, 108
Peress, Irving 387
Perry, Herman L. 148, 149, 150, 151, 265
Persons, Wilton B. 391
Peters, J. 221
Pierce, Mrs. 99
Potter, Charles 180
Powell, Adam Clayton 194
Pressman, Lee 201, 207

Rankin, John 190, 192, 214, 215
Reagan, Ronald 433, 434
Rebozo, Charles Gregory (Bebe, Beeb) 50, 446, 447

Index

Reed, Stanley F. 201
Reston, James 222
Reuther, Walter 405
Roberts, A. L. 39
Roberts, Roy 296
Rockefeller, Nelson 398, 429, 431-434
Rogers, Ted 335, 353, 407
Rogers, Will Jr. 271
Rogers, William P. 133, 135, 222, 311, 313, 318, 320, 323, 333, 337, 376, 393, 445, 446
Romney, George 433, 434
Roosevelt, Franklin Delano 1, 20, 81, 93, 105, 146, 163, 202, 205, 334, 378, 379
Roosevelt, Theodore 81, 378
Roper, Elmo 422
Ryan, Kate Halberstadt 123, 124, 125
Ryan (Thelma Catherine) Patricia 122, 123, 124, 125, 126, 127, 128, 359
Ryan, Thomas 123
Ryan, William 123

St. John, Adela Rogers 421
Sanders, H. W. 366
Sayre, Francis B. 201
Scott, Hugh 421
Seaton, Fred 415
Seeds, Sarah 5
Shell, Joseph 424
Sherwood, Jack 410
Shine, David G. 388
Shockney, Henrietta 28
Sinclair, Harry F. 52, 53
Smith, Dana 306-309, 312, 318, 341, 365
Smith, Gerald L. K. 276
Smith, Marvin 234
Smith, Paul S. 82, 84
Smith, Robert 309
Spargo, Mary 214
Sparkman, John J. 351, 352, 356
Spivak, Lawrence 238, 306
Sprague, J. Russell 296
Stassen, Harold 285, 293, 294, 296, 327, 390-394, 443
Stevenson, Adlai 202, 222, 260, 308, 317, 322, 336, 350, 351, 352, 387, 389, 405
Stewart, James 141
Strandley, William H. 196

Stripling, Robert (Bob) 193, 205, 210, 211, 212, 216, 218, 219, 224, 277, 228, 229, 240, 242, 243, 246, 249
Summerfield, Arthur 296, 305, 357, 360

Taft, Robert A. 284, 293-296, 298, 324
Taft, President William 90
Thomas, J. Parnel 190
Thornton, Governor 296
Thurmond, Strom 434
Timberlake, Philip H. 56
Tkach, Walter 403, 442, 443
Todd, Malcolm 409
Tricky Dick 305, 367, 393
Trimmer, Markaret Ann 6
Truman, Harry 2, 163, 175, 187, 202, 205, 215, 223, 248, 252, 255-259, 262, 273, 278, 289, 366, 378, 422, 445

Uncle Herman 149
Uncle West 46
Upton, Albert 120, 121, 132

Vanocur, Sander 408
Voorhis, Horace Jeremiah (Jerry) 147-175, 263, 270, 271, 393, 401, 413

Wadsworth, Sarah Ann 6
Waldman, Louis 196
Wallace, George 435
Wallace, Henry A. 269, 275
Walsh, J. 52
Waltman, Franklyn 366
Warren, Earl 148, 271, 285, 286, 292-295, 297, 316, 327
Wechsler, James A. 309
Weeks, Sinclair 296
Welch, Ola Florence 61, 62, 95
Welch, Robert 424
Welles, Sumner 247
White, Harry Dexter 203, 204, 229, 254, 298
Whittier, John Greenleaf 21, 75
Wilson, Glen 314
Wilson, H. P. 28
Wilson, Hannah 6
Wilson, Woodrow 52, 81, 378
Woods, Rose Mary 311, 330, 359, 360, 406, 409
Wroble, Lester 141

Zwicker, Ralph W. 387